THE BOTTOM LINE BOOK
OF
TOTAL HEALTH
AND WELLNESS

D1403910

THE EDITORS OF
BOTTOM LINE/Personal

BARNES
& NOBLE
BOOKS
NEW YORK

Boardroom® publishes the advice of expert authorities in many fields. The use of a book is not intended as a
substitute for legal, accounting, business or other professional services. Consult a competent professional for
answers to your specific questions.

Telephone numbers, prices, offers, and Web sites listed in this book are accurate at the time of publication,
but they are subject to frequent change.

2004 Barnes & Noble Books

ISBN 0-7607-6539-1

Bottom Line/Personal® is a registered trademark of Boardroom® Inc.
281 Tresser Blvd., Stamford, Connecticut 06901

Printed and bound in the United States of America

04 05 06 07 08 09 M 9 8 7 6 5 4 3 2 1

Contents

4 ■ Breakthrough Treatments

5 ■ Saving Money & Getting the Best Care

6 ■ Alternative Approaches

7 ▪ Healthy Eating

8 ▪ Secrets of Weight Control

9 ▪ Sports and Fitness Savvy

10 ■ Strategies for a Powerful Life

11 ■ Heart and Stroke Advisory

12 ■ Conquering Chronic Ailments

13 ■ Eyes, Ears, Mouth and Throat

14 ■ For Women Only

15 ■ For Men Only

16 ■ Relationship Secrets

17 ■ The Healthy, Safe Child

18 ■ Parenting Know-How

19 ■ Safe at Home

20 ■ Healthy Travels

21 ■ Older and Wiser

From Bottom Line Books' medical advisor...

We are facing many looming health care issues: vexing problems about the cost of care, the increasing needs of aging baby boomers and the availability of quality services for everyone. Fundamental issues have also been raised by the recent boom in complementary and alternative medicine.

Will conventional medicine, with its ever-quickening pace of technological discoveries, lead the way in the years to come? Will advances in drug therapy continue to revolutionize medicine? Will complementary and alternative medicine increasingly become part of the mainstream? Will health finally be recognized as more than simply the absence of disease but as a constellation of physical, emotional and spiritual well-being?

As far as I can tell, the answers to these four questions are yes, yes, yes and yes. Breakthroughs in computer-aided diagnostics, minimally invasive surgery, immunological treatments for cancer and drug therapy tied to the patient's genetic makeup are already changing the day-to-day practice of medicine and should be an even bigger factor in years to come.

At the same time, however, we've come to realize that in our embrace of high-tech fixes—from penicillin to the polio vaccine to open-heart surgery—something was also lost: the humanity and compassion of old-fashioned GPs. They made house calls. They knew entire families. Part of the popularity of alternative treatments is that they bring back (or never lost) what used to be very good about medicine.

But that's not the whole story. Alternative remedies have also gained popularity because many of them work—particularly for the chronic maladies that modern medicine hasn't found good answers for. Recently several herbs have been documented to be as effective as the drugs commonly prescribed for the same disorders and are often gentler, safer and a lot less expensive. Even such seemingly exotic practices as mindfulness meditation, hatha yoga, guided imagery and acupuncture have been demonstrated in scientific studies to be effective for a wide range of disorders.

Overwhelmingly, the future of health care appears to be integrative—taking the best of many approaches whether categorized as conventional or alternative. Fact is, most people don't care. They want whatever works. And they want to be given information from people with different opinions on the best approach so that they can make up their own minds.

And this is where Bottom Line Books excels. For years, they've sought out credible experts from all areas of health care and distilled their wisdom into succinct, useful advice. *The Bottom Line Book of Total Health and Wellness* collects some of the best of this information in a single, highly readable volume. If just one item helps you live a healthier and happier life, you'll have made a very good investment indeed.

I wish you good health. And I mean that broadly.

Timothy McCall

Timothy B. McCall, MD

Timothy McCall, MD, a Boston internist, medical editor of *Yoga Journal* and author of *Examining Your Doctor: A Patient's Guide to Avoiding Harmful Medical Care* (Citadel Press). He is also completing a book on yoga therapy. His work has appeared in more than a dozen major publications including the *New England Journal of Medicine, Redbook* and the *Los Angeles Times.* He can be found on the web at *www.drmccall.com*

Simple Guidelines For Better Health

Chapter 1

Strategies to Improve Your Health

Here are four recommended health-improvement strategies that you might want to try. Small changes can make a difference.

▮ Give up quick fixes—focus on the long haul for best results.

Forget about weighing yourself several times a week...going on crash diets...or beginning rugged exercise programs.

Reality: Long-term strategies for maintaining weight, diet and exercise and lowering stress have the biggest impact on your health.

Small changes in your daily habits—eating a slightly better diet...taking the stairs instead of the elevator—that are followed consistently over long periods of time yield big benefits.

One of the biggest obstacles to making meaningful changes in our lives is looking at the enormity of a task in front of us...and feeling like it's just not going to be possible to succeed.

By breaking large goals down into small ones, we are much more likely to reach them.

▮ Stop dieting—and start eating healthful food.

Focus on eating healthier things rather than trying to limit calories of unhealthful foods.

> *Example: You can eat loads of steamed broccoli and potatoes and not put on weight. Large quantities of low-fat foods, however, like frozen yogurt or low-fat cookies and cakes, are very high in calories.*

The simpler you eat, the better off you will be. In general, the more processed a food is, the more good stuff is taken out of it, like fiber, and the more bad stuff is put in, like saturated fats and sodium.

I try to get the bulk of my diet from complex carbohydrates—grains, rice, beans, fruit and vegetables.

Timothy McCall, MD, Boston internist, medical editor of *Yoga Journal* and author of *Examining Your Doctor: A Patient's Guide to Avoiding Harmful Medical Care.* Citadel Press.

With that baseline, I can allow myself to occasionally indulge—a piece of birthday cake, a great dessert in a great restaurant—and not feel guilty about it.

■ **Bring exercise into your busy life.**
It can be tough to fit exercise into your hectic schedule. While a half hour of aerobic exercise per day may be ideal, many people cannot find the time to do it.

Just a half hour of exercise a day has been shown to significantly increase your longevity. But lower levels still bring benefits—a better night's sleep …mood elevation…weight reduction…and lower risk of heart disease.

You don't need to be perfect, you just need to be consistent. Just one to two hours a week can make a big difference.

> *Example: During busy weeks, I try to get out at lunchtime or after work at least once or twice a week for a half-hour walk or run. Then I fit in a longer session on the weekend.*

Do something you enjoy. I play tennis, ride my bike or rollerblade.

■ **Get the few medical screening tests that matter.**
Despite all you hear about preventive medicine, there are only a few screening tests that have been proved to save lives. What I recommend for people at average risk…

▶ **Blood pressure.** Once a year. The ideal level is 120/80 or below.

▶ **Cholesterol.** Every three to five years. The desired level is less than 200 (HDL should be greater than 35). The test should be done after fasting overnight and the blood drawn from your arm.

▶ **Mammogram.** Nearly every medical expert agrees that women should have one yearly after age 50.

▶ **Pap smear.** Once a year for all women who have been sexually active, until three normal tests in a row…then every two to three years. If you've had a hysterectomy or are over 65 and have had normal Paps in the past, you probably don't need to continue getting Paps.

▶ **Colon cancer screening.** Starting at age 50, I recommend yearly checks for hidden blood in the stool and flexible sigmoidoscopy every three to five years.

▶ **De-stress your life.** Doctors are starting to understand all the ways stress can adversely affect health. Headaches, bowel problems, asthma and heart disease are all more likely to hit those who are stressed out. Stress consists of two elements…

▷ External factors that cause anxiety and that we can't control, such as rush-hour traffic.

▷ Reactions to those events.

Ever notice that minor irritations don't bother you after a vacation?

Helpful: Cultivate that peaceful state of mind. Exercise is probably the best stress-buster, but there are several relaxation techniques that work well.

Best: Meditation…guided imagery…a hobby you enjoy.

> *Example: Doing yoga for a few minutes each morning promotes peace of mind throughout the entire day.*

Have Fun, Get Healthy

David Sobel, MD, director of health education for Kaiser-Permanente Northern California, the large health-maintenance organization headquartered in Oakland, CA. He is coauthor of several books, including *Healthy Pleasures* (Perseus) and *Mind & Body Health Handbook* (DRx).

The healthiest, most robust people are those who dutifully work out, eat low-fat fare and follow all the other "rules" for better health. Is that right?

Yes and no. These familiar rules are obviously important. But over the past 20 years, hundreds of studies involving thousands of people have shown that one of the most important determinants of health and longevity is a tendency to enjoy sensual pleasures on a regular basis.

Here are 10 ways to indulge yourself and boost your health—at the same time...

■ Set aside time each day to pursue activities you enjoy.

This is a good way to avoid depression, which has been linked to impaired immune function and increased risk for cancer and other diseases.

A 20-year study conducted at the Western Electric Company in Chicago found that depressed men were twice as likely to die of cancer as their non-depressed colleagues.

In another key study, Edward Diener, PhD, of the University of Illinois, asked men and women to rate their happiness on a moment-by-moment basis over a six-week period. He found that overall happiness depended on *how much time* each person spent doing something that made him or her feel good. The intensity of their happiness didn't make much of a difference.

Diener's study suggests that repeated indulgence in simple pleasures—walking on a sunny day, playing a musical instrument, etc.—is more important than experiencing momentary peaks of ecstasy.

■ Satisfy your innate "skin hunger" with regular touching.

More and more doctors are beginning to recognize the importance of skin-to-skin contact.

In hospitals, premature babies are now held and touched daily. Nurses make it a point to touch adult patients, when appropriate, to stabilize heart function and blood pressure.

Touch others more—and encourage others to touch you, whether it's a friendly hug or an intimate caress. One easy way to get more touching into your life is with a regular massage given by a professional masseuse.

■ Take saunas.

Sitting in a hot sauna or steam room has been shown to promote relaxation and to alleviate chronic pain.

One Czech study found that sitting for 30 minutes in a sauna doubled blood levels of pain-killing neurotransmitters known as *beta-endorphins*.

There's even evidence suggesting that saunas can help ward off colds and other infectious illnesses. In a study of 44 German children, those who took a weekly sauna missed half as many days of school as did the control group.

■ Spend time in nature.

Humans have an innate love of natural scenes, whether it's trees swaying in a fragrant breeze...a crackling campfire beside a swiftly flowing stream ...or clouds drifting lazily overhead.

Experiencing nature is more than pleasant. People who are exposed to natural scenes recover faster from surgery, are able to tolerate pain and manage stress better. They also feel happier.

Taking a few minutes to gaze upon nature can even wipe out the effects of a stressful event. In a recent study, people were shown a disturbing film for 10 minutes, followed by a 10-minute film of trees and water.

Researchers found that watching the nature film reduced the length of time it took the participants' emotional state to return to normal following the viewing of the disturbing film.

Listen to soothing music.
Music affects respiratory rate, blood pressure, stomach contractions, brain activity and even the levels of stress hormones in the bloodstream.

In several recent studies, surgical patients recovered faster when they were allowed to listen to soothing music during the procedure.

In general, slow instrumental music is more soothing than fast, vocal music such as pop or rock.

Make time for sexual intimacy.
Sex involves not only touching, but also emotional intimacy. Both are vital for good health.

One large-scale English study found that men who had sex at least twice a week were half as likely to die prematurely as men who had sex less than once a month.

Marital happiness has been linked with reduced illness and mortality, and one key factor in marital happiness is the frequency of sexual intercourse.

Take afternoon naps.
Humans seem to be "programmed" for a midday rest, and it may be detrimental to health to forgo such downtime.

People who nap seem to enjoy reduced rates of illness. It's clear that heart disease is less common in parts of the world where an afternoon siesta is still a tradition than it is in the US.

In a Greek study of heart attack survivors, the risk for a second heart attack was 30% lower in those who took 30-minute daily naps than in non-nappers. The rate was almost 50% lower in people who napped for 60 minutes a day.

If you have trouble dozing off during the day, don't fret. Even sitting quietly for an hour in the afternoon is beneficial.

Be a moderate drinker.
Numerous large-scale studies, including the renowned Framingham Heart Study, suggest that people who consume one to three drinks a day live longer than teetotalers. (One drink means 12 ounces of beer, four ounces of wine or a mixed drink.)

Moderate drinkers suffer fewer heart attacks and face a lower risk of premature death from heart disease than either nondrinkers or heavy drinkers.

Some studies indicate that all forms of alcohol are equally beneficial. Recent research suggests, however, that wine offers the greatest benefits.

Watch funny movies and television programs.
Laughing boosts your tolerance for pain. It also lowers levels of stress hormones in your bloodstream and yields a short-term boost in immune function.

In one recent study, people who watched a Richard Pryor videotape had heightened levels of protective antibodies for an hour afterward.

Keep a pet.
Pet ownership has been shown to improve both mental and physical well-being.

In one study of heart attack survivors, those who owned pets were one-fifth as likely to suffer a second heart attack as were those who didn't own pets.

How to Declare Your Personal War Against Antibiotic Resistance

Stephen A. Lerner, MD, professor of medicine and associate dean for faculty affairs at Wayne State University School of Medicine in Detroit.

If you haven't yet been confronted by the problem of antibiotic resistance, you soon may be.

Until recently, this dangerous phenomenon—in which disease-causing germs become resistant to the antibiotics that once killed them—was thought to be limited to foreign countries and hospital intensive-care units.

No longer. Antibiotic-resistant germs—and the illnesses they cause—are showing up with increasing frequency in doctors' offices all over the country.

Result: Ear infections (otitis media), bladder infections, pneumonia and other diseases that were once easily cured with antibiotics are becoming difficult or even impossible to treat.

In one especially disturbing development, doctors now encounter strains of *pneumococcus* that are resistant to penicillin. Consequently, doctors are having fewer options for treating pneumonia and other diseases caused by pneumococcus.

It has become a race between bacteria and the pharmaceutical industry, which is hard at work on new drugs to replace old ones that no longer work.

RISKS VERSUS BENEFITS

Fifty years ago, antibiotics were seen as "miracle" drugs—a simple way to cure diseases that until then had often been deadly. In the ensuing years, however, doctors and patients alike have grown complacent in their use of these powerful drugs.

Doctors often prescribe antibiotics for the common cold and other *viral* infections, even though they're effective only against *bacterial* infections.

And—many patients who are told to take an antibiotic for a specific length of time stop taking the drug prematurely.

People who abuse antibiotics in these ways foster the growth of "superbugs"—bacteria with the genetic wherewithal to resist the effects of even the most powerful antibiotics.

This does not mean we should stop using antibiotics. They're extremely versatile drugs, and the list of their uses is growing.

ANTIBIOTICS AND THE HEART

In a study in *The Journal of the American Medical Association*, researchers linked the bacterium *Chlamydia pneumoniae* to heart attack and stroke.

The researchers theorized that taking antibiotics to kill the bacterium could dramatically reduce cardiovascular risk.

This finding poses a dilemma. If large numbers of people began taking antibiotics on a long-term basis, increased levels of antibiotic resistance would inevitably result. But if antibiotic therapy really does help prevent cardiovascular disease, it might be a risk worth taking.

Bottom line: If antibiotics are to remain effective, we must stop using them indiscriminately. Each of us must acknowledge our role in fostering antibiotic resistance…and do what we can to stop the problem from getting worse.

ANTIBIOTICS ARE DIFFERENT

Unlike other drugs, antibiotics have what doctors call a "spreading" effect.

A blood pressure medication, for example, affects only the person who takes it.

An antibiotic affects not only the person who takes it, but it also affects anyone who comes in contact with that person. This is because bacteria are so easily spread from person to person via even casual contact.

If one person begins taking an antibiotic, resistant strains of bacteria are likely to show up in family members, coworkers, classmates, etc.

WHAT PATIENTS CAN DO

Antibiotics are good for one thing only—*killing bacteria*. They're appropriate for bacterial illnesses but useless against colds, influenza, herpes and other viral infections...as well as noninfectious illnesses. (For viral and fungal illnesses, a limited number of antiviral and antifungal medications are available.)

Trap: People often assume that every sore throat is "strep" throat, caused by the *Streptococcus* bacterium. In fact, most are viral. *Here's what you can do...*

■ **Don't assume that every illness can be helped by antibiotics...**or demand that your doctor prescribe an antibiotic.

Patients often pressure doctors to prescribe antibiotics when prudence dictates that the illnesses be allowed to run their courses.

■ **Never use an antibiotic that was prescribed for someone else**—or for one of your own previous illnesses.

■ **Avoid the use of antibacterial products in your home.**
Regular use of antibacterial soaps and cleansers can create resistance. Plain soap and detergent are fine—and they do not foster resistance.

CARELESS DOCTORS

Curiously, many doctors remain unaware of their own role in the resistance problem. They continue to write antibiotic prescriptions willy-nilly.

Your doctor should be hesitant about prescribing antibiotics. He should use throat cultures and other diagnostic tests to pinpoint the cause of any health problems you have—not simply prescribe an antibiotic "just in case."

If your infection isn't too bad, tell your doctor that you'd like simply to wait it out. Minor infections generally go away on their own within a few days.

But if you have a fever of 102 degrees or higher...pain that can't be controlled with painkillers...or if you're unable to keep down fluids, antibiotic therapy is probably appropriate.

Caution: Sick children should always be evaluated by a doctor, regardless of the severity of their symptoms.

FOLLOW ORDERS CAREFULLY

If you must take an antibiotic, take it exactly as prescribed. That means taking the specified number of doses per day—for the specified number of days.

If you miss a dose or otherwise fail to comply with the doctor's orders, ask him if you should continue taking the antibiotics beyond the original expiration date.

How to Exploit the Placebo Effect for Much Better Health

Howard Spiro, MD, professor of medicine and editor, *The Yale Journal* at Yale University School of Medicine in New Haven, CT. He is author of *The Power of Hope: A Doctor's Perspective.* Yale University Press.

Before the era of modern medications and surgical procedures, doctors often relied on the *placebo response.* That's the remarkable phenomenon in which patients given a "dummy" pill (placebo) get better simply because they believe the pill will make them better.

Now, renewed interest in mind/body medicine has doctors taking a second look at the link between placebos and health…and exploring ways to harness the placebo response.

What exactly is a placebo?

In narrow terms, it's a pill that contains only sugar or another inactive ingredient. But placebos can also be thought of as any treatment believed by the patient to be capable of alleviating suffering.

This definition encompasses virtually every tool of modern medical care—not only pills, but also injections, diagnostic tests and even psychotherapy and surgical procedures.

I'm not saying that these treatments have no scientific validity. Many do. I'm saying that they may be effective in part because patients expect them to be effective.

For which illnesses are placebos effective?

They seem to be most effective at relieving pain, fatigue and other symptoms that tend to be stress-related.

That's no small matter, since 80% of all medical complaints involve stress-related ailments.

No one knows whether placebos can actually cure disease. I, for one, doubt that they can.

How do placebos work?

Since sick people often get well even without medical intervention, some researchers have theorized that it's not the placebo that helps—but simply the passage of time.

If this were true, patients given a placebo should get better no faster than patients given no treatment. That is *not* the case. Patients who take placebos faithfully fare better than those who take them more desultorily.

Placebos may work in part because patients associate them with medicines that proved beneficial in the past.

I believe that anything that reduces stress also helps curb symptoms. It may be that stress reduction causes the body to make feel-good compounds known as endorphins…or that the patients' perceptions of their problems have changed.

Most important, the placebo response is tightly linked with patients' hope, faith and anticipation of benefit.

How are placebos used?

In the first half of this century, doctors routinely doled out placebos to patients who had incurable diseases…or symptoms that defied diagnosis. These doctors told their patients that the pills contained powerful medicine that would be beneficial, if not curative.

Nowadays, it's considered unethical for doctors to dupe their patients in this way—even if doctors have their patients' interests in mind when they do so.

Today, placebos are used primarily in clinical trials of new medications.

In a placebo-controlled study, one set of experimental subjects is given a placebo that looks just like the drug under study, while another group is given the actual drug.

The placebo "arm" of the study is intended to show that any improvement experienced by the patient is the result of the drug—and not simply the result of the placebo response.

Isn't this practice a breach of ethics?

No. The subjects are informed at the start of the study that they might receive a placebo. No one is deceived.

In addition, researchers are forbidden to give placebos in place of drugs that are already known to be effective. Placebos are only given in place of experimental treatments. These treatments, in turn, are used only when there is no standard therapy.

Are placebos ever used outside of clinical trials?

A few physicians treat vague symptoms with vitamins or other medications that are of no proven value for these conditions.

I sometimes recommend vitamin B-12 injections for patients suffering from fatigue that does not respond to the usual treatments. I tell these patients only that the injections have proven beneficial for other patients—which is absolutely true. I do not promise that the injections will prove helpful in their particular case.

Can I ask my doctor to use placebos in caring for me?

Not really. What you can do is find a doctor who looks beyond science to your emotional needs... who listens carefully to your concerns...shows compassion...explains any proposed course of treatment...and expresses an openness to alternative healing techniques and to prayer.

While it's not a popular idea, I believe that much of the benefit attributed to alternative therapies stems not from the remedies themselves but from contact with the practitioners who give them.

In saying this, I exclude those herbal remedies that have been proved in years of use "in the field."

Anything else?

It's important to find a doctor who is willing to take an active role in guiding his or her patients. Some doctors are all too willing to inundate patients with information—yet unwilling to help their patients make sense of the information.

Patients should be involved in deciding which treatment, if any, is appropriate. But in my experience, patients feel better when I give them appropriate guidance.

If your doctor is optimistic about your treatment, you will feel optimistic too. If your doctor makes you pessimistic, your response to treatment may be lessened. As I always say, *hope helps*.

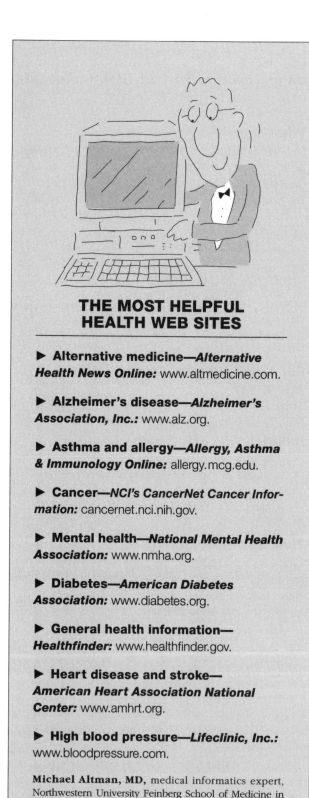

THE MOST HELPFUL HEALTH WEB SITES

▶ **Alternative medicine—*Alternative Health News Online:*** www.altmedicine.com.

▶ **Alzheimer's disease—*Alzheimer's Association, Inc.:*** www.alz.org.

▶ **Asthma and allergy—*Allergy, Asthma & Immunology Online:*** allergy.mcg.edu.

▶ **Cancer—*NCI's CancerNet Cancer Information:*** cancernet.nci.nih.gov.

▶ **Mental health—*National Mental Health Association:*** www.nmha.org.

▶ **Diabetes—*American Diabetes Association:*** www.diabetes.org.

▶ **General health information—*Healthfinder:*** www.healthfinder.gov.

▶ **Heart disease and stroke—*American Heart Association National Center:*** www.amhrt.org.

▶ **High blood pressure—*Lifeclinic, Inc.:*** www.bloodpressure.com.

Michael Altman, MD, medical informatics expert, Northwestern University Feinberg School of Medicine in Chicago.

SECRETS OF GOOD WINTER HEALTH

It's not organisms that make us sick, but our lack of ability to fight those organisms. To stay healthy, you must boost the ability of your mucous membranes—the first line of defense—to fend off those organisms and fight infection. Here are ways to boost immunity...

▶ **Eat several servings** of fresh fruits and vegetables every day.

▶ **Drink a glass of water** every few hours. Do most of your drinking away from meals.

▶ **Reduce intake of simple sugars,** cow's milk and high-fructose corn syrup (a sweetener in many prepared products, including soft drinks). These all weaken the immune response.

▶ **Take multivitamin/mineral and antioxidant supplements**—to include 15,000 to 20,000 IU of vitamin A...1,000 mg of vitamin C...400 IU of vitamin E...and 20 mg of zinc in your diet.

Note: These doses are for a 150-pound adult. Adjust for weight. Before starting any supplements, consult your health-care provider.

▶ **Engage in moderate intensity exercise consistently.**

▶ **Observe regular sleep–wake cycles.**

▶ **Wash your hands frequently throughout the day.**

▶ **Take frequent moments to breathe deeply.** This improves oxygen delivery to tissues, removes metabolic wastes and reduces stress.

▶ **Avoid antibacterial soaps**—they can actually reduce your resistance to serious infections.

Andrew L. Rubman, ND, associate professor of clinical medicine, Lane College of Integrated Medicine, Orlando, FL, and medical director, Southbury Clinic for Traditional Medicines, Southbury, CT.

How Doctors Stay Well With Sickness All Around All Day Long

Michael Janson, MD, general practitioner in private practice in Arlington, MA, and past president of American College for Advancement in Medicine, a professional nonprofit medical educational organization. He is author of *The Vitamin Revolution in Health Care.* Arcadia Press.

Doctors provide the best of their science-based knowledge about health and disease to their patients. But many of them hold off recommending alternative treatments that they themselves use.

Here's what many doctors I know believe for themselves...and how they take care of themselves to limit the likelihood of illness. Consult your doctor to be sure this advice is right for you.

▪ Vitamin supplements are essential to replenish cells with nutrients.

More than 60% of doctors say that they take supplements regularly even though they don't recommend them to their patients.

There's no question that a balanced diet is key to keeping your body functioning at its optimum level.

However, a variety of factors influence the value of nutrients in our daily diets. Factors include genetic makeup...pollution...overprocessed foods ...and stress. Stress robs the body of important immune-boosting nutrients.

Vitamin supplements enhance a healthy diet and offer protection against the many factors that negatively influence our food supply and health.

What I recommend to my patients: In addition to a multivitamin/mineral, I tell patients to take 50 to 100 mg of vitamin B6...400 to 800 mcg of folic acid...2,000 mg of vitamin C...and 6 to 15 mg of natural beta-carotene, daily.

▪ Vitamin E can protect against heart disease.

According to a recent survey, 80% of doctors said they took vitamin E.

Numerous studies have shown that vitamin E can protect the circulatory system against the consequence of cholesterol deposits. Those deposits can lead to clogged arteries—and to atherosclerosis.

Therapeutic doses range from 400 to 1,200 IU (international units) per day of natural E (d-alpha-tocopherol).

Caution: If you are taking anticlotting medications (for example, Coumadin or aspirin), you should consult your doctor before starting to take vitamin E. Its natural anticlotting properties may cause too much of that effect in your blood.

■ Niacin and glucosamine sulfate can reduce joint pain and cartilage degeneration associated with osteoarthritis—without the side effects of anti-inflammatory drugs.

Osteoarthritis—which is a degenerative joint condition that affects about 80% of people older than age 70—is effectively treated with anti-inflammatory medicines.

But these medications can cause troublesome and sometimes serious side effects for many of the patients who take them.

That's why niacin (vitamin B3) and glucosamine sulfate turn out to be an effective alternative for most of my patients.

Niacin has many uses in the body, including helping to maintain normal mental functions, energy in the cell, digestion and healthy skin.

Glucosamine sulfate is a natural compound found in connective tissue and cartilage that contributes to joint strength. Supplements help to repair joint cartilage and relieve pain within four to eight weeks.

Doses: For my patients, I recommend two 500-mg glucosamine sulfate tablets twice daily and/or two 500-mg niacinamide tablets twice daily.

■ Headaches can be effectively managed through massage and diet.

Many of my colleagues ask their spouses or partners to massage their temples or necks after the working day or they get periodic professional massages.

Reason: Massage can help to relieve headaches that may be caused by muscle tension in various parts of the body. In fact, many pain clinics use massage as part of an overall program to treat tension headaches.

Your diet can play a large role in the onset or exacerbation of headaches—particularly processed, sugary foods, which cause blood sugar levels to fluctuate.

What you can do: Before you reach for an over-the-counter pain reliever, examine the foods you've been eating. Get rid of heavily processed foods, which often contain nitrates, white flour and sugar. Satisfy your cravings for sweets by eating fruit.

Standardized extracts of the herbal medicines feverfew (25 to 50 mg two to three times daily) or ginkgo biloba (60 mg twice a day) can also reduce the frequency and intensity of headaches without the rebound effect of medicines. (As they might with any herb, pregnant women may need to take special precautions.)

■ Stress management can help lower and maintain blood pressure.

Many doctors are hesitant to discuss breathing and visualization exercises because they are still considered unconventional in most medical practices. But many doctors believe that such techniques are key to lowering blood pressure and keeping it down, with or without medications.

> **Example:** Sit in a comfortable position, and place one hand on your abdomen. While envisioning a warm, comfortable place, breathe in and out slowly, pushing your hand out each time you inhale. Do this for at least five minutes, three to four times daily.

It's also important to go to bed in a calm state. Read a relaxing book or listen to relaxing music just before bed.

■ Exercise has positive effects on more than two dozen chronic health problems ranging from rheumatism to diabetes. It's usual for

doctors to recommend physical activity for more than two dozen chronic health problems.

But has your doctor told you the reasons behind those recommendations? And how much exercise you should be doing?

Studies have demonstrated that regular exercise can improve cardiovascular health, including lipid levels, heart rate and blood pressure, and reduce breast cancer risk in women younger than age 40 by more than one third.

Researchers have also demonstrated increases in strength and bone and muscle mass, by as much as 170% among individuals over age 80.

Best routine: Walk briskly at least four to five times weekly. *Aim:* Three miles in 45 minutes.

Go as fast as you can without getting out of breath—but work up a sweat. Strength training three times weekly is a valuable addition.

BE CAREFUL BUYING DRUGS ON-LINE

Before you buy medication over the Internet, investigate how reliable the Web site is. The FDA provides some suggestions for safer on-line buying. They are…

▶ **Check** with the National Association of Boards of Pharmacy (www.nabp.net) or the Verified Internet Pharmacy Practice Sites (VIPPS) (vipps.nabp.net/verify.asp) to determine whether the Web site is a licensed pharmacy in good standing.

▶ **Do not buy** from any sites that offer to sell you a prescription drug for the first time without verification that you have had a physical exam or from any sites that will sell a prescription drug without a prescription.

▶ **Avoid** sites that do not provide a US address and phone number.

▶ **Steer clear of sites** that advertise "new cures" or amazing results" and claims that the government or researchers have conspired to suppress a product.

Protect Yourself from Your Medicine

Timothy McCall, MD, Boston internist, medical editor of *Yoga Journal* and author of *Examining Your Doctor: A Patient's Guide to Avoiding Harmful Medical Care.* Citadel Press.

Even when they are taken correctly, prescription medications can be risky. *To the rescue:* There are ways to reduce your risk of being adversely affected by prescription drugs—and limiting the mistakes of doctors and pharmacists.

RISING DRUG CONFLICTS

Health is most often compromised by drugs when two or more medications being taken interact to produce negative results…when medications trigger allergies…and when incorrect doses are prescribed.

Such mishaps are occurring with greater frequency—for a variety of reasons…

▶ **Mammogram.** Nearly every medical expert agrees that women should have one yearly after age 50.

▶ **Advances in drug therapy** are leading many doctors to prescribe more drugs.

▶ **Managed-care plans** are encouraging doctors to prescribe more drugs to cut down on clinic visits.

▶ **Managed-care plans** that encourage doctors to see as many patients as possible result in less time for doctors to explain how to take drugs properly.

▶ **A growing number of new drugs** makes it hard for doctors to keep up with the benefits and drawbacks of their uses.

▶ **Drug advertising** that is aimed at consumers is increasing demand by patients.

PRESCRIBING ERRORS

While drugs can be critical to helping patients get well fast, we need to be more wary and vigilant when they are prescribed. *Here are the most common errors doctors make and how to avoid problems…*

▣ Unnecessary prescriptions.

Many doctors are under pressure from patients who have read articles or seen ads to prescribe medications that may not be appropriate or necessary.

Examples: Weight-loss drugs for people who are not obese but only want to lose a few pounds. Antibiotics for colds or other viral infections—they are completely ineffective. Inappropriate antibiotic prescribing is also a major cause of the emergence of superbacteria that are resistant to many antibiotics.

Self-defense: Simply don't pressure the doctor for antibiotics or other drugs that are not intended for your problem.

Given how commonly medications, especially antibiotics, are prescribed inappropriately, if your doctor feels you don't need one, then you probably don't.

When a drug isn't appropriate, there's little chance it will help you, but you risk side effects—and they could be deadly.

Better: Tell your doctor that if your condition doesn't improve in a set number of days you'd like to be seen again or will call for advice.

▣ Drug allergies.

Up to 25% of all serious drug side effects are the result of patient allergies to medications.

Your doctor may be unaware of your prior drug allergy…or may forget to check your record before prescribing.

You or your doctor may not even realize the drug being prescribed is in the same class as those to which you're allergic. The drug may have a different-sounding name or may be used for different purposes.

Self-defense: When your doctor is about to prescribe a new drug, remind him or her of your prior allergic reactions. Make sure your medical record mentions your allergy. And be sure to notify your pharmacist. Any time you have an allergic reaction, write down the name of the drug and describe your reaction. Keep that piece of paper with you.

▣ Wrong doses.

Many doctors tend to take a "one-size-fits-all" approach, prescribing the same dose of each medication for most patients.

Problem: You may wind up with a dose that is too small or too large for you.

Example: A petite woman might need a smaller dose of a drug than someone who weighs 250 pounds. People with kidney or liver problems and those over age 65 may also need smaller doses because they break down many drugs more slowly. That can lead to a dangerous buildup of the medication in their systems.

Caution: Even when doctors intend to prescribe the appropriate doses, they can accidentally put the decimal point in the wrong place—1.25 mg when they mean 0.125 mg. Sloppy handwriting also contributes to this problem.

Self-defense: Ask your doctor whether the prescribed dose should be adjusted in light of your size or medical history. Before you leave the office, read the prescription back to the doctor.

Medical experts also recommend that older patients "start low and go slow" with medication. That is—begin with smaller doses, often half the standard dose. Then, if the drug is well tolerated but not as effective as desired, you can gradually increase the dose.

▣ Two doctors prescribing the same drug.

Examples: A cardiologist prescribes Lanoxin for a heart-rhythm problem. The patient's primary care doctor renews the prescription but uses the generic form of the drug, digoxin. Not realizing they are two names for the same medication, the patient takes both and winds up with a dangerous overdose. Or a doctor prescribes Motrin for a sore knee, not aware that the patient frequently takes Advil for headaches. Both are brand names for the drug ibuprofen.

Self-defense: Review all the medicines you're taking—prescription and over-the-counter—with each doctor who prescribes drugs for you.

OTHER STEPS TO TAKE

■ **Look up any drug you're prescribed before you take it.**
Even though I'm a doctor and know a lot about medications, I won't take anything until I look it up in a drug reference book or research it on the Internet. *Good resources…*

▶ ***Deadly Drug Interactions: The People's Pharmacy Guide*** by Joe and Teresa Graedon (St. Martin's Press).

▶ ***The Essential Guide to Prescription Drugs*** by James Rybacki and James Long (HarperResource).

If you have access to the Internet, Harvard Medical School hosts a site on health that includes drug information at www.intelihealth.com.

GET ENOUGH SLEEP

The average person sleeps six hours, fifty-seven minutes a night during the work week. Experts recommend a minimum of eight hours a night. Sleep-deprived people may feel better if they sleep longer on weekends, but it's impossible to make up for the adverse effect that lack of sleep has already had on their health and productivity.

Joan Goldberg, associate executive director of programs, National Sleep Foundation, 1522 K St., Washington, DC 20005…or visit its Web site at *www.sleepfounda tion.org.* for more information on sleep disorders, understanding sleep, and sleep-related research.

SEX IS GOOD FOR HEALTH

Sex relieves pain through the release of endorphins. It can lessen midlife prostate problems by emptying out fluids, and it is a calorie burner, too—a man who has sex once a week burns 2,500 calories a year. Fast, deep breathing helps the whole body—it enriches blood with oxygen, nourishing all organs and tissues.

Michael Cirigliano, MD, assistant professor of medicine, University of Pennsylvania School of Medicine, Philadelphia.

Warmer Hands and Feet, Better Sleep

Keeping feet and hands warm makes it easier to fall asleep, especially if you have reduced circulation to your extremities or are going through menopause, when the body's heat regulation can lose efficiency. For the best sleep, keep feet and hands comfortably warm while keeping room temperature cool.

Kurt Krauchi, research scientist, chronobiology and sleep, Psychiatric University Clinic, Basel, Switzerland, reported in *Prevention*, 33 E. Minor St., Emmaus, PA 18098.

Eight Symptoms Never to Ignore

Anne Simons, MD, assistant clinical professor of family and community medicine at the University of California, San Francisco Medical Center. She is coauthor of *Before You Call the Doctor: Safe, Effective Self-Care for Over 300 Common Medical Problems.* Fawcett Books.

In rare instances, seemingly minor symptoms can mean a major or even life-threatening illness. *Here are several conditions that you should not dismiss…*

CONSTIPATION

Constipation can usually be cleared up by getting more exercise…consuming more water and dietary fiber…and perhaps by taking a laxative. If these steps fail to solve the problem within two weeks, consult a doctor.

Persistent constipation can mean colorectal cancer, prostate enlargement in men and fibroid tumors or uterine cancer in women.

COUGH

A cough that lasts for two weeks or more could be symptomatic of tuberculosis, emphysema or even lung cancer.

Coughing that seems to be triggered by strenuous physical activity is also cause for a doctor visit. You may have exercise-induced asthma.

FATIGUE

Fatigue that cannot be explained by lack of sleep can be symptomatic of depression. That's especially true for fatigue accompanied by irritability and/or listlessness.

Fatigue can also be caused by different medical conditions such as diabetes, hypothyroidism, anemia, lupus, arthritis, AIDS or chronic fatigue syndrome.

FINGERNAIL ABNORMALITIES

Most fingernail abnormalities are caused by a localized problem—eczema of the nails or a fingernail infection, for instance. But certain abnormalities stem from disease processes occurring elsewhere in the body…

▶ **Bluish tinge** suggests poor oxygenation of the blood caused by lung or heart disease.

▶ **Brown or black spots** are typically a sign of infection. Discoloration that has spread to the surrounding tissue could indicate gastrointestinal polyps or malignant melanoma.

▶ **Chipped "sawtooth"** nails can be caused by vitamin deficiency or exposure to radiation or toxic chemicals.

▶ **Clubbing**—in which the nail and skin adjacent to the base of the nail bed become rounded

and bulbous—may mean cirrhosis of the liver, lung disease, heart disease or ulcerative colitis.

▶ **Horizontal grooves** can be caused by malnutrition, measles, mumps or even a recent heart attack.

▶ **Spoon nails**—in which the nails flatten or become depressed like a spoon—can be caused by anemia, thyroid disease, rheumatic fever or syphilis.

▶ **White streaks** may be a sign of kidney failure, Hodgkin's disease, sickle-cell anemia or a recent heart attack.

FREQUENT URINATION

Increased urinary frequency that is associated with fatigue, weight loss, increased thirst or sweet-smelling urine may mean adult-onset (Type II) diabetes.

Other potential causes of increased urinary frequency include sexually transmitted diseases, bladder infection, irritable bladder and prostate or kidney trouble.

HEARTBURN

A burning sensation in the chest usually means heartburn—*but not always*. Sometimes it means a heart attack.

If you experience a "funny heartburn," call 911 or have someone take you to the emergency room. Immediately chew and swallow an aspirin tablet.

Aspirin's clot-busting properties will minimize damage to your heart, should you be having a heart attack.

RECTAL BLEEDING

Most rectal bleeding stems from hemorrhoids, anal fissures or other minor problems. But some cases—especially those that involve significant bleeding—can mean intestinal ulcers or colorectal cancer.

SCALY SKIN

No doubt you already know to see a dermatologist if a birthmark or mole changes size or color. Such changes can be symptomatic of skin cancer.

You may not know that small, scaly patches on a woman's nipple can mean a precancerous condition known as Paget's disease. Any woman who notices such patches should see a doctor right away.

For Much Better Health: Decode Your Body's Secret Language

Martin Rush, MD, psychiatrist in private practice in Middletown, OH. He is author of *Decoding the Secret Language of Your Body: The Many Ways Our Bodies Send Us Messages.* Simon & Schuster.

As children, we were trained to suppress our emotional responses. Unfortunately, this process forced us to mask feelings of anger or discomfort.

Result: Negative emotions get channeled into bewildering physical symptoms. And—the actual cause of the discomfort is never appropriately addressed.

Becoming consciously aware of your emotional "triggers" is often enough to relieve the symptoms and keep you much healthier.

EMOTIONS AND HEALTH

Scientists have known for years that our emotions affect our bodies as well as our minds.

When you feel angry, threatened or upset, a series of physical changes is initiated by the hypothalamus—the area of the brain that is located on the underside of the cerebrum.

The hypothalamus sends impulses to the adjacent pituitary gland. That, in turn, sends signals to the adrenal glands to release "stress chemicals," called catecholamines, into the bloodstream. These chemicals activate the nervous system. They make your blood pressure rise, your heart beat faster, your gut contract...and they even make your hairs stand on end.

This arousal takes different forms in different situations. Your body, though, gives off signals of the upset even when you're not fully aware that something is bothering you.

STOMACH ACHE

While persistent stomach symptoms may indicate a serious illness, occasional stomachaches are often unconscious expressions of anxiety.

Reason: The stomach is the site of a dense network of nerves that are influenced directly by emotional stress.

What to do: When you feel the first twinge of cramping or discomfort in your stomach area, ask yourself the following questions...

▶ **Have I been rejected or disappointed recently?**

▶ **Am I afraid of not being accepted** by someone whose feelings are important to me?

▶ **Is there something I desire but don't believe I can attain?**

When you pinpoint the source of your anxiety, you may feel your stomach begin to relax.

Then explore the thinking behind your anxiety...

▶ **Do you have all the facts?**

▶ **Is your perceived disappointment really as threatening as you imagine?**

Look for several other alternative interpretations that are not anxiety-provoking.

HEADACHES AND MIGRAINES

While volumes have been written about headaches, I've found that they are often due to unexpressed negative feelings of unhappiness or outrage.

Reason: Headaches are thought to be the result of the sudden expansion or contraction of blood vessels leading to the brain—changes that are controlled by the nervous system.

A sudden headache should be a signal to ask yourself these questions...

▶ **Is something going on around me that I don't like or to which I object?**

▶ **Am I fantasizing about some unwanted or bothersome encounter, past or future?**

▶ **Am I angry about something** but unwilling to say so?

In my experience, once you find answers to those questions, you can usually take steps to reduce the frequency of most tension headaches.

Simply admitting that you dislike something frees your body from the need to express your outrage for you.

Next, begin to explore different responses that permit you to express your feelings to anyone who is upsetting you.

Effective alternative: Simply avoid the unwanted encounter.

NECK PAIN

During my years of helping patients decode their body's signals, I have found that neck pain can almost invariably be traced to feelings of irritation, displeasure or pique—as the result of some real or fantasized interaction.

When you receive a psychic blow, your body reacts as if you were receiving a physical one. The muscles in your neck tense up to better absorb the attack. If this tension continues, the muscles at the back of your neck can become fatigued and go into a painful spasm.

When you feel tension or pain in your neck, ask yourself...

▶ **Is something making me feel tense,** displeased or irritated?

▶ **Have I offered to do someone a favor that is more than I can comfortably handle?**

▶ **Am I being treated unfairly by someone?**

Recognize and acknowledge the source of your tension—and then mentally "release" it, telling yourself that it no longer has any hold over you. This will often cause your neck pain to vanish.

LOWER-BACK PAIN

When you feel emotionally overburdened, your body can actually translate this into a fantasized physical experience.

Reason: The lumbosacral joint—the hinge between your upper and lower back—tightens up as though you were carrying a heavy weight on your shoulders. If this continues, the muscles around the joint become fatigued and go into spasm, triggering lower-back pain.

When you feel your lower back start to ache or tighten, ask yourself...

▶ **Do I desire rest and relaxation...**or attention or acknowledgment from those around me... but won't let myself ask for it?

▶ **Am I taking care of someone else and secretly tired of doing it?**

▶ **Am I carrying a mental or emotional burden** —a secret event or hidden desire about which I feel guilty?

Then explore ways to express your feelings of being "overburdened" to those around you—and perhaps share the load.

RUNNY NOSE

Your nose speaks more eloquently about your thoughts than you might imagine—particularly if you are experiencing sadness or hurt feelings.

Reason: The nose is directly connected to large parts of the brain—including the regions associated with basic emotions—through an extensive network of nerves.

In the outer corner of each eye are tear glands. They constantly supply a small amount of tears to keep the eyes moist.

If something happens that upsets or saddens you, these glands increase their tear production, but not enough to overflow the eye and trickle down the face. Instead, they overflow into the sinuses, producing a runny nose.

The next time you have a sudden runny nose, take a moment to ask yourself these questions...

▶ **Am I feeling sad,** disappointed or dismayed about something that happened recently?

▶ **Am I upset about some ongoing situation** but don't want to admit it to myself?

Common Health Complaints... That Doctors Commonly Fail to Investigate Fully

Leo Galland, MD, director of The Foundation for Integrated Medicine, 133 E. 73 St., Suite 308, New York City 10021. He is author of *Power Healing*. Random House.

These days, doctors spend little time with patients, especially those patients who are under managed care. So there are bound to be symptoms of illness or injury doctors either miss or dismiss. Some of these symptoms, however, are signs of serious ailments.

Here are five common—and potentially serious—complaints that may signal serious disease...

FATIGUE: ANGINA

When I say "fatigue," I'm not referring to the lethargy one feels after a bad night's sleep. I mean a sudden and sustained change in your normal energy level.

You may first notice it while exercising—finding it hard to complete your usual regimen or possibly experiencing shortness of breath. Such an episode may last 20 to 60 minutes. Episodic fatigue in someone over age 40 could be caused by silent angina—clogging of the arteries in the heart without the telltale pain of regular angina, when the heart muscle is deprived of blood. Silent angina can kill.

What to do: Insist on an exercise stress test, which can detect blockages based on changes in the electrocardiogram. If the results are unclear, request a thallium stress test, in which a radioactive solution is injected into your system and follows the blood flow in the heart.

Angina treatment: The same as for coronary artery disease. There are many options—the best one depends on the individual.

RECURRENT SORE THROAT: REFLUX

When recurrent sore throat, cough or hoarse voice are not linked to a cold, influenza, allergies or strep, it could be atypical esophageal reflux. Typically, esophageal reflux appears as indigestion. But the continued irritation of the throat and larynx could produce a persistent cough, soreness or hoarseness.

Chronic reflux increases the risk of esophageal cancer. If reflux enters the lungs, the result may be asthma.

What to do: Ask your doctor about taking an acid-lowering drug, such as Prilosec or Prevacid. If it helps, your problem is likely reflux.

If neither of these drugs helps, it still could be reflux—or some other problem. You may need to undergo laryngoscopy. In this outpatient procedure, a doctor examines your throat and larynx using a very tiny camera-tipped viewing tube inserted through the mouth.

Reflux treatment: Beyond acid-lowering drugs, eating small-portion, low-fat meals may help...as may taking a dose of chewable calcium, such as Tums, with meals and at bedtime. *Also:* Don't eat within three to four hours of going to bed...and relax when you eat, rather than eating on the run.

SNORING: SLEEP APNEA

Snoring is a concern if it is loud enough to disturb others...it occurs at least three times a week...you feel tired and have memory lapses during the day. It results from trying to breathe with a partially blocked passageway. Heavy snoring is associated with obesity, high blood pressure and heart disease.

If your heart is healthy, you may be suffering from obstructive sleep apnea, in which you briefly stop breathing altogether—for a few seconds—repeatedly throughout the night. It occurs when the throat relaxes too much and closes on itself—blocking the passage of air, thereby waking up the individual. The result is a lack of oxygen to the brain and heart, which increases the risk of stroke.

What to do: Ask your doctor for a referral to a sleep specialist, who will monitor your breathing while you sleep.

Sleep apnea treatment: Lose weight...elevate the head of your bed...and wear a device to maintain an open airway. If necessary, there are also a variety of successful surgical techniques.

MEMORY LOSS: HYPOTHYROIDISM... DEPRESSION

Doctors may dismiss memory loss and difficulty concentrating as a result of stress or, in menopausal women, low estrogen levels. But they can be symptomatic of hypothyroidism (underactive thyroid) or depression.

Underactive thyroid can produce weight gain, raise cholesterol levels and increase heart disease risk. Severe depression can lead to suicide...and depressed people tend to take poorer care of their health, so their prognosis for various health conditions is worse than normal.

What to do: Insist on a blood test to measure the thyroid-stimulating hormone, which is elevated when the thyroid is underactive. Possible depression requires assessment by a skilled professional.

Hypothyroidism treatment: Thyroid hormone.

Depression treatment: A combination of medication and psychological therapy. Many effective and nonaddictive antidepressants are now available.

DIGESTIVE DISORDERS: PARASITES

Diarrhea, constipation, gas and bloating are often blamed on "nervous stomach" or irritable bowel syndrome. But they may be due to an intestinal parasite, which can be lethal. The problem is more likely to be parasitic if it develops suddenly in someone who previously had normal bowel movements...or it seems to be linked to travel or an episode of food poisoning.

What to do: Don't accept irritable bowel syndrome as a diagnosis—especially if you've never had bowel problems before. Irritable bowel syndrome typically develops in adolescence or young adulthood. Ask your doctor to have a sample of your stool evaluated by a lab specializing in tropical medicine. Sometimes more than one specimen needs to be examined.

Parasite treatment: There are several types of antibiotics, depending on the parasite.

The Most Common Health Problems Can Be Prevented Or Avoided or Delayed and Delayed and Delayed

Art Hister, MD, host of the Canadian radio program "House Calls"... and author of *Midlife Man: A Not-So-Threatening Guide to Health and Safe Sex for Man at His Peak.* Douglas & McIntyre.

There is real comfort in growing older. Middle-aged men and women are among the happiest in today's society.

At midlife, you have maximum control over many aspects of your life...you're probably making a good income...you have finished raising your children...and you are generally satisfied with who you are.

But middle age is also when an increasing number of us start dealing with physical and emotional problems.

Here are the most common health problems associated with aging and suggestions on how to delay or prevent their onset...

ALZHEIMER'S DISEASE

One instance of misplacing your car keys is not an early sign of Alzheimer's. We all forget our keys occasionally, but people with Alzheimer's forget what the keys are for.

Little is known about preventing Alzheimer's, but doctors do know something about dementia in general. *Key preventive measures...*

▶ **Regular strenuous exercise**. A brisk 30-minute run each day—outside or on the treadmill—for example, offers some protection.

▶ **Using your brain.** The more we use our minds, the less likely we are to develop dementia. The more synapses we develop, the larger "usable" area of the brain we have. This provides some cushion against deterioration from age.

CANCER

The best defense is a healthful lifestyle. Eat a well-balanced diet and get regular exercise. *Specific steps to take...*

▶ **Eat more fruits, vegetables and whole grain foods.**

▶ **Emphasize monounsaturated fats in your diet.** Monounsaturated fats come from olive oil, avocados and fish.

▶ **Limit sun exposure.** When outdoors, always apply sunblock and wear a hat. Minimize exposure to the sun during the heat of the day.

▶ **Quit smoking.** If you smoke and you do nothing else for your health, do this.

HEART DISEASE

This is the number-one killer in North America. Heart disease involves the buildup of fatty substances, calcium and clotting material on the inside of artery walls.

At greatest risk: Those who smoke...have high cholesterol...have high blood pressure...are obese...have excessive stress...or have a strong family history of premature heart disease or stroke. Strong history means a first-degree relative (parent or sibling) diagnosed with heart disease before age 55.

To lower your risk...

▶ **Keep total cholesterol below 200.** LDL ("bad" cholesterol) level should be below 130...HDL ("good" cholesterol) level should be above 35.

▶ **Reduce stress.** Mental stress is bad for your heart. Hostility has been singled out in studies as one significant personality trait linked to a higher risk of heart attack. If you are quick to anger—and often act on it—consider enrolling in a stress-management program...or talk to your doctor about taking some types of antidepressants.

▶ **Keep blood pressure below 140/90**—or, even better, 120/80. If your blood pressure is high unexpectedly, have it tested at least two more times—when you are as relaxed as possible. If it is still high and you have other risk factors for coronary artery disease, your doctor will probably recommend a lifelong commitment to a pressure-lowering medication.

DEPRESSION

About 15% of adults suffer from depression at some point in their lives...and it becomes more common as we age. If you have a family history of depression, you're at higher risk.

You are clinically depressed if you are sad or irritable most of the day every day...have a diminished interest or lack pleasure in most activities...have had significant weight loss or gain...have insomnia—or sleep too much—nearly every day...are fatigued...or have intense feelings of worthlessness.

Depression increases your chances of developing other health problems and of dying from them. It increases your risk of high blood pressure, stroke and heart attack later in life. *Treatment includes...*

▶ **Psychotherapy.**

▶ **Medication.** A slew of new synthetic drugs, known as selective serotonin reuptake inhibitors

(SSRIs), has largely replaced the older drugs, known as tricyclics. The herb Saint-John's-wort is effective for mild to moderate depression, but be sure to speak with a doctor before trying it on your own.

DIABETES

There are two types of diabetes. Type 1 appears in childhood or early adulthood.

Type 2 tends to appear more frequently in adults, although we are seeing rising numbers of cases in youngsters. Type 2 constitutes 90% of all diabetes cases.

Diabetes now affects 5% to 7% of the population...this figure is expected to rise as the population ages.

Since early symptoms are quite subtle, middle-aged men and women should have annual blood sugar tests. Readings over 126 mg/dL are considered abnormal.

Risk factors include: Being overweight...a high-calorie, high-fat diet...a sedentary lifestyle...a parent with type 2 diabetes.

Diabetes raises risk of stroke, heart attack, blindness, amputation (especially of the feet), kidney failure and perhaps dementia. It also produces nerve damage—often within 10 years.

To prevent—or at least control—diabetes...

▶ **Lose weight.** Ask your doctor for the best weight for your height and build.

▶ **Exercise regularly.**

▶ **Avoid alcohol.**

▶ **Eat a diet high in fruits and vegetables.** Limit your intake of high-calorie, high-fat foods.

OSTEOPOROSIS

Osteoporosis causes brittle bones that are fractured easily. When it affects the spine, it causes great pain and a gradual loss of height.

Risk factors include: Smoking...excessive drinking...a strong family history of the disease...a sedentary lifestyle...a diet with too much protein and too little calcium...a lack of vitamin D. Certain ethnic groups—such as Caucasians and Asians—are at higher risk.

Prevent the disease by...

▶ **Consuming enough calcium.** Generally 1,000 mg to 1,500 mg a day, either from food or from calcium supplements. *Best food sources:* Dairy products...green, leafy vegetables.

Calcium citrate is less likely to cause stomach upset than calcium carbonate.

No matter which calcium source you choose, get a few minutes per day of sun exposure. This helps your body produce enough vitamin D, which is important for proper calcium absorption.

▶ **Doing weight-bearing exercises, which increases bone density.** *Examples:* Brisk walking, jogging, jumping in place.

Secrets of Happier Recuperation after Illness... Or Surgery...or Injury

Regina Sara Ryan, wellness consultant in Prescott, Arizona. She is author of *After Surgery, Illness or Trauma: 10 Practical Steps to Renewed Energy and Health.* Hohm Press.

Convalescing after illness, surgery or injury can be frustrating and tedious—or productive and life-affirming. Much depends on how you spend your time during your period of forced confinement.

Here's how to flourish while you're recovering...

FACING YOUR EMOTIONS

Illness or injury can spark strong emotions like anxiety, anger and grief. Painful though they may be, these emotions are normal and healthy responses to what you've been through. *To express them...*

▶ **Keep a personal healing journal.** Record your feelings, sketch, write poetry, compose letters you'll never send. Don't edit yourself. Accept the full range of your emotions.

▶ **Let go by yelling.** Scream into a pillow. Or practice "silent screaming": Open your mouth …let out your breath…contort your face…and gesture as if you were shouting at the top of your lungs.

▶ **Enlist a sounding board.** Choose one or two people who agree to let you vent—uninterrupted—without advising, reassuring or judging you.

STRESS REDUCTION

Breathing and relaxation techniques reduce stress, aiding your body's efforts to heal. *Useful exercise…*

Focus your gaze on something you find soothing, like a painting or a vase of flowers. Silently count "one thousand, two thousand, three thousand, four thousand" as you inhale through your nose. Then exhale through your mouth, repeating the same slow count. Keep breathing this way for three minutes.

Next, tense every muscle in your body—jaw, fists, abdomen, calves—whatever your condition allows. Hold for a count of 10, then slowly release the tension. Breathe deeply again.

Finally, make a loud noise such as "bah" or "dah" over and over until you start to relax. Stop and repeat to yourself, "I am here, I'm alive, I can cope, I survive."

EXERCISING THE BODY

It's important to keep moving to improve muscle tone, blood flow, digestion and sleep. Do what you can. Wriggle and stretch your fingers and toes. *Or, if your doctor permits, try these in-bed exercises…*

▶ **Inner leg isometrics**. Lie flat on your back, knees bent, feet a few inches apart. Put a pillow between your thighs. Inhale, then squeeze the pillow with your legs, holding for a count of five. Exhale and release. Repeat five times.

▶ **Glute sets.** From the same starting position (but without the pillow), inhale, squeeze your gluteal (buttocks) muscles and hold for a count of five. Exhale and release. Repeat five times.

▶ **Head and neck.** Imagine that you have a pencil protruding from your chin. Inhale, turn your head left and begin to draw the biggest circle you can. At the halfway point, exhale slowly but continue to draw.

Make three circles to the left, rest, then turn to the right and make three circles.

▶ **Total body stretch.** Lying on your back, raise your arms above your head. Extend your feet and hands in opposite directions as if you were being stretched. Hold this position for 10 seconds, being sure to breathe normally. Repeat three times.

EXERCISING THE MIND

Nothing is more frustrating than feeling as if you're wasting time. But time recuperating can be time well spent…

▶ **Read about countries you'd like to visit** or heroes who inspire you.

▶ **Delve deeply into a subject that's always fascinated you**—art, astronomy, politics, economics, etc.

▶ **Use audiotapes** to practice a foreign language.

▶ **Master chess, backgammon or bridge.**

▶ **Draw or paint.** If you don't want to draw freehand, use a coloring book. Some terrific ones made for adults are available at book and art supply stores.

▶ **Listen to music.** Now is the time to enjoy entire symphonies, operas or albums.

Trap: Television can be a harmless escape …or an energy-depleting crutch. Before tuning in, ask yourself, "Does TV make me laugh more? Does it leave me feeling better about myself and my life? Does it distract me from my pain or problems?" Should you answer "no" to any of these questions, explore other, more energizing pastimes.

A HEALTHFUL ENVIRONMENT

Where you heal affects how you heal. Your immediate environment should make you feel calm and uplifted—not agitated or depressed.

▶ **Declutter your room.** Clear off surfaces…ask a friend to remove excess furniture…and toss old magazines and newspapers.

▶ **Use incandescent lights, not fluorescent ones.** Experiment with rosy lightbulbs that cast a soothing glow.

▶ **Give yourself new vistas.** Have new paintings or posters hung or old ones rearranged.

▶ **Surround yourself with mood-enhancing color.** Drape beautiful fabric over an old table or nightstand. Festoon windows with bright curtains.

▶ **Add fragrance to the room** with incense or fresh flowers.

▶ **Fill your room with plants** or grow an herb garden in an ice-cube tray on a window ledge.

WELCOMING VISITORS

Illness and injury can make visitors uncomfortable. Family and friends may be unsure of what to say or do. Put your guests at ease by voicing your wants and needs. *Be very specific…*

▶ **If talk is tiring, ask your visitor to hold your hand and pray,** meditate or do a breathing exercise with you.

▶ **Suggest a game of cards** or ask your guest to read to you.

▶ **Request a back or foot massage** from a close relative or friend.

▶ **Ask to have groceries picked up or library books returned.** Most loved ones appreciate having concrete ways to help you.

If you're too tired for visitors or need to cut a visit short, say so. Be gracious but firm. Your guests will understand.

CURBING MEDICATION SIDE EFFECTS

Even minor side effects, such as flatulence or drowsiness, can make daily life very unpleasant. *If a drug is causing trouble:* Ask your doctor about trying a lower dosage. Dosages described in medical reference texts are often needlessly high. *Rule of thumb:* If a drug has been prescribed for a chronic condition like high cholesterol, a low dosage is usually okay. It can always be raised. Drugs for infections and other acute ailments generally must be taken at specific dosages.

Jay Sylvan Cohen, MD, associate professor of family and preventive medicine, University of California, San Diego, School of Medicine. He is author of *Overdose: The Case Against the Drug Companies.* Penguin.

Promoting Personal Growth

Chapter 2

Dr. Bernie Siegel's Secrets of Happiness

Most people feel happy only when their material desires are satisfied. Consider that happiness can be found in other ways.

I have found, though, that happiness is a sensation that has little to do with external forces, such as what we possess and what we earn.

Instead, it is an emotional state that we can turn on and off at will. By embracing the talents and opportunities we're given instead of clinging to the pain we've suffered in the past, we can create internal joy at any time.

Some steps to take that will help you feel true happiness…

▪ Take responsibility for your mistakes.
We fear others will dislike us when we make mistakes, so we torture ourselves by trying to hide or deny them.

In fact, what people dislike are the excuses and the blame used to cover up mistakes. Owning up to your mistakes shows you care and helps bring resolution and healing. *Helpful…*

▶ **Forgive yourself first,** which is perhaps the biggest hurdle. Mistakes are tough on self-esteem—if you aim to be perfect. However, no one gets through life without making a few.

▶ **Apologize**—and rectify the error. Others will welcome your help, and you'll feel happier with yourself for taking constructive action.

▶ **Think of the most recent mistake you've made.** If you haven't made amends, it's probably not too late to say, "I'm sorry."

▶ **Stay in charge of your thoughts and feelings.**

Bernie S. Siegel, MD, one of the country's leading experts on the connection between a positive mind and a healthy body. He is founder of Exceptional Cancer Patients, a therapy group in Woodbridge, CT. He is a retired general and pediatric surgeon and the author of several books including *Help Me to Heal—A Practical Guidebook for Patients, Visitors and Caregivers.* Hay House.

Although you can't control events, you can manage your reactions to them. Only you can decide whether to choose harmony or turmoil.

Example: After some treasured family heirlooms were stolen from me several years ago, I realized that my anger had taken over my thoughts. Only by vividly picturing the thief using the robbery money to buy presents for his children was I able to reclaim my thoughts. Unrealistic? Probably… but instead of obsessing about the injustice, I was able to get beyond my resentment. Helpful…

▶ **Use mental imagery.** Holding a positive image in your mind crowds out negativity…and positive thoughts have been shown to create happier feelings.

▶ **Exaggerate your troubles,** stretching complaints to such hilarious limits that you end up laughing.

▶ **Take a time-out.** Go for a nature walk—the outdoors is a natural tonic. Or meditate, listen to music or give yourself a pep talk.

■ Have faith that you can overcome obstacles.

Why give up in despair when nature constantly gives us the hopeful message that we can always find a way?

Example: Jogging on a recently repaved road, I noticed one area of the new asphalt changing over a period of weeks. It first rose up several inches, then cracked, then opened like a volcano. What emerged was foliage. Trapped under the pavement, a skunk cabbage seed had grown into a plant so hardy it broke right through to the light and air.

Everyone faces walls and barriers. The unhappy choice is to let them stop you. Believing you can find an opening to grow and blossom is the joyous, life-affirming option. *Helpful…*

▶ **Be open to redirection.** When things don't go as you have planned, stop and think where this different path might be leading you. Events that at first seem to be unfortunate or undesirable may actually provide surprising advantages.

▶ **Judge each problem as an opportunity to grow.** Many patients I've treated and counseled over the years have said their illnesses taught them to value their lives and implement wonderful changes.

▶ **You don't have to "break through the pavement" in a single day.** Take troubles one step at a time. Celebrate each sign of progress before taking the next step.

■ Deal constructively with criticism.

The Sufi poet Rumi wrote, "Criticism polishes my mirror."

Regarding criticism as a threat, an insult or proof that you're worthless won't make you happy. Instead, it is better to take a more optimistic view and see criticism as a learning tool to help you improve.

I've been fortunate to have many critics among my patients. When people give you criticism, it means they feel you are willing to listen and change. *Helpful…*

▶ **Evaluate the source of the criticism.** Those who love finding fault with everyone will only scratch your mirror, not polish it.

▶ **When criticized by people you trust,** think of yourself as an athlete getting direction and support from a coach who wants to see you perform better.

▶ **Don't let criticism shake your confidence.** Use appraisals as a way to help you reach a higher level of performance.

How to Unlock the Genius Inside You

Todd Siler, PhD, inventor, writer and corporate consultant. He is the founder of Psi-Phi Communications, 6555 S. Kenton St., Suite 304, Englewood, CO 80111, which develops multimedia learning materials for schools and corporations. Dr. Siler is author of *Think Like a Genius*. Bantam Books.

Often when we hear the word *genius*, we think of a gift that is given to just a privileged few, such as great artists, scientists and inventors.

But there is some genius in all of us—if we are open to it. Thinking like a genius is in fact an innate capacity waiting to be developed.

THE GENIUS MIND

Being a genius isn't purely a matter of knowing more than anyone else. Genius isn't a matter of intelligence either, if intelligence is weighing data and solving problems rationally.

Rather, genius thinking is a free, open way of applying the mind, breaking the idea barriers of habit and convention. While most of us are gridlocked in rigid thought patterns, the genius mind leaps from one idea to another.

The genius makes connections that others can't see... explores them...and applies them to enrich his or her life and the lives of others.

Genius thinking is the development of your "mind muscle," which can stretch and strengthen with practice like any other muscle.

THINKING IN COMPARTMENTS

By the time we're in middle school, we've been taught to compartmentalize our thinking. We study science in one class and history in another. Instead of seeing the world through a wide-angle lens, we narrow it down to a series of pinholes.

As adults, we follow the same pattern, filing our relationships in one thinking compartment, our work in another and our hobbies in a third.

At work, the same thing happens. Marketing people and production people have little to do with one another.

Soon, the well-worn, collective ways in which we think about different issues become ruts.

Geniuses, however, break through the walls that keep most everyone else hemmed in. Refusing to submit to rigid patterns, geniuses go beyond the tried-and-true to the new.

Exercise: Look around your office, house or car, and choose a common object, such as a coffee cup, paper clip, pen or dish towel. Think of five new uses for it. Be as inventive as you can.

This exercise is to practice seeing things for what they could be. That is the essence of genius thinking.

The same process can transform work through innovation. In most companies, people rarely share their expertise with those in other departments.

But imagine an expert sales manager sitting in on a research and development meeting. He notes how participants fail to communicate effectively with each other.

He wonders, "Why not adapt the same techniques that my best salespeople naturally use?" They listen to the customer, finding out what the person wants and communicate the value of the product.

IDEAS ARE EVERYWHERE

The world is filled with images that can enhance your thinking—if you allow your mind to be loose and to make connections. Nature is a particularly wealthy treasure chest of inspiration for those who aren't afraid to think like a genius.

Example: A car designer I know who was stumped for new ideas took the day off and went to the zoo. In the aviary, a tropical bird swooped past him—like a race car at a speedway.

Its shape and color fascinated him. Suddenly, he envisioned "birdlike" shapes and vibrant hues in the auto design that had until then seemed flat and boring. The aviary became a wonderland of ideas to be translated into machinery.

Carry a little notepad or cassette recorder around with you so that you can record spontaneous observations, doodling and personal reflections.

Note anything that interests you—even if it seems unrelated to the work that you're doing. The goal is to let these observations stimulate your imagination.

The sense of sight is a magic wand that brings abstract ideas to life. Stimulate your connection-making capacity with pictures, diagrams and concrete representations to trigger flashes of genius and generate new thoughts about old problems.

HOW TO THINK LIKE A GENIUS

Most of us rely on a narrow field of expertise to support our ego and self-esteem. But just as you can't add water to a cup that's already full, you can't add new ideas to a mind that already knows it all.

Thinking like a genius means becoming an expert novice—being willing to let new ideas take root. The trick is learning to suspend what you know in order to discover what you don't know.

> **Example:** *Imagine a heart surgeon reading a book about Leonardo da Vinci. If he is willing to put aside his medical education and training, he may be able to make a connection between one of Leonardo's many inventions and his own work that will lead to the creation of a brilliant new surgical technique.*

Often people have moments of insight and connection, but they don't know what to do with them. Unfortunately, these moments are often lost and forgotten.

The genius contemplates the connection, weighs its significance, analyzes it, expands it and puts it to work. He "harvests" his flashes of brilliance.

FOUR STEPS TO THINKING LIKE A GENIUS

▶ **Connection.** Challenge your mind by looking for similarities and links between things that appear unrelated. For example, compare a building and a tree…or a city and a forest…or a nerve cell and a machine.

▶ **Discovery.** Investigate, explore and dig deeper into a connection you've made. For instance, how are the inner workings of a building similar to those of a tree?

▶ **Invention.** Create something meaningful based on your discovery.

▶ **Application.** Use your invention to solve a problem, fill a need, enrich your life or improve the world.

Sometimes, the route from connection to application takes place in seconds. But weeks, months, even years—and a lot of dedicated work—may need to elapse between the first flash of insight and the finished product.

Very Simple Keys to Real Happiness

Richard Carlson, PhD, one of the country's foremost experts on stress management and reduction, Pleasant Hill, CA. He is author of numerous books, including *You Can Be Happy No Matter What* (New World Library) and *Don't Sweat the Small Stuff* (Hyperion).

To be truly happy, most people think they have to solve the big problems in their lives and own what they desire most.

But achieving these things does not necessarily produce long-term happiness. True happiness is a product of your attitude, not your circumstances.

You can develop the ability to be content regardless of what is going on in your life.

Key: Pay attention to how your mind works—and learn to stop thinking in self-defeating ways.

KEYS TO HAPPINESS

■ Don't let troublesome thoughts blur reality.

Most of us give huge significance to whatever drifts through our minds. However, we forget that we're the ones creating these thoughts.

We analyze our thoughts…create mental scenes based on them…and confuse what's going on in our minds with the actual situation.

Example: *On the way to work recently, a friend heard a news item about the growing number of people who have been laid off in her field. She started to brood about whether her own job was in danger and worried about what would happen if she were laid off.*

She spent the rest of her drive to work in a full-fledged "thought attack." Even though she likes her job and hasn't heard rumors of imminent downsizing, she arrived at work tense, angry and miserable.

Self-defense: At the beginning of a "thought attack," distance yourself from the attack.

Helpful: Remind yourself that it is your thoughts that are bringing on your unhappiness...and not necessarily reality.

While it makes sense to plan how you would deal with losing your job, you'll come up with better plans if you operate from a sense of well-being rather than from tension or fear.

This is not the same as positive thinking. Trying to produce only positive thoughts and avoid negative ones takes a lot of effort. It is unrealistic to even try.

The goal here is only to take your thoughts less seriously, not to control what you think about. You do this by recognizing your thoughts for what they are—just thoughts. You created them, and you can let them pass.

◼ Let bad moods pass you by.
When you're in a good mood, you feel confident and optimistic.

When you are in a bad mood, you're hard on yourself and others, and the future looks hopeless. You think your life is to blame for your misery ...when it is really your mood.

One of the biggest mistakes people in bad moods make is attempting to figure out what is wrong and trying to fix it. The problem is that your perspective is too distorted under these conditions to come up with a good solution. You're more likely to get stuck.

Things look so intolerable that we're driven to do something—which often means confronting other people just when we're most edgy and defensive. Some of the worst tensions in relationships are caused by people trying to "work on their communication" when they're in a bad mood.

Best way to deal with a bad mood: Don't pay much attention to it. Recognize that moods are part of the human condition...and just wait it out. Postpone dealing with serious issues until your mood improves. If a situation absolutely must be dealt with immediately, recognize that your judgment is not at its best and proceed carefully.

Make allowances for other people's bad moods as well. Don't try to talk someone out of a mood or offer him or her advice—just give him room to get over it.

◼ Stay open to other people's views.
Most of us assume that others see things the same way we do...or we think they should and try to get them to change.

Most other people not only don't see things our way—they can't. Each person's view is formed by his unique life experiences.

Helpful: Instead of making yourself miserable by trying to convince people that your point of view is the "right" one, try approaching the situation with fascination...and respect.

When people sense that you are genuinely open to their way of seeing things, they become less defensive. Arguments lose their edge. A way is opened for compromise...and much more satisfying relationships.

■ Don't be afraid of negative feelings.
Like the warning light on your car's dashboard that alerts you to pull over before the engine overheats, feelings let us know when we're falling prey to dysfunctional thinking. Feelings let us know when we're on the right track, too.

If you feel angry, jealous, frustrated or just plain lousy, it's a sign you need to take a deep breath, notice what your mind has just been focusing on and relax.

Calm, contented feelings tell you that you are successfully putting into practice the principles that I have already mentioned.

Paying attention to your feelings reminds you to tune into sources of stress and change the way you react to them. You may have heard that it's a good idea to increase your tolerance for stress. *I disagree.*

People with lower stress tolerance are healthier psychologically. Their inner feedback mechanism lets them know something is wrong very early—so that instead of ruining their physical health or taking the stress out on their families, they can make quick adjustments in their thinking...and become more content.

■ Focus on the present, not past or future problems.
Dwelling on past or possible future problems causes us to miss all the present moments that make up real life.

Though understanding how the past has shaped us can be useful, this approach is too often taken to extremes. If you focus calmly on the present instead, you'll be better able to make sense of the past. That's because your mind will be more free of distraction, giving you access to your inherent wisdom and to the memories most likely to help and inspire you.

Helpful: Notice where you are right now...what you're doing...and what's going on around you. Check in with yourself throughout the day and note what you're thinking about. If you're caught up in the past or future, gently bring your attention back to your present surroundings.

It's helpful to think of the mind as a puppy. When you're training a puppy, you aren't too hard on it when it runs off—you simply call it back each time until it learns to stay where it belongs.

Similarly, when your mind wanders into the past or future, just say to yourself, "There I go again—come on back," and return your attention to the present. This process takes patience at first, but the more you do it, the more you'll notice a sense of inner balance and peace.

How to Manage Your Mind

Michael Ritt, Jr., executive director of Napoleon Hill Foundation, 1440 Paddock Dr., Northbrook, IL 60062. The organization publishes the works of Hill, one of the early pioneers of the positive thinking movement. Mr. Ritt is author of *Napoleon Hill's Keys to Positive Thinking*. Dutton.

To have a positive mental attitude, you must develop a solid, success-oriented, "I can...I will" philosophy.

You can't develop this attitude overnight or turn it on and off whenever there's something you want. A positive mental attitude must become an ingrained habit.

BECOME THE MANAGER OF YOUR MIND
The one thing in life you can command is your own mind. Whatever negative people and situations you face, you can always choose a positive attitude. But doing so requires a firm, strong commitment.

Helpful: Begin by writing a self-convincing creed—*I believe I can direct and control my emotions, intellect and habits with the intention of developing a positive mental attitude.*

Post it where you'll see it when you get up in the morning. Read it during the day, and say it aloud. Speaking an intention reinforces it.

Choose a "self-motivator"—a meaningful phrase tailored to help you reach your positive-thinking goals. *Examples...*

▶ **Counter discouragement** with the phrase "Every problem contains the seed of its own solution."

▶ **Fight procrastination** with "Do it now."

Keep your self-motivators close at hand—in your pocket or on your desk—and repeat them throughout the day to instill these important new values.

DEVELOP A LIFE PLAN

Setting short- and long-term goals each day creates a road map for your life. You identify where you're going, focus your mind on getting there and avoid many wrong turns.

Helpful: Use the D-E-S-I-R-E formula as a goal-setting guideline…

▶ **Determine** what you want. Be exact, and express the goal positively. Say what you want to be or do rather than what you don't want.

▶ **Evaluate** what you'll give in return. How much work will you do to turn your plan into action?

▶ **Set a date** for your goal. Be realistic, allowing enough time without postponing it too long.

▶ **Identify** a step-by-step plan. Devise immediate, small steps to get started.

▶ **Repeat** your plan in writing.

▶ **Each and every day,** morning and evening, read your plan aloud as you picture yourself already having achieved your goal.

Writing out your daily goals helps maintain your motivation. Keep them in your pocket or your purse to read frequently throughout the day.

THE POWER OF VISUALIZATION

Because visual images reach into our deepest mental levels, I have found pictures to be profound motivational tools.

Helpful: Make a list of personal qualities you want to develop…write down the names of people with whom you would like to have better relationships… list the material possessions you want to own.

Now clip pictures from magazines and newspapers that symbolize your goals.

> **Example:** *If generosity is your chosen quality, you could use a photo of someone with an outstretched hand.*

Put the pictures where you'll see them every day…and believe that you will get what you have visualized.

You may also create your own "mental pictures" to defeat negative thoughts, such as dwelling on past reversals.

> **Example:** *Imagine yourself in a long corridor lined with many doors, walking purposefully with a large key toward the door marked "Defeats and Failures."*
>
> *In your mind's eye, firmly close that door, lock it and pocket the key. Any time old negative thoughts appear, say to yourself, "I have locked up that thought and have the key in my pocket."*

NEGATE NEGATIVITY

You may not realize you're thinking negatively unless you consciously inspect your thoughts.

The negative ones usually are motivated by one of the following four thoughts…

▶ **You are feeling sorry for yourself.**

▶ **You are blaming someone or passing judgment.**

▶ **Your pride is hurt.**

▶ **You are being selfish.**

Each time you recognize a negative thought, counteract it with an immediate, forceful positive thought.

> **Example:** *When your coworker forgets to copy you on a memo, remember that same person covered for you when you were on vacation.*

If the thought is about you—"I can't accomplish that"—treat it as you would if you heard it from a stranger and defend yourself.

In a negative situation, look for the seed of the positive experience. Although you didn't win the new sales account, you have still learned a valuable lesson for building future success.

If your negativity manifests as worrying, use this "prescription"…

▶ **Write the best outcome** for the situation on an index card.

▶ **Focus on ways to make a positive result happen.**

▶ **Write the best outcome again,** saying that it is indeed possible that it will happen.

Whenever the worry appears, inject the message with a "dose" of optimism and confidence.

STUDY, THINK AND PLAN DAILY

Positive thinking spurs you to action. Yet it requires *planning.* Take time each day—at least 15 or 20 minutes when you can concentrate undisturbed—to study and think. *Try these techniques, using a notebook to record your results...*

▶ **Inspect your thoughts and actions.** Jot down achievements, such as reacting positively to a demanding individual or defeating a negative thought.

▶ **Evaluate your goals.** You may want to change direction or implement new steps.

▶ **Scrutinize important areas of your life.** Looking closely at your personal development, relationships, business interests, etc. inspires new insights and goals.

▶ **Stimulate creative thinking.** Write out questions, then quickly note any and all possible answers. Even seemingly impractical ones may carry the germs of workable ideas.

▶ **Analyze your accomplishments.** As you write out what works for you, you will develop a personal formula for your own success.

▶ **Read inspirational material,** even a paragraph, page or chapter. Add to your notebook the ideas that resonate with you.

MAINTAIN A POSITIVE FOCUS

Giving yourself positive experiences actually reinforces your positive attitude. *Examples...*

▶ **Treat your five senses every day.** Listen to your favorite music, taste a food you love, enjoy a beautiful view, etc.

▶ **Cultivate a sense of humor.** Laughter relaxes tension, and seeing the funny side of things helps you take yourself less seriously.

▶ **Smile when you feel like frowning.** Smile at yourself in the mirror. If this makes you laugh at yourself, the smile will be that much more real.

Now realize the optimistic face you show the world creates positive thoughts about you in everyone you meet.

How America's Top Personal Improvement Gurus Keep Their Resolutions

Joan Borysenko, PhD, psychologist and lecturer in Boulder, CO. She is author of several books, including *A Woman's Book of Life* (Riverhead) and *Minding the Body, Mending the Mind* (Bantam New Age).

Richard Carlson, PhD, one of the country's foremost experts on stress management and reduction, Pleasant Hill, CA. He is author of numerous books, including *You Can Be Happy No Matter What* (New World Library) and *Don't Sweat the Small Stuff* (Hyperion).

George Leonard, pioneer in the field of human potential and president of the Esalen Institute in Big Sur, CA, which is dedicated to the exploration of human capacities. Mr. Leonard is author of 11 books, including *Mastery* (Plume) and *The Life We Are Given* (Jeremy P. Tarcher).

Many people think of resolutions as a hopeful beginning, when they can rid themselves of old ways or old habits and start afresh. For many, though, this means making—and quickly breaking—their resolutions.

Rather than make empty promises, resolve to keep your resolutions. It's not that difficult to do.

Here's how three of the country's leading self-help experts approached their goals...and how they planned to achieve them.

JOAN BORYSENKO

Resolutions are double-edged swords. Most of us believe that drastic change will improve our lives, but then we feel bad at the first challenge in maintaining the resolution.

I don't make resolutions, but I do spend a period of time reflecting on what makes me unhappy and how I can help myself to improve my life. An area of focus for the coming year is to stop punishing myself for falling short of perfection.

> **Example:** *One year, I told myself that I would lose 10 pounds and weigh what I did in college. Although I quickly shed the pounds, they eventually came back because of my erratic travel and relatively erratic eating schedule.*
>
> *The next year I asked myself if I was unhappy because of the extra 10 pounds or because I wanted everything in my life to be ideal...including my figure.*
>
> *This awareness helped me to meet the greater challenge of accepting myself for the person I am—and how I look.*

More important: I decided to focus on tuning in to what causes me to start thinking *if only I...* thoughts. Such thoughts set us up for failure because they unfairly make our happiness contingent on impossible goals.

> **Example:** *"If only I earned twice as much as I do now, I'd be happier."*

Helpful: Thinking about what causes you to feel the way you do and making changes that are in harmony with your lifestyle are keys to reaching your goals and being happy.

Whether you want to lose weight...or exercise regularly...or break a habit, the desire to change must come from within, not from a preconceived notion of how things are supposed to be. When the motivation is internal, the resolution can be carried out externally.

Before making a resolution, ask yourself the following questions...

▶ **What is the motivation behind the resolution?**

▶ **How will I feel if I don't achieve my goal?**

▶ **Will I be able to find it in my heart to forgive myself?**

By forgiving yourself, you will be able to move on or create a new way to achieve your goal. Otherwise, you will feel as if you let yourself down... and that is never productive.

RICHARD CARLSON

The bigger the change we want to achieve in our behavior, the greater the number of related smaller changes that are needed. One of the problems with making resolutions is that they often require dramatic actions that are not aligned with our particular sets of values. So they inevitably fall short of ever becoming reality.

I look at resolutions more philosophically. I spend time regularly thinking about what I really want in life and why. Then I create a plan for how to reach my goals. It doesn't take long—less than one hour—after I've done the thinking about it.

One goal: Recently I decided to cut back on my outside obligations and allot more time for myself and my family.

As an author, I found that the year's endless stream of lectures and interviews, while necessary for relaying the messages in my books, creates an imbalance in my life and leaves me with too little personal time. *My plan to achieve my personal goal was threefold...*

▶ **I prioritized doing just a few interviews daily.**

▶ **I used to have problems saying no.** I felt guilty, and worried that I was disappointing someone. So, I started to practice saying no in a small way with friends—turning down dinner invitations in order to have more private time.

▶ **I make better use of my weekly calendar.** I formally plan personal time in advance, such as setting aside two weekends a year for camping trips with my children. Personal and work engagements are both important, so short of a dire emergency, I won't change my plans.

Resolutions can be especially helpful if they are truly relevant to one's life. A broad-stroke vow to "get healthier" may sound good on paper, but it's probably too big and unrealistic to achieve.

Better: Start with a smaller goal to do 25 push-ups and 75 crunches each morning...or to exercise three times a week. Then slowly build on the satisfaction that goes along with accomplishing what you set out to do.

GEORGE LEONARD

Resolutions are often made without much fore-thought and with little planning as to how they are to be realized. That's why I prefer to think of my resolutions as affirmations, for which I create long-term contracts with myself to make positive changes in my body, being and performance. They are written in the present tense and signed with a definite date of conclusion.

> **Example:** *Let's say you now weigh 140 pounds, but want to weigh 125. Your affirmation would be simply,* I weigh 125, *not* I will lose 15 pounds.

Of course, you know you don't weigh 125 now. The idea is to create a strong *present-tense* image in the realm of your consciousness that your weight is 125. Then you work diligently and patiently to match the mental reality with the material reality.

Recently, one of my affirmations related to my writing. I was in the early stages of a new book, still in the process of developing a style and a rhythm. My affirmation was, *I'm writing steadily and easily, with insight, power and compassion.*

My plan: I set aside four hours for writing every day. Even if I didn't write a word, that time was for getting into the flow and allowing the process to emerge.

I include my affirmations in a daily series of mind, body and spirit exercises that include stretching, deep breathing, meditation and vis-ualization. I say my affirmations aloud several times a day.

I find that four affirmations are enough for any six-month period. My fourth affirmation is always the same—*My entire being is balanced, vital and healthy.*

Important: Allow at least six months for your affirmations to become part of your life. Before you sign and date the contract, make sure they are what you really want.

Focus on changing your functioning rather than hoping to magically change the outside world. Instead of just aspiring to earn more, for exam-ple, focus on improving the way you approach your coworkers and clients. Finally, make sure the changes you want to make are physically and spiritually healthy.

Smarter Decisions, Safer Decisions

Barry Lubetkin, PhD, director, Institute for Behavior Therapy, 104 E. 40 St., Suite 206, New York City 10016. He is author of *Why Do I Need You to Love Me in Order to Like Myself?* Longmeadow Press.

It is most often assumed that making a decision is a rational process. Actually, it's very difficult to make a decision based strictly on a cost/ben-efits approach.

Typical pro and con lists don't take into account many of the key elements involved in decision making—past experiences, present mood, personal risk quotient and emotional conflict.

To make the right decision, you must look at *all* the factors, not only the rational ones. *Here's a help-ful method for making satisfying decisions...*

DECIDING TO DECIDE

The major problem: People "awfulize" and catastrophize the possible consequences of any decision. That leads to fear of making the decision itself. Any decision creates the possibility of going in a new direction, which usually means risk of some sort—personal, financial or both. Most of us are comfort junkies, and we need to increase our risk tolerance in order to get all the goodies available in life.

Some decisions don't work out. Recognizing and accepting this possibility is an important part of being human.

THE DECISION-MAKING PROCESS

▣ Define the problem clearly.
Distill it into one or two sentences.

Unclear: Should I leave my job?

Better: Break the decision into the different alternatives you've considered.

Some possibilities might be: Should I leave my job to try freelancing? Should I leave my job now on the chance that I'll find another one before my savings run out?

▣ Brainstorm.
Without sitting in judgment of any of your ideas, generate all the pros and cons. When you are considering alternative decisions, brainstorm for each option.

Key: Be nonevaluative. Sit around with a friend or relative, and allow yourself to be emotional. Progress from the most serious and rational reasons to the most emotional and absurd.

Rational: I need more money to live.

Emotional: Change drives me crazy.

Absurd: I don't like the bus driver on the route I take to work.

▣ Weigh the alternatives.
Using a scale of one to five, weigh each factor according to how likely it is to influence you and in terms of your best interests.

For instance, how important is money? It's one thing to say you need more money, but another to weigh the need. On a scale of one to five, maybe it's a two.

Example: Maybe money isn't crucial now, but if you're planning to buy a new home, it may rate a three or a four.

▣ Use imagery.
Once you've added up the numerical weights of your pro and con lists, one side will outweigh the other and the decision will be clear. However, since most people are ruled by emotion, having that information in front of you may not lead you to accept that decision. You may still feel stuck.

What to do: Close your eyes and imagine yourself following the numerically chosen decision. See what blocks come up against it. What are the nagging doubts? What are the self-condemnations? You might see yourself making a lot of embarrassing mistakes in your new job. Are you "awfulizing"? Are you *really* likely to make too many mistakes, or is this just a fear that comes from insecurity or perfectionism? Examine each block to see what basis it has in reality.

IF YOU'RE PROCRASTINATING
All of us have been in the position of knowing there's a decision we ought to make but can't bring ourselves to do it. You have to accept you're stuck. Most people start dumping on themselves. Sometimes that anger releases them, but often it causes them to wallow in self-pity.

What to do: Accept that being stuck is an OK place to be for a while. Then define the reason why you're stuck. Is it fear? Challenge the irrational ideas that are causing the fear. Keep using imagery to desensitize yourself to the block.

There's often a psychological secondary gain to being stuck. It's helpful to understand that. Poor decision makers are often committed to remaining stuck because their position is reinforced. They get more attention…or it helps them avoid what they consider a greater difficulty…or it lets them continue to see themselves as crippled.

The Sound Judgment Improvement System

John S. Hammond, DBA, management consultant, John S. Hammond & Associates, 46 Winter St., Lincoln, MA 01773, and former professor at Harvard Business School, Boston. He is coauthor, with Ralph L. Keeney and Howard Raiffa, of *Smart Choices: A Practical Guide to Making Better Decisions.* Broadway Books.

The ability to make wise decisions *consistently* is the key to success. By systematically applying tested principles, you can improve your decisions, experience less wheel-spinning and be better able to explain the soundness of your decisions to others.

THE FIVE STEPS

While some decisions are too trivial to bother spending much time and energy on, those that have lasting consequences should involve these five steps…

▨ Define the problem.

How you evaluate a problem and take it apart determines whether you identify the problem's central issues.

Your whole decision-making process will be undermined if you work on the wrong issues.

> *Example: You think your problem is how to find more time to get your daily tasks done. So you decide to work late into the evening. But perhaps you should have concentrated on how to do the tasks more efficiently or focused on which tasks to eliminate.*

Flexibility is very important in sharpening your definition of a problem. Don't be afraid to change the definition as you better understand your decision situation or as circumstances change.

▨ Clarify your objectives.

What do you want your decision to accomplish? What are your goals? Your needs? Clear, honest objectives will guide you in seeking information and evaluating alternatives.

To define your objectives, write down all the concerns you hope to address through your decision. At first, be creative rather than rigorous. Then narrow down the concerns and express each important one succinctly.

Separate the means from the ends. A common mistake is stating objectives in terms of means instead of digging for more fundamental underlying objectives.

> *Example: When my niece was house-hunting, one of her objectives was to find "a house that was less than three years old." There weren't many of those to choose from. Going beneath her initial objective, however, she realized that "a house in move-in condition" was what she really wanted. In shifting from the means ("less than three years old") to the end ("move-in condition"), she vastly expanded her options.*

The way to get down to fundamental objectives is by asking yourself—why?

> *Example: When planning a new distribution center, a company may list one objective as "to minimize construction time." If you ask why, you may find it is to get the new center operational as quickly as possible. Ask why again, and you discover it is to reduce cost and disruption of service during transition.*

Probing your fundamental objectives may suggest additional possibilities that open the decision-making process.

■ Create attractive and imaginative alternatives.

The decision you eventually make is only as good as the best alternative you present to yourself. So there is much to be gained from creating better alternatives.

Common mistakes: Repeating what you did in the past...making small changes that don't really make much difference...going with the first alternative that comes to mind...choosing among options presented by others rather than coming up with some of your own.

Helpful: Generate new alternatives by taking a fresh look at each objective and asking how it can be achieved. How can you minimize costs of a new program at work? Get your child a good education? Find a vacation spot that is both relaxing and interesting?

You may fall back on the tried and true, but you may also find something new—and much, much better.

■ Envision the consequences.

If you haven't thought out the consequences—how you'll fare with each alternative—before you make a major decision, you may not be happy with what you end up with.

Helpful: Imagine yourself in the future, living with each alternative. Then write a free-form description of the consequences, as precisely as possible.

Some alternatives may seem clearly inferior at this point. Eliminate them. Organize descriptions of the remaining alternatives into a consequences table that enables you to compare them easily.

Example: *You're choosing among several job offers. List them across the top of a page. Then list the important objectives—salary, location, vacation time, job satisfaction, job security, etc.—along the side. Fill in the chart with judgments and data about how each potential job measures up.*

■ Analyze trade-offs.

Making a decision is difficult when one alternative best meets one objective but another is superior in other ways.

Example: *Job A offers a higher salary, but Job B is more interesting...and Job C has more security and better benefits.*

You have to trade off advantages and disadvantages to find the best overall choice. Use the "even swap" method—a kind of bartering system to play alternatives against each other.

How it works: If the $200-a-month salary advantage of Job A is counter-balanced by the better promotion prospects of Job B, you can eliminate "salary" and "advancement" and base your choice between Jobs A and B on other grounds, such as satisfaction and benefits.

COMPLICATING FACTORS

Although all decisions require that you work through these five steps, some decisions are complicated by other factors, including...

■ Uncertainty.

Often you can't be sure about the consequences of your decision until after you decide.

Example: *One flight is cheaper...but if it arrives late, you'll miss a connecting flight. What to do...*

▶ **Identify the uncertainties** that most influence the consequences (whether the flight will be on time).

▶ **Determine potential outcomes** of the uncertainties (the flight will be on time or it won't).

▶ **Judge how likely each outcome is.** (What's the on-time record of the airline and flight in question?)

▶ **Determine the consequences** for each outcome. (How much of a difference would the missed flight make? For example, would you lose a day of vacation?)

▣ Risk-tolerance.

How much risk you're willing to live with is a personal matter. Investigate your feelings about risk in each situation by considering the relative desirability of various consequences.

▣ Linked decisions.

The decision today influences your future choices, so think ahead. Make contingency plans.

AVOID PSYCHOLOGICAL PITFALLS

Even savvy decision-makers can be derailed by psychological traps. *Here are some pitfalls to avoid…*

▣ Anchoring.

You tend to give too much weight to initial impressions, ideas and information.

Solution: Look at the problem from different perspectives. Get input from others, and focus on what you're likely to learn rather than on what you already know.

▣ Protecting past decisions.

You're tempted to make a decision today that will justify an earlier one, even if it means throwing good money or time after bad.

Solution: Ask yourself, "Is my decision based on trying to salvage my self-esteem?" If so, you'll need to pull your self-esteem out of the thought process if you want to come up with the best solution.

▣ Seeing what you want to see.

We tend to seek or give more weight to evidence that supports an existing predilection and discount opposing information.

Better: Expose yourself to conflicting information by getting someone to play devil's advocate. Exposing yourself to your argument's flip side often produces solutions that you hadn't considered.

How to Improve Your Adversity Quotient

Paul G. Stoltz, PhD, president of PEAK Learning Inc., an international consulting firm, 2650 Skyview Trail, San Luis Obispo, CA 93405. He is author of *Adversity Quotient: Turning Obstacles into Opportunities.* John Wiley & Sons.

Some people never seem to be affected by setbacks or crises. Adversity isn't a threat to them but a gift—a chance to test themselves and develop new solutions.

The ability to respond effectively to adversity—what I call the adversity quotient or AQ—has been shown to be more important than IQ (Intelligence Quotient) in predicting who will succeed in life.

RESPONDING TO CRISES

There are four dimensions that make up the "core" of our ability to respond to adversity…

▣ Control.

How much control do you feel you have over unexpected situations? To what extent do you feel you can influence the outcome?

People with high AQs always feel they can do something about tricky situations in which they find themselves. Even when events seem overwhelming, they focus on the elements over which they have at least some useful influence.

■ Ownership.

To what extent do you hold yourself responsible for dealing with an unexpected situation...and how accountable are you for solving the problem?

Accountability doesn't mean accepting blame for things you didn't do. But shouldering the responsibility for making things right will give you a sense of power and help you overcome self-defeating feelings of helplessness and victimization.

People with high AQs are willing to step forward and do what is necessary to overcome the obstacles before them, no matter where the problems originated.

■ Reach.

How far does the fallout from a setback extend beyond the situation at hand and reach into the rest of your life?

People with high AQs are able to keep a crisis from spreading. They recognize that whatever negative consequences exist will be limited and disappear.

The alternative, *catastrophizing*—imagining that the negative impact will spread like wildfire and cost them their jobs or destroy their financial stability—is not for them.

■ Endurance.

How long will the adversity endure?

When something bad happens, it often seems to dominate all other thoughts. In your mind, it becomes a nightmare you expect to last forever.

The ability to see beyond today's trouble is a crucial ingredient of hope and optimism. Such thinking feeds the strength to do what needs to be done.

People with high AQs vividly imagine life after the current difficulty has been overcome.

Where do these *"core" dimensions of adversity* originate? We start learning to meet challenges by watching our parents. If they throw up their hands or panic whenever the going gets tough, their children probably will learn to do the same.

As children encounter difficulties in adolescence, they naturally develop the skills to master them and they become resilient.

LEARN TO LEAD

AQ is essentially a set of learned responses. And it's never too late to learn—or relearn—them. Becoming aware of how you react to adversity and breaking down each reaction into its core components is a powerful tool that can dramatically raise your AQ.

When you encounter adversity, go through the four steps that I call the *lead* process. Ask yourself key questions, and pay close attention to the answers. In this way, you can actually reprogram the way you cope with challenges.

■ Listen to your initial response to adversity.

What thoughts go through your mind?

Do you become upset or do you stay clearheaded? How much control and ownership do you feel? Does the problem seem limited...or do you imagine that the worst will happen?

The faster you tune in to your reactions to adversity, the more effectively you can change your responses.

■ Establish your ownership.

Two questions are critical. *In the wake of what just happened...*

▶ **What do you know for sure will happen in the next 24 to 48 hours?**

▶ **To which of these events are you willing to be accountable?**

■ Analyze the evidence.

Separating fact from assumption will replace overwhelmed feelings with an action plan to address and resolve the crisis.

Specifically, what evidence is there that the situation has to be completely out of your control... or the damage has to reach into all areas of your life...or the consequences must last a long time?

You'll find that the answer to this question is nearly always, "There's no evidence at all."

■ Do something.

Pinpoint the ways you can improve, if not remedy, the situation. Come up with a firm action plan...and carry it out.

▶ **Specifically, explore what can you do to gain more control over the crisis** and make sure terrible things won't happen.

▶ **What actions will limit the fallout** in other areas of your life?

▶ **What actions will keep the damage as brief as possible** or contain it?

Goal: Sit down with pen and paper, and list as many actions you can take as possible. Then decide which step you can commit to taking first...and when you will have it completed. You will feel yourself going from helplessness to immediate, effective action.

ARM YOURSELF WITH "STOPPERS"

Whenever a crisis strikes, anxiety is a frequent—and useless—response. It also spreads like an emotional wildfire, making it impossible to apply rational steps to better cope with the problem.

Soon you start to catastrophize and feel helpless and hopeless. You squander energy and time worrying.

To avoid imagining the worst will happen, use what I call "stoppers" to regain control. *Helpful...*

▶ **When you feel overwhelmed,** slap your knee or any hard surface. Shout, "Stop!" The sting will shock you into a more rational state. Some people leave a rubber band around their wrist. When they feel anxiety, they stretch it six inches and let it go.

▶ **Focus intently on an irrelevant object,** such as a pen, the pattern of the wallpaper or a piece of furniture. If your mind is removed from the crisis, even for a moment, you can return with the calm you need to take effective action.

▶ **Take an activity break.** Just 15 or 20 minutes of brisk walking or other exercise will clear your mind, raise your energy and flood your brain with endorphins—chemicals that put you in a more optimistic mood.

▶ **Put yourself in a setting where you're dwarfed by your surroundings.** Catastrophizing makes problems larger than life. A shift in perspective will cut them down to size.

Drive to the beach and look out over the ocean...stand at the base of a large tree...gaze up at the clouds...or listen to a great piece of music and let the grandeur wash over you.

Such an exercise makes the greatest adversity seem inconsequential and more manageable. By "getting small" we become able to accomplish big things.

Simple System for Much More Effective Worrying ...Yes, Worrying

Edward Hallowell, MD, psychiatrist on the faculty of Harvard Medical School and director of the Hallowell Center for Cognitive and Emotional Health, 45 Claremont Ave., Arlington, MA 02476. He is author of *Worry: Controlling It and Using It Wisely.* Pantheon.

Most of us wish we worried less, but worrying isn't necessarily bad. In fact, we couldn't survive without at least some worry. Worry is nature's way of helping us anticipate—and avoid—danger.

The most successful people are worriers. They're constantly looking for potential problems and taking steps to forestall them. That's what I call *good worry.* It leads to constructive action.

Toxic worry does the opposite. The cascade of negative feelings immobilizes us. We become so paralyzed by our fears that we can't do anything to improve our situation.

The key to handling worry isn't to get rid of it, but to keep it within the normal—or good-worry range.

HOW WORRY GETS OUT OF HAND

Toxic worry is *ruminative* worry—going over and over the same ground without making any progress toward solving the problem. This kind of worry is self-perpetuating. It creates a psychological and physiological spiral in which stress chemicals feed back to the brain, signaling the mind to worry even more.

This is most often triggered by two factors, which I call the "basic equation" of worry—a feeling of *vulnerability*...combined with a perception of *powerlessness*.

To worry effectively, you need to combat these vulnerable and powerless feelings...and mobilize yourself for effective problem solving.

STEPS FOR WORRYING WELL

▨ Change your physical state.

One of the biggest mistakes worriers make is trying to analyze their worry—as though thinking about how worried they are will lead them to a solution. But thinking about your worry only leads to the toxic spiral previously described.

The quickest way to change your mental state is to do something physical. Whenever you catch yourself brooding, don't just sit there—go for a jog, play a game of squash or just run up and down the stairs a few times. Even brushing your teeth is better than just sitting there thinking about how worried you are.

Merely doing some activity will—at least temporarily—push the problem out of your mind.

When you return to the problem, you'll have a different perspective—and be better able to deal with it.

Physical touch is another effective way to calm yourself. Ask someone for a pat on the back or a hug...or schedule an "emergency" massage. These forms of touch can reduce emotional and physical agitation.

▨ Never worry alone.

Your imagination tends to exaggerate the danger you're in. Asking someone you trust for a "reality check" can help to reestablish your optimism and a sense of control.

Don't be shy about asking for reassurance—*Remind me that this is going to work out fine.* Hearing one simple phrase of reassurance is a surprisingly powerful way to break the worry cycle.

If worry strikes late at night—or at any other time when there's no one to talk to—write down your fears and have a "conversation" on paper. This will help put your worry into a concrete—and controllable—form.

PERFORM *EPR*— EVALUATE, PLAN, REMEDIATE

▶ **Evaluate the situation** by asking "What's the pattern here?"

Example: If you're often worried about finances, is it because you're an impulse buyer? Because you haven't planned for your financial future? Because your industry is downsizing?

If you're having trouble getting to the root of a problem, consider consulting an expert—either someone with knowledge about the problem itself (such as a financial adviser) or about how to approach problems (such as a mental health professional).

▶ **Plan.** Brainstorm ways of breaking the pattern. List steps you can take to put your plan into action.

▶ **Remediate.** Take one small step. You won't solve the entire problem today, but taking even one step will increase your sense of power and control.

PREVENTING WORRY

Over time, you can break the habit of chronic worry by doing the following...

▶ **Change what you say to yourself.** Worriers tend to talk to themselves in negative terms. When you catch yourself wallowing in self-defeating thoughts, actively challenge them.

Example: If you're worried about embarrassing yourself at an important meeting, say to yourself,

Stop! I'm going to prepare for the meeting—and I'll do fine.

This may feel forced and artificial, but if you do it consistently—it works.

▶ **Stay active.** Physical activity not only gives you a break from acute worry, but when done regularly, it can also help prevent worry. Exercise increases cerebral blood flow, so that more oxygen and stabilizing chemicals reach the brain. Eventually it will lead to positive changes in brain chemistry.

▶ **Meditate—or pray—regularly.** Although you probably shouldn't sit quietly when you're actively consumed with worry, regular meditation and prayer are as useful as exercise in preventing worry. Even five minutes of contemplation—if you do it every day—can reset the brain's circuits and have an overall calming effect.

▶ **Get connected.** Feeling that you are an indispensable part of something larger than yourself—whether it is family, neighborhood, workplace, church, community choir, sports team, etc.—is a very effective worry-buster.

There's no better antidote to insecurity, vulnerability and helplessness than knowing you can count on a group of people to support you through disappointment, failure or other setbacks…and knowing that others can count on you.

Proven Strategies to Reject Rejection

Barry Lubetkin, PhD, director, Institute for Behavior Therapy, 104 E. 40 St., Suite 206, New York City 10016. He is author of *Why Do I Need You to Love Me in Order to Like Myself?* Longmeadow Press.

Many people automatically conclude that they are personally responsible for any act of rejection. Depersonalizing rejection is the key to overcoming it.

Helpful: Look at where the rejection is coming from. It may actually have little or nothing to do with you.

CHANGE YOUR ATTITUDE

Don't take every slight personally. People can personalize any kind of rejection, even by strangers. Less rejection-prone people assume that an act of rejection is the other guy's fault. Instead of taking rejection personally, they try to generalize it whenever possible.

Recognize that others have the right to form their own opinions of you.

When you identify the thoughts that spring from an act of rejection, they're almost always overmagnified. Fight those thoughts. They lead to an endless loop in which you feel terrible about yourself.

CHANGE YOUR BEHAVIOR

Work out a strategy for coping with rejection in advance. If you're getting ready for a date or preparing to present material to someone at work, visualize the situation and play it out. *Ask yourself…*

LET IT SIT AWHILE

Creative hibernation: Like good wine, good ideas sometimes need time to age. When you put off a task or problem to think about it, you're not necessarily procrastinating. You're in *creative hibernation*. The mind needs time to consolidate and absorb new ideas. Focus on something else, and let your mind finish its creative work undisturbed.

Stanley Mason, CEO, Simco, a research and development firm in Weston, CT, and professor of entrepreneurship, Sacred Heart University, Fairfield, CT.

▶ **How will I feel if I get rejected?**

▶ **What form will the rejection take?**

▶ **How will I cope with it?**

▶ **What will I say if I'm turned down?**

▶ **What kind of relationship will I have with this person if I'm turned down?**

▶ **How can I save face?**

Imagining the worst, and defusing it, will make it easier to deal with whatever happens.

If you are rejected, quickly find activities that reinforce your sense that you are a worthy, valuable person…

▶ **Go out with someone else.**

▶ **Line up job interviews.**

▶ **Assert yourself with your boss.**

▶ **Compete in a sporting event.**

▶ **Take on a tough challenge at work.**

Best Way to Deliver Bad News

When you have bad news to give, do not delay. Choose a setting where the other person can hear the news with dignity and the two of you can handle it responsibly. Give the news in a forthright way—but with a sympathetic, supportive manner. Do not make bad news sound negotiable if they are not.

> **Example:** *If someone is being fired, the decision is not reversible. Acknowledge and respond to the other person's feelings. Whatever he says, help him find something hopeful in the situation. And help him figure out what to do next.*

Charles Foster, PhD, director, The Chestnut Hill Institute, Boston, and author of *What Do I Do Now? Dr. Foster's 30 Laws of Great Decision Making.* Simon & Schuster.

How to Fight Fear of Failure

Be willing to face failure. Before starting something new, ask yourself, *What is the worst thing that could happen?* Be prepared in case of failure—but do not expect to fail.

Helpful: Overcome fear and worry by living in the moment—not anticipating the future. Fear and worry often come from thinking too much and neglecting action. Doing what you fear makes it less fearful the next time you try it.

Robert Anthony, PhD, psychologist and author of *The Ultimate Secrets of Total Self-Confidence.* Berkley Books.

Survival Tactics for Coping with Narcissistic Personality Disorder

Psychiatrist **James F. Masterson, MD,** pioneer in the diagnosis and treatment of personality disorders. He is director of The Masterson Institute for Psychoanalytic Psychotherapy in New York and adjunct clinical professor emeritus of psychiatry at Cornell University Medical College–New York Hospital. He is author of *The Search for the Real Self: Unmasking the Personality Disorders of Our Age.* The Free Press.

The term *narcissism* comes from the Greek myth of Narcissus, who gazed into a pool and fell in love with his own reflection.

I find that the mythic label denigrates the term. Healthy narcissism is essential for emotional well-being. We need narcissism to feel confident in ourselves—and to give adequate consideration to others.

However, in the case of a narcissistic personality disorder, individuals focus exclusively on themselves, demanding that the world "reflect" back an image of idealized perfection.

If you encounter this personality type, a grasp of the underlying psychology can help you cope more effectively.

THE BIRTH OF NARCISSISTIC PERSONALITY

People with this personality disorder must constantly seek outside support and approval. If they get that support and approval, they feel complete and powerful. Without that support and approval, they feel deprived, exposed, vulnerable, angry and lonely. There's some speculation that this type of narcissistic disorder may even be genetic.

Early childhood conditioning also plays a part. The child's real or authentic self may have been ignored—or that self may have been attacked, while a demand was placed on the child to be "perfect." When that occurs, the type of behavior we associate with a narcissistic disorder is over-indulged. Fiercely driven to achieve, these children never develop the capacity to consider others' needs.

WHAT TO WATCH FOR

Most people with this disorder advertise themselves...

▶ **They seek to be the center of attention.** In search of constant approval and praise to reinforce their grandiose sense of self, they're "on stage," dominating the conversation, often exaggerating their importance.

▶ **They lack empathy for others** and have an inflated sense of entitlement, requiring others to respond to their demands and grant favors. They need everything for themselves and are envious of others' accomplishments and possessions.

▶ **Criticism or disapproval takes them back to their difficult childhoods,** sending them into a defensive fury, since any flaw or mistake means they're not perfect.

When things go wrong, they blame others because they cannot acknowledge the imperfections implicit in accepting responsibility.

▶ **Appearance matters more than substance.** Power, wealth and beauty bolster their fragmented self-image.

▶ **They may be extremely driven** because the "narcissistic fuel" of outside approval is so essential. Many are workaholics. However, this personality disorder may not always be immediately obvious. The subtle ones won't show their true colors until "deprived."

> ***Example:*** *Think of the hard-working employee who sabotages the company when passed over for promotion.*

Others may actually pursue and cater to you —if you have something they want, such as looks, money or status.

CAN PEOPLE CHANGE?

Pathologic narcissism is a personality disorder, not a neurosis. That means that, more than a behavior pattern, it is an inherent part of the person's character.

Psychoanalytic psychotherapy, which explores the origins and sources of the underlying fragmented sense of self, can free the person from his or her narcissistic defenses.

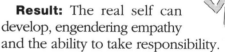

Result: The real self can develop, engendering empathy and the ability to take responsibility.

However, these people usually come for therapeutic treatment only when their behavior causes a major and painful personal crisis—or when they are sent by beleaguered families.

Reality: You won't change a person with this problem. Even constructive criticism is experienced by them as an affront and is met with anger and a sense of betrayal. Placating only results in more demands, not a return of thoughtfulness and consideration.

In fact, if you always excuse or rationalize self-absorption and give in to constant demands, you become an "enabler," actually supporting the behavior.

COPING WITH NARCISSISTIC BEHAVIOR

Sometimes the best way to deal with extreme narcissistic behavior is to end the relationship. *But since this solution isn't always possible, here are survival techniques...*

▨ Set boundaries.

Decide which demands you can meet or how much approval you're willing to give. Then stick with your decision.

Terminate a self-centered conversation if you can, or at least set a time limit on how long you'll listen. At work, having a closed-door policy or pressing deadlines can be effective protection.

▨ Support yourself.

If your resistance to them draws their anger or blame, refuse to be emotionally blackmailed.

Remember: Your time and feelings are not important in this person's eyes. This can help dispel your guilt.

▨ Use bargaining chips.

If you have something they want—such as a special expertise or solutions to problems—share it sparingly to keep their worst behavior under control.

Be aware that when you no longer satisfy them, their old ways will resurface.

▨ Avoid anger.

Any confrontation should be conducted quietly and with control. But even a tactful approach may be greeted with anger or sometimes frightening rage.

Very likely, you'll hear that the difficult situation is your problem and there's something wrong with you. Arguing will only make you feel like you're moving in circles.

Don't expect accommodation from the other person—but do give yourself points for standing up for your rights.

▨ Know when to leave.

Dealing with this personality disorder can undermine your own sense of self.

Ask yourself some questions...

▶ **Does every interaction stir up my emotions?**

▶ **Do I continually feel depressed, irritable, devalued and worthless?**

▶ **Does my anger and resentment carry over into other relationships?**

▶ **Have I stopped supporting myself in general, not treating myself well or allowing others to coerce me?**

If you've answered yes too many times, you must examine the importance of your relationship with this person.

How to Be Safe in This Increasingly Unsafe World

Harold H. Bloomfield, MD, psychiatrist in private practice in Del Mar, CA who also leads seminars on emotional well-being. He is author of several books, including *How to Be Safe in an Unsafe World.* Crown.

Our personal safety depends not only on how well we protect ourselves from physical harm, but also on how we shelter ourselves from assaults on our emotions and well-being.

In my years as a psychiatrist, I have found that the loss of control that we feel during harsh emotional encounters—with strangers, coworkers, friends or family—can be as traumatic and long-lasting as physical attacks.

Equally damaging is what I call an inner mugging, in which you are sabotaged by your own negative thoughts and feelings.

EMOTIONAL UNCERTAINTY

Our emotions function as a warning system, alerting us to threats and spurring us to take defensive action.

But unless strong emotions—fear, anger and hurt—are rationally assessed and redirected when necessary, they can dominate behavior. That curtails our confidence and effectiveness.

By developing emotional management skills, you will be better able to express your needs and expectations to yourself and others. You will be well-equipped to take the risks necessary to grow, thrive and learn from your mistakes.

When our strong emotions are left to dominate and rule our behavior, we live "disconnected" by fear from everyday life, feeling like victims even when no real threat exists.

When feelings of fear or hostility are persistent, there is also the danger that they will contribute to heart disease and high blood pressure…and compromise our immune systems.

SHIELDING YOURSELF FROM HOSTILITY

The key to regaining control over strong emotions is a series of mental/emotional shifts. You must consciously develop a strong inner reserve of calm, confidence and mental shielding from hostility.

By creating an inner core of safety, you will no longer need to raise your hand or voice in an effort to deter or defuse perceived attacks on your emotions.

▨ Cultivate a state of calm alertness.
Tension predisposes you to break under stress. However, alertness—the optimal, activated, tension-free state of the brain—enables you to observe an adversary and situation calmly and to choose your response rationally. *Exercises to cultivate a state of calm alertness…*

▶ **Think of your brain's sensory perceptions as an invisible energy field** surrounding you like a large sphere. Strong emotions sap this clear "energy balloon," while calm alertness expands

it. Mentally "inflating" the sphere to its optimum size calms you and increases your self-confidence.

▶ **Imagine a point of light a few feet from your chest.** Enlarge it into a thin wall of bright, warm light, then into a clear, glowing shield that surrounds and protects you, deflecting critical or hostile remarks while letting in friendly words and kind gestures.

▶ **Create an inner-safety anchor** that instantly connects you with a deep inner "safe space."

Example: *Sit quietly and breathe deeply until you feel completely calm. Vividly picture a real-life experience that made you feel safe. Or imagine a strong sense of safety.*

When the picture is clear, come up with a "sensory signal," such as pressing your thumb and index finger together. If you repeat the exercise frequently, you will be able to elicit the feeling of safety every time you use your anchor touch.

▶ **Maintain calm energy.** To prevent fatigue and tension from depleting your energy, routinely activate your brain's "alertness switches." These are dramatic changes in your activity that will automatically cause you to become more aware of your surroundings and other people.

Alertness switch #1: A two- to five-minute break from work at midmorning and midafternoon. Working nonstop decreases your awareness.

Alertness switch #2: Periodic physical activity. Even a few minutes of muscular movement every hour, such as push-ups in your office, increase energy and alertness.

You may also consider trying regular meditation. Two 20-minute sessions a day during which you sit quietly and breathe deeply foster mental and emotional composure.

■ Choose your battles.

Confrontations are emotionally draining and wear you down. They also rob you of the energy that you could have used more productively. The key is to use your energy on meaningful confrontations while letting others go. *Techniques to protect yourself from nonessential confrontations...*

▶ **The fishhook**. Think of all insults and criticisms as a series of fishhooks. Now see yourself as a fish in a stream. You have the choice of whether to bite or swim away.

▶ **"Anger-release" walk.** As little as five minutes of brisk walking can alter your psychological state, especially when combined with a conscious shift in mental focus.

■ Control your conflicts.

How you engage those who confront you will dictate the quality of your emotional safety. It is essential that you manage your responses from the first confrontational moment.

Strategies for sidestepping emotionally charged reactions...

▶ **Sustain your breathing.** Most of us tend to stop breathing for several seconds when stress rises, reducing oxygen flow to the brain and heightening anxiety. Consciously maintaining steady breathing promotes calm energy and clear thinking.

Key: Breathe deeply, and be sure to hold each breath for at least five seconds. You will feel more relaxed within one minute.

▶ **Be present in each experience.** The effort of blocking out unsettling situations and how they make you feel can interfere with reasoning and objective decision making.

Helpful: Practice tuning in to your physical and emotional sensations while you are calm and relaxed. This exercise will help you condition yourself to remain present and mindful under stress.

It's also beneficial to limit impulsive reactions, which can escalate disagreements and delay the best responses. Remaining calm may dissolve tension without any further action. *Helpful...*

▶ **Identify your feelings** and determine how best to guide your emotional energy. Remember, calm does not mean frozen or dispassionate.

Both withdrawal and pushing back can elevate hostility. Instead, surprise and disarm the conflict with two or more de-escalating phrases and/or two or more unexpected actions.

Examples: *De-escalating phrases such as "I understand," "Please explain" and "You seem upset" extend empathy. This understanding and acknowledgment allows a hostile person to save face, which can help defuse anger.*

Important: While you use these de-escalating phrases, keep your voice steady and at its lowest pitch but in a slightly louder-than-conversational volume. Maintain a level, rather than a questioning, intonation.

Protective actions to defuse hostility might include taking a step away...folding your arms in front of you as a symbolic shield...or combining emphatic words and actions with a turn to the side to preserve your personal space.

Practicing these principles can change the quality of your energy, allowing you to avoid hostility and keeping you safe from real or perceived challenges to your emotional safety.

Why So Many Smart People Do Such Dumb Things

Mortimer Feinberg, PhD, cofounder of the New York consulting firm BFS Psychological Associates. He is coauthor of *Why Smart People Do Dumb Things: The Greatest Business Blunders, How They Happened, and How They Could Have Been Prevented.* Fireside.

A high level of intelligence brings success, prosperity and power. But it also triggers dumb mistakes for many highly intelligent people.

History is filled with people with exceptional mental abilities who committed blunders that cost them their wealth, their good names, their freedom…and even their lives.

How can people who are so smart be so dumb? Intelligence is a double-edged sword. The same capacity to think through knotty problems can also rationalize poor judgment.

Feeling smarter than others can delude us into believing that we are above the rules everyone else must follow.

Self-defense: Being more aware of the pitfalls that can bring us down.

THE PERILS OF PRIDE

The ancient Greeks used the word *hubris* to describe the overbearing pride that brings down the great and powerful. The Greeks considered hubris a form of insolence toward the gods.

Today, hubris is considered a type of arrogance that makes some people think they're exempt from the forces of shame, decency and public opinion. It's the belief that when at the top, we have earned the right to do anything we wish.

Daily life becomes too ordinary—or too dull—for those people who come under the spell of hubris. They need the thrill of constant conquest. And that usually leads them to take greater risks.

Overconfidence plus a reckless disregard for risk is a dangerous combination. People who fit this profile don't stop pushing the envelope until they've broken all the way through—and finally fail.

THE NEEDS OF NARCISSISTS

Narcissists are so wrapped up in themselves—their power, vision and brilliance—that they lose touch with the world around them. They come to think that other people just don't matter—except when they can provide gratification.

Narcissists have no problem trumpeting their brilliance. Through sheer self-confidence, they create the impression of competence, power and superiority.

But this flamboyant strength hides a fatal weakness—disconnection from reality. They ignore the warning signs to slow down and be cautious. Narcissists are masters of denial. They ignore any challenge to their conviction that they're the greatest.

THE DANGERS OF ARROGANCE

Smart, hardworking, successful people naturally feel that their efforts should be rewarded. But this feeling, unfortunately, often turns into a sense of entitlement that grows out of control.

They eventually feel they're better than everyone else—so they believe they deserve more…and demand more.

Their "needs" frequently demand much more money, limos, larger offices, sexual favors—and lots of unnecessary new technology, too. While part of the mind urges caution, fairness and decency, those messages are no match for the intellect's ability to rationalize the desire to get everything it wants.

Sooner or later, the drive of entitlement alienates others or even runs afoul of the law.

> **Example:** *We all have read about cases in which wealthy, powerful people have been arrested for tax evasion. Sometimes when the case unfolds, we find that the illegality involved not paying sales taxes on small gifts.*
>
> *Could they afford the taxes? Of course. But their feelings of superiority—"only little people pay taxes"—arrogantly put them above the rules.*

THE THRILL OF FAILURE

It's exhilarating to be "Number One." But it's also exhausting. Being the best and the brightest carries an enormous, continual burden to defend that position. Such people often long for the day when they can stop struggling so hard.

In addition, many people who have turned their powerful minds to the successful pursuit of money, status and achievement harbor a secret sense that they're not worthy. Deep down inside, they doubt they can handle success, and at the core of their being they just don't want it.

Many of these people share a secret desire to fail, which helps explain why successful people abandon brilliant game plans in exchange for senseless risks at the brink of victory.

An impulsive desire to fail seems to come out of nowhere, flies in the face of common sense and brings them down.

HOW TO PROTECT YOURSELF

■ Question your motives.

The best defense against dumb mistakes is in becoming more aware of any changes in your personality.

Get into the habit of asking yourself whether your intelligence and success are causing you to become too filled with pride, arrogance or narcissism.

Warning signs: Always thinking you are right...failing to hear the logic of arguments that oppose your own...and believing you have super-powers or some magic touch that never fails to get you out of trouble.

■ Acknowledge your personality flaws.

One way to avoid making fatal mistakes is to admit your weaknesses as well as your strengths— without becoming puffed up with pride or crushed by shame.

Accept that there will always be some situations in life that you will handle badly. Work to improve your abilities in these areas rather than use your mind to fool yourself—and/or others.

When you've improved your abilities in these areas, assume there are other aspects of your behavior and set of skills that need work.

Never, ever fall into the trap of believing that you are perfect and do not need any more polishing.

■ Calibrate your inner compass.

Stay on course by putting your values ahead of your intelligence and ambitions. Constantly ask yourself what's most important—your ego...the respect and affection of others...your position of leadership...making more money...or service to others?

It's perfectly healthy to have several of these values, but it is dangerous to be obsessed with any one of them. When you become too focused on one, your motives and actions may be compromised.

■ Keep in touch with reality.

It's a big mistake to believe that only the lame seek the counsel of others. Share your plans and ambitions with trusted friends, savvy advisers and, above all, those you love—and those who love you.

The more you seek advice from people you trust, the better your chances of making sound decisions.

We Are What We Read

Esther Dyson, technology industry analyst and venture capitalist— and author of *Release 2.1*, which examines the complexities of human life on the Internet. Broadway Books.

Martin Groder, MD, psychiatrist and business consultant in Chapel Hill, NC. He is author of *Business Games: How to Recognize the Players and Deal with Them.* Bottom Line Books.

Alan Lakein, the country's leading expert on time management and author of *How to Get Control of Your Time and Your Life.* Signet Books.

Nancy Samalin, the director of Parent Guidance Workshops in New York City and author of *Loving Each One Best: A Caring and Practical Approach to Raising Siblings.* Bantam Books.

Michael Stolper, president, Stolper & Co., San Diego.

Sir John Templeton, the eminent financier, philanthropist and founder of the John Templeton Foundation in Radnor, PA, which supports more than 60 educational and religious programs.

E veryone has at least one or two books that have changed their outlook on life and greatly influenced their life's direction. *Here leading experts in their fields discuss the books that meant the most to them...*

ESTHER DYSON

T he books with the most profound effect on me were the works of George Orwell that warned of the dangers of ignorance and lies. *Examples...*

Such, Such Were the Joys and Other Essays is about boarding school. The young Orwell in the essay knows so little about the world that he thinks the terror he lives with is normal.

Down and Out in Paris and London and *The Road to Wigan Pier* are great models of honest reporting. He got out and about with real people and reported the truth in all its complexity.

These books didn't so much change my direction as establish it. I wanted to directly experience things, then lay out the truth in all its complexity so that others could make their own decisions.

Orwell's works insist that the truth matters and you can't sit back and let others make decisions for you. You must constantly struggle in life to determine the truth.

MARTIN GRODER

W omen Who Run with the Wolves by Clarissa Pinkola Estes, PhD, is a collection of fairy tales that has changed many lives. The book encourages people to define themselves as individuals in the world while remaining connected to the people they care about.

Through the stories, the author urges readers to reclaim their emotional lives and their natural inclination to be open and care about others. *Key lessons…*

▶ **You can make your own decisions.** You can set goals and ask others for help to attain those goals. Taking care of your own interests is perfectly legitimate.

▶ **Even if you are treated well now, you won't necessarily be treated well in the future.** These stories say, "Be alert. Guard your ability to think and act independently."

▶ **You always have a second chance.** If you've been naive and given up something of yourself, go reclaim it.

This last one is a wonderful message for people who have surrendered large parts of themselves to be on the achievement track.

ALAN LAKEIN

T he late Dr. Norman Vincent Peale's *The Power of Positive Thinking* changed my life. When I was in high school, I read many self-help books because I felt very negative about myself and wanted to change how I felt.

Dr. Peale's book offered specific techniques for helping me see that I had worth and that there were possibilities for me. *Key lessons from Dr. Peale's classic book…*

▶ **List all your strengths.** Ask friends what they see as your strengths. Combine the lists. Look at the master list every day to remind yourself of your merits and find reasons to pat yourself on the back.

▶ **Think about who and what…prompts you to have negative thoughts about yourself** and your life. Avoid them and reject their negative messages. Those messages stop you from moving ahead because they convince you that you can't succeed.

▶ **Stop discounting the positive things people say about you.** Stop acting as if you don't deserve the good things that come your way. Accept that you are worthy of new opportunities, and pounce on them. Expect the best, and you'll get it.

NANCY SAMALIN

I read *Between Parent and Child* by Dr. Haim Ginott when my kids were preschoolers, in the mid-1960s. The book focuses on the way we talk to our kids, but without psychological mumbo jumbo or vague theoretical admonitions. It is a marvelously instructive book.

Dr. Ginott uses many examples—real parent–child dialogues—to show that the way we talk to our children affects how they see themselves…how they see us…and how we deal with each other. The book focuses not just on children's *behavior* but on their *feelings* as well.

His book helped me distinguish between children's feelings and their behaviors. Acknowledging how children feel is one of the most effective and powerful ways to improve their behavior and parent–child relationships.

MICHAEL STOLPER

Enlightened self-interest is at the root of all behavior, including my own. That was the simple lesson of Ayn Rand's *Atlas Shrugged*. The book says that when you interact with people, you need to figure out where their interests lie.

Everything you subsequently do or say to them will flow from that.

David Halberstam's *The Best and the Brightest* is another favorite. It shows how some people can get slaughtered on the altar of another person's hubris and vanity. He also warns readers to avoid systems in which you surrender control. Otherwise, you wind up part of the body count for reasons that have nothing to do with merit.

SIR JOHN TEMPLETON

I discovered a slender novel called *Flatland* when I was at Yale in 1931. It was written in 1885 by an English headmaster, Edwin Abbott, whose hobbies were theology and mathematics.

This delightful novel can still make even the smartest people realize how little they know and how a greater reality can be discovered by welcoming scientific research.

The hero, Mr. Square, lives in a land where people know only length and width and have no comprehension of height. Mr. Square discovers this dimension and begins to tell people about it. For revealing that height exists, he is put in prison for life along with those whom he told, so that his heresy will not spread.

The lesson—be enthusiastic about new concepts rather than resistant to them.

In my view, science has shown that new concepts make us more broadminded and that heretics are often heroes.

How to Make Your Dreams Come True—Lessons from The Dreamers of Impossible Dreams

Steven K. Scott, cofounder of American Telecast Corp., a direct-television marketing company, 1230 American Blvd., West Chester, PA 19383. He is author of *Simple Steps to Impossible Dreams*. Simon & Schuster.

Dreams are easy to achieve if you are no longer willing to put up with mediocrity. The way to stop settling and start achieving is to overcome childhood fears that being criticized for trying an idea is worse than not trying at all. Dreams come true when we recognize that it is not bad to try and fail.

Here are the secrets of some of the world's most successful dreamers…

■ **Even the wildest dream needs a plan.**
Many people think that Henry Ford invented the automobile. He didn't. The automobile was invented in 1769 and was powered by steam. The first gasoline-powered car was built about 18 years before Ford sold his first car.

Henry Ford's impossible dream: He wanted every family in America to own its own car. That was an impossible dream early in the 20th century, when all cars were built by hand, one at a time. Automobiles were too expensive for all but the very rich. Yet Ford made the automobile available to nearly everybody by developing the moving assembly line.

Ford achieved his dream by turning it into a clear plan of action. *He did that by converting…*

▶ **His dream into specific goals.**

▶ **His goals into specific steps.**

▶ **His steps into specific tasks.**

Then he assigned a specific time to complete each task. All he had to do was follow that plan, step by step, task by task, and his dream would be achieved.

Payoff: There were about 250 other car manufacturers when Ford built his Model T assembly plant in 1908. With his assembly line, he built more cars in one day than most of his rivals could build in one month. By 1914, he was building more cars in one day than most competitors could build in one year. Between 1908 and 1928, he made more than 17 million cars.

▦ Aim as high as you can.

Most people go through life just hoping to get on base. Whether it's in their marriages, their relationships with their children, their businesses or their careers, they just want to avoid striking out. They never realize that they are capable of hitting home runs.

Babe Ruth's impossible dream: Ruth never worried about striking out. He never tried to get a walk or just hit singles, doubles or triples. His dream was to hit a home run every time he came up to bat. He didn't achieve that. But Ruth came closer than anyone in history.

▦ Set goals that are beyond your reach instead of simply setting achievable goals that are easy to reach.

Babe Ruth never lowered his sights. He never settled for what was easily attainable. He set his sights on the unattainable and dreamed how to reach it.

Nobody achieves *all* of his or her dreams. But when you dream impossible dreams, even if you do not achieve them, you wind up much closer than you would have if you had not dreamed.

▦ Seek partners who can help you achieve your dreams.

Movie director Steven Spielberg didn't know how to create the model of a dinosaur. He didn't know how to create a computerized special effect. If you put him in front of a computer and gave him a year, he still couldn't create a special effect.

Steven Spielberg's impossible dream: Even though he possessed none of the technical skills that such a project would involve, Spielberg wanted to make the most amazing movie ever

about dinosaurs. He achieved his dream so completely that when *Jurassic Park* was finished, it was so realistic it scared everyone who saw it.

Spielberg turns all of his impossible dreams into reality by finding the best people to do what he can't do. For *Jurassic Park*, he hired the best model maker in Hollywood to make dinosaur replicas. He recruited the leading special-effects company to create action and sounds.

Spielberg learned that he didn't have to do everything himself to achieve his dreams. All he had to do was find the top experts who knew how to do it. His job is to recruit and motivate people to achieve the impossible—and to direct the movie.

▦ Accept responsibility for *staying determined.*

Imagine being both blind and deaf from childhood. Imagine never seeing your mother's smile or hearing your father's voice saying, "I love you." How could anyone in such a situation dare to dream impossible dreams?

Helen Keller's impossible dream: Even though Keller was left both blind and deaf in childhood, she dreamed of leading a complete, satisfying and positive life. Against all odds, she achieved that dream. Although Keller never regained her sight or hearing, she did learn to communicate. And through her spoken and written words, she inspired millions.

Keller never surrendered to bitterness or resentment. Whatever had been taken away from her, Keller wrote, she had been left her soul. "Possessing that, I still possess the whole."

▦ Put passion into everything you do.

Passion fuels the engines that turn impossible dreams into reality. I have never known or read about any dream achiever who hasn't been driven by a passion for his dreams. Passion is the secret weapon that is shared by people who make their dreams come true.

Oprah Winfrey's impossible dream: Oprah wants to produce the most influential, most exciting, most captivating show on television. The engine that has driven her phenomenal success is her passion—her passion for life, work, people and excellence.

Even though she grew up poor, Oprah has said she discovered very early in life that there is no discrimination against excellence. The way she demonstrates her respect for excellence is through her passion. It doesn't matter who her guest is or what subject the show is featuring, Oprah becomes passionate about it.

Lesson: Most people think you either have passion or you don't. My experience—based on the lives of those successful people I have studied—is that you can bring true passion into any important area of your life.

Use It...or Lose It... the Virtues of Practice... the Dangers of Neglect

Martin Groder, MD, psychiatrist and business consultant in Chapel Hill, NC. He is author of *Business Games: How to Recognize the Players and Deal with Them.* Bottom Line Books.

The longer you neglect the talents and skills that you developed over the years, the harder it is to bring them back to their former levels of excellence.

Once you've reached the point of no return, you probably won't even make the effort.

The deterioration of our abilities occurs due to disuse. This law applies equally to mental and physical abilities—to chess as well as to tennis.

WHY WE LOSE IT

Much of the decline in strength and stamina that we blame on age is actually due to the disuse cycle. Slow down, and it gets harder to pick up the pace again—so the natural tendency is to slow down even more.

Activities as diverse as shooting pool, playing the piano, speaking a foreign language or responding

sexually are coordinated by complex interactions of nerve cells in the brain.

When you practice, these neurons actually grow microscopic filaments to connect to one another. It's a process known as arborization. When you stop practicing, these connections wither away.

Every time you learn new skills or master fresh areas of knowledge, neurons secrete growth hormones that foster arborization, thus stimulating their own growth and the growth of their neighbors.

BRAIN DRAIN

Part of the brain is devoted to learning, striving to meet challenges and dealing with frustration...while another part takes care of establishing habits and routines. Let one part atrophy, and its functions are taken over by the areas that are used more. When you stop challenging yourself and expanding your skills, that part of your brain goes quiet and brain activity shifts to its humdrum mode. The more you let yourself become stodgy and fail to challenge yourself, the harder it is to reactivate that part of your brain.

Motivation is often a major victim of this process. Once you let your skills decay, it's harder to feel excited about anything new.

> *Example: Playing piano poorly or not seeing results from exercising isn't very rewarding, so you're sorely tempted to let the activity slide altogether rather than make the effort to correct the situation or merely stay at a level that matches your innate abilities.*

A LITTLE PRACTICE

Finding the time to maintain skills in our busy lives may seem an elusive goal. But it's important to remember that in midlife or beyond, you get the most benefit from the first small effort. By practicing your skills, even just a little each week, you will be able to exercise the capacities that are important to you.

Practicing many of your skills just a little bit is more important than concentrating on just one or two. How much practice is enough? There's no universal rule, but when it comes to physical exercise, a workout every other day for 20 to 40 minutes appears to be enough to keep you in shape...and healthy. In music, too, it appears that a half-hour to an hour of practice every other day will maintain a significant level of skill.

So—using what you don't want to lose at least two to three times a week for a half-hour to an hour is a good minimum for which to strive.

MAKE PRACTICE COUNT

To ensure the time you devote to maintaining your skills is well spent, take yourself seriously enough to optimize conditions for fruitful practice.

▶ **Use the right equipment.** If you're walking to maintain fitness, get good walking shoes. Honing your piano skills? Get the piano tuned. It will make the experience more rewarding and increase the odds that you'll keep doing it.

▶ **Make practice enjoyable.** Some people like to walk, run or bike alone...while others need to feel the support of fellow strivers in a gym or health club. Ask yourself what works best for you.

Example: Will sharing your essays motivate you to keep writing? Join a workshop or organize a writers' salon on your own.

▶ **Find your level of practice...**and stick with it. Some people want to keep their skills sharp in a relaxed way, without strain, as an enjoyable leisure pursuit. Others prize the exhilaration of feeling themselves tested and stretched. Let your personal preference guide you.

▶ **Know your limits.** A big mistake is falling into the "pro" trap. Some people don't bother practicing their own skills because they know they won't ever become the champions they so admire.

Admire those who have achieved excellence, but don't model yourself after them. Realize your limitations. Remind yourself that the goal is to keep your abilities alive, not to conquer the world.

BE KIND TO YOURSELF

Attitude plays a big role in how well you perform and whether you stick to your regimen. A positive outlook fuels your determination to keep your capacities sharp, while negativity kills motivation. *Helpful...*

▶ **Be generous and accepting toward yourself,** particularly if you're trying to retain or regain competence in an area where you were once highly skilled.

▶ **Accept the role of student,** even if the activity you choose is something at which you once excelled.

▶ **Don't match your performance against memories of a younger self at the peak of your powers...**at a time when lots of practice had honed your skills.

▶ **Be a patient teacher or coach to yourself,** the kind who throws the ball to a kid a thousand times before the child learns to catch it. Summon up thoughts of past mentors. Enlist patient, supportive companions who will encourage you.

Important: Keep bad coaches and negative role models out of the picture. Listen for that nasty self-critical inner voice—we all have one —and silence it. Avoid "friends" who sap your confidence.

PRACTICE PEOPLE SKILLS

The abilities you need to get along with others— communicating, working as part of a team, compromising, making helpful judgments instead of destructive criticisms—need practice.

If you work at home, as increasing numbers of people do today, you may lack the day-to-day interaction that maintains these parts of your personality.

Solitude is important as well. People who are constantly surrounded by others—parents who have young children…anyone who works and comes home to a lively house—can lose the capacity for quiet and reflection.

Zig Ziglar's Secrets of Self-Motivation— How to Release the Awesome Power Within You

Zig Ziglar, chairman, Ziglar Training Systems, a training and development company, 15303 Dallas Pkwy., Ste. 550, Addison, TX 75001. He is author of 23 books, including *Success for Dummies*. IDG Books Worldwide.

Nearly 75% of world-class leaders whom I have studied were raised in poverty, had been abused as children or had some serious physical disability.

How did these people overcome these problems and get to the top? And how did they manage to stay there?

The key is motivation. Motivation gives you the "want to" and provides the spark. It enables you to utilize your training and experience while finding the strength, character and commitment to keep you going when the going gets tough.

MOTIVATIONAL STRATEGIES
■ Self-talk.
You *must* be in your own corner.

To start, take a 3" x 5" card and write such positive affirmations as, *I am an honest, intelligent, responsible, organized, goal-setting, committed individual whose priorities are firmly in place.*

On another card, write, *I am a focused, disciplined, enthusiastic, positive-thinking, decisive extra-miler who is a competent, energized, self-starting team player determined to develop and use all of these leadership qualities in my personal, family and business life. These are the qualities of the winner I was born to be.*

Read these positive affirmations to yourself several times a day.

■ Goal-setting.
Be specific.

Create a *Wild Idea Sheet* of everything you want to be, do or have.

Wait a day or two and then write the reason why you want to reach each goal. Ask yourself if each goal will make you happier or healthier, improve family relations, make you more secure or give you hope. Most important, will reaching each goal contribute to a balanced, successful life? Divide remaining goals into short-range (one month or less)…intermediate (one month to one year)…and long-range (one year or more).

■ Positive thinking/positive training.
When I was on the seventh-grade boxing team, I stepped into the ring with a much smaller opponent.

I was a confident, excited positive thinker.

All of those things disappeared in the flash of an eye—or maybe a fist. My opponent might have been smaller, but he had been on the boxing team since he was in fifth grade and understood the defensive aspects of boxing. He also knew that a straight punch was the shortest distance to my nose. Luckily, a compassionate coach took me aside and gave me some good instruction—fast.

Lesson: In addition to having a positive attitude and enthusiasm for what you're doing, you need to learn the skills of your trade. Education and training are essential. Enthusiasm by itself is like running fast in the dark.

■ Professional counseling.
If you broke your leg, you would not hesitate to seek professional medical help.

SURROUND YOURSELF WITH SUCCESS

Spend time with people who do what you want to do—and live as you want to live. You will pick up new ideas, possibilities and images. Read books by and about people you admire. Hear and see their music and art. Their creativity will inspire your own. Keep a self-appreciation book. When people compliment you, write down their remarks. Get in the habit of noticing praise and recording it to review later. This will boost your self-image by making you aware of your praise-worthy qualities.

Joan Steinau Lester, EdD, former executive director, The Equity Institute, diversity think tank, Berkeley, CA, and author of *Taking Charge: Every Woman's Action Guide to Personal, Political and Professional Success.* Conari.

But there are still many people who believe we should be able to take care of our emotions or our mind-sets and heal ourselves.

You get information out of books, magazines and newspapers. You get knowledge out of encyclopedias and educational institutions. Yet until you add the spiritual dimension, you're going to miss the insights, wisdom and common sense that are critical to any healing process.

Get counseling from a person who has *wisdom* as well as knowledge. Someone with knowledge has only command of the facts. But someone with wisdom has good judgment and insights into what you're facing.

Go right to the top—the best person you can identify—to get the help that you need to solve your problems.

■ Control your environment.
You might not be able to change the world, but you can change *your* world.

A sound exercise program and sensible eating habits are as important as feeding your mind good, clean, powerful positive inputs.

Even the kind of music you listen to will affect your feelings and energy level. Soothing melodies are best when you need to relax and wind down. Positive messages in songs are useful when you need to get up in the morning and get started for the day.

■ Use words that paint the right picture.
The sales manager who says to the salesperson going out to make a call, *This is our number-one client...be careful...don't foul up the deal,* paints the wrong picture and shakes the salesperson's confidence.

Such comments do more harm than good.

The right picture: *This is our number-one client. That's the reason I'm sending you out to make the call. I know you will handle it professionally and effectively.*

Use a note pad. When you catch yourself saying something that paints a negative picture, write down what you said and then later rephrase it to paint a positive picture.

> **Sample:** *Don't say,* I hope I don't forget my keys. *It's far better to say,* I'm going to remember that I placed my keys in my top drawer.

The most influential person you talk to all day long is you, and what you tell yourself has a direct bearing on your performance.

■ Last deposit.
Leave every encounter on a positive note.

If one person gives you a negative feeling, change your mood by going to an upbeat friend or acquaintance to get a quick fix. When you need to ask your spouse to run an errand or do a favor for you, save *I love you* for last.

Common Sense Remedies

Chapter 3

Alcohol–Acetaminophen Warning

Anyone who generally consumes three or more drinks containing alcohol per day should not take acetaminophen without consulting a doctor. Acetaminophen—the active ingredient in Tylenol and other pain relievers—can cause liver failure and death in alcoholics and heavy drinkers. *Self-defense:* Follow label directions. Consult your doctor before taking any pain reliever on an ongoing basis.

William Lee, MD, director, Clinical Center for Liver Diseases, University of Texas Southwestern Medical Center, Dallas, whose study of 71 cases of acetaminophen overdose was published in *The New England Journal of Medicine.*

Antibiotic Complexities

In some cases, an antibiotic should be taken with food…in others, with lots of water to wash it down so it does not irritate the stomach. Some antibiotics kill helpful as well as harmful bacteria, opening the way for yeast infections—so they may need to be taken with an antifungal drug or a second antibiotic. Eating yogurt or drinking milk limits some side effects—but dairy products can make certain antibiotics ineffective. *Bottom line:* Ask your doctor how best to use the particular antibiotic prescribed for you.

Bruce Yaffe, MD, internist and gastroenterologist in private practice, 201 E. 65 St., New York City 10021.

Back-Saving Basics

Sitting improperly causes just as much back strain as lifting improperly. Sitting slouched over stretches spinal ligaments and increases pressure on the discs, and is a major source of back injury.

Best for your back: Sit up straight in a good chair.

Elements of a good chair: The seat pad should not put pressure on the backs of the knees. Armrests should be close enough so you do not have to lean to the side to reach them—and should be adjustable. The seat back should tilt back 10 degrees, be high enough to support your entire back and have lumbar support. The chair should turn easily and have casters for movement.

Stephen Hochschuler, MD, orthopedic surgeon specializing in spine surgery, cofounder of the Texas Back Institute, Plano, and author of *Back in Shape*. Houghton Mifflin.

Do Not Heat that Bad Back

I f you have a back attack—a sudden, painful muscle strain causing severe lower-back pain —you should *not* use a heating pad. Heat will cause more swelling and pain. Use *cold* for the first 24 hours. Wrap a gel-filled ice pack in a thin towel moistened in warm water, and apply it directly to the skin. The warm moist towel lets the area chill more gradually and deeply. If you do not have an ice pack, use a bag of frozen peas or beans. See a doctor if pain lasts more than 24 hours, is very severe or is accompanied by a fever or numbness or weakness in legs or feet.

William Lauretti, DC, chiropractor specializing in pain management, Bethesda, MD.

SIT BETTER FOR BETTER HEALTH

❚mprove the way you sit for better health. *Always sit as upright as possible:* Slouching or hunching over restricts breathing and blood circulation. Keep both feet flat on the floor—if you must cross them, do so only at the ankles. Use a chair with armrests to reduce lower-back pressure. Do not keep anything thicker than a handkerchief in a rear pocket—sitting on a wallet or checkbook may cause low-back pain. Get up and move around every 30 minutes to enhance your comfort and ability to concentrate.

Porter Shimer, health and fitness writer, Emmaus, PA, and author of *Too Busy to Exercise*. Workman Publishing.

Better Back Protection

B etter back protection around the home: When lifting a box or a baby, bend from the knees— not the waist—and hold as close to your body as possible. When washing dishes, open the cabinet below the sink…bend one knee and put your foot on the shelf under the sink…lean forward so some weight is supported. When vacuuming, stand with all your weight on one foot…and step forward and backward with the other foot while pushing the vacuum forward and backward. On the phone, do not cradle the earpiece between your ear and your shoulder. When watching TV, do not use the sofa arm as a pillow.

William Lauretti, DC, chiropractor specializing in pain management, Bethesda, MD.

To Avoid Knee Injuries...

W. Norman Scott, MD, chairman of the department of orthopedics at Beth Israel Medical Center in New York. He is a member of the Association of Professional Team Physicians and team doctor for the New York Knicks. He also is director of the Insall Scott Kelly Institute for Orthopaedics and Sports Medicine in New York and author of *Dr. Scott's Knee Book*. Fireside.

Y our knees are extremely vulnerable to injury …at any age. The knee joint is a virtual crossroads connecting bones, ligaments, tendons and cartilage. *Steps to avoid injury…*

■ **Warm up knee muscles first thing in the morning to avoid accidental injury.**
Use a stationary bike or walk on a treadmill at a comfortable pace for 5 to 10 minutes. Or gently stretch for 5 to 10 minutes to improve flexibility.

Sit on the bed with one leg extended on the surface and the other leg on the floor. Or sit on the floor and extend both legs.

Slowly bend from the waist and reach toward the toes of the extended leg. Hold the stretch for about 30 seconds. Then do the exercise with the other leg.

Repeat these stretches 10 times with each leg.

Important: Never grab the underside of your knee and pull...never force a stretch...and never bounce while stretching.

■ **Condition your knees if you run or jog.**
Runners and joggers must keep in mind that with every step they are forcing hundreds of pounds through their knee joints.

People who run should condition their knees by exercising the muscles three times a week to maintain knee strength.

High-torque activities—such as skiing, tennis and other racket sports—require even more rigorous conditioning on those days.

Basic conditioning: Spend 30 to 45 minutes, three times a week, stretching and using the leg-extension and leg-curl machines at a gym.

Also use the abduction and adduction machines. Those are the ones on which you recline and work your inner and outer thigh muscles. Add three sets of 10 calf lifts, also known as toe raises, in which you stand, rise up on your toes and come back down.

If you love to run, I recommend that you run for speed rather than distance. Otherwise, the continuous force on your knees inevitably will cause pain, which may or may not be an indication of destruction.

Instead of running continuously for 30 minutes, spend 10 minutes alternating sprints with your regular jogging speed. Then walk rapidly for 20 minutes. Think in terms of time, not distance.

For arthritis sufferers: I recommend a nonimpact exercise program that strengthens the muscles without stressing the knee joints.

Activities such as swimming, riding a stationary bike or using a cross-country ski machine strengthen muscles and reduce pain.

Avoid impact activities such as jogging, jumping and running, which put too much force on knee joints.

Too Much of a Good Thing Can Be Dangerous

Timothy McCall, MD, Boston internist, medical editor of *Yoga Journal* and author of *Examining Your Doctor: A Patient's Guide to Avoiding Harmful Medical Care.* Citadel Press.

D id you ever notice," a friend asked me the other day, "that marathon runners never look healthy?" I don't think that's true in every case, but I knew what she meant. Even healthful activities such as running can be detrimental to health when taken to the extreme.

With running, there's little extra cardiovascular benefit after the first few miles—or the first few times per week—and lots of wear and tear on the knees, ankles and lower back. And while it affords an excellent workout, running is harder on the body than walking, biking or swimming—each of which can provide similar aerobic benefits.

Believe it or not, some "ultramarathoners" find that the 26.2 miles of a marathon isn't enough—and run even longer distances. No one can possibly believe that's good for them.

I see the same problem in many areas of health. People figure that if a little is good, more is better. Many patients, for example, are convinced that the more tests the doctor orders—or the more medications he or she prescribes—the greater the benefits. Yet we know that diagnostic tests can cause serious side effects. They can also yield "false positives," leading not only to needless anxiety, but to additional testing and procedures. Similarly, drugs can work miracles—but can be harmful if used inappropriately.

The same applies to nutritional supplements such as vitamin C. While the findings on this antioxidant vitamin are equivocal, I believe that it's reasonable for most people to take 250 milligrams (mg) to 500 mg per day. Who knows? Maybe it will turn out that 1,000 mg or even 2,000 mg per day is more beneficial. But many people are taking 10 times that much, and some alternative medicine "experts" recommend intravenous vitamin C in dosages of up to 200,000 mg a day. Supposedly, this much vitamin C can "reverse" everything from cancer to AIDS to chronic fatigue syndrome.

I realize people who are seriously ill may be desperate enough to try something such as this. But I know of no credible evidence that massive dosages of vitamin C can help. And there's reason to believe such a practice may do harm—particularly to people already weakened by illness.

Perhaps the best evidence for a sensible middle path comes from alcohol. Moderate consumption of red wine and other forms of alcohol is known to lower the risk for heart attack and the most common form of stroke. Women who have more than one drink a day raise their risk for breast cancer. More than a couple of drinks a day contributes to high blood pressure and obesity. For millions of people, of course, a few drinks a day begins the slippery slope that ends in alcoholism.

More than 2,000 years ago, the Greek poet Euripides advocated a policy of moderation in all things. So rather than doing one form of exercise to excess, why not take his advice and mix things up? Take a walk one day and go for a bike ride the next. Play tennis on the weekend. By varying activities, you'll be using different muscles and will be less likely to overwork any particular muscle or joint.

The same strategy applies to treating many medical conditions. Yes, the new cholesterol-lowering "statins" can bring your cholesterol down even if you continue to eat loads of fat. But isn't it more sensible to eat sensibly and take a lower dose of the drug? You'll save money and lower your risk for side effects. And you'll probably drop a few pounds, too.

How to Prevent and Treat Foot Problems

Daniel McGann, DPM, podiatrist in private practice in El Monte, CA, and chief of podiatry at Alhambra Hospital in Alhambra, CA. He is author of *The Doctor's Sore Foot Book*. William Morrow.

By inspecting your feet and toenails each day, you can catch early signs of foot problems and treat them at home. *How to take care of the most bothersome foot problems...*

FUNGAL INFECTIONS

Fungal infections of the toes or toenails afflict 85% of the US population—though many don't know it.

Signs of fungal infections include itching…broken, white or cracked skin between the toes…toenail discoloration, thickness and/or brittleness…and separation of the nail from the nail bed. You're likely to attract a fungal infection—such as athlete's foot—by not wearing socks, especially during athletic activities or when using a public shower. A sweaty foot in the dark environment of your shoe invites dirt and fungi to come in and multiply.

Prevention: Dry your feet carefully after washing them daily with soap and water. Pay particular attention to drying between the toes.

Treatment: Use a nonprescription fungicidal cream, lotion or powder to control the growth of fungi.

INGROWN TOENAILS

You can tell you have the beginning of an ingrown toenail when the area around your nail becomes inflamed, red and tender. It is often caused by improper cutting of the nail and/or wearing too-tight shoes or socks.

Prevention: Cut your toenails straight across and even—use a nail file to even out the pointed ends. Don't cut lower than the fleshy part of your toe or into the corners. And don't dig into the toe or along the groove.

Self-treatment: Soak your foot so that the flesh around the nail remains soft and nonresistant to nail growth. Apply an over-the-counter topical antibiotic ointment to the nail. If the area around the nail becomes very painful or red, see a podiatrist or your primary care doctor for treatment. You may need oral antibiotics or minor office surgery.

BLISTERS

Blisters usually develop because of improperly fitting shoes or tight socks—both cause friction and perspiration.

Prevention: Wear loose-fitting shoes and socks …apply a moisturizer to your feet before putting on socks to reduce friction.

Self-treatment: Soak and dry your foot, apply antibiotic ointment to the blister and put a bandage

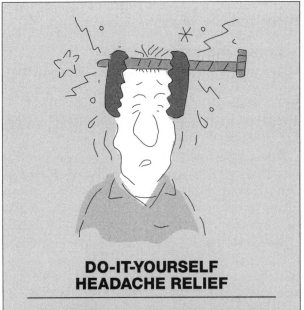

DO-IT-YOURSELF HEADACHE RELIEF

▶ **Replace fluorescent lamps with incandescent lamps.** The almost imperceptible flicker of fluorescent lights can possibly trigger a headache.

▶ **Visualize yourself on a hot beach.** Doing so raises your body temperature and eases your headache pain.

▶ **Hold a bag of crushed ice to the area of your head that hurts, while soaking in a hot bath for about 30 minutes.** The cold shrinks the inflamed blood vessels that cause pain.

▶ **Have a cup of coffee.** Caffeine constricts the blood vessels, reducing blood flow to the head. However, limit your consumption to no more than two cups a day—any more than that can worsen headaches.

▶ **Breathe deeply to reduce tension.** Inhale for four seconds…exhale for four seconds. Repeat six times.

▶ **Talk with your doctor about taking 400 milligrams (mg) a day of chelated magnesium.** It has been shown to help relieve migraines.

Alexander Mauskop, MD, director, New York Headache Center, and associate professor of clinical neurology, State University of New York, Brooklyn.

over it until it heals. Never pop a blister—it invites bacteria into the wound.

CORNS AND CALLUSES

Corns are the most common foot ailment. They develop on the upper portion of the foot, on top of or between the toes.

Calluses emerge on the bottom—usually on the ball of the foot.

Prevention: Any ill-fitting shoes may cause corns or calluses. Check the interior of all shoes for rough spots that may rub against your foot. Pad those areas, or discard the shoes. Also, vary the height of the heels you wear.

Self-treatment: Soak your feet in warm water until the skin softens. Gently rub the area with a pumice stone or callus file. It may take more than one soaking to remove all the dead skin.

In between, apply moisturizer to the area and cover it with a moleskin or a foam-rubber pad to ease pain.

Don't cut off corns or calluses by yourself. See a podiatrist.

Beware: Avoid over-the-counter chemical corn removers or medicated corn pads. They contain acids that eat away at a corn—and your healthy skin. Every week, I see at least one patient with a chemical burn resulting from the use of these products.

AVOID FOOT ODOR

Spray antiperspirant on your feet. Or soak feet in black tea, which contains bacteria-fighting tannic acid. *Recipe:* Brew two tea bags in one pint of water for 15 minutes...add two quarts of cool water...soak feet 20 to 30 minutes daily for about a week. *Also helpful:* Scrub feet with an antibacterial soap while bathing, then dry them with a blow-dryer. Wear cotton socks or sandals...let shoes air out for at least 24 hours between wearings...and buy shoes made of leather and other materials that "breathe."

Michael Ramsey, MD, dermatologist, Penn State Geisinger Health System, Danville, PA.

HEARTBURN CONTROL

Control heartburn after meals by chewing gum for at least 30 minutes.

Chewing stimulates production of saliva, which neutralizes stomach acid and washes it out of the esophagus.

Heartburn results when stomach acid "backs up" into the esophagus.

Robert Marks, MD, medical director, Alabama Digestive Research Center, Birmingham.

Age-Old Practical Wisdom

Tim Clark, executive editor of *The Old Farmer's Almanac* for 20 years. The *Almanac* is published each year in four regional editions. Yankee Publishing, Box 520, Dublin, NH 03444.

The *Old Farmer's Almanac* publishes weather predictions, planting tables, unusual facts, age-old advice and novel solutions to everyday problems. *Here are some favorites from recent editions...*

WHAT TO DO IF YOU'VE TOUCHED POISON IVY OR POISON OAK

► **Up to three to four hours after exposure:** Swab the skin with rubbing alcohol, and wash with lots of warm water. Harsh laundry soap is no more effective than other kinds of soap, but soap alone won't do it. Water is the key.

▶ **If the rash has broken out:** All you can do is treat the symptoms. Cortisone cream relieves minor itching. Calamine lotion may also bring temporary relief. Prescription cortisone gels are needed in many cases, especially when the sores are in the weepy stage. Make sure to wash any clothing, garden tools or other objects touched by poison ivy.

▶ **How to get rid of poison ivy and poison oak plants:** It is never safe to burn poison ivy or poison oak. The toxins are carried in the smoke. Also, avoid pulling up the plants. Broken-off rootlets may sprout next year. Some of the worst cases of poison ivy and poison oak come from grubbing out the plants and roots.

Best: Even many environmentally conscious gardeners favor chemicals to combat these poisonous plants. Use chemicals found at plant and garden stores to destroy the plants.

REMOVING A RING FROM A SWOLLEN FINGER

Push a piece of string two or three feet long up under the ring. Hold the short end firmly with the ring-hand's thumb while winding the long end tightly around the finger and knuckle over which the ring must slide. Then unwrap the string by pulling the short end toward the tip of the finger. The ring will slide off.

Better Skin Examinations

Make sure your doctor checks the entire skin surface. Skin cancer can develop anywhere, even between the toes and in other areas protected from the sun. The exam should be in a well-lit room. The scalp should be examined by parting the hair a little at a time or using a hand-held hair dryer. If your physician finds any potentially cancerous moles, see a dermatologist.

Neal Schultz, MD, dermatologist in private practice, 1130 Park Ave., New York City 10128.

Check Those Moles

Check moles every six months for any changes. See a physician if a mole meets any of the **ABCD** conditions…

Asymmetry means the two sides don't match in shape or color. **Border** is irregular, ragged or notched—or seems blurred. **Color** varies in different parts. **Diameter** is more than one-quarter inch.

Very important: A skin biopsy should be read by a *dermatopathologist*—a physician who is specially trained in interpreting the test. Do this even if your insurance won't cover the cost. *Danger:* Many early-stage melanomas are missed on biopsies.

Robert Friedman, MD, clinical assistant professor of dermatology, New York University Medical Center.

BEWARE OF CHANGES IN MOLES

Mole changes during pregnancy may be a serious problem. Pregnant women often think any changes they experience are caused by the pregnancy. But this is not true of moles. Moles do not normally grow significantly during pregnancy. Pregnant women with moles that are unusual in size and appearance should see a dermatologist every three months.

Perry Robins, MD, president, The Skin Cancer Foundation, New York City.

Foods to Help You Sleep

Foods that help you sleep better include cauliflower, broccoli, soybeans and other nondairy sources of calcium. Dairy sources, such as milk, can be hard to digest.

Also: Foods containing L-tryptophan, like spinach, peanuts, cashews and all high-protein foods (best eaten at lunch). And—foods rich in B vitamins, like fish, whole grains, peanuts, bananas and sunflower seeds.

Foods to avoid: Sugar, which can cause you to wake up in the middle of the night…alcohol…salt …caffeine.

Helpful: Drink eight glasses of water a day to help flush toxins out of the body and allow you to get the rest you need.

Katherine Albert, PhD, MD, director of the sleep laboratory at New York Hospital–Cornell Medical Center, New York City.

WHY YOU SHOULD SLEEP IN THE DARK

Sudden exposure to light while you sleep upsets your internal clock—even if it does not wake you up. It changes the body's secretion of the hormone melatonin, which controls the sleep/wake cycle.

David Klein, PhD, chief of neuroendocrinology, National Institute of Child Health and Human Development, Bethesda, MD.

SELF-DEFENSE AGAINST DEHYDRATION

Common dehydration symptoms: Fatigue, dry skin and headaches. Symptoms are often attributed to other causes—usually stress. But they may simply indicate too-low water consumption. *Self-defense:* Drink at least 8 eight-ounce glasses of water, milk, juice or decaffeinated soft drinks every day. Drink more if you have had a caffeinated or alcoholic beverage—caffeine and alcohol rob the body of water.

Barbara Levine, RD, PhD, associate professor of nutrition in medicine, Weill Medical College of Cornell University, New York City.

Adult Diphtheria Protection

Adults need diphtheria boosters every 10 years. This bacterial disease is usually considered a childhood ailment—but susceptible adults can get it, too. Vaccinations protect for about 10 years. The last childhood booster is usually given by age 12.

Walter Orenstein, MD, former director, national immunization program, Centers for Disease Control and Prevention, Atlanta.

The Key to Better Vitamin Absorption

For better vitamin absorption, look for the letters USP on a supplement's label. Products complying with US Pharmacopoeia quality standards break down properly, releasing vitamins and minerals for absorption. Some manufacturers use their own assurance wording, saying *proven release* or *release assured*—while others say nothing. If your brand has no printed statement, call the company and find out if the product passes a 45-minute dissolution test. *Best:* Rely only on products with the USP label.

Vitamins, Minerals and Dietary Supplements by **Marsha Hudnall, MS, BS.** Chronimed. She is also a registered dietitian for the American Dietetic Association.

How to Protect Yourself From UV Rays

Wear dark clothing when you're outdoors in summer. *Reason:* While you might feel a little warmer, dark colors protect skin better than light-colored clothing by absorbing more of the sun's UV rays.

Rodney Basler, MD, dermatologist and assistant professor of internal medicine, University of Nebraska Medical Center, Lincoln.

KEEPING BUGS AWAY

To keep mosquitoes away, avoid using scented soaps, deodorants, colognes and hair gel. Those sweet-smelling toiletries attract mosquitoes and other bothersome bugs.

Also effective: Insect repellent containing 5% to 30% DEET.

James H. Runnels, MD, former head of the travel medicine service at Baylor College of Medicine in Houston, and now a physician in private practice in Baton Rouge, LA.

Effective Bug Repellent

Bug repellents containing DEET are the most effective—and are safe if used as directed. *Best:* Apply before getting dressed—but only to skin that will be exposed. Deet should not be used in a concentration higher than 50%. It should be used only lightly in skin folds.

Neal Schultz, MD, dermatologist in private practice, 1130 Park Ave., New York City 10128.

Off-Season Colds— A Symptom-by-Symptom Guide to Quick Relief

Ronald Eccles, PhD, DSc, director of the Common Cold Centre at Cardiff University in Cardiff, Wales.

The best advice for avoiding the all-too-common cold are the following four easy-to-remember precautions…

▶ **Wash your hands several times a day.**

▶ **Avoid touching your hands to your mouth or eyes.**

▶ **Eat a balanced diet** that contains lots of fresh fruits and vegetables.

▶ **Try to relax.** Anxiety lowers resistance to infection.

If you come down with a cold despite your best efforts at prevention, here's how to treat the most troublesome symptoms…

COUGH

There is little evidence to suggest that cough remedies containing *dextromethorphan* are effective for coughs due to colds.

But hot, spicy foods, including soups and curries, provide relief by promoting saliva flow and by stimulating the production of mucus in the throat.

You can also unclog your chest with a steamy shower…or a bath with eucalyptus oil added.

FEVER/HEADACHE

Aspirin, acetaminophen and ibuprofen are all equally effective. However, acetaminophen is less likely to cause stomach upset.

These drugs also relieve the chills and muscle aches that often go along with fever.

NASAL CONGESTION

One of the most effective strategies is also one of the oldest—inhaling steam from a kettle of boiling water.

Adding a drop or two of menthol, peppermint oil or eucalyptus oil to the water adds a pleasant cooling effect.

A brisk walk can help ease congestion for about an hour. Moderate exertion causes a transient rise in blood pressure, which helps narrow nasal blood vessels that are dilated as a result of inflammation.

Alcohol's dehydrating effect exacerbates nasal congestion, especially when you lie down.

You'll breathe easier, especially at night, if you use an over-the-counter decongestant nasal spray an hour or two before bedtime. The most effective decongestants are *xylometazoline* (Otrivin) and *oxymetazoline* (Afrin).

Caution: Chronic use of decongestant nasal spray can lead to "rebound" congestion, in which congestion becomes worse than before. To avoid this phenomenon, use a spray for no more than one week.

SINUS PAIN

If acetaminophen, aspirin or ibuprofen doesn't help, consider trying an oral decongestant such as *pseudoephedrine* (Sudafed).

Caution: These drugs can be risky for people who have high blood pressure, heart disease, glaucoma or prostate enlargement...and for anyone taking a monoamine oxidase antidepressant, such as *phenelzine* (Nardil). Check with a doctor first.

SNEEZING

Sneezing is common with colds. But if sneezing persists for more than a couple of days—especially if your eyes and/or nose are itchy—the problem is more likely to stem from an allergy to dust mites, animal dander or pollen. An over-the-counter antihistamine such as *chlorpheniramine*

(Contac) or *doxylamine* (Tylenol Flu) is often helpful.

SORE THROAT

The same hot foods and beverages that relieve cough also ease sore throat pain. For additional relief, gargle with salt water or use an anesthetic throat spray such as Chloraseptic.

Caution: If severe throat pain makes it difficult to swallow or breathe—and is accompanied by an earache—see a doctor. You may have a bacterial infection, which calls for treatment with antibiotics.

ALTERNATIVE REMEDIES

Despite its reputation, vitamin C is ineffective at preventing colds, but very large dosages (1 gram [g] to 2 g a day) may help reduce the severity of an existing cold.

The immunity-boosting herb *echinacea* seems to reduce the risk of catching a cold—but is of no use if you're already sick.

What about zinc? Some studies show no benefit. Others suggest that sucking on a zinc lozenge at the first sign of a cold may speed recovery.

FEED A COLD

Foods that help handle a cold: Chicken soup really makes you feel better faster—though researchers do not know why. Sweeteners like honey, molasses and sugar soothe sore throats. The sour taste of lemon tea and sour-lemon drops help saliva flow—also soothing the throat. Hot peppers, horseradish and onions make it easier to blow your nose and cough up mucus.

Nutrition for Dummies by **Carol Ann Rinzler,** New York–based author of numerous health-related books. IDG Books.

FEWER WINTER ALLERGIES

Wash outerwear regularly—dust mites build up in items that are washed less often, such as sweaters and jackets. Use the hottest washing temperature possible. Washing in cool water, then drying for 15 minutes at a high temperature, also kills mites. If high temperatures cannot be used, freeze clothing overnight—or have it dry-cleaned.

Martha White, MD, director of pediatric allergy and research, Institute for Asthma and Allergy, Washington Hospital Center, Washington, DC.

Cold and Flu Self-Defense

Keep at least three feet between you and anyone who is sick. That is about as far as most airborne droplets from a cough or sneeze can travel. *Vital reminders:* Turn away from the sick person when he or she coughs…wash your hands immediately after any contact…avoid rubbing your eyes and nose—that can easily deposit cold and flu germs onto your mucous membranes.

Dennis Murray, MD, fellow of the Pediatric Infectious Diseases Society (PIDS). He is a professor of pediatrics and Chief of the Section of Infectious Diseases at the Medical College of Georgia Children's Medical Center.

Winter Hair Care

Reduce static electricity by using brushes with natural bristles. Leave-in conditioning sprays and foams will also help. *Favorites:* Irridiance by L'Oreal (leave-in foam)…Framesi Biogenal (leave-in spray), available in salons.

Robert Craig, hair colorist, Rokari Hair Arts Center, 249 W. 21 St., New York City 10011.

How to Recognize Frostbite

*S*ymptoms of frostbite: Pale skin, from lack of blood reaching the affected area…numbness or pain as tissues start to freeze…blistering. In more serious frostbite, skin turns white and hard and eventually freezes solid. *Self-defense:* Prevent frostbite by insulating the body carefully and completely. Watch out for metal objects, such as eyeglass frames and earrings—they can cause frostbite when making contact with skin. Rewarm a mildly frostbitten area through direct contact with another person's warm skin. Get medical attention for more severe cases.

Appalachian Mountain Club Guide to Winter Camping by **Stephen Gorman.** Appalachian Mountain Club Books. He is a wilderness emergency medical technician in Exeter, NH.

In-the-Ear Thermometer Warning

*I*n-the-ear thermometers can spread disease. The problem isn't the tip—they are disposable—but the handheld base unit. *Problem:* Since few hospitals or doctor's offices sterilize the units, germs are transmitted from patient to patient. *Self-defense:* Ask medical personnel to clean the thermometer base with an alcohol wipe. Make sure he or she washes his hands after touching the thermometer and before touching you.

Wesley Kozinn, MD, clinical assistant professor of medicine, Medical College of Pennsylvania/Hahnemann University, Philadelphia. His study of hospital thermometers was presented at an Interscience Conference on Antimicrobial Agents and Chemotherapy in San Diego.

Pet Allergy Basics

No dog or cat breed is truly hypoallergenic—all can cause an allergic reaction in some susceptible people. *Helpful:* Before selecting a pet, spend at least one-half hour with the animal to test your tolerance to a specific breed. *However:* Allergies sometimes develop after a period of weeks or years. Allergies can also subside on their own over time. *Good news:* Often, allergies can be successfully treated with desensitizing injections. Symptoms can be minimized by bathing the animal regularly.

Stefanie Schwartz, DVM, veterinarian and pet behavior consultant, Brookline, MA, and author of *True Facts About Pet Care.* Random House.

Dogs Need Warmth, Too

Protect your dog from winter chills by letting it live in your house, even if it stays in a doghouse during the rest of the year. If that is not possible, make sure the doghouse is properly designed for cold weather, well insulated and equipped with appropriate bedding.

R.J. Schuff, DVM, veterinarian in private practice, Woodruff, WI.

HOW TO AVOID RABIES

To avoid rabies, stay away from animals that show little fear of people. Avoid any nocturnal animal you see during daylight—bats…foxes…raccoons …skunks. Make sure children are aware of the danger, and tell them to report any animal behaving oddly. *Note:* A rabid animal can spread the disease not only by biting but also by licking. The virus is present in saliva.

Peter Bromley, PhD, department extension leader, zoology, North Carolina Cooperative Extension Service.

TRICKS TO GET RID OF TICKS

▶ **To protect your dog from ticks and the diseases they may carry:** Have your dog wear a tick collar containing amitraz.

▶ **Mow your lawn often,** and clear leaves from your yard to reduce tick-friendly areas.

▶ **Consider having your dog vaccinated against Lyme disease** if you live in or near an area where it is common.

▶ **And—check for ticks every day.** The ticks that can transmit Lyme disease are very, very small. If you spot one, remove it with tweezers. Grasp the tick close to the dog's skin …pull gently and steadily.

Linda Ross, editor in chief, *Your Dog.* Tufts University School of Veterinary Medicine, 200 Westboro Rd., North Grafton, MA 01536.

Hypothermia in Dogs

If a dog gets too cold, it may develop hypothermia—it will shiver noticeably and then become lethargic because of a lower body temperature. *What to do:* As soon as possible, dry the dog with towels and then wrap it in blankets warmed in a clothes dryer. Use a hair dryer on a warm setting to dry off moisture. If the dog seems mentally confused or is comatose, take it to a vet immediately.

R.J. Schuff, DVM, veterinarian in private practice, Woodruff, WI.

How to Care for Minor Injuries

Disinfect dogs' minor injuries with chlorhexidine or with hydrogen peroxide. Both are effective and do not usually hurt. Use alcohol as a disinfectant only if you must—it works, but stings on contact.

R.J. Schuff, DVM, veterinarian in private practice, Woodruff, WI.

Breakthrough Treatments

Chapter 4

Improvement with Hepatitis B Drug

The drug most widely used for the life-threatening liver disease hepatitis B—*interferon alpha*—works in only 20% of patients and can cause severe side effects.

In a recent one-year study, 56% of hepatitis B sufferers given the prescription drug *lamivudine* (Epivir) showed marked improvement. Lamivudine seems less likely than interferon alpha to cause severe side effects.

Ching-Lung Lai, MD, professor of medicine, Queen Mary Hospital, Hong Kong. His one-year study of 358 hepatitis B patients was published in *The New England Journal of Medicine,* 10 Shattuck St., Boston 02115.

Migraine Headache Breakthroughs

About 26 million Americans suffer from migraine headaches, yet 40% of them don't bother to see a doctor. Many of them believe there isn't anything that doctors can do to prevent or treat migraines.

In fact, there are several ways to prevent and treat the problem—including new drugs that have recently approved by the Food and Drug Administration (FDA).

CAUSES OF MIGRAINES

A migraine headache—unlike the more common tension type—has distinct physical symptoms.

Migraine headaches typically start on one side of the head and can be preceded by visual sensations,

J. Keith Campbell, MD, past president of the American Association for the Study of Headache and former editor of *Headache,* its journal. He is an emeritus neurologist affiliated with the Mayo Clinic in Rochester, MN.

such as zigzagging lines. Migraines can cause nausea. They throb with your heartbeat. They also make you extremely sensitive to light or sound—sometimes both.

About 70% of migraine sufferers have family members with the condition.

TREATING MIGRAINES

▪ **Triptan family of drugs.**
Triptan drugs are prescription medications taken as tablets—or as a nasal spray or self-injected. The big four Triptan drugs are...

- ▶ **Rizatriptan** (Maxalt)

- ▶ **Sumatriptan** (Imitrex)

- ▶ **Naratriptan** (Amerge)

- ▶ **Zolmitriptan** (Zomig)

▪ **Midrin** comes in capsule form and often is a doctor's first choice in migraine treatment. Not only does it work for people with mild to moderate migraines, it is also less costly than the Triptans.

▪ **Excedrin Migraine** was approved by the FDA. It is three drugs in one—acetaminophen, aspirin and caffeine. It is available over the counter.

Fast-Acting Migraine Drug

An oral migraine drug usually brings relief within two hours. Rizatriptan benzoate, sold as *Maxalt*, is available by prescription either in conventional tablet form or as pills that dissolve on the tongue. Maxalt can relieve pain, nausea and light-

and-sound sensitivity. Most people report that side effects are temporary and mild—but heart patients and people taking certain other medicines cannot use Maxalt.

Seymour Diamond, MD, director and founder, Diamond Headache Clinic, Chicago. He is also director of the Inpatient Headache Unit at Saint Joseph Hospital, Chicago.

Migraine Relief

Nose drops relieve migraine headaches fast. Within five minutes of using prescription drops containing the topical anesthetic lidocaine, 31% of headache sufferers felt relief...58% of headache sufferers experienced relief within 30 minutes.

Morris Maizels, MD, family practitioner and headache researcher, Southern California Kaiser Permanente Medical Group, Woodland Hills, whose seven-month study of 131 migraine sufferers was presented at a meeting of the American Society for the Study of Headache.

VITAMINS EASE MIGRAINES

Vitamin B2 eases migraines. More than half the migraine sufferers who took 400 mg of vitamin B2 daily for four months reported at least a 50% drop in headache frequency. Vitamin B2 seems to be as effective as drug treatments for migraines, with fewer side effects. Talk with your doctor before trying B2 supplements.

Fred Sheftell, MD, cofounder, The New England Center for Headache, Stamford, CT.

NEW TECHNOLOGY FOR BONE AILMENTS

Heel spurs and tennis elbow may soon be treatable without the bother of cortisone injections, physical therapy and the other usual treatments. *Orthopedic lithotripsy* (orthotripsy) uses "spark plug" technology to direct tightly focused shock waves into the injured bone or tendon. The doctor simply holds the affected body part against an orthotripsy device. The waves cause minor changes in bones and tendons, encouraging the growth of new blood vessels that spur healing. Orthotripsy—which is similar to the lithotripsy devices used to treat kidney stones—has a 90% success rate for treating heel spurs, 65% for tennis elbow and 65% to 70% for rotator cuff tendinitis.

Robert Gordon, MD, orthopedic surgeon, Institute of Sports Medicine, Toronto.

Combination Treatment For Bell's Palsy

Bell's palsy patients recover faster when they take a combination of *acyclovir* (Zovirax) and the steroid *prednisone* (Deltasone) than when they take prednisone alone. Combination therapy is most effective if begun within 72 hours of the onset of the primary symptom, facial paralysis. *Good news:* Patients on combination therapy for 10 days recovered muscle control sooner and were less likely to develop permanent nerve damage. *Best of all:* Without treatment, 90% of all Bell's palsy patients eventually recover.

Paul G. Auwaerter, MD, assistant professor of medicine, Johns Hopkins University School of Medicine, Baltimore.

Less Steroids for Asthma Patients

Asthma patients can get by with lower doses of inhaled steroids when the prescription inhalant *formoterol* (Foradil) is added to their regimen. A long-acting beta-2 agonist, formoterol starts working within three minutes of inhalation. Patients who tested the drug duo reported fewer daytime symptoms, such as wheezing and shortness of breath. They said it helped them sleep better, too. Headaches, tremor and other side effects were short-lived. Steroids should be used sparingly, since long-term use can lead to hoarseness, skin thinning and decreases in bone density.

Anthony D'Urzo, MD, MSc, lecturer, department of family and community medicine, University of Toronto Faculty of Medicine.

New Drug Fights Asthma

Anew drug has been shown to reduce asthma attacks by more than 50%. *Omalizumab* (Xolair) also allows patients to reduce their use of inhaled corticosteroids, which can cause side effects. The drug, which is injected once or twice a month, is for patients with moderate to severe allergic asthma that can't be adequately controlled by other drugs. *Caution:* Patients given omalizumab in clinical trials had slightly higher cancer rates than placebo patients, but the difference was not statistically significant. Patients with a personal or family history of cancer should discuss risks with their doctors.

Thomas Casale, MD, chief of allergy and immunology and director of clinical research, Creighton University, Omaha.

BETTER NARCOLEPSY DRUG

Unlike the stimulants now used to control this neurological disorder, the prescription drug *modafinil* (Provigil) does not cause the jitters.

New finding: Once-a-day modafinil significantly reduced daytime sleepiness in most patients who took it.

Joyce Walsleben, PhD, director, sleep disorder center, New York University School of Medicine, New York City.

NEW ANTIHISTAMINES MUCH BETTER

Brompheniramine, chlorpheniramine, diphenhydramine, hydroxyzine and other "first-generation" (older) antihistamines are riskier than once thought. They cause not only drowsiness but also delayed reaction time and impaired thinking. Even when people do not feel drowsy after taking them, data suggest that these antihistamines can lead to automobile accidents and poor academic performance in children. *Self-defense:* Use a newer nonsedating antihistamine, such as *loratadine* (Claritin) or *fexofenadine* (Allegra). If you do take a first-generation antihistamine, exercise the same precautions as you would if you were to drink alcohol.

Mark S. Dykewicz, MD, professor of internal medicine and director of the training program in allergy and immunology, St. Louis University School of Medicine.

Advances Against Acne

New acne medications seem to have fewer side effects than Retin-A, the prescription face cream that helps clear up acne but can also irritate skin and increase sun sensitivity. New medications—available by prescription only—are *adapalene gel*, sold as Differin…and *azelaic acid cream*, sold as Azelex.

Neal Schultz, MD, dermatologist in private practice, 1130 Park Ave., New York City 10128.

Vitamin Protection from Colon Cancer

Colon cancer risk can be reduced through vitamin use. In a recent study conducted at the Fred Hutchinson Cancer Research Center in Seattle, people who took a one-a-day multivitamin for at least 10 years reduced their risk of colon cancer by 51%. Vitamin E alone had an even greater effect—reducing colon cancer risk by 57% for people who took 200 IU a day. Vitamins may be particularly helpful for smokers, whose risk of colon cancer stays relatively high even after they quit.

Edward Giovannucci, MD, assistant professor of medicine at Harvard Medical School, Boston.

Cow Bile Drug Used in Fight Against Pancreatic Cancer

Cow bile may revolutionize the treatment of pancreatic cancer. Researchers at the University of Nebraska tested a bile-derived immunity-boosting drug called Virulizin on 26 pancreatic cancer patients. Survival among the group averaged six to seven months—up to three months longer than patients given the standard drugs for pancreatic cancer, *gemcitabine* (Gemzar) and *5-fluorouracil* (5-FU). Bleak statistics, true, but the hope is that by combining the two drugs, doctors can extend survival significantly. Each year, 29,000 Americans are diagnosed with pancreatic cancer…80% die within one year.

University of Nebraska.

Double-Duty Sunscreen Ingredient

A sunscreen ingredient blocks ultraviolet A (UV-A) as well as ultraviolet B (UV-B) light. That's important because UV-A is now thought to contribute to premature aging of the

skin…and ordinary sunscreen protects mostly against UV-B. *Avobenzone* (Parsol 1789) is as effective against UV-A as opaque barrier sunscreens such as zinc oxide and titanium dioxide—but it is lighter and smoother.

Lorraine H. Kligman, PhD, research professor of dermatology, University of Pennsylvania School of Medicine, Philadelphia.

SOUNDER SLEEP FOR SNORERS

Snorers troubled by daytime sleepiness should ask a doctor about *continuous positive airway pressure* (CPAP). This treatment involves wearing an air-delivery mask during sleep. In a recent study, CPAP patients reported improved mood and less fatigue than similar patients given nasal strips and counseling.

The CPAP mask can be inconvenient, but it's often the best measure against repeated wakenings at night associated with snoring.

Susan Redline, MD, MPH, chief of clinical epidemiology, Rainbow Babies and Children's Hospital, Cleveland. Her eight-week study of 111 snorers 25 to 65 years of age was published in the *American Journal of Respiratory and Critical Care Medicine,* 1740 Broadway, New York City 10019.

NEW PILL FOR ALCOHOLISM

A new pill for alcoholism, widely used in Europe, may soon become available on this side of the Atlantic. In recent studies, half of the alcoholics who took *acamprosate* abstained from drinking for a full three months. That's the period during which heavy drinkers are most likely to fall off the wagon.

Tanning Beds Can Fight Psoriasis

Phototherapy for psoriasis involves treatment with ultraviolet-B (UV-B) light. If UV-B treatment is not available at the dermatologist's office, a tanning bed, which emits some UV-B light, may provide some relief. *Caution:* Tanning salon staff are not trained in phototherapy, and the potency of UV-B light may vary. You should try this only if your doctor recommends it, and use only a facility that he/she chooses. Most insurance companies cover this form of phototherapy, but you might need preapproval by your carrier.

Christopher S. Carlin, MD, research fellow, department of dermatology, University of Utah Health Sciences Center, Salt Lake City, and leader of a study of 26 psoriasis patients, presented at the annual meeting of the American Academy of Dermatology.

The New World Of Office Surgery

Ervin Moss, MD, executive medical director of the New Jersey State Society of Anesthesiologists in Princeton Junction and clinical professor of anesthesiology at Robert Wood Johnson Medical Center in New Brunswick, NJ.

Surgery has moved outside the hospital surgical suite. Thirteen percent of all surgical procedures are now done in doctors' private offices. By 2005 that figure is expected to rise to 20%. That's almost 10 million operations a year. These include cataract surgery…biopsies…hernia repairs…cosmetic and plastic surgery…and ear tube insertions.

Office surgery costs less than similar procedures done in hospitals or outpatient surgical facilities. It can be more convenient and "patient friendly," too. But office surgery also poses potential risks.

Even the best-equipped doctor's office lacks the state-of-the-art surgical suites and extensive support staffs found in hospitals. Some in-office surgeons lack the training required of their hospital counterparts. And office surgery generally isn't regulated by state or national agencies.

That's not to say that surgical procedures can't be done safely in doctors' offices. *But before bypassing the hospital, patients should ask the surgeon…*

▣ Do you have hospital privileges to perform this procedure?

Surgeons earn hospital privileges—the right to operate in the hospital—by undergoing intensive scrutiny. Only surgeons who provide exemplary care get the privileges.

Surgeons who work in office settings may not have those privileges. And if they have a high rate of poor outcomes, they normally aren't required to report it.

Also important: Ask your doctor if he or she is board-certified for the type of surgery to be done. Certification means that the surgeon has passed written tests and keeps up with developments in his specialty through continuing medical education courses.

▣ How many similar procedures have you performed?

Surgeons get better with practice. A surgeon who has done only a few dozen procedures is still learning. Patients should choose surgeons who have performed many operations similar to the one they will undergo.

▣ Who will administer the anesthetic?

The person administering the anesthetic should be a board-certified anesthesiologist or a certified nurse-practitioner-anesthetist. That's a registered nurse (RN) who has had two years of specialized training in anesthesiology.

States have standards regarding the types of anesthetic that nurse-anesthetists can administer in the hospital and the circumstances under which they can do so. These standards vary among states. Ask your doctor which standards his hospital follows. His in-office surgical practice should follow the same standards.

▣ Is your office prepared for emergencies?

Are resuscitation and life-support equipment and medicine on hand in case things go wrong during the surgery?

At a minimum, this equipment should include a "crash cart" with a defibrillator and airway resuscitation equipment.

▣ Do you have an ongoing relationship with an ambulance company?

The drivers should know exactly where the office is…the best routes to get there and from there to the hospital…and which entries and exits are large enough to accommodate a stretcher.

▣ Who staffs your office?

The doctor's office should employ at least one RN who, like the surgeon and anesthesiologist, has training in advanced cardiac life support.

All nurses assisting during surgery should be RNs specializing in operating room procedures. And—all RNs caring for patients after surgery should be specialists in post-anesthesia recovery.

▣ Has your facility been accredited?

Several agencies inspect physicians' offices, protocols and procedures to certify that they meet standards for quality in-office surgery.

The most demanding agency is the Joint Commission on Accreditation of Healthcare Organizations (JCAHO).

Facilities offering in-office surgery aren't required to be JCAHO-accredited, but some go through the procedure voluntarily. Ask to see the accreditation certificate. It assures you that the facility is well-run and up-to-date.

■ **How long will my procedure take?**
In-office surgery is safest when it does not exceed four hours. Any operation lasting longer should be done in a hospital.

Attention Deficit Disorder Troubles Adults, Too. How to Recognize It... Treat It...Beat It

John J. Ratey, MD, associate professor of psychiatry at Harvard Medical School in Boston. He is coauthor of *Driven to Distraction: Recognizing and Coping with Attention Deficit Disorder from Childhood through Adulthood.* Pantheon.

The ability to concentrate is something most of us take for granted. We have no trouble focusing on the task at hand, whether it's work, recreation, conversation, etc. When something needs to be done, we plan each step and carry it out.

But many adults—perhaps 10 million in the US—find it hard to focus. These people are easily distracted. They procrastinate. They miss appointments. They are unable to keep details straight. Instead of files, they have piles of papers and unfinished projects.

If this sounds familiar, you—or someone close to you—may be suffering from attention deficit disorder (ADD).

NOT JUST FOR KIDS
A decade ago, doctors thought that ADD affected only children...and that these children eventually outgrew the condition. Now we know that childhood ADD persists into adulthood in roughly half of all cases.

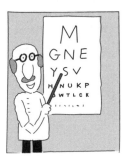

ADD appears to be a subtle disorder of the brain's attentional system—neural circuits that govern the ability to focus and concentrate.

Because the attentional system has links to many other regions of the brain, ADD can cause a wide range of troubling symptoms...

▶ **When *arousal* circuits are affected, people with ADD have difficulty sleeping**—or staying awake. Many people with ADD are restless—in constant motion. Others are lethargic.

▶ **Disruption of the brain's *motivational* circuits makes many people with ADD easily bored.** They crave new sensations—and are prone to engage in risky behavior.

Many ADD patients have substance abuse and/or gambling problems.

▶ **Disruption of the *executive* function weakens inhibitions that help us behave prudently.**

ADD sufferers are often irritable and/or impulsive, acting and speaking without considering the consequences.

The executive function also encompasses the ability to set priorities and plan effectively. Disruption of that function can set the stage for chaotic schedules, missed appointments and, in general, a disorganized lifestyle.

Many people with ADD have low-level jobs despite their obvious intelligence. Others become skilled professionals—but feel they could accomplish even more if only their symptoms didn't get in the way.

Taken alone, each of these symptoms is nothing unusual. From time to time, even the most psychologically healthy person is apt to feel bored, disorganized or scattered. But with ADD, there is a telling *pattern* to these symptoms.

Anyone who exhibits more than a few of these symptoms should seek an evaluation from a psychologist or psychiatrist who specializes in ADD.

LIFESTYLE STRATEGIES
Knowing that the problem is *biological* rather than a character flaw helps control feelings of self-blame.

Similarly, family members, coworkers, etc., are less likely to belittle ADD sufferers once they understand that the problem isn't laziness or a lack of concern.

ADD sufferers often get significant relief from troublesome symptoms simply by changing their environment to compensate for their problems. *Successful strategies…*

▶ **Use lists and reminders.** Hang a wall calendar in an obvious place to record important personal and business engagements. Color-code entries to keep things straight.

▶ **Prepare a written schedule for each day.** Use a Palm Pilot, computer calendar or date book—whichever works best. Create rituals. Do the same thing, in the same order, every day.

▶ **Break down large tasks into small ones, and attach deadlines to each.** Big jobs often lead to procrastination because they're overwhelming. Little tasks are more manageable.

▶ **Use the *OHIO* principle with all paperwork— Only Handle It Once.** When receiving written material, respond to it at once…toss it…or file it permanently. Don't put it in a "to do" box or add it to some pile.

▶ **Notice how and where work gets done best.** In a noisy room? A quiet one? While listening to music? People with ADD often perform best under conditions that others would find tremendously distracting.

> ***Examples:*** *Carrying on a conversation while surfing the Web…reading while watching TV.*

▶ **Exercise vigorously and regularly. Exercise works off excess energy and aggression…**and calms jangled nerves. Many people with ADD find that exercise improves their concentration all day.

HELPFUL MEDICATIONS

Two classes of medication get at the root of ADD, "normalizing" brain functions.

Psychostimulants like *methylphenidate* (Ritalin) and *dextroamphetamine* (Dexedrine) activate the brain's limbic system and frontal cortex. These regions are involved in mood and rational decision making. Instead of feeling revved up, those who take the drugs feel calm and in control.

Certain antidepressants, including *bupropion* (Wellbutrin), *desipramine* (Norpramin) and *venlafaxine* (Effexor), help regulate levels of brain chemicals essential for sustaining attention.

Whether to take medications for ADD is a personal choice. But most people disabled by the disorder find they need medication along with lifestyle changes to function well.

For more information about ADD, contact Children and Adults with Attention-Deficit/Hyperactivity Disorder, 8181 Professional Pl., Landover, MD 20785. 800-233-4050. *www.chadd.org.*

Free "Electronic" Facelift

A free "electronic" facelift service shows your post-surgical appearance before you go under the knife. *How it works:* Mail or E-mail a photo of yourself, along with a description of the procedure you're considering. In 48 hours (E-mail) or four weeks (regular mail), you'll receive a computer-generated image of the predicted result.

Robert Kotler, MD, clinical instructor, head and neck surgery, University of California, Los Angeles, School of Medicine. Mail photo to Dr. Kotler, Suite 201, 436 N. Bedford Dr., Beverly Hills, CA 90210…or send it via E-mail to *cssmg@bb4faces.com.*

Saving Money & Getting the Best Care

Chapter 5

Shrewder Vitamin Shopping

Buy generic multivitamins—they work as well as brand names and cost much less…forget the hype about natural vitamins— your body absorbs natural and synthetic vitamins the same  way…check expiration dates—avoid vitamins with only six to nine months left until expiration…look for the letters USP on the label, which indicate that the vitamin meets standards for dissolving properly. *Important:* Take multivitamins at mealtime— some nutrients are absorbed only when the stomach is full.

Neva Cochran, spokeswoman, American Dietetic Association, 216 W. Jackson Blvd., Suite 800, Chicago 60606.

Save on Vitamins

Taking too many vitamins can be bad for your health—and a waste of money. Vitamins provide benefits only *up to a point.* Taking them in excess dosages is a waste of money—and can lead to medical complications. *Best:* A well-balanced diet provides all the vitamins needed by most people who don't smoke, drink excessively or have specific medical problems. A standard vitamin supplement may make up for a particular lack in your diet—but more than that is not better.

Walter Bortz II, MD, clinical associate professor of medicine at Stanford University Medical School, Portola Valley, CA.

Returning Prescription Drugs

Most states and pharmacies prohibit returning prescription drugs. *Reason:* Once the medicine has left the pharmacy's controlled environment, there is no way to know if it was tampered with.

Self-defense: When starting a new drug, ask your doctor for a starter prescription—one week's to one month's worth. By then, you will know if the medication works or has side effects.

Mitchel C. Rothholz, RPh, vice president for professional practice, American Pharmacists Association, Washington, DC.

Hospital Bill Savvy

Review hospital bills carefully. If you don't understand a charge, ask about it. Watch out for fancy language—a $15 *thermal therapy* kit may simply be a plastic bag filled with ice cubes. If charges seem too high, contact the hospital's patient representative, hospital administrator or your insurance company.

Mike Donio, MPA, The Institute for Safe Medication Practices.

DENTAL EXPENSE SELF-DEFENSE

Get a pretreatment estimate before having major dental work done. This will show exactly how much your dental plan will pay. If the dentist's fees are higher than the insurer's reimbursement rate, try negotiating with the dentist to waive the balance. If the dentist refuses, you will have to pay the balance yourself—or find another dentist.

Gary Rainwater, DDS, a Dallas dentist and past president, American Dental Association.

HOW TO FINANCE SURGERY

New way to pay for elective surgery: Financial services companies now make loans for such treatments as cosmetic, dental and laser eye surgery that are not usually covered by health insurance. The one- to two-year loans sometimes carry low interest rates. *How it works:* Patients generally fill out their loan applications at participating doctors' offices and receive word of approval in about 10 minutes.

Jeffrey Yager, MD, cosmetic plastic surgeon, New York Aesthetic Center.

Saving Money on Prescription Drugs

Timothy McCall, MD, a Boston internist, medical editor of *Yoga Journal* and author of *Examining Your Doctor: A Patient's Guide to Avoiding Harmful Medical Care.* Citadel Press.

With some prescription drugs now costing up to $15 a pill, patients often ask me what they can do to keep their drug expenses down.

Some patients cut costs by skipping doses or by simply not filling prescriptions. Either approach can be dangerous. But there are many ways to lower costs without compromising your care.

▪ Ask your doctor the cost of each drug prescribed.
Doctors often wildly underestimate the costs of the drugs they prescribe. By inquiring, you let your doctor know that price matters to you. Doing so also lets you assess just how aware of costs your doctor really is.

If the estimate is way off, let your doctor know. The doctor may then make another suggestion. At the very least, future patients may benefit from your inquiry.

■ Tell your doctor how you pay for drugs.

About 75% of Americans with health insurance are covered by a plan that pays for at least part of each prescription. If you're not one of the lucky ones, tell your doctor. Similarly, if meeting copayments is a concern for you, let your doctor know.

■ Ask your doctor if there are cheaper alternatives.

In general, generic drugs are just as safe and effective as name brands—sometimes at less than one-tenth the price. And most drug plans charge lower copayments when patients use generics or other "preferred" medications. Ask, too, if there's an entirely different medication that might work just as well for your condition at lower cost.

Each time your doctor prescribes a drug for you, ask if there's any reason *not* to use the generic version. Occasionally, there are good reasons to stick with the name brand. Be wary of doctors who always oppose generic substitution.

■ Ask your doctor about nondrug alternatives.

For many illnesses, it's possible to forgo medication—or use lower dosages—if nondrug therapies are used.

Losing weight, for example, can reduce the need for medication in many cases of diabetes, arthritis and high blood pressure. Acupuncture can lessen dependence on pain pills. Some herbs, such as saw palmetto for prostate enlargement, are effective but cost less than prescription drugs.

■ Ask your doctor to prescribe medication in large quantities.

Pharmacies often give discounts to patients who purchase more than 100 pills at a time. Similarly, a four-ounce tube of a salve may cost only a bit more than a one-ounce tube.

If you've never used the drug before, however, stick with a small quantity. That way, you won't wind up with an excess of a drug that didn't work well for you—or that caused unacceptable side effects.

Another way to save money is to buy pills in a higher-than-needed dose and then divide the pills. If you take 20 mg per day, for example, ask your doctor if you could buy 40-mg tablets and cut them in half. Be careful, though. This strategy works only with "scored" pills, which have a groove down the middle.

WHEN TO BUY MAIL-ORDER DRUGS

Buying prescriptions by mail can be economical. But many mail-order pharmacies use nonpharmacists to fill prescriptions. While a pharmacist does a final check, the volume of drugs being processed is high—and mistakes are possible. *Also:* You lose the benefit of a face-to-face meeting with your pharmacist, who can warn you about drug interactions. *Bottom line:* Use mail order only for drugs with which you are familiar.

Donald L. Sullivan, RPh, PhD, a Columbus, OH, pharmacist and author of *The Consumer's Guide to Generic Drugs: The Complete Reference Book for Anyone Using Prescription Drugs.* Berkley Books.

SAVE MONEY ON MEDS

A prescribed medication may be cheaper than a similar over-the-counter one if the prescribed one is in your insurer's formulary of drugs that qualify for benefits. *Examples:* Prescription treatments for yeast infections, asthma inhalers and pain relievers such as *Motrin* (ibuprofen) are available in slightly higher dosages than over-the-counter products, which health insurers never cover. *To reduce your copay further:* Ask your doctor to prescribe generic brands where appropriate. *Helpful:* Clip coupons for over-the-counter medications you use, and compare the cost to your copay for the prescribed version.

Frank Darras, partner, Shernoff, Bidart, Darras & Arkin, a law firm that specializes in claims against health insurers, 600 S. Indian Hill Blvd., Claremont, CA 91711.

Medical Bill Gifts

If you pay medical or tuition bills for relatives or friends, the payments aren't counted against the annual limit—$10,000 per recipient—on tax-free gifts. *Caution:* Payments must be made directly to the doctor, hospital or educational institution. Don't give the money to the friend or relative.

Sidney Kess, Esq., attorney and CPA, 10 Rockefeller Plaza, Suite 909, New York City 10020.

How to Know if Long-Term-Care Insurance Is for You

Joseph Matthews, JD, an attorney in San Francisco. He is author of *Beat the Nursing Home Trap: A Consumer's Guide to Choosing & Financing Long-Term Care.* Nolo Press.

Many insurance companies now pay nursing home reimbursements for geriatric conditions. And home health care coverage now is part of all good long-term-care policies.

But does it pay to buy a policy?

WHEN COVERAGE IS A WASTE
If you can afford to pay 20 to 30 years of annual premiums, you probably don't need long-term-care insurance.

Reason: You can afford nursing home or home health care if needed.

A person's odds of spending a long period in a nursing home are relatively low. So—most people who purchase this insurance collect few, if any, benefits because they simply don't need a long stay at a nursing facility.

Better: Consider investing the money you would spend each year on premiums in a separate investment account. This way, if you don't need long-term care, you will have the assets for other things or for inclusion in your estate.

THE IDEAL CANDIDATE
Even though the likelihood that you'll need a lot of long-term care is low, coverage may make more sense for some people than for others.

> **Example:** *People in their 60s and 70s who can't afford care...or have a small family that wouldn't be able to care for them...or have family members who live far away.*

When considering coverage, remember that national health care costs rise faster than inflation, and your policy may not keep up with the cost.

Helpful: Be sure your policy includes inflation protection, although rapidly rising health costs may require you to pay more out-of-pocket when you need care.

Is Variable Universal Life Right for You?

Alvin Singer, CLU, president of Singer Nelson Charlmers, insurance brokers, 1086 Teaneck Rd., Teaneck, NJ 07666.

When you buy a variable universal life insurance policy, part of the premium goes to pay for life insurance coverage while the rest is invested in mutual funds. The policy is especially attractive because it offers a tax-deferred way to save for retirement and invest in the stock market at the same time.

WHY VARIABLE UNIVERSAL IS HOT

Like universal life, variable universal life insurance offers flexibility—you can change the amount of life insurance you carry, raising and lowering the face amount simply by amending the policy.

> *Example: You might not need as much life insurance when your children are grown and out of school. In this instance, reducing the portion of the premium going toward insurance would increase the amount invested in stocks.*

You also can invest additional amounts, over and above the required premium, in the funds offered by the policy. Many policies have eight to 10 funds from which to choose.

The ideal candidate for this type of policy is a person with at least 20 years to ride out stock market ups and downs.

FINDING THE IDEAL POLICY

Start by looking at the funds you like. Then call the funds to see which insurers in your area are offering those funds in variable universal plans.

Important: Read the funds' prospectuses to find out the fee structures.

If you already work with an insurance agent, find out which companies offer variable universal coverage. A few companies offer lower-cost policies…and have very thoughtful mutual fund options.

> *Examples: Aetna has minimal front-end charges and Ameritas has no front-end charges on their variable universal policies. General American, Lincoln National Life and Nationwide are other companies with lower-than-average fees.*

WHAT YOU NEED TO KNOW ABOUT DISABILITY INSURANCE

Income-replacement disability policies insure against loss of income due to sickness or accident. Unlike occupation-specific disability policies, which pay monthly benefits if you cannot perform the substantial and material duties of your occupation, these policies have clauses requiring that you return to any reasonable occupation. Your annual premium can be increased to reflect poor claims experience. Discuss this type of policy with a trusted insurance agent or broker.

Frank Darras, partner, Shernoff, Bidart, Darras & Arkin, a law firm that specializes in claims against health insurers, 600 S. Indian Hill Blvd., Claremont, CA 91711.

Build Your Nest Egg with Health Savings Accounts

James Shagawat, fee-only financial planner at Baron Financial Group, Fair Lawn, New Jersey. He has done extensive research on HSAs because they might be useful to his clients, many of them corporate executives. *www.baron-financial.com*

You can get big tax breaks for medical and long-term-care insurance costs with new health savings accounts (HSAs) created by recent Medicare drug legislation.

Bonus: These accounts also offer a new way to build wealth.

If you have an HSA, you still can contribute to an individual retirement account (IRA), a 401(k) and a flexible spending account (FSA).

LIKE AN IRA—ONLY BETTER

HSAs are so much like IRAs, they could be called "health-care IRAs." *Benefits...*

▓ **Money grows tax-deferred,** potentially for decades.

▓ **You can contribute up to $2,600 a year** ($5,150 for a family) and deduct the amount from your federal income tax.

Taxpayers age 55 and older can contribute an additional $500.

▓ **Tax benefits are more generous** than those for traditional or Roth IRAs.

Contributions are tax deductible, *and* with-drawals used to pay health-care expenses are not taxed. In comparison, traditional IRAs offer deductible contributions but withdrawals are taxed. Roth IRA withdrawals are tax free, but contributions are not deductible.

▓ **Money can be withdrawn for any purpose** without penalty after age 65—but you will have to pay income tax if expenses are not health-related.

Before age 65, if cash is used for other purposes, you'll be hit with income tax and a 10% penalty.

▓ **An HSA can be transferred to a spouse or other beneficiary upon the account holder's death.**

If transferred to a spouse, the account remains an HSA, so no tax is owed. If transferred to another beneficiary, the account is no longer an HSA. The beneficiary must include the fair market value of the assets as of the date of the HSA owner's death in his/her gross income.

▓ **An HSA can be established** at any financial institution, just like an IRA, although many institutions don't yet offer them because they are so new.

(Until HSAs are readily available, keep money in a traditional IRA.) An HSA can invest in stocks, bonds, mutual funds, etc.

Requirements: You must be under age 65 and have health insurance with an annual deductible of at least $1,000 ($2,000 for a family).

Many corporations are expected to introduce high-deductible plans during the next benefits open-enrollment period this fall in order to trim insurance costs. Some firms might use a portion of the money they save to contribute to employees' HSAs—as they do for 401(k) plans.

IS AN HSA FOR YOU?

You are a good candidate for an HSA if...

▓ **You have a high-deductible health plan through your employer.**

▓ **You are self-employed.** The HSA tax write-off can help ease the burden of paying your own medical costs.

▓ **You are in a high tax bracket.** Affluent people can use HSAs to generate tax-free savings.

For maximum tax benefits, let money in an HSA grow for as long as possible and pay deductibles and other medical costs from taxable accounts. An HSA holder is never required to spend the money in the account.

HSAS VS. FSAS

Some experts now believe that HSAs eventually will replace FSAs because FSAs have the following drawbacks...

▶ **IRS regulations require that FSA holders forfeit any unused balance at year-end.** Participants must plan carefully. With an HSA, unspent dollars grow tax-free.

► **FSA holders have to provide documentation of medical expenses before being reimbursed for them.**

This isn't necessary with an HSA. Nevertheless, you should maintain evidence of medical expenses in case of a tax audit.

COMPARING HEALTH PLANS

With health insurers gearing up to offer high-deductible plans to corporations and individuals, it pays to shop around. To compare high-deductible health insurance policies, contact Insure.com, 800-556-9393. Also check *www.ehealthinsurance.com.*

Before signing up with an insurer, check its consumer complaint history at the National Association of Insurance Commissioner's Web site, *www.naic. org.* Search under "Consumer Information Source."

If and When to Buy Long-Term-Care Insurance

Lee Slavutin, MD, CPC, CLU, a principal of Stern Slavutin-2 Inc., insurance and estate planners, 530 Fifth Ave., New York 10036 says that about 11% of those turning age 65 can expect to spend a significant amount of time in a nursing home.

The cost of nursing home care is high. In a number of areas in the country it can top $100,000.

How are you going to cover such a huge expense if the need arises? *The answer depends on your income and net worth...*

► **The "poor"**—and those who spend down their assets to become poor—can rely on Medicaid to cover the cost of a nursing home stay.

► **The "wealthy"** can afford to use their incomes to pay for such care without affecting their assets or standard of living for other family members.

► **Those in the middle**—individuals with a net worth, say, of between $500,000 and $5 million—should consider buying a long-term-care policy.

Here are some factors to weigh in deciding whether to buy a long-term-care policy, and when...

CAN I AFFORD IT?

Premiums for long-term-care policies aren't cheap. Like life insurance policies, the younger you are when you take out the policy, the lower your premiums will be.

Caution: Premiums for long-term-care policies are considered "level premiums"—that is, they don't increase as you age. *However*—the insurance company has the right to increase the premiums for a whole *class* of policies. This could happen with long-term-care policies as insurance companies gain more experience and find they've underpriced them.

Cost of the premium depends on...

► **The person's age** when the policy is first purchased.

► **The benefit per day.**

► **The period for which benefits will be paid** — three years, five years, life.

► **The "elimination period"**—the time before benefits will start.

► **Other factors,** such as a cost-of-living adjustment to the daily benefit.

TYPES OF POLICIES

The type of policy you buy really depends on what you can afford.

The best of policies: Lifetime coverage for the maximum benefit, with a short elimination period.

But if you find the cost of such coverage prohibitive, consider a more modest daily payout for a shorter period than life, or with a longer elimination period.

In comparing policies offered by different companies, there are nuances to consider that can affect your choice.

Example: Be sure you understand how each company counts days of care for purposes of the

OUTSMART THAT COLLECTION AGENCY

To stop harassment by a collection agency, write the agency and demand it stop calls and other troublesome activities. A copy should also go to the creditor. Under federal law, the activities must stop. *Other laws affecting collection:* Collectors must keep your debts private—they may contact others to try to find you, but may not indicate that they are trying to collect a debt. They must send you written notice of the debt within five days of contacting you. They cannot threaten, lie or use profanity.

David Gilbert, partner, Mintz, Levin, Cohn, Ferris, Glovsky & Popeo, PC, One Financial Center, Boston 02111.

elimination period. Say someone needs three days of care per week. Does this count as an entire week for the elimination period or will it take seven calendar days to equal one week for the elimination period?

▇ Get professional help.
Use an insurance professional who can guide you through the intricacies of long-term-care insurance.

▇ Experience counts.
Stick with an insurance company that has experience with long-term-care policies, such as GE Capital, Travelers, John Hancock, Fortis and Conseca.

Tax break: A portion of the premiums can be treated as a deductible medical expense based on your age, thereby offsetting some of the cost for those who itemize their medical expenses.

CAN YOU AFFORD NOT TO?
If you are in the middle—not rich and not poor—you may not accumulate enough through savings to pay for nursing home care. If you are in this situation, you should consider buying a long-term-care policy.

> *Example: At age 60, you buy a $100 per day benefit at a cost of $519 per year—a three-year policy with a 90-day elimination period.*

Then assume at age 80, you require nursing home care. You would have paid $10,380 over the 20 years of coverage.

Had you used that same $519 each year to invest for an after-tax return of 6%, you have only $20,237 after 20 years.

This would cover just 203 days in the home (at $100 a day). The policy would cover 1,095 days.

WHEN TO BUY A POLICY
Those who are 55 years old or older should start to look seriously at long-term-care policies.

If you don't have employer-provided coverage, then look into individual coverage. The younger you are when you start the policy, the lower your premiums will be.

But if you buy at 55, won't you be paying premiums for 20 or 30 years before needing benefits, if ever? Does that make sense?

While your chances are better than 50% that you'll never put in a claim, should you need to do so, you're likely to come out ahead financially if you have a policy.

> *Example: Suppose a 55-year-old buys a policy to provide $250 a day for a lifetime if needed (with a 90-day elimination period). She would pay $3,452.20 a year in premiums.*

If she should need long-term care after just one year of paying premiums, she would recover her entire outlay in just 14 days in a nursing home of average cost.

Five years of premiums would be recovered in 69 days, 10 years in 138 days. And—20 years in 276 days.

Even if this 55-year-old were not to need any benefits until age 85, her 30 years of premiums would be recovered in 414 days.

How to Protect Your Full Rights as a Patient

Charles Inlander, health-care consultant and president, People's Medical Society, a consumer health advocacy group in Allentown, PA. He is author of more than 20 books on consumer health issues, including *Take This Book to the Hospital with You: A Consumer Guide to Surviving Your Hospital Stay*. St. Martin's.

B eing ill or injured is a stressful experience— some injuries/illnesses, of course, are more stressful than others. The general feeling is one of being out of control—at the mercy of the "system."

You want answers…information…state-of-the-art treatment. You want to be treated with respect. And you want your medical information kept confidential.

Knowing your rights as a patient can protect you from abuse by the system.

GETTING COMPLETE INFORMATION FROM YOUR DOCTOR

In the past, many doctors viewed patients as unable to understand diagnoses, and so shared little about patient conditions and treatment alternatives (beyond what was required to obtain "informed consent").

Today, patients are savvier and demand more from their doctors. *How to proceed…*

■ **Demand the time that is needed to tell your doctor about your symptoms.** And— demand the time to hear his or her explanation of possible diagnoses and courses of treatment.

Helpful: Write down your symptoms so you don't overlook them in conversation with your doctor.

If you don't think your doctor is listening to you or giving you the time you need—speak up!

■ **Get a second opinion before surgery or other invasive treatment.**
Most insurers are willing to pay for this—since a second opinion may indicate a less drastic and less costly course of action.

■ **Do your own research.**
While you aren't licensed to practice medicine (even on yourself), there's plenty of easy-to-understand medical information available on the Internet (try *www.ivillage.com* and *www.seekwellness.com*).

Also check InteliHealth at *www.intelihealth.com*. Of course, don't rely solely on any information you find. Discuss it with your doctor.

PATIENT BILL OF RIGHTS
Most hospitals nationwide have adopted some or all of the 12 rights enumerated in the *Patient Bill of Rights* approved by the American Hospital Association in 1992. *These rights include…*

▶ **Right to receive considerate and respectful care.**

▶ **Right to obtain relevant, current and understandable information** about diagnosis, treatment and prognosis from doctors and other caregivers. This includes disclosure of the financial implications of the alternatives presented.

▶ **Right to make decisions about the plan of care.** This includes the right to refuse a recommended treatment.

▶ **Right to have an advance medical directive—a living will or a durable medical power of attorney.** These documents permit you to express the kind of care you want and *don't* want.

▶ **Right to every consideration of privacy.** This extends not only to a patient's body during examination and treatment, but also to case discussions.

▶ **Right to expect confidentiality** for all communications and records pertaining to treatment.

▶ **Right to review records pertaining to personal medical care.** This includes the right to have such information explained.

▶ **Right to expect a reasonable response from a hospital** to a request for appropriate and medically indicated care. That may require transfer to another medical facility.

▶ **Right to be informed about business relationships among the hospital, doctors and others that may influence a patient's treatment and care.**

> *Example: The urologist owns an interest in the lithotripsy center, where kidney stones are sonically blasted. The urologist will be inclined to send you there even though there may be alternative treatments.*

▶ **Right to consent or decline to participate in clinical studies** of an ailment that you suffer from.

▶ **Right to expect reasonable continuity of care.** You don't want a different doctor every other day.

▶ **Right to be informed of hospital policies and practices**—such as how to resolve billing disputes.

WINDOW DRESSING?

These rights sound great, but they're only "window dressing." Hospitals that say they support these rights might not. *Instead...*

▶ **Doctors may not adequately inform patients of a prescribed drug's side effects.**

▶ **Hospitals may not prepare itemized bills.**

▶ **Hospitals may not even have a doctor in the emergency room 24 hours a day.**

Reality: No one else will be looking out for your rights.

If you're a patient and believe your rights have been or are being violated, you can take action.

Ask to speak with the hospital's patient advocate, a person employed by the hospital to be a go-between for patients and the hospital's administration.

You'll find the name and number of the patient advocate (sometimes called a patient representative) on your hospital admission papers or posted in your hospital room.

Vocal objections to treatment you've received or failed to receive may just be the case of the "squeaky wheel" getting the grease it needs.

REVIEW YOUR MEDICAL RECORDS

Review your medical records to ensure that there are no mistakes that could produce problems for you down the line.

The best course of action: Ask your doctor for a copy of your records. Hospitals that have adopted the Patient Bill of Rights are supposed to provide your records upon request.

Even the Best Doctors Make Dangerous Errors

Richard N. Podell, MD, internist at Podell Medical Center in Springfield, NJ. Dr. Podell is a specialist in chronic fatigue syndrome and fibromyalgia. He is author of several books, including *The G-Index Diet.* Warner.

Physicians now face time and financial pressures that make it impossible to spend as much time as they want to with each patient. And most patients are too timid or embarrassed to ask for more time—even if they need it.

In their rush to see as many patients as possible, some doctors are making big mistakes. *Here's how to deal with a doctor's mistakes and make sure your medical needs are fully met...*

MISTAKE: Not asking if you have any questions. A good doctor won't be offended if you question him or her or ask for an explanation of something he has said or is about to do.

Key: At the beginning of your visit, tell your doctor exactly what topics you want to discuss while you're there.

A verbal outline prepares the doctor for the likelihood of your questions along the way and keeps him from viewing your questions as challenges. As a doctor, I find it frustrating when a patient brings up a major concern while I'm wrapping up the consultation. When you mention all your concerns at the outset, you and your doctor can pace the available time to make sure everything is covered.

MISTAKE: Failing to ask about what vitamins, minerals and herbs you are taking. Many of these supplements can interact with the drugs you're taking or affect your symptoms.

> *Examples: Ginkgo biloba can thin blood—and is particularly dangerous for patients taking blood thinners. Licorice root can cause potassium loss.*

If your doctor doesn't ask, it's your responsibility to inform him.

Helpful: Before you visit the doctor, prepare a list of all the vitamins, minerals, herbs and prescription and nonprescription drugs you're taking. Even if you mentioned them during a previous visit, remind him again. Your prescription regimen or health may have changed since your last visit.

MISTAKE: Not ordering a biopsy for a breast lump that doesn't disappear after a menstrual period. Even if a mammogram has shown no evidence of cancer, any persisting lump has the potential to be malignant.

Most lumps are not, but looking at a mammogram or feeling the lump can't tell you for certain if a lump is cancerous.

Roughly 15% of breast cancers don't show up on mammograms. Any new lump that doesn't disappear with a menstrual cycle must be biopsied or the patient should be referred to a specialist—regardless of mammogram results.

MISTAKE: Failing to prescribe potassium supplements for patients who are taking thiazide-type diuretics. Thiazide diuretics, such as *Hydro-DIURIL*, are used to lower blood pressure by decreasing fluid retention.

These drugs increase the outflow of potassium and magnesium in the urine. That raises the risk of dangerous heart-rhythm abnormalities.

What to do: If you're taking a thiazide diuretic, potassium levels should be monitored within one month of starting the medication...and then every three to six months thereafter. Also ask whether you need to be taking potassium or possibly magnesium supplements. Magnesium levels can also fall when taking diuretics, although measuring blood levels does not always reveal this.

Don't try to stabilize potassium levels yourself by taking over-the-counter supplements. Potassium levels need to be monitored carefully by your doctor. Besides, over-the-counter supplements don't have enough potassium to be effective in this situation.

MISTAKE: Missing signs and symptoms of depression. Depression is extremely common, but many people who suffer from it don't realize they have it. The primary mental symptom of depression is loss of pleasure in things you used to enjoy. Depression also manifests as vague physical symptoms, such as fatigue, headache, backache, etc.

Self-defense: Mention any troublesome symptoms to your doctor and that you suspect you may be depressed. Otherwise, your doctor may not take the kind of history necessary to properly diagnose depression.

Psychological therapy and antidepressant drugs are among the effective treatments for depression. But the problem can't be treated unless it's diagnosed.

MISTAKE: Not asking how you're sleeping. Insufficient sleep is a major contributor to both physical and mental illness. Yet doctors rarely ask patients about their sleep patterns. Not all doctors realize that sleep is one of the body's most powerful natural healing processes.

Tell your doctor if you are not sleeping well. There are specific disorders that can disrupt rest—and they can usually be treated with drugs and/or behavioral therapy, and/or other measures.

> **Examples**: Periodic leg movement disorder, in which small muscles twitch throughout the night ...sleep apnea, in which the individual stops breathing for brief moments throughout the night.

How to Make Tough Medical Decisions

Peter Clarke, PhD, professor of preventive medicine and director of the Center for Health and Medical Communication at the University of Southern California School of Medicine in Los Angeles. He is coauthor of *Surviving Modern Medicine: How to Get the Best from Doctors, Family & Friends.* Rutgers University Press.

Bypass surgery or angioplasty? Massage for a bad back—or muscle relaxants? What's the best remedy for varicose veins?

Medical decisions can be *very* hard to make. Your well-being, comfort—perhaps even your life—depend on making the right choice. And there are often many, many options.

> **Example:** Even a minor ailment such as bronchitis can now be treated with 31 different medications—each with its own pros and cons.

Beset by confusion and anxiety, many people simply accept the first option suggested by their physician—"Whatever you say, doctor."

This is *not* the best approach.

PATIENTS SHOULD DECIDE
Doctors can guide you in your decision—but watch out. Each has biases that can interfere with proper decision making.

> **Example I:** A surgeon may be more likely than an internist to recommend surgery for prostate cancer.

> **Example II:** A holistic doctor may be more likely than a cardiologist to recommend nutritional therapy for heart disease.

Your goal, of course, is to select the course of action that's best for you. It may or may not coincide with your doctor's biases.

There's another reason patients should make their own decisions. If you take time to explore all your options yourself, you'll have a satisfying sense that you're in control of your care. Feeling in control contributes to the healing process.

Finding: Surgical patients who felt they had carefully weighed all their options needed less pain-killing medication...experienced fewer complications...and were discharged from the hospital sooner than similar patients who had been more passive in their decision making.

DECIDING UNDER PRESSURE
Most medical decisions are made under pressure. Often, the doctor presents a diagnosis, recommends a course of treatment and expects to be given the go-ahead—all during the same all-too-brief appointment.

In such a stressful situation, few people can think clearly—much less weigh complicated options rationally.

Good news: While a tight deadline may be convenient for the doctor, it's *almost never* justifiable on medical grounds. Rare indeed is the illness that requires immediate action.

In most cases, it's safe to postpone the decision for a few days, a week or even longer. Immediate action is called for only rarely—for example, when heart or lung function is in steep decline...or infection rages.

If a doctor urges a quick decision, ask if your life is in jeopardy. If not, tell the doctor you'll have a decision within the next week or so.

Delaying the decision gives you a chance to do your own medical research and get a second—or even a third—opinion.

Even if the second opinion confirms the first, you'll feel better knowing that you've gotten good medical advice.

A DECISION PRESCRIPTION

No one can say for sure what the consequences of medical treatment will be. But the more you know about various treatments, the less uncertainty you'll have to endure.

Scour bookstores and libraries for relevant material. The Internet can be an excellent resource. *Three Web sites are especially helpful...*

▶ **www.cdc.gov.** This site includes an A to Z index of diseases and conditions.

▶ **www.medscape.com.** Intended for the medical community, Medscape can be a bit technical for laypeople. But it's a great way to search for abstracts of relevant studies.

▶ **http://health.nih.gov.** This is the official site of the National Institutes of Health.

Once you know your options, you'll no doubt have new questions for your doctor...

▶ **How long will surgery affect my day-to-day activities?**

▶ **How do my treatment options compare** in terms of discomfort and length of convalescence?

▶ **What percentage of patients experience complications**...and what are the most common ones? What are the most serious ones?

▶ **Will this drug interfere with my appetite or sex life?**

Do *not* phone your doctor with these questions. Instead, fax or E-mail your questions. Ask that the doctor fax or E-mail the answers back to you...or suggest a time when you can talk.

GET THE RIGHT DOCTOR FOR YOUR CONDITION

If you have a chronic illness and are in an HMO, you cannot count on the provider directory to help you find the right primary-care doctor. Try calling specialists at high-quality hospitals and ask them to name primary-care physicians they consider good at treating patients with conditions like yours. Or get recommendations from a chronic-illness support group at a hospital, social service agency or the local branch of a national group focusing on your condition.

Peter D. Fox, managed care consultant, Chevy Chase, MD, quoted in *The Wall Street Journal.*

A NEW WAY TO COMMUNICATE WITH YOUR DOCTOR

More and more patients are corresponding with their doctors using E-mail. E-mail is often a convenient way to discuss matters with doctors, given their hectic schedules. Next time you see your doctor, consider asking for an E-mail address.

Tom Ferguson, MD, professor of health informatics, University of Texas Health Science Center, Houston.

DEFINE RISKS CAREFULLY

Doctors often use vague language when explaining the risks and benefits associated with various treatments. But vague language isn't very helpful when you're making a life or death decision. *Insist on clarity.*

If the doctor says complications are rare with a particular surgical procedure—or that a particular drug seldom causes side effects—ask that he quantitate the appropriate rate for you.

Similarly, find out what the doctor means by "successful" treatment. Does that mean you'll be able to go hiking following surgery for your arthritic knees? Or does it mean only that the operation will make your knees a bit less painful?

Helpful: Ask someone to accompany you to your next doctor's visit. Tell your companion in advance about the questions you have...and encourage him or her to pursue any other questions that arise during the discussion.

The last step in making a sound medical decision is to take time to think things over.

Find a quiet, solitary place, and spend 15 minutes envisioning each scenario you can imagine.

You may even want to prepare a written list of all the pros and cons for each option.

How to Get the Best Care from Your Doctor— Simple Strategies That Work Wonders

Richard L. Sribnick, MD, an internist in private practice in Columbia, SC. He is coauthor of *Smart Patient, Good Medicine: Working with Your Doctor to Get the Best Medical Care.* Walker & Co.

The doctor–patient relationship, like any other, requires effort to make it work. *Strategies that can help...*

■ Speak clearly and concisely when describing your symptoms.

Though a physical exam and lab tests may follow, the first—and often critical—ingredient for an accurate diagnosis is how well you describe your symptoms.

A good description reduces the risk of misdiagnosis...and helps you avoid needless diagnostic tests and surgical procedures.

Helpful: Prepare your questions ahead of time—in writing. If you wait until you're in the doctor's office, you may have a hard time expressing your thoughts clearly. *Four important issues...*

▶ *When* **did the problem first appear?**

▶ *Where* **is it located?** Be specific. "Pain in the temples" is better than "a headache."

▶ *How* **does it feel? Is it a stabbing pain?** Throbbing? How often does it occur? How long does it last?

▶ *What* **brings it on or makes it worse?** What relieves it? What other symptoms occur at the same time?

If you have several problems, list all of them as soon as the doctor walks into the examination room. Let the doctor decide which to pursue first.

Say you've been experiencing chest pain. How do you describe your symptoms to the doctor?

Wrong: "My chest feels funny sometimes at work. It's probably just stress."

A busy doctor may dismiss that problem as trivial, and not investigate further.

Right: "I feel like there's a fist tightening in the center of my chest. This chest pressure began several weeks ago and lasts for a couple of minutes each time. I first noticed it after walking up two flights of stairs at work. I felt better after I stopped to rest."

Such a description will alert the doctor to the possibility of heart disease, and the need for diagnostic tests like stress tests.

▪ Be calm—but not stoic.

If you don't look like you're in pain, the doctor may fail to appreciate just how much it hurts. If you make light of a symptom, he is likely to do so as well.

Important: Share your concerns. If you fear that your headaches are being caused by a brain tumor, for instance, say so. But do so *after* you've described your symptoms. That way, the doctor's thinking won't be biased.

Whatever you do, *don't* panic. If you do, the doctor may be tempted to order needless tests and procedures to comfort you.

▪ Adopt a positive attitude.

Some patients exhibit a negative, almost accusatory attitude when talking to the doctor. It's an attitude exemplified by statements such as, "I want what's due me here, and I don't want you to cut any corners."

Such an attitude puts the doctor on the defensive. That can lead to hostility, and it's hard for a doctor to provide good care when he's mad at you.

If you tend to leave your doctor's office feeling shortchanged of time or attention, you may need to find another doctor.

If you have that same feeling with several different doctors, odds are you need a new attitude. Discuss the situation with a friend or relative whose judgment you respect.

▪ Don't tolerate rudeness.

If you feel you have been treated poorly by the doctor or his staff, let him know. Just be sure to do so diplomatically. Make it clear that your purpose is problem-solving, so you can work better together.

Wrong: "Why do I always have to wait? Isn't my time important too?"

Right: "How can I minimize the time I have to wait?"

Always wait until the *end* of your visit to air any complaint. That way, the doctor can turn his full attention to your medical problem—without being distracted by his own defensiveness.

LOOKING FOR A GOOD DOCTOR?

Good ways to find a good doctor: Ask a hospital's vice president of nursing for a recommendation…talk to a chief resident (a doctor in the last year of residency) at a teaching hospital…call a health reporter for a large newspaper…speak to a pathologist—since pathologists do many autopsies, they see the results of good or poor treatment by other doctors. If looking for a surgeon, ask an operating room nurse—they see surgeons in action.

John Connolly, EdD, former president, New York Medical College, and president of Castle Connolly Medical Ltd., a medical publishing company in New York. He is author of *Buyer's Guide to the Best Health Care.* Castle Connolly Medical Ltd.

BETTER DOCTOR'S APPOINTMENTS

When making a doctor's appointment, know how much time the doctor will have and adjust your questions accordingly. Bring along a pad and pen so you can take notes on what the doctor and nurses say. Plan ahead to focus on the most important issues.

Molly Mettler, senior vice president, Healthwise Inc., a consumer health information group, Boise, ID, quoted in *Investor's Business Daily*, 12655 Beatrice St., Los Angeles 90066.

CONFIDENTIAL RECORDS —A MUST

To make sure that your medical records are kept private, confirm with your physicians that they will not send anything about you out of the office without first showing it to you and getting your approval. *Especially important:* Information on mental health…and substance abuse. If you see anything ambiguous in your record that could cause legal problems for you later, discuss it with your doctor or medical provider and find replacement terminology that is mutually acceptable.

Harold J. Bursztajn, MD, associate clinical professor of psychiatry, Harvard Medical School, Boston, and psycho-analyst in private practice, Cambridge, MA.

■ Take steps to avoid frustration.
Minimize waiting for appointments by scheduling routine visits for the first slot after the doctor's lunch hour. If that slot is unavailable, ask for the first appointment in the morning.

If the doctor agrees to "work you in" between appointments, ask in advance how long you'll have to wait. That will give you a sense of control—and reduce your frustration.

Phone strategy: Unless it is a true emergency, don't expect to speak with the doctor right away.

Tell the receptionist you would like the doctor to call you as soon as it's convenient.

In an emergency, of course, don't hesitate to ask the nurse to interrupt the doctor.

Prescription refills: Call during office hours, not on evenings or weekends. Call from home or work—not the pharmacy. Ask the doctor or nurse approximately when the prescription will be phoned in.

■ Show your appreciation.
Like everyone else, doctors want to feel good about their work…and they have affection for patients who express their appreciation for their efforts.

That is especially true nowadays, when doctors feel they are under attack by the media and the general public.

Don't be afraid to say "thank you" to your doctor. A simple note can really make a doctor's day—and improve the quality of your care.

Medical Rights You May Not Know You Have

Charles Inlander, health-care consultant and president, People's Medical Society, a consumer health advocacy group in Allentown, PA. He is author of more than 20 books on consumer health issues, including *Take This Book to the Hospital with You: A Consumer Guide to Surviving Your Hospital Stay.* St. Martin's.

Several years ago, a woman I know had the local sheriff called in when a hospital refused to discharge her. She had no cash, credit cards or checks with her, and the hospital wouldn't let her go until she paid $20 for services not covered by her insurance. Her husband called the sheriff and said that she was being held for ransom.

He was right. When the sheriff arrived, she was freed, and the hospital immediately changed its policy. Hospitals do not have the right to deny discharge if the patient can't pay.

Knowing your medical rights is important. *Here are some rights you may not realize you have...*

■ **Access to your medical records.** You have the right to copies of your medical records.

It's especially important to get them when a major condition, such as cancer or diabetes, has been diagnosed or major surgery is performed. Even though only 26 states have specific statutes that give this right, no state has laws that allow providers or facilities to deny you access to your records. But remember, the operative word is "copy." The record itself legally belongs to the provider. In most states, providers can charge a "reasonable" fee for copying costs. Check with your state's health department to learn the maximum allowable copying fee.

■ **Special Medicare rights.** Medicare beneficiaries have some special rights not given to other consumers.

> *Example: If a doctor tells a Medicare patient that a service is covered by Medicare and it turns out it is not, the doctor can't charge you. It is illegal for a doctor to bill any Medicare beneficiary under such circumstances. Even though it may seem uncomfortable, ask the doctor to put it in writing that Medicare will cover the charges. That's the best way to protect your rights (and your money).*

■ **Discharge rights.** If you are a Medicare beneficiary and think you are being discharged

before you are medically ready, tell the hospital that you wish to appeal.

The hospital must then give you a "Notice of Noncoverage," which starts the appeals process. You are not required to pay for hospitalization during the one to two days that it takes for the appeal to be decided by an outside organization retained by Medicare.

Similarly, anyone has the right to check out of a hospital at any time. If the doctor disagrees, you'll be asked to sign an "Against Medical Advice" form. This form releases the hospital from any liability.

■ **Nursing-home rights.** If you or a family member has any type of problem in a skilled nursing home, you have the right to seek help from your state's nursing-home ombudsman.

This federally mandated program helps resolve, free of charge, any problem or disagreement related to care or rights in these facilities. By law, the

nursing home must give you the phone number and address to contact the ombudsman.

Finally, if you think "there ought to be a law" about some medical right, there probably is. Call your state's attorney general's office for more information.

FAKE CERTIFICATES YOU NEED TO KNOW ABOUT

Beware of doctors' certification. Some may be meaningless. The official certifying organization is the American Board of Medical Specialties in Chicago. But another 125 groups claim to provide certification. Some insist on substantial training—others do not. *Self-defense:* Call ABMS at 866-275-2267 to find out if a doctor is officially certified.

How Not to Let Your HMO Take Advantage of You

Vikram Khanna, MHS, head of State Health Policy Solutions, a health-care legislative and market strategy research firm in Columbia, MD. From 1986 through 1991, he directed the health education and advocacy unit of the Office of the Attorney General of Maryland in Baltimore. He is author of *Managed Care Made Easy.* People's Medical Society.

Health-maintenance organizations (HMOs) get plenty of bad publicity, but the vast majority of people who belong to an HMO are satisfied with the care they receive. *Here's how to get good care from an HMO...*

CRUCIAL FIRST STEPS

Study the HMO's enrollment materials. Find out exactly which services are covered...and what steps you must follow to ensure that your care is covered.

Take special care in familiarizing yourself with the procedures for emergency and out-of-town care. HMOs sometimes refuse to cover such care because patients fail to follow procedures that are spelled out clearly in the enrollment materials.

Next, check your HMO membership card. Make sure that your name, Social Security number and any other information printed on it is correct.

Using a card with faulty information can cause months of billing problems.

YOUR HEALTH INVENTORY

Upon joining an HMO, you'll be required to select a primary-care physician. This doctor—in most cases an internist, a gynecologist or, for children, a pediatrician—provides routine care and may control your access to specialized care.

To help you pick a doctor, the HMO should provide you with a list of doctors in its network, along with pertinent information about each doctor.

You'll want a board-certified doctor whose office is convenient to your home or workplace ...and who has admitting privileges at a reputable hospital.

Before contacting any of the doctors who meet these basic criteria, however, it's a good idea to prepare a "health inventory" about your family.

What to do: On paper, briefly describe the overall state of each family member's health. Detail any recent, recurring or chronic medical conditions... and list all medications each person takes.

A health inventory might begin something like this...

I'm 41. I'm pretty healthy, although I suffer from mild psoriasis. I work out regularly, but I'm about 10 pounds overweight.

My 12-year-old daughter wears braces and has mild asthma.

PICKING A DOCTOR

Use the basic criteria to narrow your search to three doctors. Then schedule a five-minute, face-to-face interview with each one.

During this initial meeting, go over your health inventory with the doctor. Ask how much experience he or she has in treating the conditions that affect you...and what approach the doctor would use in treating you.

Find out, too, whether the doctor thinks you should sign up for any extra-cost coverage offered by your employer—for vision care, dental care, mental health care, etc.

Most important: Make sure you and the doctor get along.

Some doctors don't charge for an initial get-acquainted interview. But don't be put off if the doctor charges you for a regular office visit.

Once you've picked a doctor, schedule your first official visit. Take along all pertinent health information—names and phone numbers of doctors you've seen in the past year…copies of recent X rays and test results…a list of all drugs you take, including prescription and nonprescription drugs and herbal remedies.

PREVENTIVE CARE

HMOs typically cover a wide range of preventive care. This may include childhood immunizations…physical exams…and screening tests for cholesterol, glaucoma, colon cancer, prostate cancer, breast cancer, etc.

Review your plan materials to find out what sorts of preventive care are covered. Ask your primary care doctor which tests you should be getting and how often.

Good news: Many HMOs offer classes or even individualized counseling in weight loss, smoking cessation, stress management, childbirth, etc.

SPECIALIZED CARE

If you need surgery or other specialized care, your HMO may require you to get a second opinion from a doctor who belongs to its network.

Caution: Some HMO doctors aren't very good about telling their patients about certain costly treatment options. To avoid being misled, ask your doctor if there are any other treatment options you should know about—even if the plan will not pay for them.

If your condition is particularly serious, consider going outside the network for your second opinion—even if you must pay for it yourself. That way, you can reduce the risk that you're not being told of all the options open to you.

If a child needs specialized care: The child should be referred to a pediatric specialist—not an adult specialist who sometimes sees children. If the HMO has no in-network pediatric specialist, the HMO should pick up the tab for an out-of-network referral.

IF HOSPITALIZATION IS NECESSARY

HMOs have something of a reputation for forcing hospital patients to go home prematurely. But no matter what the HMO's official policy is regarding the length of hospital stays, your doctor is the only person who can authorize your discharge. Ask your doctor what criterias he will use in determining when you are ready to go home.

Within a few days of being discharged from the hospital, you should get a detailed bill, a copy of your medical records and the names, addresses and phone numbers of the doctors who treated you. You'll need this information if there's a payment dispute.

FILING A COMPLAINT

Minor complaints can often be resolved with a single call to the HMO's customer service department. Even so, it's a good idea to keep detailed notes of all conversations you have with plan representatives.

Record the date of each discussion, the names of customer service representatives and supervisors you spoke with, what they said, etc.

If customer service doesn't help, file a written grievance with the HMO's medical director. Explain what went wrong and what you've done to try to resolve the problem. Be sure to enclose supporting documents—a statement from your doctor, copies of your medical records, etc.

If you exhaust your HMO's internal grievance process, contact your state insurance commission, health department or attorney general's office.

If your HMO is unwilling to tell you how to conduct an external appeal, call your state health department for guidance.

CALL A SPECIALIST

Your doctor is four times more likely to refer you to a specialist if you ask him/her to. Instead of waiting for him to suggest it, speak up if your doctor is uncertain about your diagnosis or treatment. This is especially important when complications arise or when a specialized procedure is needed.

Richard Kravitz, MD, professor and director, University of California, Davis, Center for Health Services Research in Primary Care, Sacramento.

Managed Care Danger

Managed care plans are pressuring doctors to save money by switching patients not just from brand-name drugs to generics but to different drugs altogether. That practice can seriously affect the patients' health.

Self-defense: Drug substitutions can cause side effects and may not work as well as your doctor's first choice. Be sure you understand the reason for any medication change and verify that all prescribed drugs make sense for your condition. If you suspect a switch is made to reduce costs, tell your doctor you are worried about the decision. Your doctor may be able to make an exception or a case on your behalf to the managed care plan.

Timothy McCall, MD, a Boston internist, medical editor of *Yoga Journal* and author of *Examining Your Doctor: A Patient's Guide to Avoiding Harmful Medical Care.* Citadel Press.

DRUGS WITH *TWO* NAMES

Some drugs have two brand names. When a medication may be prescribed for different purposes, the manufacturer will sometimes give it different names—one for each use. *Danger:* A patient needing treatment for two conditions might get prescriptions for the same drug, under two names, from different doctors. Taking a double dosage could cause side effects. *Self-defense:* Make sure your pharmacy has drug-interaction computer programming. *Also:* Be sure each doctor and pharmacist knows all the medicines you take.

Susan Proulx, PharmD, president, Medical Error Recognition and Revision Strategies, Inc., Huntingdon, PA.

PUZZLING PILLS

Undissolved pills sometimes show up on X rays —and are thought by doctors to be gallstones or kidney stones. Iron and potassium pills are most likely to be misidentified in this manner. *Self-defense:* Before having an X ray, let your doctor know about any pills you have taken.

Jonathan M. Evans, MD, associate professor of internal medicine, University of Virginia Health System.

Plastic Surgery Woes...

Did you know that half of all plastic surgery patients suffer depression afterward? That's the highest rate of any surgical procedure. *Possible reason:* The contrast between the patients' high expectations and the swollen and bruised image they see the first time they look in the  mirror. *Also:* Sedatives used before and after surgery may deplete the brain's serotonin, a chemical involved in mood regulation. *Good news:* In most cases, depression is mild and lasts only two to three months.

Oscar M. Ramirez, MD, plastic surgeon, Esthetigue Internationale, Baltimore.

Questions to Ask Before Having an Operation

Charles Inlander, health-care consultant and president, People's Medical Society, a consumer health advocacy group in Allentown, PA. He is author of more than 20 books on consumer health issues, including *Take This Book to the Hospital with You: A Consumer Guide to Surviving Your Hospital Stay.* St. Martin's.

We readily grill a salesperson when we are buying a car. Yet when it comes to surgery, we routinely accept medical opinions without question.

That's a mistake—one with potentially serious consequences. Questioning surgical procedures—all of them—and being an involved, participating patient is your most important consideration when you are facing surgery.

Before any procedure…

ASK THE DOCTOR...

■ What are the alternatives to this procedure?
For example, temporary pacemakers are commonly implanted during cardiac surgery. But noninvasive pacemakers, with electrodes attached outside the chest, have proven to be effective in 94% of patients. This is typical of the alternatives to many surgical procedures that should be discussed with your physician.

■ How much experience do you have with this procedure?
Studies show that surgeons who perform specific procedures more often tend to do them better. Experience, though, isn't the only factor when selecting a surgeon. Many veteran surgeons, for instance, continue to perform outdated operations that are avoided by younger physicians who are attuned to more modern technologies.

This illustrates, incidentally, the importance of second opinions. Nearly 80% of certain procedures may not be recommended by a second opinion. If there is disagreement between your first and second opinions, don't hesitate to seek a third or even a fourth opinion. The key here is consensus.

■ What are your fees?
You should ask, and get in writing, the doctor's fees—from the doctor, not the secretary. *Important:* Fees are often negotiable.

ASK THE HOSPITAL...

■ What are your nosocomial infection rates?
Nosocomial infections are those that originate in the hospital. About 10% of all patients get them, usually because of flaws in hospital sanitation procedures.

Hospital personnel are usually reluctant to discuss their nosocomial infection rates. If so, your doctor should be able to provide them. If the rates are around 5%, the hospital is probably doing a good job controlling infections.

■ What kind of training and experience does the surgical support staff have?
Insist on meeting your anesthesiologist. In a non-hospital setting—a hospital outpatient department, physician's office or freestanding surgery center—the anesthesiologist's qualifications are crucial.

The anesthesiologist should be board-certified in anesthesiology. Like others on the surgical staff, he or she should be trained in CPR. Also ask to see the certified nurse anesthetist, if one is going to be present during the operation.

Discuss what he or she will be doing throughout the operation.

State laws vary governing surgery outside of hospitals. Some facilities may use surgeons who are board eligible, but you're better off with one who is board-certified...so check.

◼ How do you handle emergencies?
This is especially important in nonhospital surgery.

For example, is an ambulance on standby to transport you to a hospital if an emergency arises? Does the facility have a written agreement with a nearby hospital to accept patients in trouble immediately, or will you have to be processed through an emergency room? Every surgical facility should be happy to discuss the ways in which surgical complications are handled.

◼ How often is this procedure done here?
Recovery rates for coronary bypass surgery are noticeably higher in hospitals where 100 or more of them are done annually. The hospital should be able to inform you of its experience with specific operations.

ASK THE ANESTHESIOLOGIST...

◼ What kind of anesthesia will be used?
Local (anesthetizing a small portion of the body for a short time), regional (affecting a larger body area, like the epidural that numbs the entire abdominal region and below) and general anesthetics (which affect the whole body for an extended time) are all possibilities.

Be sure you know which anesthesia will be used during the procedure and why.

◼ What's going to happen to me?
Your anesthesiologist can be helpful by explaining exactly what you'll experience while he or she prepares you for the operation...what happens when you're "under"...and what to expect as you come out of the anesthesia.

These kinds of questions may seem excessive. *However, they serve two vital functions...*

▶ **They provide you with valuable information.**

▶ **Your questions alert doctors** and hospital personnel to the fact that you're informed and interested.

Several studies have shown that involved patients who question surgical procedures receive treatment that is above average during their hospital stays.

When you interact with your surgeon, anesthesiologist and others on the surgical staff, you're no longer "the laparoscopy in room 213." You're an individual personality.

By your involving yourself in the operation, the doctor and hospital staff become involved with you, and they're much more likely to do their best with someone they know.

HOSPITAL STAY ADVISORY

Don't stay in the hospital longer than necessary. *Danger:* Picking up more infections. Hospital patients have less resistance to disease than people who are well—and many bacteria in hospitals are resistant to antibiotics. *Self-defense:* When you're about to be examined, ask doctors and nurses politely if they have washed their hands. Many are remiss about this vital precaution. *Also*—don't touch your dressings yourself. This can infect your wounds.

Frank Lowy, MD, professor of medicine at Columbia University College of Physicians and Surgeons in New York, and an infectious disease expert.

Hospitalization Does Not Have to Be Traumatic

Theodore Tyberg, MD, assistant professor of medicine at New York Hospital–Cornell Medical Center. Dr. Tyberg is coauthor of *Hospital Smarts.* HarperCollins.

Being knowledgeable about your condition and treatment can improve your chances of receiving the best possible care during a hospital stay.

Of course, there's a fine line between being knowledgeable and being obnoxious. Try not to cross that line…but do not let yourself be ignored or mistreated.

BEFORE ADMISSION
■ Meet every doctor who will be involved in your care.

If you are scheduled for surgery, you will want to meet the surgeon and the anesthesiologist.

Key questions to ask…

1. Are you board-certified?

2. How many similar cases do you handle in a year? If the number is 25 or fewer, ask your doctor why. Consider finding a new doctor or hospital.

3. Is this hospital appropriate for my condition? For common medical problems and low-risk surgical procedures, a community hospital is fine. But teaching hospitals have more experience with serious conditions and complex, high-risk procedures.

■ Learn hospital routines.

Call the hospital a week or so before your admission to inquire about admitting procedures, parking regulations, charges for telephones and televisions, etc.

Ask about the discharge routine. Will you be in a wheelchair? On crutches? Will you need an escort? Must you follow a special diet or other restrictions after you go home? Confirm details with your doctor.

■ Appoint a health-care advocate.

It's the job of this trusted friend or family member to speak on your behalf should you be temporarily unable to make decisions (during recovery from surgery, for example). Pick someone who is level-headed—and *assertive.*

To give your advocate more authority, sign a legally binding proxy. Obtain a proxy form from the hospital's patient services department—or from your lawyer.

If you have a living will, your advocate must make sure the doctor respects your wishes. Your attending physician may not be aware of your living will, particularly in emergency situations. Be sure that your patient advocate makes it clear to the doctor that you have one.

■ Pack wisely.

Take pertinent medical records, a list of allergies you have and a supply of drugs you routinely take. Don't forget books, magazines and a list of telephone numbers of friends, family members and doctors.

What about clothing? Bring slippers, pajamas and a bathrobe. Leave jewelry and other valuables at home.

DURING YOUR STAY
■ Take an active interest in your care.

When unfamiliar people enter your room, ask who they are and what they're going to do. Consent to tests and procedures only after you've discussed them with your doctor.

Each time you see your doctor, ask what will happen next…and when to expect the next visit. Save questions about food, mail, etc. for a nurse or another nonphysician staff member.

■ Guard against mistakes involving drugs, food, etc.

Remind the staff of your condition and the treatment you expect. Have someone identify each drug before it's administered.

Examples: "Is this the blood thinner?" "Another IV bag! What's in that one?"

If your doctor tells you not to eat before surgery and housekeeping delivers a food tray, ask for an explanation.

A patient of ours who had surgery recently put a sticker on one leg that said, "Operate on this one"…on the other leg, "Don't operate on this one."

■ Insist that the staff wash their hands or if they're wearing rubber gloves make sure they're a fresh pair—especially if you have a fresh surgical incision.

FACTS ABOUT HOSPITAL BED RAILS

Hospital bed rails can be deadly—especially for patients who are impaired by medication or dementia and/or weakened by illness or age. These patients sometimes suffocate after becoming trapped between the upper and lower rails…or sliding between the mattress and the rails. Most patients—even older, frail or confused patients who have fallen before—are better off without rails.

Steven Miles, MD, professor of internal medicine, University of Minnesota Medical School, MN.

Steering Clear of Incompetent Doctors and Hospital Staffers

Martin L. Gross, an investigative journalist and a social critic who lives in Connecticut. He is author of *The Medical Racket: How Doctors, HMOs, and Hospitals Are Failing the American Patient.* Avon.

Is your doctor competent? How about the staff at your local hospital? There may be good reason to wonder, says Martin L. Gross, a leading critic of the US health-care industry.

According to Gross, too many health-care workers are either incompetent or dangerously sloppy. *Gross identified the threats consumers face—and what we can do to protect ourselves…*

■ What sorts of incompetence exist?

Let's start with physicians. American doctors are generally well-trained, but a surprisingly large number are woefully inept in one way or another.

Consider these disturbing findings…

▶ **Poor stethoscope skills.** Many doctors simply don't know how to use a stethoscope, the most basic of all diagnostic tools. In a study involving 453 medical residents, only one in five heart abnormalities that should have been easily diagnosed with the stethoscope was correctly diagnosed.

▶ **Bad care for diabetes.** The most important diagnostic tool for the treatment of adult-onset diabetes is the glycosylated hemoglobin test. Yet in a Medicare study of 97,000 diabetics, 84% of doctors failed to administer the test.

▶ **Misread mammograms.** Radiologists fail to spot malignant breast tumors that are present on mammograms 46% of the time, a Yale study found.

▶ **Bad care for people with pneumonia.** Doctors often fail to follow crucial guidelines when treating older pneumonia patients. In a study of more than 14,000 pneumonia patients, many doctors failed to take blood cultures and to give antibiotics correctly and on a timely basis.

How to tell if a particular doctor is competent.

There's no easy way for a layperson to tell. The best you can do is look for evidence that other *medical experts* have judged the doctor competent.

In addition to a medical school diploma and admitting privileges at an accredited hospital, doctors should be board-certified in their specialty.

To learn if a doctor is board-certified, consult the *Official ABMS Directory of Board Certified Medical Specialists* or look on the Web site *www.docsearch.com*. It is available at most municipal libraries or at *www.abms.org*. Another helpful resource is the American Medical Association: *www.ama-assn.org*, and go to "Doctor Finder."

For most people, the best bet is to find a private practitioner who has a faculty appointment at a medical school. Such doctors tend to be more up-to-date than other doctors.

If you have a particular medical problem, call the nearest medical school. Speak with the chair of the appropriate department or one of his colleagues. Ask if he takes private patients. Many do.

How to find out if a doctor has been disciplined.

On request, the state of Massachusetts will send—free of charge—a dossier on any doctor practicing in the state. In other states, citizens must write to the agency that oversees the licensing of physicians—this varies from state to state—and ask for information on a particular physician.

The Washington, DC–based consumer advocacy group Public Citizen publishes *20,125 Questionable Doctors*. The book lists physicians who have run afoul of their licensing boards or who have been hit by malpractice suits or some other trouble.

Some doctors whose names appear on the list may be perfectly competent. After all, plenty of good doctors are sued at some point during their careers.

But inclusion on the list should lead you to question your doctor closely about why he has this dubious distinction.

If you can't find a copy of the book at your library, you can call 202-588-1000 to order a report covering your home state.

Obviously, friends or relatives who are doctors may have privileged access to information about doctors in your area. By all means, ask what they know.

What to look for in a hospital.

Better hospitals tend to have been accredited "with commendation" by the Joint Commission on Accreditation of Healthcare Organizations (JCAHO). "Regular" accreditation is virtually meaningless.

On request, JCAHO, a not-for-profit agency, will send a free report on any hospital. It can be reached at One Renaissance Blvd., Oakbrook Terrace, IL 60181 (630-792-5800/or at *www.jcaho.org*).

If no nearby hospital has the top JCAHO accreditation, opt for the nearest university (teaching) hospital. For complicated medical problems at least, teaching hospitals tend to offer better care than community hospitals.

Common threats faced by hospitalized patients.

There are two primary threats—medication errors and infections.

To avoid being given the wrong drug and/or the wrong dosage, take pills only if they are offered to you by a registered nurse (RN), licensed practical nurse (LPN) or physician.

Your doctor should tell you all the pertinent facts about any drug prescribed for you. That includes its generic and trade names, the size and color of the pills, how many pills you should take and how often—and any possible side effects, too.

For intravenous (IV) drugs, you should know the drug's name and how often the bag should be changed.

Medication errors and side effects kill an estimated 50,000 Americans each year.

How to avoid infections while hospitalized.

Some hospitals are better than others at stopping hospital-acquired (nosocomial) infections. Unfortunately, there's no way for consumers to find out a particular hospital's infection rate.

The best tool for minimizing your risk is hand-washing—especially by doctors and by nurses who give bedside care and maintain IV lines. Sites where the IV line enters your body are especially vulnerable to infection.

The Centers for Disease Control and Prevention estimates that nosocomial infections kill 90,000 Americans each year.

Nondrug Arthritis Remedies

Exercise.

Exercise increases flexibility, strengthens muscles to reduce strain and improves condition of joints.

By aiding weight loss it can further reduce strain on arthritic joints. Exercise also promotes sound sleep.

Consult your doctor about best exercises and precautions that may be necessary due to your specific condition.

Heat and cold treatments.

These can ease pain and inflammation when applied to sore areas. A warm soak can soothe and loosen a painful joint.

Massage.

This can reduce pain and loosen tight muscles that compound arthritic discomfort.

Acupuncture.

Treatment by a trained professional often relieves pain for many. Consult your doctor.

Mayo Clinic Health Letter, 200 First St. SW, Rochester, Minnesota 55905.

HOSPITAL DISCHARGE SAVVY

Take charge of your hospital discharge. Before being admitted, have your doctor describe a typical length of stay for someone in your condition who is undergoing the same procedure. Ask what criteria the doctor will use to decide if you are well enough to go home.

Make it clear that you expect all criteria to be medical—not financial or based on managed-care schedules.

Before being discharged, have your doctor discuss self-care and other post-hospital steps you will need at home. If you do not have someone to help you at home, ask if your doctor can order home care for a limited time after hospitalization.

Vikram Khanna, MHS, director, State Health Policy Solutions, LLC, Columbia, MD, and author of *Managed Care Made Easy.* People's Medical Society.

Alternative Approaches

Chapter 6

Meditation Has Enormous Mental and Physical Benefits—Here's How to Get Started

Do you meditate? If not, you're missing out on a safe, effective way to boost your mental and physical health.

As countless studies have shown, as little as 20 minutes of daily meditation can have profound effects on the body. *Consider this evidence...*

■ Chronic pain.
When chronic pain patients began practicing a simple form of meditation known as the relaxation response, the number of times they visited a pain clinic in the ensuing two years fell by 36%.

(From the Mind/Body Medical Institute at Harvard Medical School in Boston.)

■ Depression and anxiety.
People who completed an eight-week course in a form of meditation known as *mindfulness* experienced a sharp decline in depression, anxiety and other psychological problems.

They also reported having a greater sense of control over their lives.

(From the University of California at Irvine.)

Meditation has also shown at least some effectiveness against high blood pressure, heart disease, backache, headaches and digestive problems.

Despite its myriad benefits, meditation is practiced on a regular basis by less than 10% of the US population.

Why don't more Americans meditate? *Most people's excuses are based on misconceptions about the process...*

Excuse: I don't know how to get started.

The basic elements of meditation are actually quite straightforward...

■ Sit comfortably.

■ Pick something to pay attention to.
It might be your breathing...or a silent syllable or

Lorin Roche, PhD, a meditation teacher in Marina del Rey, CA, for the past 30 years. He is author of *Meditation Made Easy*. Harper San Francisco.

phrase. Some people use their name for God—Jesus, Jahweh, Elohim, Allah, etc.

■ **When your mind wanders**—as it inevitably will—simply return to this focus.

Don't exert any effort at "mind control."

One easy way to start is simply to sit on the sofa, let out a deep breath and say, "Whew."

When you resume breathing normally, pay close attention to the air as it flows into and out of your nostrils…your belly rising and falling…and any other physical sensations that you become aware of.

Feelings of relaxation may give way to intrusive thoughts. *That's fine.* Gently return your attention to your breathing or other focus.

Do this for three minutes or so each day for one week. (It's okay to check your watch.)

After one week, extend your meditation to at least 10 minutes a day—up to 20 minutes twice a day, if you wish.

Excuse: I can't sit cross-legged.

There's nothing magical about this position. It just happens to be the way people sat in Asia when meditation techniques were evolving.

Most Americans do better sitting on a chair or sofa, with a pillow to support the lower back and feet on the ground. That's perfectly acceptable.

Excuse: Meditation is too hard.

Not true. In fact, if you've ever been swept away by beautiful music, a tranquil nature scene, etc., you already know how to meditate.

Ultimately, meditation is really nothing more than just *restful alertness.* Meditating on a daily basis helps you reach this condition more quickly and stay there longer—and thus reap bigger health benefits.

Go easy on yourself. Approach meditation not as a long list of rules to follow but as a favor you're doing for your mind and body. That way it won't seem like a chore.

Excuse: I can't empty my mind.

Often while meditating, you'll find yourself planning, rehearsing, reviewing and otherwise being caught up in thoughts and worries.

This does not mean that you have failed. The brain does this kind of processing whenever you

rest. The trick is to *accept* your thoughts, then gently return to your focus. Do not resist this mental "housecleaning."

Excuse: I don't have time to meditate.

You can get a lot out of meditation even if you can spare only a few minutes a day. And most people find that the more time they spend meditating, the more they like it…and the more time they're willing to set aside to practice it.

These "mini-meditations" take only a minute or so to do…

▶ **Take a conscious nap.** Sit with eyes closed for five minutes. Let your mind drift.

▶ **Do the slump.** Periodically, as you're seated, let your head droop slowly toward your chest.

Notice the weight of your shoulders and the gentle stretch through your spine. Take a few breaths. Slowly return to an erect posture.

Excuse: I don't have a quiet place in which to meditate.

Most people can meditate even in the midst of loud noises and bustling activity.

Have you ever become engrossed in a book while waiting in a crowded airport? Ever fallen into a deep slumber in front of a blaring television or radio? If so, you can certainly learn how to meditate in less-than-perfect circumstances. Treat noise during meditation the same way you deal with your own thoughts. Notice the distraction, then return to your focus.

If noise is still a barrier, try meditating…

▶ **At the office.** Close your office door for 10 minutes and ask not to be disturbed.

▶ **In your car.** Meditate in your driveway before getting out of your car and walking inside.

▶ **At bedtime.** Sit up in bed while your partner reads quietly beside you.

Excuse: I keep falling asleep.

Fine! Most busy people have a huge sleep debt. Nodding off may be exactly what you need.

When you wake up, don't try to return to your focus right away. Give your brain a few moments to come back to consciousness. Then continue meditating.

Herbal Supplements to Protect Your Health

Daniel B. Mowrey, PhD, president of the American Phytotherapy Research Laboratory, a nonprofit research facility in Lehi, UT. He is author of several books on herbal medicine, including *Herbal Tonic Therapies.* McGraw-Hill.

Many herbal supplements have an impressive array of health benefits. These health benefits include increased energy and stamina…heightened immunity…reduced risk of heart disease…improved liver function…reduced joint inflammation.

Unlike drugs, herbal preparations are not regulated by the FDA. Ask the store clerk to recommend a reputable brand.

You can take each of these herbs on a daily basis. Or you can rotate through the list, taking each herb for a few weeks at a time. The doses listed below are based on capsules containing 850 milligrams (mg) to 900 mg of the herb.

Caution: Consult a doctor before starting any herbal regimen—especially if you have a heart ailment or another chronic illness and/or you are using prescription or over-the-counter medications. Herbal remedies can interact dangerously with certain drugs.

Certain remedies are inherently unsafe. *Comfrey, borage, chaparral* and *coltsfoot* can cause liver disease…*ma huang* can cause a rise in blood pressure that is particularly unsafe for those with heart or thyroid disease or diabetes…*yohimbé* can cause tremors, anxiety, high blood pressure and rapid heart rate.

If you develop a rash, nausea, hives, headaches or hay fever–like symptoms while taking an herb, stop using it immediately.

CAYENNE

Cayenne is good for the cardiovascular system. The herb also helps maintain muscle tone in the stomach and intestinal walls and aids in digestion. Cayenne is also an excellent "activator herb," amplifying the benefits of other herbs you take.

Daily dose: Two capsules. Or use ground cayenne as a spice.

ECHINACEA

Echinacea fights illness on two levels. First, it boosts levels of white blood cells, B- and T-lymphocytes and phagocytes—the key components of a healthy immune system. Second, it neutralizes invading microorganisms.

German researchers have shown that echinacea stops staph, strep, fungal infections and a variety of viruses.

Daily dose: At the onset of symptoms—two capsules. Be sure the capsules contain the whole root in powdered form, not extract.

Used intermittently, liquid extract of echinacea is soothing for sore throats. Use an eyedropper and let a few drops fall against the back of your throat.

GARLIC

This spice helps prevent heart disease by lowering cholesterol levels and blocking formation of fatty deposits in the coronary arteries. It also boosts levels of T-cells, a critical component of the immune system.

Animal and human studies have shown that garlic also relieves arthritis. It contains sulfur compounds, which are known to have significant anti-inflammatory properties.

Daily dose: Two pills. Or use a garlic clove or garlic powder in your cooking.

GINGERROOT

Gingerroot is an excellent remedy for indigestion, constipation, diarrhea and nausea (including morning sickness). My research suggests that ginger is even more effective than Dramamine at preventing motion sickness. It is also effective against the flu.

Be sure to buy capsules made from the whole gingerroot—not extract.

Daily dose: For mild motion sickness, two capsules 15 minutes before you depart (and two to four more every hour or whenever symptoms return). For serious gastrointestinal upset, take six to 12 capsules an hour.

PAU D'ARCO

Pau d'arco, also known as lapacho, contains naphthoquinones (N-factors), compounds that have antiviral and antibiotic properties. It's effective at preventing colds, flu and bacterial infections.

Taken in capsule or tea form, pau d'arco soothes painful joints...boosts energy levels...and stimulates activity of enzymes in the liver, enhancing its ability to remove toxins from the blood.

In Brazil, pau d'arco is used to treat leukemia and cervical cancer, and pau d'arco salve is used to treat skin cancer. Studies suggest that the herb may also be effective against breast cancer.

Make tea by simmering the purplish paper-thin inner lining of the bark in hot water for 20 minutes, then strain and let cool. Leftover tea can be refrigerated.

Daily dose: To prevent illness, four capsules or two cups of tea. To treat an infection, six capsules or one to two quarts of tea.

MILK THISTLE

One of the world's most studied plants, milk thistle is very good for the liver. By stimulating protein synthesis, it boosts levels of key liver enzymes, speeding regeneration of damaged liver tissue. It also inhibits lypoxygenase, an enzyme that destroys liver cells.

Recent studies show that milk thistle can help reverse the effects of hepatitis and cirrhosis.

Daily dose: Two capsules.

PYGEUM EXTRACT

Derived from the bark of an African tree, pygeum has been shown to prevent—and even cure—benign enlargement of the prostate. It contains phytosterols, potent anti-inflammatory compounds.

Pygeum also contains triterpenoids, compounds that have an antiswelling effect.

Daily dose: To prevent prostate enlargement, two capsules. To shrink an enlarged prostate, four capsules.

YERBA MATÉ

This South American herb boosts energy and stamina without causing the jitters that caffeine can cause. Anecdotal reports suggest that yerba maté is also effective against asthma and allergies, though the mechanism is unknown.

Yerba maté is best taken as a daily tea. Pour boiling water over yerba maté leaves, let sit for 10 minutes, then strain and serve.

Daily dose: Two to four cups.

HERB/MEDICINE INTERACTIONS

Herbs and medicines may not mix. Just as some drug interactions can be dangerous, so can some mixes of herbs and medications—prescription or over-the-counter. *Example:* Many herbs are blood thinners—including ginkgo, garlic, ginger, ginseng, white willow bark and others. If combined with prescription anticoagulant drugs—or aspirin—they could cause bleeding or even a stroke. Herb/medicine interactions are largely unexplored. To minimize risk, learn how herbs work—and inform your doctor about all supplements you take.

Varro Tyler, PhD, ScD, distinguished professor emeritus of pharmacognosy, Purdue University, West Lafayette, IN.

What Conventional Doctors Are Saying About Alternative Medicine

Wendy Harpham, MD, internist in Dallas and on staff at Presbyterian Hospital, Dallas. She is author of *Diagnosis: Cancer—Your Guide Through the First Few Months.* W.W. Norton.

Timothy McCall, MD, Boston internist, medical editor of *Yoga Journal* and author of *Examining Your Doctor: A Patient's Guide to Avoiding Harmful Medical Care.* Citadel Press.

Terry Shintani, MD, JD, MPH, associate chair, department of complementary and alternative medicine, the University of Hawaii School of Medicine. He is author of several books, including *The Hawaii Diet Cookbook.* Health Foundation Press.

A growing number of doctors who practice conventional medicine are beginning to consider the role that alternative treatments play in boosting and maintaining their patients' health.

The National Institutes of Health has established an office to assess the scientific value of complementary and alternative practices, and a growing number of HMOs are now covering some alternative therapies.

Here, three outstanding conventional physicians discuss which treatments they consider safe for their patients...which ones they feel are risky...and how to better integrate conventional and alternative treatments.

WENDY HARPHAM, MD

I'm a strong believer in conventional treatments because they are backed by sound scientific testing. This distinction can be useful when considering alternative therapies, which have not undergone rigorous, controlled study.

Yet I have found that some alternative therapies have a place in the care of patients. They bring benefits when used in conjunction with conventional therapy. Many nonconventional treatments have an element of healing and support that conventional medicine often lacks.

> *Example: Visualization—imagining a desired outcome in your mind—and **hypnosis** offer many patients effective relief of the pain and nausea that is associated with chemotherapy and boost the patients' mental attitudes toward overcoming the illnesses.*

Before trying alternative treatment...

■ Get a thorough examination and diagnosis from a conventional doctor.

One of the risks of alternative therapy is that, too often, it does not include the appropriate workups to identify exactly what is wrong with the patient.

> *Example: An herbal preparation such as gingerroot may ease the pain associated with a sore throat. But that can increase the risk that something more serious will be overlooked once relief is achieved. Strep throat, if not treated with appropriate antibiotics, can lead to rheumatic fever, even though the sore throat is resolved.*

■ Discuss alternative treatments with your doctor.

Many patients fail to do this because they fear these treatments will be ridiculed. However, discussing them with your doctor helps ensure that it is safe and allows the doctor to adjust concurrent conventional treatments accordingly.

▶ Approach alternative treatments with the same skepticism used for conventional ones.

Ask your conventional doctor and alternative therapist...

▷ What are the cure rates?

▷ How long will the treatment last?

▷ How long will the benefit last?

▷ What side effects and risks are associated with the treatment?

▷ What are the credentials of the alternative practitioner?

▷ How many patients has the alternative practitioner treated?

■ Seek sound, objective information before making any decisions about alternative treatments.

If your doctor does not embrace an alternative route and refuses to support you, try to find a doctor who is open to considering it—provided the risks are addressed and that your conditions are closely monitored.

The key is to have communication. Regardless of the treatment, the ultimate goal for any doctor is to get the patient well and to provide as much comfort as possible.

TIMOTHY MCCALL, MD

My expertise lies in conventional Western medicine, and for the most part, that's what I practice. However, many times patients see doctors for problems that may not readily be helped by conventional treatments.

This is especially true of illnesses that are exacerbated by emotional stress and other psychosocial factors. Here, alternative therapies—such as meditation, herbal supplements and acupuncture—may have a real, beneficial role to play.

Example: Certain herbal preparations, such as ***echinacea*** *(which may boost the immune system) and* ***valerian root*** *(which promotes relaxation and combats insomnia) have been used quite effectively for hundreds of years. I wouldn't hesitate to recommend them when appropriate.*

However, it's important for people to realize that an "alternative" label does not automatically guarantee safety.

Examples: Melatonin has been promoted as a cure-all for everything from jet lag to osteoporosis. It isn't an herbal supplement—it is a human hormone in pill form that has not undergone extensive testing for safety and toxicity. The same

is true for DHEA, which has been said to delay the aging process. There is no scientific basis for most of these claims. And we know nothing about their long-term safety.

The key is to weigh the risks and benefits of any treatment—conventional or alternative—before you try it. A frank discussion with your doctor is important and can be very helpful. Regardless of the type of therapy you choose, keep in mind that every treatment carries potential risks, including the most seemingly harmless treatments.

Example: In megadoses, vitamins can act like drugs and cause harmful toxicities, which is why it's a good idea to discuss with your doctor any vitamin supplement you are considering.

Many doctors trained in conventional medicine do not yet recognize the value of certain alternative therapies. However, the patient's values—not the doctor's—should dictate the care delivered.

If you believe something may help you and your doctor is not willing to try it, you may want to consult another doctor.

TERRY SHINTANI, MD

I'm formally trained in conventional medicine, and I have training in nutrition and Oriental medicine. This combined approach has given me a much broader perspective on alternative treatments and how I treat my patients than most traditional doctors have.

Two of the most important things to remember about most of conventional medicine and some alternative therapies is that they are temporary measures, and they work primarily on symptoms.

Ultimately, the best approach is one that takes into account the whole person, including spiritual, mental, emotional and physical aspects. This may require an integration of conventional and alternative practices.

Other key points to keep in mind when considering alternative therapies...

■ If a conventional doctor suggests an alternative treatment that requires you to see another practitioner, the doctor and the practitioner must be in communication.

This concept of seamless or integrative care ensures that the two types of therapies are in sync, which works in favor towards the patient's health.

▧ Patients need to be cautious.

Patients should be wary if the alternative practitioner totally repudiates conventional medicine. If he or she suggests that you not follow your doctor's advice, you should seek another opinion.

> *Example:* Hodgkin's disease is a highly treatable form of cancer when conventional methods are used. If anyone recommends delaying treatment in favor of an alternative in this situation, he could be putting the patient's life in jeopardy.

▧ Learn as much as possible about what conventional and alternative therapies can do for your medical problem before seeking treatment.

Many people mistakenly believe that only one type of treatment will alleviate their medical problem. The reality is that each approach may have its merits and shortcomings.

When any doctor or alternative practitioner suggests a treatment, ask questions. What is the effectiveness of the treatment? What are the risks? What is your training and success rate for treating this condition? Is there any literature published on the treatment for me to review? Do your own research on the practitioner's credentials and track record.

Improve Your Sex Life

Sexual problems triggered by antidepressants respond well to treatment with ginkgo biloba supplements. After taking 60 milligrams (mg) to 120 mg daily, the majority of subjects in a recent study reported improvements in their sex lives. Women were more responsive—91% reported positive effects...and men, 76%. *Advantages over Viagra:* Increased desire and the ability to achieve orgasms again.

Alan J. Cohen, MD, psychiatrist in private practice in Berkeley, CA, and assistant clinical professor of psychiatry, University of California at San Francisco, whose study was published in the *Journal of Sex & Marital Therapy.*

CHAMOMILE TEA DOES MORE

Chamomile tea may do more than calm an upset stomach, aid digestion and relieve gas, bloating and intestinal cramps. New evidence suggests that it helps with more serious digestive disorders, including irritable bowel syndrome and peptic ulcers. *Helpful:* Drink three or four cups a day between meals. Chamomile has long been used as a sleep aid, although no studies have been conducted to confirm this effect.

Mindy Green, director of educational services, Herb Research Foundation, Boulder, CO.

RELAXATION BREATHING

To control psychological stress during even the most hectic periods, inhale slowly for eight seconds. Then hold your breath for eight seconds...and then exhale for eight seconds.

Richard Swenson, MD, family physician in private practice in Menomonie, WI. He is author of *Margin/The Overload Syndrome.* NavPress.

Fast Psoriasis Relief

Ultraviolet B (UVB) light is highly effective against the scaly, inflamed skin of psoriasis—and listening to relaxation tapes can make UVB therapy even more effective.

Recent finding: Psoriasis lesions healed after a median of 84 days when patients listened to a relaxation tape during daily UVB sessions. Lesions in similar patients who didn't listen to tapes during the sessions took 98 days to heal.

More: Psoriasis patients who got a similar treatment known as photosensitizer psoralen ultraviolet-A (PUVA) along with tapes healed in only 46 days, compared with 95 days for those who got PUVA without listening to tapes.

Overall, psoriasis sufferers who listened to tapes healed four times faster than those who didn't. Listening to tapes during light therapy also helps offset the increased cancer risk from UV light by limiting the amount of time spent under the lights.

Jon Kabat-Zinn, PhD, associate professor of medicine, University of Massachusetts Medical School, Worcester. His study of 37 psoriasis patients was published in *Psychosomatic Medicine,* 428 E. Preston St., Baltimore 21202.

HERB WORKS AGAINST ALCOHOLISM

Drunken rats may show the way to a new treatment for alcoholism. When the rats—they're bred to drink—were given St. John's wort, their alcohol intake fell by 50%. Researchers are now investigating whether St. John's wort safely fights alcohol cravings in humans.

The Medical Tribune.

NATURAL WAY TO PREVENT CANCER

Powerful, natural cancer fighter: The nutrient *glucarate.* It detoxifies cancer-causing agents in the environment, such as carcinogens in barbecued meat. In recent studies, it dramatically reduced the incidence of breast, colon, prostate, lung and other cancers—in some cases by more than half. *Rich sources:* Apples…bean sprouts…broccoli …brussels sprouts…cabbage…cauliflower… grapefruit. *Best:* Daily supplement of 1,000 milligrams (mg) to 2,000 mg. Capsules are available at health food stores and pharmacies—but talk with your doctor first. Glucarate has no known side effects, and your body will excrete any excess.

Zbigniew Walaszek, PhD, a scientist at AMC Cancer Research Center in Denver, an independent not-for-profit research institution focused solely on cancer prevention and control.

Music, Music, Music— To Improve Your Health and Your Mind

Don Campbell, who established the Mozart Effect Resource Center, 3526 Washington Ave., St. Louis 63109. He is author of several books, including *The Mozart Effect.* Quill.

Music has a potent impact on the mind, body and spirit, and it can be used to effect healthful changes.

More and more doctors are using music as part of their treatments to help patients stay healthy and recover more quickly from illness. *Examples…*

▶ **Heart patients derived the same benefits** from listening to 30 minutes of classical music as they did from taking 10 mg of the antianxiety medication Valium…at a Baltimore hospital.

▶ **Music and relaxation therapy were used together** to lower heart rate and blood pressure in patients with heart disease…at a Dallas hospital.

▶ **Migraine sufferers were trained to use music, imagery and relaxation techniques** to reduce the frequency, intensity and duration of their headaches…in a California State University study. Music also has an impact on our intelligence and productivity. *Examples…*

▶ **Students who listened to 10 minutes** of Mozart prior to taking SATs had higher scores than students who weren't exposed to music…at the University of California.

▶ **People who listened to light classical music for 90 minutes** while editing a manuscript increased accuracy by 21%…in a University of Washington study.

THE MUSIC–MOOD CONNECTION

Music affects the body and the brain in three ways simultaneously…

▦ Music's rhythms affect your heartbeat.

The heart tends to speed up and slow down to match the pace of the music that's playing.

Rhythms also alter our brain waves and breathing patterns. Other types of music induce us to move our bodies. In addition to hearing music, we feel the vibrations of music and other sounds on our skin and in our bones. It is the impact of these vibrating sounds on the body that subtly alters our mood and many of our body functions—particularly blood pressure, pulse and body temperature.

▦ Melodies stay in your head like a second language.

Music with strong, hummable melodies takes on a greater meaning—and affects your mood just by recalling them.

Researchers have found that whatever an individual's music preferences, music by Mozart—more than any other composer—invariably calms the listener's mind and body rhythms, improves spatial perception and promotes better communication of emotions, concepts and thoughts.

Background: The highly organized structure and many rhythms, melodies and high frequencies of Mozart's music stimulate and charge the creative and motivational regions of the brain.

However, you don't have to listen only to Mozart—or even classical music. Everything from Gregorian chant to New Age, jazz, big band, Latin, dance and rock compositions can produce different benefits.

▦ **Harmony affects your emotions,** helping you to release painful or angry feelings or boost happy feelings.

MUSIC THAT CHANGES YOUR MIND

▶ **To stimulate the mind:** Choose a composition that will charge you up—music that is moderately fast with high frequencies. The music will activate your brain, enhance mental alertness and boost your mental organization.

Examples: Mozart's Violin Concertos, especially Nos. 3 and 4.

▶ **To stimulate the body:** Put on your favorite dance or swing music.

Examples: I like the Flashdance…What a Feeling soundtrack and Riverdance, which features Irish dance music. The lively beat demands that you move your body.

▶ **To relieve anxiety:** Select music that is slow and has lower tones. It will slow your breathing and your heart rate. Quieting the body releases physical tension and calms the mind.

Examples: Baroque music, such as Pachelbel's Canon & Gigue in D for Three Violins & Continuo…or New Age works by Paul Winter and Kenny G.

▶ **To lift the blues:** Listen to slow blues. It was created to help people access and release painful emotions.

Examples: The **Lady Sings the Blues** *soundtrack is a favorite of mine, as is Eric Clapton's* **From the Cradle**.

▶ **To boost your imagination:** Tap your unconscious mind by first stimulating your body. Listen to upbeat instrumental music to stimulate the creative, right side of the brain.

Examples: Beethoven's **Pastoral Symphony** *…Dvorak's* **New World Symphony** *…and* **Giant Steps** *by jazz saxophonist John Coltrane are excellent choices. These compositions have a basic but unpredictable structure that encourages your imagination to run wild.*

▶ **To help you concentrate:** Classical selections that have a constant, easy beat and light melodies will help pace you to read, focus, memorize and study better.

Examples: Many Baroque compositions by Vivaldi, Bach and Handel are ideal.

▶ **To help you relax:** Select slow music, which will calm your heartbeat and breathing rate, lower your blood pressure and release muscle tension.

Examples: The **Out of Africa** *soundtrack…or* **Sun Singer** *by Paul Winter.*

▶ **To relieve anger:** Play a piece that is driven, energetic and intense to help you release your strong emotions.

Example: Brahms's **Piano Concerto No. 2.**

Follow with any of the relaxing pieces of music mentioned earlier.

ADVANCED LISTENING TECHNIQUES

To have a positive effect, you must listen to music—rather than just hear it as background noise.

When you hear music, you are actually hearing all of the sounds around you. Listening to music, however, refers to the selective process of focusing only on certain sounds in your environment. *Helpful…*

▶ **Choose a quiet room, and have a pen and paper at hand.** Put a mood-appropriate CD in your CD player. Dim the lights, and sit or lie down on a comfortable chair or couch.

▶ **Close your eyes—your sense of hearing is more acute when you can't see—**and listen to one movement. Let your mind wander.

▶ **After the movement ends, write down how the music made your body feel,** both as it began and as it progressed. Note if any images entered your mind or if you felt any strong emotions.

▶ **Bring up the lights, and replay the same** movement while sitting upright and keeping your eyes fixed on a blank spot on the wall in front of you.

▶ **When the music ends, again write your feelings and perceptions.** Compare how the two scenarios changed your experience of the music.

Natural Pain Relievers That Really Work

Mark A. Stengler, ND, naturopathic physician in private practice in La Jolla, CA, and associate clinical professor at Bastyr University in Kenmore, WA, and the National College of Naturopathic Medicine in Portland, OR. He is author of *The Natural Physician's Healing Therapies.* Bottom Line Books, Box 436, Stamford, CT, 06901.

For most people, prescription and over-the-counter (OTC) pain relievers are fine for occasional use, but they carry increasing risks the longer they are taken.

Aspirin and other nonsteroidal anti-inflammatory drugs (NSAIDs), such as *ibuprofen* (Advil), *naproxen* (Aleve) and *ketoprofen* (Orudis KT), can cause digestive problems, including internal bleeding. *Acetaminophen* (Tylenol) is potentially toxic to the liver and kidneys after months of use. Prescription drugs that contain either barbiturates, such as *phenobarbital*

(Solfoton), or opiates, such as *oxycodone* (OxyContin), are potentially habit-forming.

These are among the reasons why many people are turning to natural pain relievers—vitamins, minerals, herbs and homeopathic remedies (highly diluted natural substances made from plants, minerals and animal products).*

Natural pain relievers aren't as strong as pharmaceutical products, so they may not work as fast. But because they are less toxic, they typically are much safer over the long run, especially for treating chronic pain.

Both drugs and natural pain relievers block the body's pain signals, but natural remedies also enhance the body's own recuperative power to repair injured tissue and fight disease. *My favorite natural pain relievers...*

ARTHRITIS AND BACK PAIN

Methylsulfonylmethane (MSM). This compound, which occurs naturally in living organisms, acts as a potent anti-inflammatory. It reduces muscle spasm and slows down the overactive nerve impulses that may cause this condition.

Because most back pain is the result of muscle spasm and inflammation, MSM often brings lasting relief and can prevent future episodes. In addition, it has been shown to ease the pain associated with fibromyalgia and osteoarthritis.

Typical dosage: For preventive purposes (for arthritis, chronic back pain, fibromyalgia, etc.), 1,000 milligrams (mg) to 2,000 mg daily, indefinitely. For relief of acute pain, the effective dose depends on individual factors, such as weight and age. Start at 3,000 mg per day and increase in increments of 1,000 mg every two to three days, until you experience relief or reach 6,000 mg daily.

Helpful: Take MSM with food to minimize digestive upset.

Boswellia. This herb, which is widely used in Ayurvedic (Indian) medicine, is another anti-inflammatory that treats both rheumatoid arthritis and osteoarthritis. A review of 11 German studies found that boswellia brought substantial benefits

to 260 people who had not responded to conventional medical treatment. Most were able to curb their intake of anti-inflammatory medication.

Typical dosage: 1,500 mg of a standardized preparation (containing 60% to 65% boswellic acid), three times a day for six weeks. For long-term use, reduce the dosage to 750 mg, three times a day.

Rhus toxicodendron. This homeopathic remedy, derived from poison oak, is particularly helpful for rheumatoid arthritis or osteoarthritis pain that is worse in the morning and improves with motion and activity...or that flares up before a storm or in damp weather.

Typical dosage: For long-term use for chronic pain, take a 6C potency pellet, two to three times daily.

INJURY

Arnica. When pain is the result of a bump or bruise, this homeopathic remedy is extremely effective, sometimes within minutes. It also is very helpful for muscle soreness after overexertion.

Typical dosage: Dissolve two 30C potency pellets under your tongue every 15 minutes for a total of up to three doses per day, until the pain goes away.

Arnica is also available as a cream or tincture. Apply it directly to the painful spot.

Rhus toxicodendron. This homeopathic remedy, also used for arthritis, is ideal for strains and sprains. Besides relieving pain, it speeds recovery.

Typical dosage: Dissolve a 30C potency pellet under your tongue, two to three times daily for two days.

Bromelain. This protein-dissolving enzyme is found in pineapple stems. It effectively reduces the swelling and bruising that cause pain for days after injury. Bromelain breaks down the blood clots that form as a result of physical trauma, restoring circulation and healing damaged tissue.

Typical dosage: 500 mg, three times daily between meals. Look for a bromelain preparation standardized to 1,600 MCU (milk-clotting units) per 500 mg.

Caution: Bromelain has a slight blood-thinning effect. Check with your doctor before taking it if you're on blood-thinning medication, such as *warfarin* (Coumadin).

---

*Even when a natural remedy (or drug) effectively relieves pain, it is important to discover and treat the underlying cause. Consult your doctor, especially if muscle or joint pain or other symptoms worsen.

NERVE PAIN

Capsaicin. A potent compound found in cayenne pepper, capsaicin apparently blocks the messenger chemical substance P from carrying pain signals along the nerves.

It can be highly effective against the often severe pain of shingles (herpes zoster). Capsaicin also relieves diabetic neuropathy, the pain that develops usually in the legs and feet of diabetics because of nerve damage.

Typical dosage: Apply a cream that contains 0.025% to 0.075% capsaicin extract to the painful area, two to four times daily.

How to Strengthen Your Immune System Easily

Jamison Starbuck, ND, naturopathic physician in family practice and a lecturer at the University of Montana, both in Missoula. She is past president of the American Association of Naturopathic Physicians and a contributing editor to *The Alternative Advisor: The Complete Guide to Natural Therapies and Alternative Treatments*. Time Life.

Strengthening the immune system is a popular concept these days. But if you're like many of my patients, you don't know what comprises the immune system—much less whether yours needs help.

In conventional medical parlance, the "immune system" consists of white blood cells, the lymphatic system, adenoids, thymus, spleen, tonsils and parts of the mucous membranes of the gastrointestinal and respiratory tract. As your body's disease-fighting system, these organs and tissues are activated whenever you encounter microorganisms, foreign substances like soot and/or allergens, such as pollen and animal dander. But immune health is affected not only by blood cells and lymph tissue but also by emotional stress, physical activity, nutrition and liver function.

Symptoms of a flagging immune system include chronic fatigue, frequent colds, flu or sinus infections. *If you've had two or more of these symptoms for one week per month for three months or more, consider trying this immune-boosting protocol…*

1. See your doctor to rule out disease. Ask for a physical exam and lab tests, including a complete blood count…a blood chemistry panel, including cholesterol and glucose levels…a thyroid panel, which measures levels of thyroid-stimulating hormone (TSH) and the thyroid hormones T3 and T4…and an erythrocyte sedimentation rate (ESR) test—a marker of inflammation and illness.

2. Get enough vitamins. The liver needs hefty supplies of vitamins A, C and E to give your immune system the energy it needs to keep you well. Dark-green veggies, such as spinach, kale and broccoli, as well as orange fruit, such as mango, cantaloupe and apricots, are rich in vitamins A and C. Nuts and soy are high in vitamin E. Nourish your immune system by consuming four vegetables, three fruits, two whole-grain or legume servings and 64 ounces of water daily. Sugar is an immune system depressant, so avoid cola, sweetened cereal, juice and desserts. Eat no more than one serving of sweetened food per day.

3. Choose gentle exercise. If your immune system is fatigued, shun strenuous exercise, such as jogging, tennis and cycling. These activities stress the muscles and bones, which can increase inflammation. Instead, walk or swim and/or perform yoga or tai chi.

A BETTER MASSAGE

To give a better massage, apply pressure throughout the process, using different hand pressure in different places. Keep hands as loose and flexible as possible. Keep both pressure and speed even. Changes of speed and pressure should always be gradual. Apply pressure with your weight, not your muscles—simply by leaning the weight of your upper body into your hands. Maintain physical contact until the massage is completely finished. To avoid tickling, press hard but without causing pain.

George Downing, massage and body-awareness teacher, The Esalen Institute, San Francisco, and author of *The Massage Book*. Random House.

4. Keep your mood balanced and upbeat. Avoid disturbing situations whenever possible. Decline social invitations that are not enjoyable. Choose comedies or romances over violent films. Solve disputes or misunderstandings right away rather than letting them stew.

5. Take medicinal mushroom extracts. In Asia, mushrooms have been used as an immune-enhancing medicine for centuries. Modern studies confirm this benefit. My favorite mushrooms include Cordyceps, Maitake, Reishi and Shiitake. They are available in powdered or liquid form. Mushroom extracts are safe to use for six months, but, if you have a chronic illness, check with your doctor first. For the appropriate dosage, follow the directions on the label.

How to Change Your Whole Approach to Life— One Breath at a Time

Andrew L. Rubman, ND, associate professor of clinical medicine, Lane College of Integrative Medicine, Orlando, FL, and medical director, Southbury Clinic for Traditional Medicines, Southbury, CT.

The recognition of breath's intimate attachment to health and also to appreciation of life is as old as recorded history. Some of the first references to the mental benefits of breath control can be found in Vedic writings from India that are more than 4,000 years old.

Today, the focus of virtually all the schools of physical arts—yoga, tai chi and other martial arts, even the physical conditioning techniques used by the military—includes the conscious awareness and modulation of breathing.

BENEFITS OF BREATH CONTROL

Controlling your breathing is not difficult. It's actually very easy to practice, and takes only a few seconds to have a noticeable effect.

I was skeptical when I first tried using the technique more than 30 years ago, but the impact was so profound that I quickly became a believer.

I found my concentration and energy were enhanced—and, more important, my whole approach to life changed.

Instead of worrying incessantly about things I had little control over, I discovered that I was living more in the moment, at peace with the present and less fearful of the future. All this simply from practicing a few slow, purposeful breaths.

HOW BREATH CONTROL WORKS

We often choose to dwell on negative thoughts—fears, anxieties or other emotional baggage—that have nothing to do with what we're experiencing in the moment. These thoughts are carried primarily in our subconscious, but they frequently drift up into our conscious thoughts as well, where they cause distraction, angst and physical dysfunction.

Addressing these chronic fearful thoughts is at the core of the popular brand of psychology known as *cognitive therapy*. But you can also banish them in a simpler way—by modulating your breath.

Reason: As subconscious fears begin to color your conscious thoughts, this shift can be observed most readily by changes in your breathing—it becomes faster, shallower and less regular. When you consciously shift your breathing to a deeper, slower, more regular pattern, you are literally disconnecting yourself from this subconscious mental influence.

This means you'll move yourself to living more in the present moment, experiencing life with a sense of untroubled peace and enjoyment that may surprise you.

It certainly surprised me!

HOW TO START...

Breath control, at its most basic, involves three simple principles...

▶ **Breathe slowly and deeply.**

▶ **Aim for an inhalation/exhalation pattern of 1 to 2** (if you count four beats each time you breathe in, for example, try to make each out-breath last for eight beats).

▶ **Use visual imagery as you breathe.**

You can start practicing right now, by taking one slow, controlled breath…

▶ **Sit in a comfortable position.**

▶ **Breathe in at a slow, comfortable rate, counting as you do.** *Concentrate on this visual image…*

Imagine a cloth bag is being held up to your torso with the open end just at neck height. As you breathe in, imagine sand is slowly being poured into this sack. As you inhale and focus on this image, feel a sense of fullness and weight spread through the front and back of your lower abdomen (which supports your lungs). Your ribs will automatically lift and move out, as your rib cage expands.

▶ **At the end of your inhalation, pause briefly before you begin to exhale.** This is known as a "still point."

▶ **Gently exhale, picturing the same sand-pouring process happening backward, only more slowly—exactly as if it were a movie being run in reverse at half speed.** Try to make your exhalation last twice as long as your inhalation. (At first, many people can only maintain a 1 to 1.5 ratio—with practice, however, your out-breaths will get longer.)

You can repeat this process as many times as you like. But you'll find that even one slow, purposeful breath will leave you feeling less anxious and more energized and centered.

FITTING BREATH CONTROL INTO YOUR DAILY ROUTINE

When you first start practicing purposeful breathing, it's important to concentrate on doing it correctly.

PRAYER HEALS

Four-hundred-sixty-six heart patients who were the object of other people's prayers during their hospital stay had 11% fewer complications than did 524 patients who were not prayed for. Patients did not know prayers were said for them. Those who did the praying knew only the patients' first names…and prayed only for "a speedy recovery with no complications." The researchers note that, statistically, such a difference between the groups would occur by chance only one in 25 times.

William S. Harris, PhD, heart researcher, Lipids and Diabetes Research Center, Saint Luke's Hospital, Kansas City, MO. His study of 990 coronary care unit patients was published in the *Archives of Internal Medicine,* 515 N. State St., Chicago 60610.

This will ingrain the breathing pattern into your subconscious. Once you're comfortable with the technique, you can begin incorporating it into your day-to-day life.

Whenever you have a few seconds to spare—during a TV commercial, for instance, or when you're stopped in your car at a traffic light, or when waiting for someone to answer the telephone—use this opportunity to take one slow, purposeful breath, using the same method and imagery described above.

In the same way that driving a car becomes a subconscious act over time—even though it seemed awkward and difficult at first—this style of purposeful breathing will become second nature as you practice it. If you do this technique several times a day, within a few weeks you'll find that your breathing has become more controlled and purposeful throughout your day, even when you're not consciously striving for breath control.

Better still, you'll find that your improved breathing patterns will instill your day-to-day life experience with a pervasive feeling of calm and optimism—as your subconscious fears and worries float away in the breeze.

Garlic Power

Varro Tyler, PhD, professor emeritus of pharmacognosy—the study of natural medicine—at Purdue University in West Lafayette, IN. He is author of more than 30 books, including *Tyler's Honest Herbal.* Haworth Press.

Garlic—long valued as a great flavor enhancer—is also a boon for better health. Its effects stem mainly from a sulfur-rich compound called *allicin.* Research suggests garlic's health benefits include....

▨ Reduced blood pressure.
Researchers at Flinders University of South Australia in Adelaide recently analyzed seven placebo-controlled studies involving more than 400 people who took garlic.

Finding: A daily dose of 600 milligrams (mg) to 900 mg of garlic powder pills significantly lowered systolic pressure (the first number in a reading) in three studies. Diastolic pressure (the second number) was significantly lowered in four studies.

▨ Increased aortic elasticity.
The aorta is the large artery that delivers oxygen-rich blood from the heart to the rest of the body. It becomes less elastic with age. That contributes to high blood pressure.

A two-year study at Ohio State University tracked the progression of aortic stiffness in 100 people 50 to 80 years of age.

Finding: Daily doses of 300 mg of garlic powder pills markedly reduced the progression.

▨ Reduced risk for atherosclerotic plaques.
These are fatty deposits that block coronary arteries and reduce blood flow. This can cause angina pain and, eventually, heart attack.

The best study of garlic's effect on plaque formation was conducted at Humboldt University in Berlin. It involved several hundred people. All had some degree of atherosclerosis. Daily doses of 900 mg of garlic powder pills reduced plaque formation up to 13%.

In some cases, garlic *reversed* plaque buildup—a feat rarely achieved in any clinical study of atherosclerosis.

▨ Lowered blood lipids.
Many studies have found that garlic lowers cholesterol and triglyceride levels.

But this benefit remains uncertain. Some studies have found no effect.

▨ Reduced blood clotting.
Ajoene, a compound derived from allicin's breakdown, inhibits the clumping of blood cell fragments called platelets.

Platelet clumping is a key step in the formation of blood clots that cause heart attack and stroke. Sixteen studies have shown that garlic is as effective as aspirin at preventing clotting.

▨ Tumor inhibition.
Pennsylvania State University researchers found that garlic powder supplements slowed development of breast tumors in mice by an average of 70%.

Other animal studies suggest that garlic slows the activity of carcinogens linked to colon, rectal and esophageal cancers.

The benefits for humans remain unproven. But studies suggest that consumption of garlic is linked to a reduction in the incidence of stomach and intestinal cancer.

No one would suggest that garlic can cure or treat cancer in humans. But it may help lower the risk. That effect is probably due to garlic's antioxidant activity. Antioxidants combat "free radicals"—highly reactive substances that damage cells.

■ Infectious disease prevention.

Some 20 studies have shown that garlic inhibits the growth of bacteria, viruses and fungi.

Implication: Garlic helps prevent or reduce the severity of colds, flu and other bacterial and viral infections.

HOW TO GET YOUR GARLIC

Allicin is destroyed by heat. This means that cooking garlic robs you of most of its benefit.

Eating raw garlic is not necessarily a solution, however. The stomach's digestive acids inactivate the enzyme that catalyzes allicin's formation from precursor compounds. *But you do have two options for fully exploiting garlic's health benefits...*

Option I: Each day, chew one large or two small cloves for *at least one full minute* before swallowing.

You can also add the equivalent amount of chopped raw garlic to dressings, sauces, spreads and dips. Chew *each bite* for at least one full minute.

You may hate the taste—and friends may shun you—but you will get the allicin's full effects. That's because the allicin will be released in your mouth and absorbed through the cheek's mucous membranes.

Option II: Take enteric-coated garlic powder tablets. The coating lets the powder pass through the stomach undigested. Allicin can then be absorbed through the small intestine.

Even with high-quality garlic powders, you may experience mild garlic taste and odor. Split your daily intake into several small doses to minimize this effect.

Garlic tablets are sold under several brand names. Most studies of garlic's health benefits have been conducted with Kwai supplements. Other quality supplements include Garlicin...Garlitrin...and Garlinase 4000.

Kyolic, a popular product, is an aged garlic preparation that does *not* produce allicin. Most researchers believe it is not as active as powdered garlic tablets.

Important: Check garlic supplement labels for allicin content. For maximum benefit, the daily dose should provide at least 5 mg of allicin. That's equivalent to chewing one large or two small cloves of raw garlic.

Natural Year-Round Allergy Remedies

Richard Firshein, DO, physician practicing in complementary medicine in New York. He is author of *A Guide to Nutritional Therapies: The Nutraceutical Revolution*. Riverhead. Dr. Firshein answers health-related questions at *www.drcity.com.*

More than 20 million Americans suffer from springtime allergies. Over-the-counter and prescription antihistamines, decongestants and steroid nasal sprays may help—but they can cause drowsiness and nasal bleeding and may have other yet-unknown effects.

Here are some natural remedies that can often be used instead of—or in conjunction with—medications. Consult a doctor before trying any of these, especially if you are pregnant or trying to get pregnant, planning surgery or taking other medications.

■ Quercetin.

This supplement is a bioflavonoid—the component in fruits and vegetables that gives them their vibrant color. It has natural antihistamine and anti-inflammatory effects.

Typical dosage: Start taking quercetin when spring weather begins, and continue through the end of June. Take 300 milligrams (mg) twice a day for one week. If that doesn't work, increase to 600 mg.

If you also suffer from fall allergies, begin again in mid-August and continue through the first frost. In hot climates, you may need to take quercetin year-round.

Stinging nettle.
Like quercetin, this plant extract is an excellent antihistamine and anti-inflammatory. It can be used in conjunction with quercetin or on its own.

Typical dosage: 400 mg twice a day during allergy seasons.

On-the-spot treatment: If you find yourself in the throes of an allergy attack despite taking quercetin and/or stinging nettle regularly, take an extra dose. I tell my patients to reach for these remedies whenever they would take an antihistamine.

Most allergy sufferers find quercetin and/or stinging nettle highly effective. But if they don't work for you, one of the following natural antihistamines and anti-inflammatories may help—either in conjunction with each other or alone. Try them in this order—but, of course, talk with your doctor first.

Vitamin C.
Take 1,000 mg once or twice a day during allergy season. This should be reduced or eliminated during the off-season.

Recent studies suggest vitamin C in high doses may cause thickening of arteries and interfere with certain cancer therapy. Caution is advised for patients with these conditions.

Pycnogenol.
An antioxidant derived from the bark of pine trees.
Take 50 mg twice a day.

Ginkgo biloba.
Take 60 mg twice a day. Once symptoms subside, stop taking this herb. Used in excess (more than 200 mg per day), it can cause diarrhea or sleeplessness.

Caution: People using blood thinners should avoid ginkgo biloba.

Feverfew.
Buy a product standardized to contain at least 0.7% *parthenolide*.

That is the component of this herb that reduces swelling in the sinuses. Take 500 mg two or three times a day.

MORE ALLERGY DEFENSES

▶ **Rinse pollen out of your nasal passages before bedtime.** Use a saline nasal spray, or make your own nasal wash by dissolving one-half teaspoon of salt in one-half cup of water. Place a few drops of the solution in your nose with a dropper, then blow your nose.

▶ **Keep home and car windows closed—to keep pollen outdoors.** Run an air conditioner continuously to filter air and fight different types of allergy-causing molds.

ARE HERBAL REMEDIES BETTER?

Herbal remedies are not necessarily better or safer or even cheaper than prescribed medication. People who use natural therapies to treat or prevent illness are using the herbs as drugs. *Example:* A popular dietary supplement is no safer or better at lowering cholesterol than a leading drug. Both products contain the same active ingredient, but the supplement isn't covered by insurance and is therefore more expensive.

Leo Galland, MD, director of The Foundation for Integrated Medicine, New York, and author of *Power Healing.* Random House.

▶ **Run a HEPA filter all the time during allergy season**—to purify your air of pollen and other allergens. A HEPA vacuum cleaner may also help.

▶ **Shampoo your hair, eyebrows, eyelashes, mustache and beard at bedtime and after outdoor activities.** Dust mites and other allergens cling to hairs. Change clothes when you come inside.

▶ **Strengthen your immune system.** Better overall health means reduced allergy symptoms. Take a daily multivitamin/mineral supplement… eat healthfully…get adequate rest…exercise regularly…and don't smoke.

Adaptogenic Herbs Prevent Colds and Flu

For years, naturopaths have recommended echinacea as a means of treating colds and flu. But researchers from the National College of Naturopathic Medicine (my alma mater) reported at the convention that echinacea is significantly less effective at preventing illness than "adaptogenic" herbs—so named because they help the body adapt to stress.

As a result of this finding, I'm changing my prescribing practices for my patients who suffer from frequent colds and flu. Instead of waiting until the onset of illness, I'll urge my patients to prevent colds and flu by boosting their immune system with an adaptogenic herbal formula containing Siberian ginseng, astragalus and ashwaganda. Combine tinctures of these three herbs and take one-half teaspoon of the mixture daily during periods of high stress. If a cold develops anyway, use echinacea to treat mild symptoms. Thirty drops of echinacea tincture every three hours typically suffices.

Jamison Starbuck, ND, naturopathic physician in family practice and a lecturer at the University of Montana, both in Missoula. She is past president of the American Association of Naturopathic Physicians and a contributing editor to *The Alternative Advisor: The Complete Guide to Natural Therapies and Alternative Treatments.* Time Life.

Healthy Eating

Chapter 7

Five Healing Foods for Your Regular Diet

Of all the questions I get from my patients, none is more common than, "Doctor, what foods should I eat?" Here are my favorite foods. They're tasty, easy to prepare and available in grocery or health-food stores. And unlike white flour products, luncheon meats, soft drinks and the other foods that many of us subsist on, these foods can help prevent—and even treat—certain illnesses.

■ Beets.

Both the red root—the part we ordinarily eat—and the green tops—the part we throw away—are full of magnesium and iron.

These minerals are essential to good health. But watch out. Like spinach, beet tops are rich in oxalic acid. This compound has been linked with formation of kidney stones. Beet tops are off-limits for anyone with stones or a history of stones. The red part is safe.

Beet tops can be torn like lettuce and added to salads. They can be steamed and added to soup—or served as you would serve spinach.

You can also eat beet roots raw. Grate directly into salad...or onto a sandwich made with lettuce, onion, tuna or fresh turkey and whole grain bread.

■ Kale.

I eat this dark, leafy green veggie at least twice a week during winter and early spring.

At this time of year, the body's need for vitamins and minerals rises—the result of reduced exposure to sunlight and consumption of fresh food.

Kale is a fabulous source of calcium, iron, vitamins C and A, folic acid and chlorophyll. Unlike corn, beans and tomatoes, kale can be found fresh all year long.

Jamison Starbuck, ND, naturopathic physician in family practice and a lecturer at the University of Montana, both in Missoula. She is past president of the American Association of Naturopathic Physicians and a contributing edi1tor to *The Alternative Advisor: The Complete Guide to Natural Therapies and Alternative Treatments.* Time Life.

Kale improves circulation and helps ward off colds. The compounds that give kale its bitter flavor help improve digestion and decrease the production of mucus.

Lightly steamed kale is delicious. It tastes a bit like spinach, though more flavorful. I eat the whole leaf, but you may want to avoid the stems. They can be tough.

■ Nuts.

Brazil nuts, almonds, filberts and walnuts are packed with minerals, folic acid, vitamins B and E and beneficial oils.

I recommend buying nuts in the shell—for two reasons. First, the shell keeps nut oil from going rancid. Second, the effort required to crack each nut by hand helps ensure that you won't eat too many of these nutritious—but calorie-dense—treats.

■ Parsley.

Though best known as a garnish, parsley has much more to offer. It improves digestion, freshens the breath and curbs breast tenderness associated with premenstrual syndrome.

It's also a tonic for the adrenal glands, which can become "exhausted" as a result of hard work or stress.

I like to add abundant amounts of chopped raw parsley to salads or pasta, or simply eat sprigs as a snack. Ounce for ounce, parsley contains three times as much vitamin C as an orange.

Women who are pregnant or nursing should have no more than a sprig of parsley per day. More than that, and it can cause breast milk to dry up. It can even cause premature labor.

■ Sweet potatoes.

This starchy vegetable is rich in vitamin A and other carotenoids, which are necessary for healthy eyes, skin and lungs.

Bake them or combine with onions, garlic, tomato and chickpeas to make a hearty stew.

Veggies for Breakfast

Eat vegetables at breakfast so you do not need to crowd your daily servings later. Make vegetable-rich cream cheese by mixing low-fat cream cheese with carrots, zucchini and raisins. Or prepare a vegetable omelet with red or yellow peppers, spinach, chopped tomatoes or cut-up broccoli florets. Try a sweet potato sprinkled with cinnamon and sugar…broccoli florets with yogurt-based dip …even vegetable leftovers from last night's dinner.

Tufts University Health & Nutrition Letter, Six Beacon St., Boston 02108.

BEST FORTIFIED FOODS

Best fortified foods: Calcium-fortified orange juice. Check the package to make sure that it is 100% orange juice. *Avoid:* Fortified imitation orange juice. *Not necessary:* Orange juice with added antioxidants—orange juice has plenty of antioxidants (vitamin C). *Whole-grain cereals with added vitamins and minerals.* A serving usually supplies one-quarter of the recommended daily levels of about a dozen vitamins and minerals. *Trap:* Kids' fruit snacks with added vitamins—they don't change what is essentially candy into a healthful food.

Bonnie Liebman, nutrition director, Center for Science in the Public Interest, Washington, DC 20009.

Smart Food

Food to keep you sharp at work: Eat a grilled chicken breast for breakfast on a day when you need to be super-alert before lunch. If you have an important lunch meeting, order starches without fats or oil to get calming carbohydrates without high-fat foods that slow thinking and make you sleepy. *Good choices:* Pasta with fresh tomatoes and basil...rice with vegetables or fruit.

Nutrition for Dummies by **Carol Ann Rinzler, MA.** IDG Books. She is author of numerous health-related books.

Better Whole-Wheat Bread

Better whole-wheat-bread shopping: Be sure the first ingredient listed on the package is whole-wheat flour. If it is not, the bread was made with refined flour. Do not be fooled by words like wheat, unbleached, enriched or stone-ground.

Richard Podell, MD, clinical professor of family medicine, University of Medicine and Dentistry of New Jersey, New Brunswick.

Great Smoothie Recipe

Quick and healthful breakfast: Fruit smoothies —made in a few seconds in a kitchen blender. Combine bananas...berries...pineapple...or melon with orange juice...nonfat yogurt...tofu...or skim milk. Add ice to make the drink frosty. A smoothie with these ingredients contains fiber and vitamins— and tastes great.

Gail Frank, DrPH, RD, professor of nutrition, California State University, Long Beach.

ROASTED VEGETABLES ARE BETTER

Roast vegetables to intensify their flavor and enhance their natural sweetness. All vegetables can be roasted, then served plain or with a splash of citrus juice or vinegar. Spread vegetables in a single layer on a baking tray. When figuring quantities, allow for shrinkage during roasting. *Examples:* Roast onions and shallots at 375° on a lightly oiled baking tray...winter squash and sweet potatoes in ¾-inch-thick pieces on an oiled tray at 375°...asparagus or mushrooms lightly coated with olive oil at 400°. Roasting time varies...it can take from about 10 minutes to 30 minutes, depending on the vegetable.

Mollie Katzen's Vegetable Heaven by **Mollie Katzen.** Hyperion. She is a cookbook author based in Berkeley, CA, as well as a cooking-show host.

QUICK AND EASY PARTY DIPS

Into a container of sour cream or yogurt, stir a packet of dried seasoning mix. *Tasty examples:* Ranch dressing...herb dressing... cheese-and-garlic dressing...Caesar salad dressing...or the old reliable onion soup. *Best:* Refrigerate for several hours before serving.

The Culinary Sleuth, Box 156, Spring City, PA 19475.

▶ **Erewhon Instant Oatmeal with Added Oat Bran**, 130 calories/four grams of fiber.

▶ **Arrowhead Mills Instant Multigrain Cereal**, 100 calories/three grams of fiber.

▶ **Quaker Instant Oatmeal**, regular, 100 calories/three grams of fiber.

▶ **Erewhon Instant Oatmeal**, flavored, 130 calories/three grams of fiber.

▶ **Roman Meal Instant Delights Cream of Rye**, 100 calories/three grams of fiber.

Jayne Hurley, RD, senior nutritionist, *Nutrition Action Healthletter,* 1875 Connecticut Ave. NW, Washington, DC 20009.

Most Nutritious Greens

▶ **Beta-carotene**—dandelion greens, kale, turnip greens, spinach.

▶ **Vitamin C**—kale, mustard greens, turnip greens, watercress.

▶ **Folic acid**—turnip greens, spinach, mustard greens, chicory.

▶ **Calcium**—turnip greens, dandelion greens, arugula, kale.

▶ **Iron**—dandelion greens, Swiss chard, mustard greens, turnip greens, kale.

Ronald Ruden, MD, internist and nutritionist in private practice, 121 E. 84 St., New York City 10028.

Start the Day with Hot Cereal

Instant whole-grain hot cereals are a significant source of fiber, nutrients and phytochemicals, which may protect against cancer, heart disease and diabetes...and they are a warm start to the day. *Cereals with no more than 20% of calories from sugar and no more than 200 mg of sodium per serving...*

BEST ANTIOXIDANT VEGETABLE

Best antioxidant vegetable: Kale. Other vegetables high in antioxidants—which can reduce the risk of cancer and other diseases—are beets, red peppers, broccoli, spinach, potatoes, sweet potatoes and corn. *Best antioxidant fruits:* Blueberries and strawberries...followed by plums, oranges, red grapes, kiwi, pink grapefruit, white grapefruit, white grapes, apples, tomatoes, bananas, pears and melons.

Ronald Prior, PhD, scientific program officer, and Jean Mayer USDA Human Nutrition Research Center on Aging, Tufts University, Boston.

How to Cook Fish

Before cooking fish, remove visible fat and skin whenever possible. This limits exposure to toxic substances. *Also helpful:* Bake or broil on a rack or grill to let any other fat drip away.

Elisa S. Zied, RD, writing in *Environmental Nutrition,* 52 Riverside Dr., New York City 10024.

The Healing Power Of Nuts

Gene Spiller, PhD, director of the Health Research and Studies Center, an independent research facility in Los Altos, CA. He is coauthor of *Nutrition Secrets of the Ancients* (Diane Publishing) and *Healthy Nuts* (Avery).

Most health-conscious people think of nuts as a delicious indulgence, too full of fat to enjoy on a regular basis.

But the most recent research suggests that nuts are actually *good* for you. Eaten in moderation, they lower cholesterol levels even more effectively than olive oil, which has been highly touted for its cholesterol-lowering properties.

GOOD AND BAD FATS

It's true that nuts are fatty. The average nut derives more than half of its calories from fat. Some nuts, including Brazil nuts and macadamias, are approximately 70% fat.

But when it comes to heart health, fats are not equal.

Saturated fat—the kind that predominates in meat, dairy foods and many packaged foods—raises cholesterol levels.

But *unsaturated* fat (monounsaturated and polyunsaturated) has the opposite effect. And nuts are a terrific source of unsaturated fat.

Study after study has shown that a diet rich in unsaturated fat lowers heart attack risk even more effectively than the low-fat diet advocated by the American Heart Association.

Good news: More than 60% of the fat in almonds, hazelnuts, macadamias, pecans and pistachios is monounsaturated. And roughly 70% of the fat in walnuts is polyunsaturated.

NUTS VS. HEART DISEASE

In a study published in the *Journal of the American College of Nutrition,* 45 men and women with elevated cholesterol levels were divided into three groups. One group got most of its dietary fat from dairy products...one mostly from olive oil...and one mostly from almonds.

After four weeks, researchers measured the participants' cholesterol levels.

Result: Total cholesterol levels were significantly lower in the almond group than in the dairy group or the olive-oil group.

The same pattern was observed with regard to LDL (bad) cholesterol. The almond eaters' readings averaged 33 points lower than those of the dairy group...and 16 points lower than those of the olive-oil group.

Similar news came out of another study, which looked beyond cholesterol to the bottom line—the incidence of heart disease.

In the study—published in the *British Medical Journal*—women who ate at least one ounce of nuts more than five times a week were less likely to develop heart disease than were women who ate nuts less frequently. This finding corroborated that of an earlier study conducted at Loma Linda University in Loma Linda, CA.

In that study, 34,000 people were followed for eight years. Those who habitually ate a handful of nuts four or five times a week had fewer fatal heart attacks than those who ate nuts less frequently.

WHAT'S GOOD ABOUT NUTS

The monounsaturated fat found in nuts isn't the whole story. Nuts also contain protein and dietary fiber. Each of these has its own cholesterol-lowering effect.

Also, nuts are rich sources of heart-healthy phytochemicals (plant-based chemicals)...

▶ **Plant sterols.** These cholesterol-like compounds lower cholesterol levels.

▶ **Tocopherols.** These antioxidants—which include vitamin E—block the oxidation of cholesterol, a process that leads to clogged arteries.

▶ **Magnesium and potassium.** These minerals are crucial for controlling blood pressure.

No one knows just which of these nutrients is most important for cardiac function. For this reason, it's best to eat a variety of nuts—to make sure that you get *all* the beneficial nutrients.

Among nuts, almonds, hazelnuts, macadamias, pecans and pistachios are the best sources of monounsaturated fat. Walnuts have more polyunsaturated fat, which is effective against cholesterol and blood clots.

Some studies of nut consumption have included peanuts. While they're actually not nuts at all—they're legumes—peanuts are also a good source of monounsaturated fat.

WON'T NUTS MAKE YOU FAT?

Eat too much calorie-dense food, and you'll gain weight. That's true whether your weakness is nuts, cake, cookies, whatever.

But some dietary fat is necessary. It provides a feeling of satiety that counterbalances the tendency to overeat.

In one study, people were asked to eat three ounces of nuts each day—and yet they didn't gain weight. The nuts made them feel full, so they didn't *want* to overeat.

In another study of 101 overweight people, those who followed a high-monounsaturated fat diet—35% of calories from nuts, peanuts, olive oil, etc.—lost just as much weight as those who followed a low-fat diet with equivalent calories.

After six months, nearly two-thirds of those in the high-monounsaturated fat group were still sticking to their diet. Fewer than half of those in the low-fat group had stuck with theirs.

HOW TO EAT NUTS

For maximum benefit to the heart, eat one ounce of nuts daily. That's about a handful.

Nuts should be a substitute for other foods you ordinarily eat—not something you eat in addition to these foods.

Carve a place for nuts by cutting back on meat, cheese and other animal proteins.

It makes no difference whether nuts are eaten raw or roasted without oil. But minimize your consumption of salted nuts if you have high blood pressure.

If you have trouble controlling what you eat, stick with unshelled nuts. The extra effort required to crack the shells discourages overeating.

Milk Alternative for the Lactose Intolerant

Trouble with milk? Try yogurt. Even people who have difficulty digesting the lactose in milk can usually eat yogurt containing live active cultures. The cultures help digest the lactose. A cup of plain low-fat or fat-free yogurt has 35% to 40% of the recommended daily intake of calcium—compared with 30% to 35% in a glass of 1% or fat-free milk. Fortified milk does have one thing yogurt lacks—vitamin D. Yogurt eaters who do not drink milk need to get enough of this vitamin from other sources.

Bonnie Liebman, nutrition director, Center for Science in the Public Interest, writing in *Nutrition Action Healthletter,* 1875 Connecticut Ave. NW, Washington, DC 20009.

HOW TO DE-FAT MEAT

Wash chopped meat to lower its fat content. Cook it in a pan until it browns. Pour off the fat, put the meat in a strainer, then pour three cups of hot water over it—one cup at a time. Use the de-fatted meat in spaghetti sauce or similar dishes. Every tablespoon of fat you remove cuts about 100 calories—and cuts cholesterol and saturated fat.

Nutrition for Dummies by **Carol Ann Rinzler, MA.** IDG Books. She is author of numerous health-related books.

More Healthful Fast-Food Eating

Plan your meals before walking in to a restaurant. Order regular, junior, small or single portions—not large ones. Make special requests if you are willing to wait for your food and the restaurant seems accommodating. Eat slowly—spend at least 15 to 20 minutes eating. When you eat too fast, you hardly taste the food—so your hunger remains unsatisfied. Also avoid drive-through windows. They encourage speedy ordering and in-car, speedy eating.

The Restaurant Companion: A Guide to Healthier Eating Out by **Hope Warshaw, RD.** Surrey Books. She is a Washington, DC-based nutritionist.

Are You Sure You Want That Hot Dog?

Most hot dogs are unhealthful despite labels like *lean* and *lite*. A two-ounce reduced-fat turkey frank may have 40% less fat than a regular frank made from beef or pork. But it may still contain 10 grams of fat—and a hefty dose of sodium, too. *Self-defense:* Always check labels carefully.

Pat Kendall, PhD, RD, food and nutrition specialist, Colorado State University Cooperative Extension, Fort Collins.

Watch What You Eat

Eating large amounts of meat and processed foods lets harmful sulfur-eating intestinal bacteria multiply at the expense of healthy carbohydrate-consuming microbes. These bacteria produce corrosive sulfides, which are suspected to cause ulcerative colitis and other intestinal problems. Rich sources of sulfur include meat, highly processed foods, dried fruit, alcoholic drinks and fruit juices preserved with sulfur dioxide and similar chemicals. *Self-defense:* Eat a balanced diet with plenty of fresh fruits and vegetables. Protein should provide only about 15% of your daily calories.

John H. Cummings, MD, senior scientist at the Faculty of Medicine and MRC Dunn Clinical Nutrition Centre, Cambridge University in England.

WHEN EATING ON THE STREET

Be very wary of food prepared by street vendors. Cast a careful eye over the vendor and the cart, paying special attention to cleanliness...whether raw and cooked foods are handled separately...how long food is left out in the open...whether food is cooked thoroughly and served piping hot. *Riskiest:* Foods with multiple ingredients prepared on the cart, such as chicken and rice. *Best bet:* Hot dogs.

Robert Gravani, PhD, professor of food science at Cornell University, Ithaca, NY.

Dairy Food—Anticancer Aid

Colon cancer risk may be lowered by eating dairy foods. Researchers monitored a group of people at risk for colon cancer. At both 6 and 12 months, those who upped their intake of low-fat or nonfat dairy foods showed a reduction in markers of risk for colon cancer. Calcium has long been thought to play a role in colon cancer prevention, but other nutrients found in dairy, including vitamin D, may also help.

Peter R. Holt, MD, professor of medicine, Columbia University College of Physicians and Surgeons, New York City.

FACTS ABOUT SALT SUBSTITUTES

Salt substitutes give much of the flavor of table salt—but are not usually used in cooking because they can give foods a bitter taste. Also, salt substitutes are made by combining potassium—instead of sodium—with chloride, so they add a considerable amount of potassium to users' diets. This can be healthful—*or harmful.* Some diuretic medicines deplete the body's potassium—so salt substitutes help users. Other diuretics conserve potassium—so salt substitutes should not be used. Talk to your doctor before starting to use salt substitutes.

Ronald Ruden, MD, internist and nutritionist in private practice, 121 E. 84 St., New York City 10028.

Feisty Salmonella Strain You Need to Know About

An antibiotic-resistant salmonella is unfazed by most antibiotics. And it may develop resistance to currently effective antibiotics. Like other strains of salmonella, DT-104 causes stomach upset, diarrhea, nausea and low-grade fever. Most people get better in a few days. But without effective drugs, DT-104 can be deadly—especially to children, the elderly and those with weakened immune systems. *Self-defense:* Keep raw food refrigerated …cook meat thoroughly…carefully clean everything that comes in contact with raw meat…refrigerate leftovers immediately.

Irmgard Behlau, MD, a member of the Food Safety Initiative at New England Medical Center, Boston.

Frozen vs. Fresh Vegetables

Frozen vegetables are as good for you as fresh ones. Frozen produce is on ice within hours of being picked. But fresh vegetables often go two weeks from the time they are picked to the time you eat them—losing up to 50% of nutrients in the process.

Barbara P. Klein, PhD, food scientist, University of Illinois at Urbana, and leader of a research project comparing the nutritional value of fresh and frozen vegetables.

More on Frozen vs. Fresh

Frozen fruits and vegetables are sometimes more nutritious than fresh fruits and vegetables. Frozen green beans, for instance, contain twice the vitamin C as fresh ones that have been sitting for nearly a week on store shelves. Fresh produce is generally more nutritious—but only if eaten soon after being picked.

Franca B. Alphin, MPH, RD, assistant clinical professor, department of community and family medicine, Duke University, Durham, NC.

The Whole Truth About Dietary Fiber...And Its Role in Preventing Cancer, Heart Disease And Diabetes

David J. A. Jenkins, MD, PhD, DSc, professor of medicine and nutritional sciences at the University of Toronto Faculty of Medicine.

For decades, doctors have been assuring their patients that a high-fiber diet could reduce the risk for colon cancer.

Then a study published in *The New England Journal of Medicine* indicated that fiber appeared to make no difference.

Researchers had followed 89,000 women for 16 years. They found that those who consumed moderate amounts of fiber developed colon cancer at the same rate as those who ate a diet low in fiber.

Many people were stunned by the study. Consumers started to wonder whether all those years of eating bran cereal had been worth the trouble.

KINDS OF FIBER

Dietary fiber refers to any of the indigestible portions of plant foods we eat. Although we talk about fiber as a single entity, there are actually many kinds of fiber. *The different types of fiber can be grouped into two broad classes...*

▶ **Soluble fiber**—found in high amounts in fruits, oats and beans—dissolves in water, forming a gel.

▶ **Insoluble fiber**—found in vegetables, wheat bran and whole grains—does not dissolve in water.

Instead, it absorbs water to become bulky, which increases the weight of feces and the speed at which waste passes through the intestines and out of the body.

Typically, of all the fiber eaten, two-thirds is insoluble and one-third is soluble.

WHAT FIBER CAN DO

The same study that found that fiber did not protect against colon cancer showed resoundingly that eating a high-fiber diet helped prevent heart disease and diabetes.

How fiber in the diet helps prevent heart disease is poorly understood. It may alter clotting factors in blood, reducing the risk of *thrombosis*—blockage in an artery that can cause a heart attack.

Fiber also may cut heart disease risk by lowering cholesterol levels, reducing the rate at which fatty deposits form within arteries.

Normally, we excrete small amounts of cholesterol in the feces. Soluble fiber binds more cholesterol as bile acids and carries it out of the body.

High-fiber foods protect against diabetes, a major cause of health problems in Western countries. Exactly how fiber helps prevent diabetes remains unknown.

Fiber also guards against....

▶ **Diverticular disease.** Fiber is the standard treatment for prevention of *diverticula*. Those are small sacs that balloon out from the colon wall as the result of pressure exerted by feces and intestinal gas.

▶ **Constipation and hemorrhoids**. Fiber makes stools softer and more bulky. That allows them to pass easily out of the body without the need for straining.

▶ **Obesity.** High-fiber foods tend to be lower in fat and calories than low-fiber foods. Diets that include lots of high-fiber foods tend to have fewer calories than diets that stress low-fiber foods.

And because fiber adds indigestible bulk, it makes you feel fuller longer.

WHAT ABOUT COLON CANCER?

Despite *The New England Journal of Medicine* study, it's premature to write fiber off as a means of reducing colon cancer risk.

The average American consumes about 15 grams (g) of fiber a day. For the past 10 years, researchers have been saying that we should be getting at least twice as much fiber. A truly high-fiber diet may contain 40 grams (g) to 60 g of fiber a day.

In *The New England Journal* study, women who ate the most fiber got only about 25 grams (g) a day. Obviously, that's less than the recommended level of fiber intake—and far short of a real high-fiber diet.

Bottom line: The study did not really investigate the effects of a high-fiber diet.

DIETARY RECOMMENDATIONS

For most people, it's not especially difficult to get 30 grams (g) to 40 g of fiber per day from food sources. *Here's a workable strategy…*

▶ **Start each day with a high-fiber breakfast cereal,** such as Bran Buds, All-Bran or Fiber One. Add these to your usual cereal until you get used to the taste and texture, then make the transition, gradually, to the high-fiber cereal only.

▶ **Substitute whole-wheat products for white flour products—**bread, pasta, bagels, crackers, etc.

▶ **Eat at least five servings of fruits and vegetables a day.** Seven servings is better, and 10 will easily put you in the high-fiber range.

▶ **Eat at least one serving of peas or beans every day.**

Fiber supplements should not be used instead of a proper diet. But the supplements can be beneficial when used in addition to such a diet.

One good fiber supplement is psyllium, which is found in Metamucil and other products. High in soluble fiber, psyllium has been found to lower serum cholesterol…flatten blood glucose levels after meals…and keep insulin levels from rising too high.

You can dissolve Metamucil in water and drink …or sprinkle it on breakfast cereal or other foods.

Food manufacturers have begun to add psyllium to certain foods. Kellogg's, for example, has introduced a line of psyllium-enriched foods called Ensemble. The line includes cookies, bread, cereals, pasta and frozen entrées.

Restaurant Food

Restaurant food is much higher in fat—and lower in nutrients—than meals prepared at home. On average, meals eaten at a restaurant derive 40% of their calories from fat, compared with 32% in homecooked meals. Restaurant meals contain less dietary fiber, calcium and iron, too.

Elizabeth Frazao, PhD, economist, Economic Research Service, US Department of Agriculture, Washington, DC.

NUTRITION MATTERS AND YOUR DOCTOR

Very important to your health: Having a doctor who uses nutrition to prevent and treat such illnesses as obesity, diabetes and hypertension, along with medication if necessary. *Alarming:* Medical schools still offer virtually no training in nutrition—even the best medical schools. Younger physicians…and those who have MPHs (advanced public health degrees) tend to know more than older ones. *Bad sign:* A doctor who views weight gain as inevitable. It isn't—and it has an enormous impact on health.

Franca B. Alphin, MPH, RD, assistant clinical professor, department of community and family medicine, Duke University, Durham, NC.

Secrets of
Weight Control
Chapter 8

Weight Loss Is Good for You

E ven a small weight loss significantly cuts risk of heart disease. Losing 5% of body weight is associated with lower blood pressure. Losing 10% is associated with lower cholesterol. *Bottom line:* Even if you want to shed a lot of weight, focus first on losing a little. *Caution:* Diet drugs are not recommended for long-term weight control—and doctors consider obesity a lifelong condition.

Robert Eckel, MD, vice chairman, nutrition committee, American Heart Association, Dallas.

The Sleep–Weight Connection

G etting enough sleep helps you lose weight. Research suggests that appetite increases when humans are deprived of sleep. This may help explain why so many Americans are obese. Even just 40 years ago, people slept eight to nine hours a night. Today it's down to seven or eight hours. *Also:* The extra hours awake often are spent in front of the TV, snacking on high-fat foods.

Pat Kendall, PhD, RD, professor and associate department head, food science and human nutrition, Colorado State University, Fort Collins.

Few Overweight People Eat Because They Are Hungry

Lawrence J. Cheskin, MD, director of Johns Hopkins Weight Management Center and associate professor of International Health, Johns Hopkins Bloomberg School of Public Health, Baltimore. He is author of *Losing Weight for Good: Developing Your Personal Plan of Action.* Johns Hopkins University Press.

D ieting is a national obsession in America. Yet as few as 10% of dieters who lose weight keep it off for five years or more.

Most people fail at dieting because they don't correct, in a permanent way, the basic psychological behavior that leads them to overeat.

Losing weight and keeping off the pounds requires more than just going on a diet. You must change your behavior.

WHY WE EAT THE WAY WE DO

Few overweight people eat because they are physically hungry. Instead, they tend to eat for a variety of psychological reasons—and out of habit.

Our desire to overeat is not genetically programmed behavior. It is a learned habit that we may not even be aware we're doing.

We learn to misuse food in childhood, largely through exposure to TV commercials and parenting messages that use fattening foods as rewards for good behavior, finishing dinner and completing homework or chores.

Eating salty, sugary or fatty foods becomes a habit when we're adults because they continue to reward us. During times when we're upset, eating these foods distracts us from our bad feelings.

When we develop such habits, pathways emerge in our brains that make it easier for us to engage repeatedly in the behavior. In order to break the habit, you have to develop new pathways.

> **Example:** *Break the habit of reaching for potato chips when you watch TV by replacing the chips with a healthy habit—such as walking on your treadmill.*

It also has been found that overweight people tend to eat fast. Since it takes about 20 minutes for the brain's appetite center to get the message that you're full, you may eat a lot more than you should in just 20 minutes if you eat quickly.

To lose weight for good, you must find the personal "whys" that trigger you to overeat and gain weight. There are numerous learned behaviors that lead to excess eating. *The most common behaviors are...*

▶ **Food as comforter:** "I'm feeling lonely, so I need to eat something."

▶ **Food as stress reliever:** "I'm really busy at work, and I don't have the time or energy to eat healthy right now."

▶ **Food as reward:** "I finished a project today—let's have dinner and celebrate."

▶ **Food as boredom reliever:** "There's nothing to do, so I'll just snack."

▶ **Food as social facilitator:** "Sure, I'll eat something if you're eating, too."

▶ **Food as habit:** "It's 6 pm, so I'll eat dinner even if I'm not very hungry."

IDENTIFYING YOUR TRIGGERS

Most people are unaware of the ways in which they use food inappropriately to manage their stress and the difficulties they face each day.

To get a handle on your individual learned behavior, undertake a one-week observation period. Keep a log of what you're eating and the circumstances under which you're eating.

Here's what a sample entry in your log might look like...

▶ **Date and time:** Saturday, March 10, 2004, 8 pm.

▶ **Place:** At home in the kitchen.

▶ **Who I was with:** No one.

▶ **What I ate:** A large slice of chocolate cake.

▶ **Why I ate:** Busy day at work. Cake was left over from party.

▶ **Was I hungry?** Not really.

▶ **How did I feel?** Tired, stressed.

During the observation period, eat in your usual manner and be honest with yourself in your journal. This will allow you to best assess when and why you eat and determine how to change your eating habits for the better.

Look for situations in which you ate immediately after a stressful situation even though you weren't hungry. Then think of behavior that you can substitute for eating in those situations.

One of the best things about the observation period is that it puts you in touch with your unconscious behavior and with every piece of food you eat.

You also can count calories, carbs or fat grams. If you're under age 55 and not very physically active, it takes about 12 calories for each pound of body weight to maintain your weight. A 150-pound person can eat about 1,800 calories a day and not gain weight, and should eat slightly less as he or she gets older. You can eat more if you exercise three days a week for one-half hour or longer at a time.

So—if you count calories during the observation period and find you're exceeding your weight-maintenance calorie count, that's a good indication that you need to cut calories.

HOW TO OVERCOME YOUR TRIGGERS

Identifying the situations that prompt you to overeat and the unconscious and ingrained eating habits you've formed over a lifetime is half the battle.

Next, develop a personal plan of action—a better set of responses—for countering these inappropriate eating cues to help you keep the weight off.

After the one-week observation period is over, continue to keep your journal but add a new category—"What could I have done in this situation instead of eating?" *Examples...*

▶ **Eating to relieve loneliness, anger or other emotions:** In the instance where you ate the chocolate cake because you were tired and stressed, instead of eating, learn to meditate... listen to a CD...take the dog for a walk.

▶ **Eating to relieve stress at work:** Rather than heading to the vending machine, go for a quick walk around the office...or clean your files or your shelf.

Best of all: List the top three things you need to do and complete the first one.

▶ **Eating to reward yourself:** It's fine to allow yourself occasional indulgences. But buy one portion at a time. Don't bring foods that you have trouble resisting into your home. Eat them only at restaurants.

▶ **Eating out of boredom:** Many times, when we sit down to watch TV, we're bored and tired. TV commercials for fatty foods encourage us to use these foods as rewards. As a result, we eat recklessly while we're watching TV. *Helpful...*

▷ Don't eat anywhere but in the kitchen or dining room, sitting at the table.

▷ Turn off the TV if you can't watch without eating fatty foods. Just realizing that ads are part of the problem will make you conscious of what you're eating.

▷ Make two lists—one that reminds you of the tasks you need to accomplish, such as returning videotapes and picking up shampoo...the other that reminds you of the things you'd like to do. These dream activities may include reading a book...planning a party...playing with your kids.

When you're bored and find yourself watching TV or reaching for food, engage in an activity from one of your two lists.

▶ **Eating on the run:** Instead of eating a pastry at the last minute, prepare a fast, nutritious breakfast the night before—fresh fruit, fat-free yogurt or cereal in a plastic container. Grab the prepared breakfast on your way out the door.

Correcting your inappropriate eating behaviors will not be easy. Habits are notoriously hard to break, especially ones that encourage us to use food as a replacement for happiness and self-satisfaction.

Secrets of the Diet Masters

Anne M. Fletcher, MS, RD, registered dietitian and former executive editor of *Tufts University Diet & Nutrition Letter.* She is author of *Eating Thin for Life: Food Secrets & Recipes from People Who Have Lost Weight & Kept It Off* and *The Thin for Life Daybook,* all from Houghton Mifflin.

People who lose weight and keep the pounds off for longer than three years are true diet experts. To learn their eating and exercise secrets, I surveyed 208 women and men whose average weight loss was 64 pounds.

Here's what they said works…

▓ Drink a glass of water before eating.

There really is no metabolic reason why drinking water should make you shed pounds.

But to my surprise, two out of every three people I questioned told me they make a serious effort to drink water to control their weight.

While downing a glass of water (8 to 10 ounces) won't necessarily stem the craving for a candy bar, the water will fill you up. Having a glass of water before or between meals leaves less room in your stomach and is likely to help you eat smaller portions.

If water is not appealing, drink sparkling water with lemon or lime…or flavored sparkling water… or even diet soda.

When you feel hungry or have a craving between meals, try drinking a glass of water and waiting 20 minutes to see if the desire to eat passes. If not, have a small amount of the item you desire—along with a big glass of water.

▓ Kick the red meat habit.

For years, health experts have been telling us to get less of our protein from meat—particularly steaks and burgers, which tend to be high in total fat and the saturated fat that is linked with heart disease.

The people I interviewed cut back dramatically on their consumption of red meat. Most told me they eat little or no red meat, with more than half indicating that at most they eat meat once or twice a week. Instead of meat, they favored poultry, seafood and legumes—all of which are lower in fat and calories.

From a nutritional standpoint, there is no reason to shun lean meats. But red meat seems to be associated with past unhealthy ways of eating that maintainers want to avoid.

Helpful: Think of meat as a condiment rather than as the main course. When you eat red meat, your portion should be no bigger than a deck of cards.

Substitute a three-ounce portion of skinless poultry, fish or shellfish for meat. On other nights, have a meatless pasta dish…or a vegetarian meal consisting of a hearty bean soup or rice and beans.

> ***Example:*** *A filling, tasty combination is rice, seasoned canned beans and salsa. Mix and warm, then top with some reduced-fat cheese or fat-free sour cream.*

▓ Eat low-fat and fat-free foods carefully.

There is evidence suggesting that when some people see the words "low-fat" or "fat-free" on food labels, they eat much more.

The diet masters consume reduced-fat foods carefully, watching their portion sizes. Given a choice between two similar foods with similar calorie values, they tend to choose the one with less fat but they consume it in a portion equal to the regular one.

Helpful: The next time you reach for a bag of low-fat chips or cookies, read the label and parcel out only the amount listed as a "serving size." Then put the bag away. Also, compare labels of reduced-fat and regular versions of the same foods to see if there really is much of a difference.

My rule of thumb: If there is no more than a two- to three-gram fat difference and no more than a 25-calorie difference per serving, the reduced-fat item probably doesn't have much of an edge.

To stick to reasonable portions of all snack foods, have a piece of fruit along with each snack or sweet you eat.

■ Keep track of what you eat.

Most diet masters do not obsessively weigh and measure the foods they eat. But they do track it occasionally.

Some count calories or keep track of food groups, while others keep food diaries, writing down the foods they eat as the day progresses.

Keeping a food diary pinpoints where your extra calories are coming from if you get stuck at a plateau while losing weight. It also makes you stop and think before grabbing a handful of snacks.

Helpful: Buy yourself a lined notebook or a weight-loss journal. For one week, write down what you eat, the amount and the total calories in the portion. There is no need to count sugar-free beverages or gum.

Women trying to lose weight should stick with 1,200 to 1,500 calories a day…for men, the daily caloric intake should be 1,500 to 2,000 calories.

■ Don't let exercise become boring.

Exercise is a cornerstone of successful weight control. Most diet masters told me that they exercise at least three times a week, with 25% of them working out five or six times weekly. Many of them had more than one way to keep physically fit.

Example: Six out of 10 people engage in at least two different forms of exercise, such as walking and light weight training. Some change their exercise with the season—outdoor cycling in the summer and aerobics in the winter.

Others vary their exercise within a workout session. Spending 45 minutes on a treadmill is boring,

ALLERGY–WEIGHT-GAIN LINK

Allergies can make you fat. People who were tested for food sensitivity and who stopped eating foods to which they were allergic lost three pounds of fat and gained one pound of muscle in 30 days. People following weight-loss diets but not eliminating foods to which they were allergic gained fat and lost lean muscle. *Self-defense:* If you are overweight and have at least two other disease symptoms—such as migraine headaches and gastrointestinal trouble—ask your doctor about being tested for food allergies.

Gilbert Kaats, PhD, director, Health and Medical Research Foundation, San Antonio, whose study of 100 overweight individuals was published in *The Bariatrician*.

but spending 15 minutes on each of three different pieces of equipment is more bearable.

Helpful: Since exercise goals that are too rigorous are usually short-lived, start small, start easy and do a form of exercise that you enjoy.

Begin by walking for 15 to 20 minutes, the top form of exercise among diet masters. After a few weeks, increase to 30 minutes, and on alternate days, ride your bike or lift weights.

Important: Give yourself a break—schedule some days off from exercise each week, and don't feel you have to quickly increase your exercise to benefit. That's a good way to get hurt or discouraged.

What You Can Do About Your Children's Weight

Best ways to prevent children from becoming overweight...

■ **Feed kids only when they are hungry.** If they aren't hungry at mealtimes, don't insist that they eat.

■ **Observe how your children signal real hunger,** versus other dissatisfied states such as boredom, loneliness and frustration.

■ **Discourage physical inactivity— especially sitting in front of the TV.** Get into outside activities with your kids—they will be more likely to engage in exercise if you play with them.

■ **Be a good role model.** Eat healthfully and in moderation—and don't be a couch potato. Children with an obese parent are twice as likely to become obese adults.

Robert Whitaker, MD, assistant professor of pediatrics at Children's Hospital Medical Center, Cincinnati.

It Takes More than Fat To Make You Fat

It's not just fat in your diet that makes you fat. No matter what you eat, you will put on weight if you take in more calories than you burn. Pound for pound, fat contains more calories than carbohydrates or protein—but that does not mean you can eat as much low- or nonfat food as you want.

In fact, the national rate of obesity has soared to record levels, even as Americans have been consuming less fat. *Bottom line:* Watch what you eat— and look for opportunities to burn more calories, through formal exercise or by becoming more active in your everyday life.

Walter Willett, MD, DrPH, chair of the nutrition department at Harvard School of Public Health, Boston.

Healthier Eating

Give yourself time to get used to less fat. Fat has a wonderful *mouth feel* for people who eat it regularly—but once you spend a month drinking skim milk, you won't enjoy regular milk anymore. *In the meantime:* Give yourself a healthful taste treat by using the freshest, most seasonal products you can find. Fresh herbs add a lot of flavor...can be grown inexpensively at home...and are much more flavorful than dried herbs.

Heart Fitness for Life: The Essential Guide to Preventing and Reversing Heart Disease by **Mary McGowan, MD.** Oxford University Press. She is director, Cholesterol Management Center, New England Heart Institute, Manchester, NH.

HOW TO BENEFIT FROM BROKEN RESOLUTIONS

Even broken resolutions have benefits. People who make New Year's promises to change bad habits and then break the resolutions within a month are at least twice as likely as people who make no resolutions to change the habits anyway within the next six months. *Helpful:* Change your attitude when making a resolution. *Example:* Instead of focusing on losing weight by no longer eating indulgent foods, concentrate on the health benefits of exercise and better nutrition.

James Prochaska, PhD, director, Cancer Prevention Research Center, University of Rhode Island, Kingston.

How to Lose Weight Without Feeling Deprived

Barbara Rolls, PhD, professor of nutrition at Pennsylvania State University in University Park, and past president of the North American Association for the Study of Obesity.

Is there any realistic way to lose weight and keep it off? After studying people's eating habits for more than 20 years, Penn State researcher Dr. Barbara Rolls says the answer is *yes*.

■ Why do diets so often fail to bring lasting results?
Because they're simply too hard to follow.

They require you either to adopt eating habits dramatically different from your current habits…or to follow complicated rules about which foods can be eaten and when.

Few people have the patience to incorporate such programs into their lifestyles.

■ What's more important in weight loss—reduced calorie intake or reduced fat intake?
Assuming your exercise level remains constant, the only way to lose weight is to take in fewer calories than your body expends.

Many popular weight-loss diets focus on reducing the proportion of fat in the diet. But whether your diet is 20% or 45% fat, lowering the total number of calories is the *only* dietary strategy that leads to weight loss.

■ Are you saying that it doesn't matter how much fat I eat?
No. Too much fat raises the risk for heart disease and certain forms of cancer—and, of course, fatty foods tend to be high in calories.

But fat feels good in the mouth. If you cut too much fat out of your diet, eating will cease to be pleasurable. You won't feel satisfied, so you'll have a hard time sticking to your weight-loss plan.

■ Isn't exercise important, too?
Exercise burns calories, so you'll lose weight faster if you cut calories and exercise more. But cutting calories is much more important.

■ What's the secret to feeling satisfied without overeating?
To avoid feelings of deprivation, you must be able to eat the same foods you ordinarily eat—and in satisfying quantities.

■ How can I eat the same old foods and still lose weight?
Lower the foods' *energy density*.

That's the number of calories per ounce. Fortunately, it's possible to do this without significantly compromising flavor or texture.

If you like lasagna, for example, use as much cheese as you always do. Just raise the vegetable content a bit…and use a *blend* of whole-fat and reduced-fat cheese. Today's reduced-fat cheese tastes better than the bland, rubbery stuff that was on the market just a few years ago.

If you eat lots of sandwiches, opt for whole-wheat bread. It's more satisfying than white bread—and more nutritious.

Instead of topping your sandwiches with cheese or mayonnaise, top them with garlic, onions or pepper sauce.

Love chili? Instead of beef, which is high in energy density, make chili with lean turkey breast, which is lower in energy density…or skip the meat altogether and make vegetarian chili.

Carrots, celery, onions and tomatoes are *very* low in calorie density.

■ Isn't it smarter simply to treat certain foods as "off-limits"?

I'm against that. If you try substituting carrots for ice cream—or broccoli for a cheese-laden casserole—you won't stay on that diet for long.

You'll feel so deprived that you might lose control and overeat.

It *does* make sense to limit the portion sizes of any calorie-dense foods you eat. If you love chocolate candy, for example, you might indulge in a piece or two after a filling meal. Do not snack on chocolate candy.

If you've been known to eat half a box of cookies in one sitting, try buying only one cookie at a time. Do not keep boxes of cookies on hand.

For more variety, stock up on nonfat yogurt, frozen blueberries, angel food cake (only 100 calories per slice) and other low-calorie foods.

■ Is counting calories a good idea?
That can get tedious. It's more realistic to write down in a notebook everything you eat.

This forces you to pay attention to what you put into your mouth.

■ How can I keep calories down when eating at restaurants?
Instead of bread or chips before the meal, have soup. When people start with soup, they eat fewer calories during the rest of the meal.

Make sure the soup you order is broth-based, not cream-based.

Choose entrées that are grilled or steamed, not fried. Ask that dressings and sauces be served on the side. Split one dessert among all of your dining companions.

Don't be shy about asking your waiter how a dish is prepared. If he or she doesn't know, politely request that he check with the chef.

Restaurant portions are often enormous. Don't feel you must eat everything on your plate. Ask for a doggie bag.

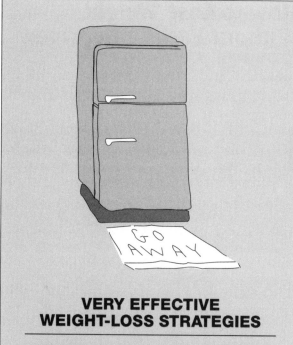

VERY EFFECTIVE WEIGHT-LOSS STRATEGIES

▶ **Restaurants:** Avoid the *10-minute* problems—the first 10 minutes with the bread basket and the last 10 minutes with dessert.

Skip breads altogether. Have a tomato juice or shrimp cocktail instead. For dessert, have sorbet…fruit…or cappuccino with skim milk. *Best:* Have an apple…low-fat yogurt…or some other healthful snack *before* you go out.

▶ **Travel:** Do not eat desserts until the last day of your trip. If you eat them earlier, you are likely to do it throughout the entire trip.

Airports: Stay away from newsstands— they stock high-sugar snacks. *Better:* Bring your own fruit.

▶ **Watching TV:** Don't snack in front of the TV—sip hot or cool liquids instead.

Effective strategies wherever you are: Resist cravings for 10 minutes—they may go away. *Also:* Avoid going longer than three or four hours without a healthful snack or meal. Eating at regular intervals will keep your blood sugar stable and keep cravings at bay.

Stephen Gullo, PhD, psychologist in New York City and author of *Thin Tastes Better: Control Your Food Triggers Without Feeling Deprived.* Dell.

FAT-FREE TRAP

Going fat-free can backfire. In a recent study, men were fed a lunchtime shake made with either skim or whole milk, then monitored to see what they ate later in the day. They didn't know which shake they got. *Result:* The men who drank the skim-milk shake tended to eat more fat later in the day than did the other men. *Implication:* Eating meals containing a little fat will help you avoid fatty foods all day.

John Allred, PhD, professor emeritus of nutrition, Ohio State University, Columbus.

Cut Fat Slowly

Cut dietary fat slowly to give your body time to adjust to new flavors, textures and tastes. Use just one tablespoon of sour cream instead of two tablespoons...replace some oil or butter in a recipe with wine...*toast* foods to bring out fuller flavor. Replace half the oil in a recipe with plain nonfat yogurt or applesauce. Sauté vegetables in dry white wine or broth instead of butter or oil.

Tailoring Your Tastes by **Linda Omichinski, RD,** president, Hugs International, which develops health promotion products, Winnipeg, Manitoba, Canada. Sterling.

Disadvantages of Protein Bars

Expensive protein-packed bars, shakes and foods aren't the best way to boost energy or lose weight. *Reason:* Protein isn't the most efficient energy source...and is already over-consumed by most Americans. *Health danger:* Some products that have a concentrated type of protein are also high in saturated fat and calories...make your kidneys work overtime (avoid these products if you have kidney problems)...and may cause dehydration, constipation and bad breath if not combined with adequate high-fiber, carbohydrate- containing foods. *Best:* A balanced diet...and healthful snacks, such as whole-grain bread, vegetables or fruit, if needed.

Wahida Karmally, MS, RD, director of nutrition at Irving Center for Clinical Research at Columbia–Presbyterian Medical Center in New York City.

THE SUGAR SUBSTITUTE WITH ALL THE ADVANTAGES

The latest sugar substitute on the market—*sucralose,* or Splenda—is the first sweetener in a decade to be approved by the Food and Drug Administration. *Advantages over other sugar substitutes:* Unlike aspartame (Nutrasweet), it retains its sweetness when subjected to processing and high temperatures. And, unlike saccharin, it has no bitter aftertaste. Sucralose-sweetened diet drinks and other products are available now, and it has been approved for use as a tabletop sweetener and an additive in baked goods, chewing gum, frozen desserts and other foods. But—the most powerful weapons in the weight-control battle remain the tried-and-true triad...exercise, a moderately low-fat diet and portion control.

Pat Kendall, PhD, RD, professor and associate department head, food science and human nutrition, Colorado State University, Fort Collins.

Break the Sugar Habit—Lose Weight, Feel Great

Morrison C. Bethea, MD, cardiac, thoracic and vascular surgeon with Tenet's Memorial Medical Center in New Orleans. He is author of *Sugar Busters: Cut Sugar to Trim Fat.* Ballantine.

Refined sugars and overprocessed carbohydrates can wreak as much havoc on weight gain and health as eating too much fat.

Fortunately, there are ways to make more healthful choices about the foods we eat—without sacrificing the need to satisfy our sweet tooth.

INSULIN AND WEIGHT GAIN

During digestion, carbohydrates are converted into glucose—the body's primary fuel. This raises blood sugar levels and triggers the release of insulin, a powerful hormone. Insulin directs glucose into the cells for immediate energy needs…or it converts glucose so that it can be stored by the liver and muscles.

However, because the body can store only a small amount of glucose at a time, all excess is converted to fat in the liver and transported to fat cells for storage.

Insulin contributes to weight gain by blocking the action of hormone-sensitive lipase, an enzyme critical to the breakdown of stored fat into fuel.

Insulin also stimulates the liver to produce very low-density lipoprotein (LDL) cholesterol, the "lethal" type of cholesterol.

HEALTHIER CARBOHYDRATES

Not all carbohydrates stimulate the same amount of insulin. So—the type and the total amount of carbohydrates you eat ultimately will affect the rate of sugar absorption and subsequent release of insulin.

Carbohydrates that provoke large amounts of insulin have what is called a *high glycemic index* (HGI). This means that they are quickly digested and result in high blood-sugar levels. HGI carbohydrates are generally highly processed and contain very little fiber.

Examples: *Fine white and wheat flour pastries and cakes, ice cream, honey, molasses, white rice, pasta, potatoes, corn products—including corn syrup.*

Better: Carbohydrates that have a *low glycemic index* (LGI). These raise blood-sugar levels slowly, stimulating lower amounts of circulating insulin.

Examples: *Unrefined, whole or cracked grain products that have little or no added sugar. They include whole-grain bread products and pastas …bran…sweet potatoes, which have a high fiber content…peas…beans…and most fruits and nuts.*

Eating fewer insulin-stimulating carbohydrates can help boost weight loss, reduce circulating insulin levels and help prevent illnesses—particularly heart disease and diabetes.

OTHER SUGAR-BUSTERS

■ **Limit your intake of seemingly "pure" carbohydrates, which rate high on the glycemic index.**

These carbohydrates include potatoes, corn, beets, carrots and other root vegetables.

All are starch, which upon digestion is quickly converted to sugar.

Helpful: If you crave a potato, scoop out and discard the inside and eat the skin.

■ **Avoid fruits that have high glycemic indexes.**

These fruits include watermelon, bananas, pineapple and raisins.

But you can have plums, apricots, peaches, mangoes, oranges and grapes.

Alternatives: If your sweet tooth is acting up, try artificially sweetened yogurt or ice cream. Dark chocolate that contains 60% or more cocoa is also an acceptable treat. The higher the cocoa, the less the sugar content.

■ **Eat lean meats, and reduce your intake of saturated fats and hydrogenated oils, such as margarine.**

Use monounsaturated types instead—such as olive oil or canola oil.

■ Don't combine fatty meat with a high glycemic carbohydrate.

Those two together can cause a greater insulin response.

The combination of meat and potatoes not only promotes the storage of sugar as fat but also forces fat to be stored more aggressively. Insulin promotes the storage of fats as well as the storage of sugar.

Better: Sweet potato with a lean meat such as turkey or chicken.

■ Eat fruit 30 minutes before—or two hours after—a meal.

Eating fruits with protein and fats can produce gastric upset and bloating.

Additionally, most fruits contain fructose, a sugar that stimulates insulin secretion less than glucose. *But* when fruit is combined with other carbohydrates, this benefit is often lost.

Unsweetened and fresh-squeezed fruit juices can be consumed with other foods, including carbohydrates, because fluid passes through the digestive tract faster than solids.

■ Exercise at least 20 minutes, four times a week.

No matter how carefully you eat, it is still important to raise your resting heart rate.

There's nothing like exercise to help you reduce weight, maintain optimum insulin levels and stay healthy.

COOKING OILS THAT ARE BETTER FOR YOU

Instead of cooking with melted butter or margarine, use fats that are liquid at room temperature—such as corn oil or canola oil. They contain fewer trans fatty acids, which can raise cholesterol levels. *Also:* Choose softer fats— like soft margarines—instead of the harder ones when you need something to spread.

Alice Lichtenstein, DSc, associate professor of nutrition, Human Nutrition Research Center, Tufts University, Boston, and author of the American Heart Association dietary guidelines on trans fatty acids.

WHY FIBER WORKS

Eating high-fiber food can help you lose weight. Fiber may bind with protein and fat, making the body less able to absorb them. People who ate the most fiber absorbed less protein and fat. And doubling the amount of fiber eaten from 18 to 36 grams a day will prevent absorption of up to 130 calories from other foods.

David Baer, PhD, research physiologist at the USDA's Human Nutrition Research Center, Beltsville, MD.

Best Tasting Fat-Free Foods

Here are the best tasting of all the fat-free foods. *Baked goods:* Entenmann's Fat-Free Light Raspberry Twist. *Cheese:* Kraft Free Singles, American Flavor...Healthy Choice Fat-Free Mozzarella. *Cold cuts:* Louis Rich Free No-Fat Oven-Roasted Turkey Breast...Oscar Mayer Fat-Free Bologna. *Ice cream/ frozen yogurt:* Edy's Fat-Free Vanilla...Häagen-Dazs fat-free yogurts. *Chips and snacks:* Nabisco Pretzel Air Crisps...Louise's Fat-Free Caramel Corn.

Ann Russell, editor, *Living Fit,* 21100 Erwin St., Woodland Hills, CA 91367.

Lower-Fat Peanut Butter Sandwiches

Use only one teaspoon of regular peanut butter per sandwich for a low-fat meal—or one tablespoon for moderate fat. *Great-tasting variations:* Add two slices of fat-free or low-fat cheese…a mashed banana…fruits like sliced strawberries, raspberries, blueberries, raisins or dried cranberries…or fat-free or reduced-fat cream cheese.

Lowfat Cooking for Dummies by **Lynn Fischer.** IDG Books. She is the founder of the National Women's Health Awareness Forum, Washington, DC.

Reduced-Fat Gravy

Use a fat separator to skim the fat from pan juices. Add some nonfat chicken broth and evaporated nonfat milk mixed with flour to thicken the gravy. *For added flavor:* A splash of sherry.

Low-Fat Living Cookbook by **Leslie L. Cooper.** Rodale Books. She is a nutrition and health educator, Ann Arbor, MI.

How Yogurt Can Be Less Fattening

Avoid fruit-on-the-bottom yogurt. The fruit is often in the form of jam—which can contain almost as much sugar as a can of soda. *Alternative:* Plain fat-free yogurt that doesn't contain fruit. Add fresh berries or use two teaspoons of fat-free hot chocolate powder to make a chocolate yogurt.

Stephen Gullo, PhD, a psychologist in New York City and author of *Thin Tastes Better: Control Your Food Triggers Without Feeling Deprived.* Dell.

Fidget Factor

We all know lucky folks who stay slim even when they overeat. *A study from the Mayo Clinic reveals their secret:* They burn excess calories by fidgeting—stretching, standing up, moving their legs, etc. The take-home message, say the Mayo researchers, is that every little motion counts toward weight control.

Science.

Lose Belly Fat and Save Your Life

Arthur Agatston, MD, cardiologist and associate professor of medicine, University of Miami School of Medicine, FL, and consultant, National Institutes of Health Clinical Trials Committee, Bethesda, MD. He is author of *The South Beach Diet.* Rodale.

The size of your waist is a better indicator of health risks than your weight. Men whose waists measure more than 40 inches and

HEALTHY ALTERNATIVES TO POPULAR HIGH-FAT FOODS

▶ **Butter and margarine.** Use reduced-fat margarine, light butter or…
For baking: Applesauce, low-fat yogurt, mashed sweet potatoes, puréed fruit, mashed bananas.
For sautéing: Broth or stock…low-fat or fat-free salad dressing…flavored vinegar…fruit juice.

▶ **Mayonnaise and salad dressing.** Use fat-free or low-fat versions…buttermilk…fat-free mayonnaise mixed with nonfat plain yogurt …low-fat or fat-free cottage cheese.

▶ **Ground beef.** Extra-lean (at least 90% fat-free) ground beef… ground turkey breast with less than 10% fat.

▶ **Eggs.** Use egg substitutes or two egg whites (for one egg)…three egg whites, or one whole egg and one or two egg whites (for two eggs).

Karen Bellerson, recipe developer specializing in healthful ingredients, Phoenix, and author of *Low-Fat No-Fat Cookbook.* Avery.

women whose waists measure more than 35 inches usually have excess visceral fat. Large amounts of visceral fat—which wraps around internal organs, such as the heart—greatly increase your risk of diabetes, heart disease, stroke and cancer.

CARBOHYDRATE CONNECTION

Diet is the key to reducing visceral fat—specifically, a diet that contains little or no refined carbohydrates.

The carbohydrates that dominate the typical American diet—white bread, pasta, cereal, snack foods, cakes, cookies, candies, etc.—are stripped of fiber during processing. These foods are quickly digested and absorbed as glucose, the form that sugar takes in the bloodstream.

The body must produce ever-increasing amounts of insulin to remove excess glucose and fat from the blood. Elevated levels of insulin promote fat storage in the abdomen.

High insulin levels end up removing too much glucose from the blood. The resulting low blood sugar, called *reactive hypoglycemia*, triggers food cravings. The more you give in to the cravings, the more weight you gain.

I have developed a three-phase plan that reduces insulin resistance and food cravings without dramatic calorie reductions. People typically lose eight to 13 pounds in the first two weeks and one to two pounds a week thereafter.

PHASE 1

For 14 days, eat all the lean meat, chicken, turkey and seafood you want. Eliminate refined carbohydrates—bread, pasta, rice, baked goods, candy and alcohol. These foods have high glycemic indexes. The glycemic index measures the amount by which a specific food raises blood glucose levels.

Eliminating these foods for 14 days reduces cravings for carbohydrates and helps normalize glucose levels. Eventually, you will be able to add some high-glycemic foods back into your diet.

Fruits and root vegetables such as carrots and potatoes also have high glycemic indexes and should be avoided in this phase. You can have as much as you want of other vegetables. To find the glycemic index of various foods, go to *www.telus planet.net/public/dgarneau/health3b.htm.*

You also can have mono- and poly-unsaturated fats, such as olive and canola oils. These satisfy appetite, reduce food cravings and help lower levels of harmful triglycerides and LDL cholesterol—key risk factors in people with large stores of visceral fat.

Nuts also are allowed. They are filling and contain mainly monounsaturated fats. Nuts are high in calories, so limit yourself to about 15 almonds or cashews, 30 pistachios or 12 peanuts (technically a legume) daily.

Don't worry about overeating. Eat until you're satisfied—you'll still lose weight. Most of the weight loss that occurs during this phase will come from your midsection.

PHASE 2

During week three, you can reintroduce refined carbohydrates into your diet. Your body will respond more normally to insulin's effects. You can allow yourself a small serving of bread, pasta, potatoes or rice twice a day. Cookies, cakes, candy, alcohol and snack foods, such as potato chips, still should be avoided.

Continue to focus on foods that have low glycemic indexes. Foods that are rich in fiber, such as brown rice, whole-grain breads, etc., have the lowest glycemic numbers because they are digested slowly and release glucose into the bloodstream gradually.

Helpful: Prepare foods whole, or chop them as coarsely as possible. The more work the stomach has to do to digest the food, the more slowly glucose enters the bloodstream. Finely chopped foods—shredded potatoes in hash browns, for example—allow glucose to enter the bloodstream more quickly. Whole fruit is better than juice for the same reason.

Other Phase 2 strategies…

▣ Fat fish at least twice a week.

The omega-3 fatty acids in fish have been shown to reduce heart attack and stroke risk. Salmon, mackerel and herring are particularly rich in omega-3s.

▣ Eat a high-protein breakfast.

Morning protein suppresses food cravings and promotes weight loss. People who skip breakfast experience morning drops in blood glucose that trigger cravings. They also tend to eat more calories during the day. A study of teenagers found that those who ate sugary breakfast cereals consumed 80% more calories over the following five hours than those who ate omelettes.

Try an omelette with cheese or vegetables, such as asparagus or broccoli, or have Canadian bacon, turkey bacon, low-fat cottage cheese or farmer cheese.

■ **Snack when you're hungry.**
Always try to keep some food in your stomach. It is the best way to prevent sudden food cravings.

Rather than grabbing fast foods that are high in glucose-raising carbohydrates, try cheese sticks or a serving of sugar-free yogurt. These foods are ideal because they provide appetite-suppressing protein with very little sugar.

PHASE 3

This is the maintenance phase of the diet. Once you have reached your desired weight, continue to limit refined carbohydrates to keep food cravings under control, minimize insulin resistance and maintain low levels of visceral fat.

Take-It-Off and Keep-It-Off Diet Magic

Susan Estrich, JD, a professor of law and political science at University of Southern California and a syndicated newspaper columnist. She is author of *Making the Case for Yourself: A Diet Book for Smart Women.* Riverhead.

For most of my adult life, I have been disciplined and have reached almost every career goal that I set for myself.

Examples: I was a law clerk for Supreme Court Justice John Paul Stevens...I was the first woman to run a presidential campaign...I became a tenured professor at Harvard Law School...I was the first female editor of Harvard Law Review...I have written several books—and I'm not even 50 years old.

Yet I haven't been able to resist a pastry—a weakness that caused my weight to balloon several years ago by 40 pounds.

Then I realized that I could use the same disciplined strategies that helped me succeed in my career to lose weight and keep off the pounds.

CHANGING YOUR MIND

My wake-up call occurred in the dressing room of a clothing store. I was 40 years old, and 40 pounds overweight. I had been a size 10 before my son was born a few months earlier, but I had grown to a size 14.

I had been on diets for most of my life, but I was still heavier than I wanted to be.

In that dressing room, I decided that losing weight was not just important—it was going to be my top priority. I knew that I had the power and determination to do it.

I decided I would approach my diet the same way I approached everything else in my life—as if it were a career objective. In just five months, I lost the 40 pounds.

Like many adults, I used to approach dieting with the mind-set of a teenager. I ate the latest fad diet foods...set my weight-loss goals too high...restricted my calories too much...bought all the trendy weight-loss gadgets...and overexercised—*and burned out.*

I threw common sense to the wind. I risked my health and sanity to lose a few pounds, only to gain them back.

The secret of weight loss: Any healthful diet will work if you stick to it. The key is getting your mind to go along with your diet. How you think about dieting and exercise is more important than what you eat and how you feel.

MY BIG DIETING ADVANTAGE

At work, you assess a situation critically. You do some research, brainstorm strategies, set reasonable goals and come up with a plan.

When the plan goes awry, you adjust it. You don't give up. You don't blame others—at least not if you want to succeed. Instead, you take responsibility and move forward.

Example: I used to blame my weight on my lack of discipline. That was ridiculous because I am nothing if not disciplined at work.

■ Make a contract with yourself.

Declare your weight-loss intentions—in writing, as if you were writing a memo or a contract outlining the terms of a project.

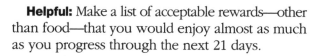

Start with a 21-day commitment. Why 21 days? Because that's how long experts say it takes for a new behavior pattern to take root.

Memos and contracts are good because they are binding. What you declare on paper you are obligated to accomplish. Memos also make you think out whether your goals are reasonable and achievable.

THE DIET CONTRACT

■ Mission statement.

Describe exactly what you agree to do over the next three weeks.

> *Example: I promised to follow a low-calorie diet for 21 days. I promised to devote one hour every day, for each of the 21 days, to exercise. I even promised to mark the scheduled hour on the days of my calendar right away.*

The diet you choose to follow isn't important as long as it is healthful and low in calories—but not less than 1,200 calories a day.

Your attitude is the key to your success, not the specific diet.

■ Planning statement.

Devise a statement that covers how you plan to cope with hazardous situations—parties, office birthday cakes and family gatherings.

> *Example: I promised myself to plan in advance for every event that involves eating over the next 21 days. I wrote that I considered my diet a valid and legitimate reason to decide not to go somewhere.*

■ Reward clause.

We often eat the wrong foods in an attempt to reward ourselves. Or we do it because we have nothing better to do with our time.

Helpful: Make a list of acceptable rewards—other than food—that you would enjoy almost as much as you progress through the next 21 days.

> *Example: After one week on my diet, I rewarded myself with a new book. After two weeks, a massage.*

■ Evening eating component.

Most of us break our diets at night, eating 70% of our calories after 5 pm.

Devise strategies that will help you to circumvent junk-food eating.

> *Example: I promised myself to stop eating by 8:30 pm on weekdays and 9:30 pm on weekends.*

■ Cheating clause.

A promise not to cheat doesn't mean much.

But a promise to cheat only after giving the situation thought has a chance of acting as a deterrent.

> *Example: I promised to write down why I was going to eat a muffin or chips or cookies before eating them. In most cases, writing down my answers gave me just enough time to catch myself and give up the craving.*

■ Nonderailment clause.

We've all cheated on diets and let slipups ruin our days or diets.

Make that reaction unacceptable behavior.

> *Example: I wrote that if I cheated, I would not use it as an excuse to abandon my diet. When I strayed, I resumed my strict adherence to the 21-day plan as if I had never cheated.*

The 21-day diet is just the start of a weight-loss regimen. Continue on the course...and remind yourself of your goals. Your workplace skills will prod you to lose the weight—and keep it off.

An Old-Fashioned Approach to Weight Loss

Jamison Starbuck, ND, naturopathic physician in family practice and a lecturer at the University of Montana, both in Missoula. She is past president of the American Association of Naturopathic Physicians and a contributing editor to *The Alternative Advisor: The Complete Guide to Natural Therapies and Alternative Treatments.* Time Life.

When it comes to weight loss, I'm old-fashioned. Diet pills and fad diets—including the high-protein regimen that's now popular—seldom bring lasting weight loss. Worse, they can damage your heart, liver and kidneys.

In my experience, the only things that work for weight loss are smart food choices...regular exercise ...and a commitment to your emotional well-being.

Here's the eating plan I recommend to my patients who want to lose weight...

▶ **Eat only whole foods.** I'm talking about fresh fruits and vegetables, whole grains and beans— things that still look pretty much the way they did the day they were harvested.

▶ **Avoid packaged and fast foods, refined sugar and flour.** That means no bread—not even whole-grain bread—no pasta and no baked goods. Instead, eat brown or wild rice, barley, oats and whole-grain hot cereals.

▶ **Eat at least two pieces of fruit per day.** At least one of these should be a citrus fruit.

▶ **Eat at least four daily servings of vegetables.** Two of these servings should be raw vegetables. Raw carrots, cucumber, radish and celery make good choices.

▶ **Avoid salty foods.** No pickles, chips, soy sauce, etc. If you really crave salt, have no more than a dash.

▶ **Avoid dairy products.** That means no cheese, cottage cheese, ice cream or milk—even skim milk. The only exception I permit is plain low-fat or nonfat yogurt with live bacterial cultures— up to eight ounces a day.

▶ **Avoid red meat and chicken.** They contain far too much fat for weight loss to occur. Four ounces of turkey or fish per day are permitted.

▶ **Limit oil intake to two tablespoons of olive or flax oil per day.**

▶ **Drink at least 60 ounces of water per day.** Bottled spring water is best. Or—you can buy a charcoal or reverse-osmosis filter for your tap.

▶ **Drink digestion-enhancing tea.** Each day, have one to three cups of green, dandelion, burdock, yellow dock or chamomile tea.

I also urge my overweight patients to become more physically vigorous. If you're not much of an athlete, walking is often the best approach. I've seen people lose 75 pounds simply by adding a 20-minute walk to their daily routines.

Successful weight loss also requires mental and emotional balance. Too often we use food as a substitute for other needs—affection, creativity and play. A psychologist friend of mine teaches a course called "Feeding the Hunger Within." Her title captures the essence of what weight loss is really all about for many people. Many of my patients have found her approach—understanding the emotional roots of overeating—to be remarkably effective.

If you're having trouble losing weight on your own, look for a counselor who specializes in weight loss and body image issues. Or pick up a copy of *Overcoming Overeating* by Jane R. Hirschmann, MSW, and Carol H. Munter (Fawcett Books). This self-help book can help you understand the link between emotions and diet.

Remember, if you have heart or kidney disease, diabetes, asthma, arthritis or any other chronic condition, consult a doctor before beginning any weight-loss program.

Don't Let Pets Get Overweight

Overweight pets are more likely to have health problems—just like overweight people. Fat pets get arthritis at a younger age...are more likely to have trouble with inherited problems...and have a higher incidence of diabetes and liver and bladder disease. *Solution:* Give low-fat treats sparingly— break them into small pieces and offer them one at a time. Make sure your pet gets exercise—ask your veterinarian how much walking or other exercise is safe and desirable.

Alison Knox, DVM, veterinarian in private practice, South Burlington, VT.

Sports and Fitness Savvy

Chapter 9

How to Get Back in Shape—Realistically

Most Americans are not as physically fit as they could be—and should be. Only 40% of adults engage in some form of moderate activity each week. About 50% of us are totally sedentary.

Moderate exercise can stave off many of the effects of aging and improve your quality of life. Those who are physically fit are less depressed, feel ill less often and have a better self-image and a more positive attitude toward life.

Exercise need not be strenuous or overly time-consuming. My exercise program is easy to perform, represents a realistic level of activity for most people and minimizes the risk of musculoskeletal injury.

BEFORE YOU START
■ Get your doctor's approval.
Make sure your doctor endorses any form of exercise program that you intend to start.

Ideally, your doctor should perform a physical examination that includes both a resting and a stress electrocardiogram. These tests should be repeated every three years or as often as your doctor recommends.

■ Start out slowly.
In my experience, when people over the age of 40 suit up to work out after a period of inactivity, the first thoughts that enter their minds are memories of their school-age athletics.

These memories of a trim, fit youth can be dangerous if they propel you to mimic the athletic routine you had as a student.

Important: Don't rush into exercise. It may have taken you 20 years to get out of shape. If you try to get back into shape in 20 days, you can injure yourself. Plunging into activity too fast can even be potentially fatal.

Kenneth Cooper, MD, MPH, who invented aerobics in 1968 and who founded Cooper Aerobics Center, 12200 Preston Rd., Dallas 75230. He is author of numerous books, including *Faith-Based Fitness* and *Can Stress Heal?*, both from Thomas Nelson.

Aim for 30 minutes of moderate-intensity exercise, four or more days a week.

Even an exercise program that is that modest offers significant health and longevity benefits.

Moving from a sedentary lifestyle to exercising at moderate intensity has been shown to reduce the risk of death from all causes by 58% over a 10-year period.

Try to stay active for the entire period outlined, but even breaking up the workout into 10- or 15-minute sessions has health benefits.

You can also count everyday activities, such as walking the dog, cleaning the house and gardening vigorously toward your 30-minute goal.

THE 40-PLUS PROGRAM

Walking is a great activity. I've created a six-week walking program for my patients at the Cooper Aerobics Center that is ideal for men and women over age 40.

Note: Walking five times per week is appropriate at first because speed is quite slow. Once you walk faster than 20 minutes per mile, frequency can decrease to four times per week.

▶ **WEEK 1: Walk one mile in 24 minutes...**five times a week. Ideally, try to walk first thing in the morning—exercise tends to be most consistent when it is performed before breakfast.

Start out at a normal walking speed. As the weeks progress, you'll be able to increase your speed to match the set time limits.

If it is not possible to walk in the morning, take a brisk walk an hour or two after dinner. Bring your spouse along...or a friend...or your dog.

▶ **WEEK 2: Walk one mile in 22 minutes...**five times a week.

▶ **WEEK 3: Walk one mile in 20 minutes...**five times a week.

▶ **WEEK 4: Walk one-and-a-half miles in 30 minutes...**five times a week.

▶ **WEEK 5: Walk one-and-a-half miles in 29 minutes...**five times a week.

▶ **WEEK 6: Walk two miles in less than 40 minutes...**five times a week.

ADVANCED PROGRAM

At the end of six weeks, if you haven't developed any musculoskeletal problems, you may wish to move on to a more vigorous regimen...

▶ **WEEK 7: Walk two miles in 38 minutes...** four times a week.

▶ **WEEK 8: Walk two miles in 36 minutes...** four times a week.

▶ **WEEK 9: Walk two miles in less than 35 minutes...**four times a week.

If you'd like to vary your routine, try another type of activity besides walking. Alternatives such as cross-country skiing, swimming and cycling offer equal health benefits.

STRENGTH TRAINING

It's critical to maintain total fitness—not just aerobic fitness—as you age. That means you also need to work out with handheld weights or weight machines or perform calisthenics.

With strength training, you'll also substantially improve your flexibility and coordination and reduce your risk of injury.

> **Example:** *Thanks to strength training, at 66 years of age I can ski continuously for five to six hours. Before I started lifting weights, I'd have to stop and rest after two hours because of intense burning in my quadriceps.*

Although we lose muscle mass as we get older, a now-famous Tufts University study has shown that muscle mass can be rebuilt by engaging in strength training.

For strength training, I recommend a circuit program in which you utilize at least 10 different stations, lifting at 65% of your maximum capacity, 10 to 12 repetitions in 30 seconds. Rest 30 seconds between stations. Two complete cycles in 30 minutes twice weekly will result in considerable muscle strengthening and training.

As you age, however, you need to increase the percentage of time that you spend strength training and lessen your aerobic activity. *Here are my ratios...*

▶ **In your 40s:** Spend 70% of your weekly exercise regimen doing aerobic activity/30% of the time doing strength training.

Example: Walk for 30 minutes five days a week, and strength train two days a week.

▶ **In your 50s:** 60% aerobic exercise/40% strength training.

Example: Walk four days a week, and perform strength training three days a week.

▶ **In your 60s and 70s:** 50% aerobic exercise/ 50% strength training.

Example: Walk three days a week, and strength train three days a week.

You can strength train on the same days you perform aerobic activity or on alternate days.

EXERCISE SAFETY

To prevent injury and cardiac arrhythmias that can occur with intense exercise, it is important to carefully observe good exercise skills, no matter what your age. *Follow these three basic guidelines...*

▦ Warm up for three to five minutes before stretching.

Then stretch out for three or four minutes before exercising.

Stretching the Achilles tendons and the hamstrings should always be included in a warmup.

Important: Many people age 60 or older injure their hamstrings and Achilles tendons when they stretch because their bodies aren't as supple as they used to be. So I encourage them to walk for about one-quarter mile before stretching.

▦ Cool down for five minutes after working out.

Just keep walking around slowly.

Don't lie down, or go right into your car and drive away. And never go directly into a sauna or steam room after exercising. The dramatic heat increase can cause heart problems right after exercise.

▦ Do enough—but not too much.

Moderation is the key...and avoid dehydration.

How do you know if your exercise routine is too strenuous for you?

At the end of your five-minute cool-down, take your pulse for 15 seconds and then multiply that number by four.

▶ **If you're between ages 40 and 50:** The number should be less than 120.

▶ **If you're over age 50:** The number should be less than 100.

SAVE MONEY AT THE HEALTH CLUB

Best way to use a health club: Join a chain—many individual clubs have gone bankrupt, leaving members stranded. Start with a monthly membership—half the people who join fitness clubs drop out within six months. Find out about different classes of membership—some clubs charge less if you give up use of certain facilities or features. Ask about off-peak discounts. Read the contract carefully, looking for escape clauses—for instance, if you move or become disabled.

Jon Robert Steinberg, senior finance editor, *New Choices,* 28 W. 23 St., New York City 10010.

EXERCISE ALWAYS HELPS

Exercise does not wear out bodies. We should all exercise more…farther and faster are better, but not beyond our limits. Exercise does not reduce life span. Athletes who die young generally die from one of the usual causes of premature death—alcohol or drug abuse, congenital abnormalities, auto accidents. Star college athletes who become sedentary live no longer than anyone else. But people who start exercising later in life seem to gain many of the same benefits as lifelong exercisers. *Bottom line:* Exercise improves health no matter when you start.

Ralph S. Paffenbarger, Jr., MD, professor emeritus of epidemiology, Stanford University School of Medicine, Stanford, CA, leader of an ongoing study of 52,000 men who entered college between 1916 and 1950.

EXERCISE EVERY DAY

Build physical activity into your everyday life—do not make it something extra to add to an already crowded schedule. *Helpful:* During working hours, take short walks instead of coffee breaks…walk at least part of the way up or down in office buildings…park farther away from the office, or from a store when shopping…walk every day at lunch time…stand and move around while talking on the phone.

Bob Anderson, physical education instructor, Palmer Lakes, CO, and author of *Stretching at Your Computer or Desk*. Publishing Group West.

The Busy Person's Exercise Guide

James M. Rippe, MD, associate professor of medicine at Tufts University School of Medicine in Boston and director of the Rippe Lifestyle Institute, 21 N. Quinsigamond Ave., Shrewsbury, MA 01545. He is author of *Fit Over 40* (Quill) and *Fit for Success* (Random House).

Most of us want to exercise on a regular basis, but our busy schedules always seem to get in the way.

Yet a few years ago, when I surveyed Fortune 500 CEOs for my book *Fit for Success,* I was surprised to find that those busy executives were three times more likely than others to exercise.

Two-thirds said they engaged in aerobic exercise at least three times a week. Why? Because it reduces stress…gives them energy…enhances their health…and, of course, boosts their productivity.

Lesson: If people with such crammed schedules and levels of responsibility find time for physical activity, anyone can.

YOU MAY BE EXERCISING TOO HARD

The good news is that you don't have to schedule strenuous aerobic exercise sessions to enhance your health.

Minimum exercise guidelines were introduced by the Centers for Disease Control and Prevention and the American College of Sports Medicine in 1995. All adults should accumulate 30 minutes or more of moderate-intensity physical activity on most—if not all—days of the week.

This activity should be continuous in motion and strenuous enough to make you breathe at least a little faster.

Adjectives that describe the intensity you should strive for include "brisk" and "determined." A leisurely stroll doesn't qualify.

Convenient: Break exercise activity into 10- to 15-minute segments throughout the day.

You can count everyday activities, such as taking care of your house and garden…walking the dog…and climbing the stairs.

FINDING THE TIME

I've found that many people set up barriers to exercise. Only when you learn how to overcome these obstacles will you find it easy to fit physical activity into your busy daily schedule. *Follow these steps...*

Stop thinking you don't have time for exercise.

Be honest with yourself about your excuses, and look for strategies to counter them.

> *Example: If you loathe exercise, ask yourself why. If it's because it takes too long, find a more convenient gym—or work out at home. If you don't like being out of breath, start out with activities that don't require much exertion.*

If you follow the new moderate-intensity guidelines, you'll only be slightly winded and you shouldn't feel pain.

If you feel too tired to exercise—another big excuse—take a brisk walk or perform another physical activity to revive you.

You might even schedule exercise to coincide with your post-lunch energy slump—and boost your afternoon productivity.

Find an activity you enjoy.

Exercise doesn't have to mean an aerobics class or a highly competitive game of tennis.

> *Example: You might find, as many do, that you enjoy hitting a tennis ball against a wall...or playing doubles tennis, which will let you socialize with others. Or you might better tolerate walking on a treadmill if you combine it with watching television, listening to tapes or reading.*

Be on the lookout for exercise opportunities in your daily life.

Walk part of the way to work each day.

Take the stairs instead of the elevator. Walk over and hand-deliver messages to colleagues at the office instead of over the phone or by E-mail.

Find an activity that you can perform consistently.

It should be something that easily fits in with the rest of your life.

> *Example: Walking is an ideal activity for everyone because there are so many opportunities to do it.*

A BUSY PERSON'S DAILY WORKOUT

▶ **In the morning, walk for 10 minutes before breakfast.** Walk at a determined four-mile-per-hour pace. To approximate that pace, stride as though you are late for an appointment and can't waste time.

▶ **At lunch, take a 10-minute walk**—again at four miles per hour—with a coworker before you go back to your job.

▶ **In the evening, walk for 10 minutes** at the same speed as in the morning.

▶ **On the weekends, add gardening to your list.** Or, mow the lawn, perform home repairs, play golf, play tag or catch with your children and add Frisbee or any other leisure activity that will require continuous movement as you work toward your 30-minutes-a-day goal.

DON'T LET HOLIDAYS DISTRACT YOU FROM YOUR GOAL

A holiday exercise program will prevent you from spending the first months of the new year trying to regain fitness. Many people stop exercising as shopping, parties and vacations crowd the holiday season. That leads to substantial loss of cardiovascular fitness in just two weeks. Once fitness levels drop, it takes three times as long to get them back. *Self-defense:* Reduce exercise frequency instead of stopping completely. If you cannot keep up full intensity, stay at 70% to 75% of your maximum. This will limit deconditioning and make it easier to get back on track in the new year.

Rick Gerwin, MS, exercise physiologist, Good Samaritan Fitness Center, Oakbrook Terrace, IL.

Stretching Exercises for Happier, Healthier Posture

Leonard McGill, DC, director of Life Chiropractic Center in Salt Lake City. He is author of *The Chiropractor's Health Book: Simple Natural Exercises for Relieving Headaches, Tension and Back Pain.* Crown.

By practicing a few easy exercises every day, you'll get your body used to the correct position for good posture and strengthen your back muscles. You'll even reduce tension and improve your health.

EXERCISE ONE

Repeat this exercise 30 times in a row at a relatively quick pace...

▶ **Sit in a chair with your back straight,** and imagine the bottom of your jaw parallel to the floor. Keep shoulders down, as if someone is pressing on them.

▶ **Gently pull your chin straight back.** Your head and neck should be aligned, and you should feel tension underneath your skull at the back of your neck. This is the proper position for good posture.

▶ **Hold for five seconds,** relax and repeat.

EXERCISE TWO

Practice a few times daily...

▶ **Stand against a wall,** with head straight and shoulders down as if someone is pressing on them. Place your heels against the wall.

▶ **Try to get rid of all the space behind your neck, lower back and knees** by pressing your body against the wall. Keep your head straight.

▶ **Step away from the wall.** Your body will be naturally aligned.

EXERCISE THREE

▶ **Get on the floor on all fours, keeping your back straight.** Stretch out your left arm in front of you and your right leg behind you.

▶ **Lift your outstretched arm and leg toward the sky** and hold them there for three breaths.

▶ **Relax.** Switch to your right arm and left leg, and repeat the exercise. This exercise should be repeated three times for each side.

Benefits of Walking With a Weighted Vest

Walking with a weighted vest can turn a stroll into a brisk workout. Vests with weighted pockets are available at sporting-goods stores for $50 and up. The vest balances weight evenly, helping pull shoulders down and back—giving you more erect posture. Walking with a vest works most major muscle groups. Add wrist weights to tone arms. *Bonus:* Walking is a weight-bearing exercise that can stimulate bones to maintain calcium content—reducing the risk of osteoporosis in later life.

Viisha Sedlak, national director, American Walking Association, Box 4, Paonia, CO 81428.

SHORT WORKOUTS OK

Several short workouts can be just as beneficial to the heart as one long one. *Recent finding:* Three 30-minute jogging sessions in a single day were just as effective at controlling triglyceride levels as a single 90-minute jog.

Jason Gill, exercise physiologist, Human Muscle Metabolism Research Group, Loughborough University, Loughborough, Leicestershire, England. His study of 18 men was published in *Medicine and Science in Sports and Exercise,* 3500 Camp Bowie Blvd., Fort Worth, TX 76107.

Walk Your Way to Better Health—Physical, Mental, Emotional, Too

Sara Wilcox, PhD, assistant professor, department of exercise science, School of Public Health, University of South Carolina, Columbia.

Walking is one of the best forms of exercise. Anyone can do it…it's easy to fit into your lifestyle…and it doesn't overly tax the body. Also—you don't need any special equipment…and you are more likely to stick with it.

Important: You can achieve both physical and mental benefits from walking on a regular basis.

WALKING FOR PHYSICAL HEALTH

There is impressive scientific evidence to show that people can substantially improve their health when they go from being sedentary to being even moderately active.

The benefits of going from a moderate to a strenuous level of activity are also significant but probably not as crucial.

Walking at a brisk pace is a great form of moderate activity. It improves your cardiovascular functioning…and strengthens your bones and muscles.

Walking also lowers your risk of heart attack and stroke…helps you lose weight…and improves your blood pressure and cholesterol levels.

Beware: Leisurely walking, while pleasant and excellent for getting started and forming a health routine, probably does not offer substantial health benefits. Walk at a determined clip to make significant strides in your health.

The Surgeon General and the Centers for Disease Control and Prevention recommend that all adults get 30 minutes or more of moderate-intensity exercise most days of the week.

Here's a walking program that is used in our research that will help you achieve that goal…

Important: Don't progress to the next week's level if you have aches or pains. Remain at the level at which you feel comfortable but challenged.

▶ **WEEK ONE:** Walk for 20 minutes at a brisk pace, as if you were late for an appointment. Do it for five days the first week. You may be slightly out of breath, but you should still be able to carry on a conversation. In heart-rate terms, you should be walking at 60% of your maximum heart rate.

To calculate your maximum heart rate: Subtract your age from 220. Multiply that number by the percentage target heart rate you're trying to reach.

Example: 220 minus 45 years old equals 175. Multiply 175 times 0.60, and you get 105 beats per minute.

To measure your heart rate: Place your middle and index fingers on your wrist and find your pulse. While looking at a watch with a second hand, count the beats for 15 seconds. Start with zero as the first beat you feel. Multiply the beats you count by 4 to find your beats per minute.

▶ **WEEKS TWO and THREE:** Increase your duration of activity to 30 minutes, five days a week, at 60% of your maximum heart rate.

▶ **WEEK FOUR:** Increase the intensity of your walking to 65% of your maximum heart rate. Continue to walk 30 minutes, five days a week.

▶ **WEEK FIVE:** Increase the intensity to 70% of your maximum heart rate, 30 minutes, five days a week.

▶ **WEEK SIX and BEYOND:** Pick the pace up to 75% of your maximum heart rate, 30 minutes, five days a week.

If you are inactive or have any health problems, start walking at a lower intensity and build your program more gradually. Always consult your physician before beginning an exercise program.

WALKING FOR MENTAL HEALTH

Sedentary people often say that walking is boring. But this belief need not be true. It is important that you find your own ways of making walking interesting and fun.

Some people like to walk with a partner to socialize. Other people use this time to think through their days and set goals for tomorrow. Still others like to escape from daily hassles by listening to music or books on tape. It is important to choose whatever works best for you.

Walking and other forms of exercise can offer a "time-out" from your problems.

Research shows that walking helps to reduce stress and improve mood. Walks can also be used as ideal problem-solving sessions. *Example...*

▶ **STEP ONE:** Identify a problem to solve. Be clear about what is bothering you about the situation.

▶ **STEP TWO:** Identify what you would like to see happen in this situation. Make your solutions specific and realistic.

▶ **STEP THREE:** If the problem is one that is long-standing, think through the obstacles you need to overcome to resolve it.

▶ **STEP FOUR:** Isolate the steps you need to take to resolve the problem.

▶ **STEP FIVE:** Rehearse what you plan to say to the other person involved in the problem.

▶ **STEP SIX:** Visualize your delivery of this message and the person's response—and then modify the script.

WALKING Q&A

Q: Is walking on a treadmill just as beneficial as walking outdoors? Absolutely. In some ways, a treadmill has certain advantages. You can walk no matter what the weather or time of day...you

can get a readout on how fast and far you go ...and you can watch television or a video for distraction.

> ***Example:*** *Collage Video (800-433-6769) offers tapes that make it seem as if you're walking on roads in different parts of the world.*

As with the outdoor program we recommend, begin your treadmill walking program at an easy pace. Gradually increase your speed so that by week six you're walking at 75% of your maximum heart rate for 30 minutes, five days a week. You can, of course, mix and match treadmill and outdoor walking sessions.

You can also use the incline feature to mimic outdoor conditions...increase your heart rate...and work off more calories. Start on a flat surface and then progressively raise the grade.

Important: If you experience discomfort—pain or labored breathing—reduce the inclined angle of the treadmill.

You can also use programmed cycles, which feature different preset inclines and intensities.

Avoid built-in programs that are only 20 minutes long—including the warm-up and cool-down. You want to get at least 20 minutes of activity at your goal heart rate.

Q: Is it worthwhile to carry weights on your arms or legs while walking? I don't recommend wearing ankle weights. They place too much stress on your knee and ankle joints and can injure them.

Light (one- to two-pound) handheld or wrist weights can be beneficial, once you have an established walking program. They help to increase your heart rate. Swing your arms normally as you stride to get your heart rate up...burn extra calories...and give your upper body a workout.

Q: What types of walking injuries are most likely to occur—and how can they be prevented?
One of the great things about walking is that major injuries aren't common. Those that do occur are sprains or twisted ankles…shinsplints…pulled muscles…and blisters on the feet.

To avoid injuries, warm up for each session by walking at a slow pace for five minutes. Then stretch for 5 to 10 minutes before walking for 20 to 30 minutes at your desired heart rate.

After walking, repeat the slow-paced walking and stretching routine to cool down your body and muscles. While walking, don't push yourself beyond your comfort level.

Wear appropriate walking shoes that offer good foot and ankle support…have ample cushioning…and aren't so constricting that they cause blisters and calluses.

COLD WEATHER SMARTS

When exercising outdoors in cold weather, drink plenty of fluids. Although it may seem that you don't sweat as much as in the summer, winter winds quickly evaporate perspiration. *Also:* You lose more water with each breath…heavier clothing makes you perspire more…and people tend to produce more urine in cold weather. *Bottom line:* Drink 16 ounces of water or other plain fluids two hours before exercising—and four to six ounces every 15 to 20 minutes during exercise.

Edmund Burke, PhD, director of exercise science, University of Colorado, Colorado Springs, whose study of fluid loss among skiers was published in the *Penn State Sports Medicine Newsletter.*

Fast Stretches when You Are Too Busy To Limber Up

Beth Barrow, a former ballerina who has been dancing professionally for more than 13 years.

■ The butterfly.
Sit on the floor. Put the bottoms of your feet together so that your knees are bent and open in a butterfly position. With the soles of your feet together, gently slide your feet close to your body. Then slowly curl your upper body forward and over your legs. Exhale as you bend forward into the stretch. Hold the position for four seconds. Then slowly sit up. Repeat this exercise eight times.

Muscles stretched: The backs of your legs and torso.

■ The sitting "L."
Remain on the floor. Place your legs straight out together in front of you. Sit up so your back is perpendicular to your legs. Your body should form an L shape. Reach your hands out toward your toes, head down as close to your knees as possible. Hold this position for 10 seconds. Sit back up. Repeat this exercise eight times.

Muscles stretched: Back, shoulders and legs.

■ The standing "L."
Stand with your feet parallel to each other, about 10 inches apart. Raise your arms straight up in the air, palms facing each other. Bend forward at your hips so your back is absolutely flat and straight, arms outstretched in an inverted L. While in this position, suck in your stomach and round your back like a Halloween cat. Keep your hips in place. Hold for four seconds. Do this exercise four times.

Muscles stretched: Hamstrings, along the backs of your legs.

■ The reach.
Stand with your left hand on your left hip. Raise your right arm straight over your head. Bend your body slowly toward the left and stretch your right hand. Hold for four seconds. Do not bounce.

Exhale as you stretch. Inhale as you come up. Bend to your left side slowly eight times, then switch arms and bend to your right eight times.

Muscles stretched: Arms, sides of torso and lower back.

Better Power Walking

Warm up by marching in place and doing gentle shoulder, hip, ankle and knee circles. Focus on posture, standing tall with your abdominal muscles contracted, chest lifted, elbows at right angles and arms swinging forward and back. Don't walk with weights. Instead—walk faster and include hills on your course.

Barbara Harris, editor, *Living Fit,* 21100 Erwin St., Woodland Hills, CA 91367.

SAFER EXERCISE BIKES

To avoid injury, watch your form. Do not round your shoulders and back. Keep your chin pulled in…head up and centered over shoulders…and wrists straight. Warm up before exercising—stretch afterward. If you develop back or neck strain, stay off the bike until pain subsides.

Len Kravitz, PhD, associate professor of exercise science, the University of New Mexico, Albuquerque.

EXERCISING WHEN YOU HAVE A COLD

Exercising when you have a cold is all right if you confine yourself to easy workouts—*and* drink lots of fluids while exercising. If you are taking antihistamines, avoid treadmills and barbell squats—coordination may be affected by the medication. Reduce the intensity and duration of your usual workouts.

Peter Bruno, MD, internist in private practice in New York City and team internist for the New York Knicks.

Weight-Lifting Risk

Weight lifting can harm hearing. Overexertion can rupture membranes in the inner ear—which can cause hearing and balance problems. *Self-defense:* When lifting, exhale during the muscle contractions to prevent buildup of potentially damaging ear pressure.

Ross J. Roeser, PhD, director, Callier Center for Communications Disorders, University of Texas at Dallas.

Watch Out for Weight-Lifting Belts

Caution—weight-lifting belts worn during workouts can slow development of abdominal and lower-back muscles. People who do not wear the belts use more of those muscles to balance the load—so they develop more quickly. *Also:* Many people use the belts because they think the belts will prevent injury—but they won't. *Bottom line:* Unless you are lifting exceptionally heavy weights, you'll get a better workout if you don't use a belt.

Sohail Ahmad, MD, longtime weight lifter and chief resident physician in orthopedic surgery, Albany Medical Center, Albany, NY, whose study was presented at a meeting of the American Academy of Orthopedic Surgeons.

WHY REST TIME IS IMPORTANT IN WEIGHT TRAINING

Did you know that you achieve more strength gains from shorter rests during weight training? In one 12-week period, men who took 30-second breaks between sets gained 6% more strength than men who rested for 90 seconds. In women, the additional gain was 12%. *Possible reason:* Less rest may force different muscle fibers into action. *Caution:* Do not suddenly change your between-sets rest time—decrease it gradually over a few weeks.

Frank Kulling, PhD, associate professor, health and human performance, Oklahoma State University, Stillwater, and leader of a study of 55 men and women taking a 12-week resistance training program, published in *Medicine and Science in Sports and Exercise.*

Better Beach Running

Run along the water in an "S" pattern that takes you both close to the surf, where the sand is harder, and higher up the beach, where the softer sand gives a better workout. When you've finished running, swim in the surf for 15 minutes to add a good upper-body workout to your routine.

Ed Burke, PhD, professor, department of exercise science, University of Colorado, Colorado Springs.

Shinsplint Warning

New runners and joggers often get shinsplints —any of several minor but painful injuries to the front of the lower leg. *Treatment:* Ice the area for 20 minutes three times a day...take anti-inflammatory medication, such as aspirin or ibuprofen...do not run if it hurts...stretch calves several times a day to relieve tightness that can contribute to injury. *The good news:* As your legs get used to the exercise, shinsplints won't occur as often.

Julie Colliton, MD, sports medicine specialist in private practice, Frisco, CO.

Shinsplint or Stress Fracture?

Figure out the kind of injury by pushing with fingers on the tender area. Shinsplints and similar injuries cause pain over a broad area. In a stress fracture, the pain is localized at a single spot. *Caution:* If rest and ice do not solve any sports-injury problem within a few days, see a doctor.

Andrew Cosgarea, MD, associate professor of orthopedic surgery, Johns Hopkins University, Baltimore.

Runners—Eat Right

Eat before running—but be sure to eat the right foods. Bananas, apples and whole-grain foods like oatmeal give plenty of energy for a brisk morning workout. But breakfast foods like toast, waffles and cornflakes give only a short-term energy boost. Some people who eat those refined starches before exercising actually tire faster than people who skip breakfast altogether.

John Kirwan, PhD, associate professor of physiology, Case Western Reserve University, Cleveland.

The Truth About Energy Bars

Energy bars won't make you feel more energetic. Those chewy, high-carbohydrate confections can deliver needed energy to people running marathons or involved in other lengthy, high-intensity exercise. But they are not a panacea for stressed-out or worn-out people. And…athletes can find a cheaper source of needed calories.

Bonnie Liebman, MS, director of nutrition at Center for Science in the Public Interest, 1875 Connecticut Ave. NW, Suite 300, Washington, DC 20009.

Best Sports Socks

Choose sports socks carefully for your needs. If you tend to get blisters, consider thicker socks with padded toes. If your feet sweat, get socks made of wicking materials, such as acrylics and synthetics, that draw away moisture. For arch problems, try socks with reinforced arches.

Arnold Ravick, DPM, podiatrist in private practice, Washington, DC.

GIVE YOURSELF A TREAT

Make exercise clothes a reward—not something you buy when starting a fitness program. This helps to associate the clothing with continuing success.

Jeff Galloway, Atlanta–based former Olympic runner and author of *Galloway's Book on Running.* Shelter Publications.

BEST EXERCISE CLOTHING

Synthetic fabrics can be more comfortable than cotton in hot weather. Exercise clothing that is made of fabrics like CoolMax and Supplex is better than cotton at getting sweat away from your body. These synthetics are also lighter than cotton and are usually woven more loosely for extra comfort.

Sarah Bowen Shea, Portland–based sports and gear writer.

How to Combat Jock Itch— Men and Women, Too

The germs that cause jock itch are common in men and women. *To prevent infection:* Keep groin area dry—pat dry after showering, and get out of wet clothes as soon as possible after exercising or swimming…don't use much soap in the groin area—it can make infection worse. *For itching:* Use an over-the-counter powder, such as *Zeasorb-AF* (active ingredient—tolnaftate, an antifungal), which fights the fungus and absorbs moisture. See a dermatologist if it does not improve after a week. *Interesting:* Jock itch and athlete's foot are caused by the same fungus. To minimize transfer from foot to groin, some people put on socks before underwear. But—germs are likely in both places. While jock itch is far less common in women, they should take the same steps to prevent it in themselves and prevent transferring it to their partners.

Neal Schultz, MD, dermatologist in private practice, 1130 Park Ave., New York City 10128.

Safest Bike Helmets

▶ **Do not buy by price**—some inexpensive helmets outperform some costly ones.

▶ **Select a helmet with bright colors**—it will make you more visible.

▶ **Buy a helmet molded in the shell,** the best construction method.

▶ **Good fit is essential for maximum protection.**

▶ **Helmets have stickers indicating which safety standards they meet.** The best safety standard is the Snell Foundation's B-95. *The next best*—Snell's B-90 or the CPSC or ASTM safety standard.

Randy Swart, The Bicycle Helmet Safety Institute, 4611 Seventh St. South, Arlington, VA 22204.

BETTER BICYCLING

▶ **When climbing a hill, mentally break it into small pieces.** Find a landmark ahead of you, and focus on riding to it. Then set a new goal.

▶ **Use a gear that balances the climb between your legs and lungs.** Breathe deeply while pedaling.

▶ **Keep rest stops to two minutes or less.** Straddle the bike while resting—do not get off completely.

▶ **Ride as far right as is comfortable, and stay highly aware of your lane position.** Be prepared to "take the lane" by riding in the middle of the lane if it would be unsafe for cars to pass—especially at tops of hills and on blind curves to the right.

▶ **Use low gears when appropriate** so you can sit while climbing.

Donald Tighe, director of education, League of American Bicyclists, Washington, DC.

SOCCER SHOCKER

Years of "heading" the ball and colliding with other players can cause permanent brain damage, UCLA researchers report. Tests confirm that professional soccer players are more likely than other professional athletes to exhibit impaired memory, planning ability and recognition skills.

Safer Ice Skating

When skating, have kids wear knee pads, elbow guards and bicycle helmets—or at least knitted stocking caps rolled at the bottom. Layer kids in thermal underwear, turtlenecks and sweaters. Don't use gloves with smooth palms— simple knitted gloves, which help kids get up from the ice when they fall, are safer. *Important:* Give children basic skating lessons, including lessons on how to fall. Encourage them to skate slowly until they know the moves and are comfortable on the ice.

Judith Caulfield, executive director, Ice Skating Institute, Buffalo Grove, IL.

Super Swim Goggles

Buy swim goggles with hypoallergenic seals to avoid the raccoonlike rashes often caused by neoprene seals. *Also:* Low-elasticity straps help to prevent the overtightening common with rubber band–type straps. And shatterproof, antifog lenses help avoid injuries.

Barbara Paulsen, editor, *Health*, Two Embarcadero Center, San Francisco 94111.

HEALTH CONCERNS FOR POOL SWIMMERS

Here are some common concerns—and what to do about them…*breathing chlorine vapor from indoor pools with poor ventilation:* Swim outdoors whenever possible. *Athlete's foot from pool decks:* Wear flip-flops instead of going barefoot. *Eye irritation from chlorine in pools:* Do not open eyes under water or swim with contact lenses. *Infections caused by bacteria in pool water:* Be sure pools are properly disinfected, filtered and chemically balanced.

Timothy McCall, MD, a Boston–based internist, medical editor of *Yoga Journal* and author of *Examining Your Doctor: A Patient's Guide to Avoiding Harmful Medical Care*. Citadel Press.

Good for Golfers

Gray sunglass lenses are highly recommended. They allow golfers to retain a true view of the course while protecting against UV light. *Best:* Wraparound lenses to keep out sunlight.

Paul Berman, OD, team optometrist for the New Jersey Devils and an optometrist in private practice in Hackensack, NJ.

Safe In-Line Skating

In-line skating wrist guards only help prevent cuts and scrapes, but not hand or wrist fractures in a high-speed fall. *Helpful:* Practice falling to the side rather than forward onto your outstretched arms. *Also:* Avoid skating on walkways…don't weave in and out of lanes…know how to stop quickly.

Peter Sharkey, MD, orthopedic surgeon, Thomas Jefferson University, Philadelphia, whose study was published in the *American Journal of Sports Medicine*.

WHY YOU SHOULD CHECK YOUR HEART BEFORE SCUBA DIVING

Scuba divers should be screened for a heart defect that could place them at risk for diving-related brain damage. The test checks for *patent foramen ovale* (PFO), a hole between the heart's right and left upper chambers (atria). PFO lets dissolved nitrogen pass into the arterial system. As a diver ascends, expanding nitrogen bubbles can cause brain lesions akin to those seen in strokes. Divers who test positive for PFO should dive less deeply and for shorter periods…and take more decompression stops while ascending.

If you dive—or if you intend to start—ask a neurologist about having echocontrast transcranial Doppler testing to check for this problem.

Stefan Ries, MD, neurologist, University of Heidelberg Medical School, Germany.

Strategies for a Powerful Life

Chapter 10

A Bad Attitude Takes Its Toll

People with negative personalities are at high risk for repeat heart attacks. In a recent study, researchers gave psychological tests to men who had reduced heart function after a heart attack. Patients who tested high on negative emotions—anxiety, insecurity and social inhibitions—were more than four times as likely to have another heart attack within the next decade. *Self-defense:* People with heart disease who frequently feel negative emotions should consider seeking professional advice to help find ways to overcome negative moods.

Robert Carney, PhD, professor of medical psychiatry at Washington University School of Medicine, St. Louis.

Better Stress-Busting

Identify exactly which problems are troubling you instead of trying to deal with stress in general. Identify specific conversations and actions that cause you to feel stress. Neutralize internal causes of stress by challenging stress-producing conversations and disrupting stress-producing actions. *Example:* Try looking at a situation from a different perspective to short-circuit a stressful response.

Morton Orman, MD, internist in private practice in Baltimore, MD, and author of *The 14-Day Stress Cure.* Breakthru Publishing.

Don't Get Stressed

Beware: Heart-attack risk rises the week after a high-pressure deadline or high-stress job event —such as laying someone off. Receiving a promotion also increases stress—and therefore increases the risk of heart attack. *Self-defense:*

Mentally rehearse stressful situations before going into them...and regularly practice meditation or other relaxation techniques.

Murray Mittleman, MD, DPH, associate professor of medicine, Beth Israel Deaconess Medical Center at Harvard University, Boston, whose study was presented at a meeting of the American Heart Association.

Stress Affects Hay Fever, But Relax

People with hay fever are often anxious throughout allergy season—and the heightened stress can worsen allergic  reactions. *Self-defense:* Lie down in a comfortable place, and visualize yourself in a peaceful, safe setting—away from allergies. Think of an image to help you visualize cleansing your sinuses. *Example:* Imagine a brush coating your sinuses with a soothing protective substance.

Martin Rossman, MD, co-director, Academy of Guided Imagery, Malibu, CA.

RELIGION/HEALTH CONNECTION

In a recent survey, older people who attended religious services at least once a week were much less likely than non-attendees to have high blood levels of an immune-system protein associated with many age-related diseases. *Possible reason:* Going to religious services may help counteract stress.

Harold Koenig, MD, co-director, Center for the Study of Religion/Spirituality and Health, Duke University Medical Center, Durham, NC, whose study was published in *The International Journal of Psychiatry in Medicine.*

Assertiveness Power— Very Effective at Alleviating Stress

Sharon Anthony Bower, president of Confidence Training, Inc., an assertiveness and public speaking training company in Stanford, CA. She is coauthor of *Asserting Yourself* (Addison Wesley), which details her DESC method, and author of *The Assertive Advantage* (National Press Publications).

We all know that psychological stress takes its toll physically as well as emotionally. Stress has been linked to high blood pressure, increased susceptibility to colds and greater sensitivity to pain.

Stress also contributes to headache, backache, peptic ulcers, digestive problems and insomnia.

Meditation and other relaxation strategies help curb stress. So does aerobic exercise. But it's better to *prevent* stress in the first place. One highly effective—and often overlooked—way to do this is simply *to be more assertive.*

WRITE YOUR OWN SCRIPT

Many perfectly intelligent people avoid speaking up for themselves because they fear they'll get flustered and be forced to back down.

It's helpful to have a "script" to follow. Committing your thoughts to paper forces you to clarify the situation...figure out what you want...and come up with the best way to get it.

You needn't memorize your script word for word. But by practicing your main points, you'll develop the confidence to stand up for yourself.

Helpful: As you rehearse your script, breathe slowly and deeply. Say to yourself, "I can meet this challenge." Visualize yourself speaking with confidence and power.

THE DESC METHOD

To write an effective script, use the "DESC" method...

▶ **Describe** the behavior that bothers you. Do not waste time trying to identify the other person's motives. Instead, focus on the specific behavior or behaviors that bother you.

Example: *"Several times during the past few weeks, you asked me to baby-sit at the very last minute."*

▶ **Express** your feelings about the troublesome behavior. Be calm but firm. Use "I messages" to avoid putting the other person on the defensive.

Example: *"I'm inconvenienced when you ask me to baby-sit on short notice. I'm also frustrated because I then act tense with the kids."*

▶ **Specify** what you want the other person to do. Make sure your request is reasonable.

Example: *"I'd like you to give me at least two days' advance notice when you ask me to baby-sit. Will you do that?"*

▶ **Consequences.** List the benefits the person will reap if he or she agrees to your conditions.

Example: *"Given two days' notice, I'll be happy to watch the kids two or even three times a month. Since I'll feel relaxed, the kids and I will be better able to enjoy our time together."*

In some cases, you'll have to specify *negative* consequences that will come to pass if the other person doesn't cooperate. Negatives should be used *only* if the positive approach fails.

Example: *"If you fail to give me advance notice, I'll say no next time you ask me to baby-sit."*

Not every situation calls for a detailed four-step script. Often, you can get your point across in a single sentence, such as "This radio has a defective speaker" or "The line starts back there."

If you're caught off guard by someone's behavior and find it hard to be assertive right then and there, simply say, "Let me think about that. I'll get back to you in an hour." Use the time to write an assertiveness script.

Good news: Once you write a few DESC scripts, you'll find it easier to assert yourself on the spur of the moment.

DEALING WITH DETOURS

What if the other person keeps you from sticking to your script...or tries to "detour" the conversation? Imagine his reactions and objections—in advance—and prepare a detailed response.

Good ways to respond...

▶ **Persist.** Repeat your main point—the "specify" part of DESC—as many times as necessary.

▶ **Agree...but.** Begin to acknowledge that the other person has a right to his feelings...but disagree with the notion that you must feel the same way.

▶ **Disagree.** Say something like, "I hold a different view" or "I see it another way."

▶ **Emphasize your feelings.** Give more details about your feelings or thoughts...or state them more firmly.

Common detours...

Put-off detour: "Let's not go into that now"...or "I'm too busy right now." *Reply:* "It's important to me that this be settled. If this isn't a good time, please name a time today when we can talk."

Reinterpreting detour: "I only meant that remark as a joke." *Reply:* "Perhaps so, but I didn't think it was appropriate. I felt hurt."

Blaming detour: "You're going through a tough stage now. You'll see things differently in a few weeks." Reply: "This is no stage. The problem isn't me, but the way you've been treating me."

HOW TO GET STARTED

Each day for the next few weeks, try one of the following exercises. Each time you try one, observe what happens—and how you feel...

▶ **Ask for clarification.** If someone criticizes you—or *seems* to be criticizing you—ask for more details.

Example: *"I'm not sure what you mean when you say I've been defensive. In what ways have I been defensive?"*

▶ **Ask for help.** When you feel overwhelmed, get help. Don't feel that you must be a superperson all the time.

Example: *"I want to do a good job on this project, but I'm feeling overwhelmed. Could we hire an assistant?"*

▶ **Fight the urge to justify yourself.** You have every right to your feelings. Devise simple statements that show you won't be drawn into an argument.

> **Example:** *"That's how I feel about the issue, and I don't have to supply you with more reasons. Let's get back to the issue at hand."*

▶ **Use assertive body language.** Make eye contact, but shift your gaze every few seconds. Staring makes you seem aggressive.

Eliminate distracting gestures—covering your mouth, touching your hair, clearing your throat, shifting your weight back and forth, etc.

Practice your DESC message with a friend or in front of a mirror—or record yourself and play it back—until you can use it comfortably.

How to Be Assertive Without Being Aggressive Or Impolite...Or Boorish

Nathaniel Branden, PhD, psychotherapist and corporate consultant who specializes in issues of accountability and self-esteem, The Branden Institute for Self-Esteem, Box 2609, Beverly Hills, CA 90213. He is author of numerous books, including *Self-Esteem at Work: How Confident People Make Powerful Companies* and *A Woman's Self-Esteem: Struggles and Triumphs in the Search for Identity*, both from Jossey-Bass.

I s it possible to be assertive without being obnoxious? Are there ways to become effectively assertive without turning off the very people you're trying to win over?

To find out where the middle ground exists, read what Nathaniel Branden, PhD, one of the country's leading authorities on assertiveness and self-esteem, has to say...

■ What is assertiveness?
Assertiveness isn't about being pushy or negatively aggressive.

To be assertive means behaving in a direct and honest way and not faking what you think or feel in order to be liked.

■ Why is assertiveness so important?
It is an essential part of self-respect.

Whenever you keep quiet about your thoughts, feelings and desires because you are afraid people will disapprove of you, you're putting yourself second. This is humiliating.

You can't live according to your values without being assertive. Without assertiveness, you're not likely to get what you need in life—nor are you likely to make much of a contribution.

As a corporate consultant, I've seen people keep quiet even when their ideas might contribute to the resolution of a problem—because they're afraid to rock the boat. The company suffers, and so does the person's self-esteem.

■ Is it possible to be too assertive?
Many people confuse assertiveness with having to get their own way all the time.

Being assertive doesn't mean demanding to be the center of attention...elbowing to the front of the line...or being rude to intimidate others.

Assertiveness is a matter of being authentic—not obnoxious. It's about having the courage to stand up for your beliefs in appropriate ways.

When we have viewed assertiveness negatively, that so-called assertive person usually invaded our space. Such behavior is beyond assertive. That can be confrontational, aggressive, impolite.

We can't expect to have our rights respected if we don't respect others' rights.

■ Where is the line between inappropriate and appropriate levels of assertiveness?
Inappropriate assertiveness includes shouting down another person...interrupting so that you're the only one who gets a chance to speak...insulting someone...and other behaviors that treat people as though they exist only to make the offensive person's life more convenient.

Appropriate assertiveness is saying what you think—even if you don't know if your listeners agree. It could mean telling someone that his or her behavior is unacceptable—without name-calling. Paying a genuine compliment is assertive—positively assertive. Even silence can be assertive—such as when you refuse to laugh at an offensive joke.

Appropriate assertiveness advances your cause through courage—but not at the expense of others.

▧ What's a good way to deal with an inappropriately assertive person?
Stay calm, describe the behavior to which you object, and state what you want and/or intend to do.

By refusing to meet the other person's aggression with hostility, you retain dignity and control—and your words will be much more effective.

Examples of what to say to an inappropriately assertive person...

▶ **"If you're unwilling to lower your voice and speak in a normal manner,** I'm unwilling to continue this conversation now."

▶ **"I don't find hostility productive for getting problems solved**—so I'm going to wait until you're willing to have a nonhostile discussion with me."

Asking the other person a question about the way he's acting is also effective. It invites him to stop and think—and possibly change what he is doing. *Examples...*

▶ **"Do you think that shouting louder will make you more convincing?"**

▶ **"Do you feel a need to go on talking or arguing** even though I've made it absolutely clear that I'm not going to do what you want?"

▶ **"Is it your intention to be insulting right now?"**

That doesn't mean you should never get angry. Some people won't pay attention unless you have an edge to your voice or use strong language. But I've never seen any good come from losing control, being insulting or saying anything you might regret later.

▧ How can we learn to assert ourselves more often?
One of the best ways is to spend a few minutes a day doing sentence-completion exercises.

This process is extremely simple and takes no more than 10 minutes a day. But it produces powerful change. *How to do it...*

Every morning, soon after you wake up, write the following sentence stem...

▶ **"If I were 5% more self-assertive today..."**

Then write 6 to 10 endings for that particular sentence, without stopping to think. Don't worry about whether your endings are "right" or "wrong."

Next write 6 to 10 endings each for a few more sentence stems...

▶ **"If I had the courage to treat my needs as important..."**

▶ **"If I don't stand up for my thoughts and feelings..."**

▶ **"If I am willing to ask for what I want..."**

Do this every morning for a week. On the weekend, reread the week's sentences. Then write 6 to 10 endings for this sentence...

▶ **"If any of what I have been writing is true,** it might be helpful if I..."

Some examples of sentence endings are..."I'd tell people what I think"..."I'd be more honest about what I feel"..."I'd let people know what I need."

As you do these exercises, you will become more aware of the situations in which you censor yourself...and less willing to remain silent when it's appropriate to be assertive.

Facial Tics

Many facial tics are stress-related and disappear as long-term stress is controlled. *Also helpful:* Reduce caffeine intake…practice relaxation techniques in particularly tense situations. Stress-related tics are most common in children. Parents should not call attention to the twitches—that only makes them worse. *When to seek help:* If a tic persists throughout the night or lasts a full day or more, consult a neurologist. Medication or surgery can help tics caused by "cross-talking" nerves. Only a small number of tics reflect an underlying disease.

Richard Hughes, MD, chief of neurology, Denver Health Medical Center.

Control Your Temper—Stay Healthier

A low anger threshold increases the chance of heart disease and makes a person more likely to contract many illnesses, from colds to cancer. *To control your temper:* Admit it to yourself when you feel angry. To learn what regularly angers you, keep an anger journal. Then imagine the things that make you angry—and devise ways to handle them without blowing up. *Examples:* Take a break from the angering situation…step back and take a deep breath…try to find humor in the situation that is making you feel angry.

Raymond Novaco, PhD, professor of psychology and social behavior, University of California, Irvine, quoted in *Investor's Business Daily*, 12655 Beatrice St., Los Angeles 90066.

Writing About Stress Boosts Health

Among patients with mild to moderately severe asthma or rheumatoid arthritis, those assigned to write about the most stressful events of their lives

showed more improvement after four months than those told to write about neutral subjects. *Reason:* Unknown. But you can test this idea on yourself and benefit physically by writing down negative memories.

Joshua Smyth, PhD, department of psychology, State University of New York at Stony Brook. His study of 112 patients with either asthma or rheumatoid arthritis was published in *The Journal of the American Medical Association*, 515 N. State St., Chicago 60610.

PUNCHING A PILLOW

Punching a pillow—or similar cathartic techniques—may increase aggressive feelings rather than dissipate them. *Better than catharsis:* Expressing your feelings verbally or in writing in a constructive way—preferably before anger builds…looking closely at situations that provoke your anger to see whether you can view them differently. *Example:* If a driver cuts you off, it is not directed at you. *Helpful image for managing anger:* Visualize a fish in a pond. A hook drops down. The fish can bite…or it can move on. Tell yourself, "That's a hook"…and choose not to bite. *Important for parents:* Violent video games increase aggression…and violence on TV, even in cartoons, interferes with learning constructive ways to deal with anger.

James Blumenthal, PhD, professor of medical psychology, Duke University, Durham, NC.

Simple Secrets of the Power of Confidence

Confidence is an essential quality in determining our degree of success. Confidence helps us approach the people we want to meet...and need to meet...and helps us ask for what we need and for what we deserve.

Confidence is not the same as self-esteem, although the two are related. Self-esteem is an inner attitude—it refers to the way we regard ourselves.

Confidence is the ability to project this positive self-regard when in public situations. It comes across as poise—even when we are feeling under pressure. Though confidence may seem like something you're born with, it can be acquired. Shy people can acquire it, too. *Simple strategies for projecting confidence...*

▨ Always focus on the other person.

It's hard to seem poised when you're worrying about how you look or whether you are saying the right thing. In order to lose this debilitating self-consciousness, focus your attention on others instead of on yourself.

To accomplish this quickly, use the simple four-L technique:

> ▶ **Look** at the other person with interest.

> ▶ **Lean** forward slightly, as though to catch every word.

> ▶ **Lift** your eyebrows.

> ▶ **Level** or equalize your conversation style. Talk at the same level as the other person. If the person you're talking to is sitting, then sit down next to her. If he is standing, then you should stand up so that you are making eye contact at the same level.

These simple physical acts generate the appearance and feeling of interest in others—which then attracts people to you.

Try it. You'll find it's impossible to be lethargic, distracted or preoccupied with yourself when your body language shows animation and a strong interest in others.

▨ Smile broadly.

I know some people believe smiling makes them look naive or not in control. But a smile draws people to you involuntarily.

Whether you're at a party, a conference or a job interview, it's very hard to resist a genuine smile.

That word *genuine* is important. Many people think they're smiling when their face is actually set in a grim mask of anxiety.

If you remain concentrated on your fears—such as "I hate talking in front of a large group"—those fears will show up on your face, even when you try to smile.

So change what you tell yourself. Try, "What I'm saying will help people to do their jobs more efficiently"—and you will appear open, receptive and confident.

▨ Become an instant insider.

People commonly feel ill at ease walking into a conference, networking event or other occasion where they don't know many people.

To get over this fear and build instant connections, ask for help—or offer your help to others.

Because our culture prizes self-sufficiency, asking for help may not sound like a good way to create confidence. Yet people love to feel needed—we're all yearning to make a difference in the world.

When you ask for help or offer help, you're empowering both yourself and the person you're asking help from or assisting. You'll come across as someone who is friendly and outgoing, which translates into confidence.

▨ Take the initiative.

People love when you walk up and introduce yourself. It means they don't have to look for someone to talk to.

Don't worry about a clever opener. Just smile warmly, introduce yourself and add a line about what you do or where you live.

Taking the initiative works especially well at luncheon meetings, where groups of eight or 10 near-strangers are seated around a table.

> *Example: People are invariably grateful when someone says, "We've got about 20 minutes before the program starts, and we haven't had a chance to meet each other. Why don't we go around the table and introduce ourselves?"*

This initiative won't be perceived as overly aggressive or inappropriate because you're not grabbing the conversational ball for yourself. People wind up exchanging useful information, sharing ideas and showcasing their expertise—thanks to your act of confidence.

■ Sell yourself with a sound bite.

When people ask, "What do you do?" have an answer that you have prepared in advance that makes them want to know more about you.

> *Example: "I'm a loan officer at a bank" is flat when compared with "I meet with small business owners and help finance their growth."*

Easy conversation starter: Asking other people, "What's your favorite thing to do when you're not working?" is a great way to get a lively discussion going. It puts both you and others at ease right away and makes you appear confident.

■ Make good mistakes.

Someone once said that the only "bad" mistake is one from which you don't learn.

Confident people take thoughtful risks—but don't beat themselves up when things fail to turn out as they had hoped. They see mistakes as lessons, not failures. They're self-coaches, not self-critics. And they focus on the future, not the past.

Use Your Critical Thinking

Edward de Bono, PhD, the world's leading authority on the teaching of thinking and cognition. He has held faculty appointments at Oxford, Cambridge and Harvard.

Intelligence isn't solely the result of what we've read and what we've experienced. To be a real thinker, you need to go beyond skillful analysis and judgment, which tell you "what," and integrate creativity and design into your problem-solving process so that you understand "what can be."

SEEKING THE TRUTH

The human mind works by organizing information into familiar patterns that can be used to trigger a course of action.

> *Example: Recognition of people's voices allows us to greet them. And...the recognition of patterns of printed words on a page enables us to read.*

But far too much of this patterning depends on searching for the truth through critical thinking...analysis...judgment...and criticism. In order to understand a problem or situation, most people analyze it and break it down into the small pieces that their brains can judge and criticize.

In other words, people use established thinking patterns and experiences to find the cause of problems. Then they react to fix them.

This form of thinking, called critical thinking, often produces flawed results. We prevent ourselves from thinking deeper to find solutions to problems for which there may be no easy answers.

Critical thinking locks us into limited solutions. Many businesses operate under the assumption that new ideas come only from analyzing existing information. Coupled with the attitude that "if it ain't broke, don't fix it," this complacency prevents businesses from exploring the potential and success of new ideas.

Example: In the 1960s, American auto manu-facturers began to make compact cars. Because car dealers complained that the smaller vehicles weren't producing large enough profits, carmakers returned to full-size models.

Then oil prices rose. But manufacturers' reluctance to go back to making smaller cars left the door open for Asian imports, which have since established a strong foothold in the compact-car market.

THE RISE OF DESIGN THINKING

Though we cannot predict the future, we do know actions that are taken now will have consequences at some later point.

By continuously striving to discover what can be—rather than what is—we open the door to a realm of possibilities.

Unlike critical thinking, which only allows us to look for solutions to problems by searching through our many experiences, design thinking forces us to use new approaches.

Design thinking uses ideas, perceptions (the way we look at things) and creativity (the search for alternatives) to come up with solutions we may never have considered.

We rarely look for alternative ways of performing tasks or solving problems when there is no immediate need to do so. But—when you acknowledge that the best solutions may exist outside of what you know now, you will begin to think about the possibilities.

■ Exercise I:

The next time you are faced with a problem, ask yourself, "Why are things done this way?"

When you come up with an answer, ask yourself "Why?" again. Continue this process until you have considered a few new solutions.

Example: Why do employees have to meet every Monday? Because that's the start of the week. Why is that good for employees? Because it starts their week out right.

By continuing with the "why again" sequence, you may discover that Monday meetings are not the most economical or efficient use of employees' time and that meeting Friday afternoons makes much more sense.

Key: Think about all the factors that "shape" a concept or rule. Then systematically challenge these factors—even if they appear to be sensible and fully justified.

Important: Omit "either/or" polarizations in your challenges, such as "Either we do this…or we do that."

Instead, consider how an existing concept may be limiting…or if there are any issues that are being avoided by continuing a certain practice.

■ Exercise II:

Provoke your mind with outrageous ideas to find new solutions.

Example: Consider the statement, "Airplanes can land upside down." We all know that airplanes land right-side up. But this sentence deliberately reverses the norm and provokes new ideas.

After you've laughed to yourself and said that airplanes do not and cannot land upside down, you may find yourself in new territory. You may find yourself wondering, "What if the pilot's windshield were at the bottom of the passenger plane's nose, not at the very top? Could the pilot get a better view for landing?"

This may lead you to consider where pilots actually sit in airplanes. Maybe it makes more sense for them to sit on top, where they sat at the start of aviation.

Maybe that's not the best placement for pilots. Perhaps pilots could sit somewhere else if video cameras were installed to help give them a better view of the runway.

As you can see, the key to unlocking creative thought and designing new opportunities is mental movement. Don't wait for inspiration to create new opportunities. Break free of constraining thought patterns and focus on moving to new approaches to ideas or problems.

Take the time to pause and pay deliberate attention to your thoughts. From these creative pauses come the points of value that are contained in a simple germ of an idea.

How to Think Your Way to Warm and Wonderful Success

Roger Fisher, director of Harvard Negotiation Project and professor emeritus at Harvard Law School, Boston. He is one of the country's leading authorities on negotiating tactics and is author of *Getting It Done: How to Lead When You're Not in Charge.* HarperBusiness.

When trying to solve any problem—whether it is a personal issue or a complex negotiation between two groups—we tend to jump randomly from one idea to the next and confuse facts with impressions.

This scattered approach invariably leads to thinking in circles—revisiting ideas that you've discussed before—and unwittingly skipping over key steps in the solution process.

At the Harvard Negotiation Project, we recommend a specific way of organizing your thoughts in order to tackle difficult problems. *This type of thinking involves two steps...*

▶ **Carefully defining your goal.**

▶ **Using a "quadrant approach"** to divide all ideas into four different categories—data, diagnosis, direction and do next.

DEFINING THE PROBLEM

Before you can begin working on a problem by yourself or with others, you must define exactly what result you are hoping to achieve.

Success will then be measured by the final product—and how well it matches your original expectation.

Helpful: Rather than letting yourself become bogged down trying to identify a single goal, try to come up with several goals.

These goals should include an inspiring long-term objective...a mid-distance goal that is a worthy objective in itself...and a short-range goal that you can start working on at once.

> *Example: A lawyer starts out with a law firm whose motto is "Always aim for excellence." Over time, he finds himself unmotivated by this vague goal. Instead of looking for others to provide him with a list of goals, this lawyer sets his own series of concrete goals...*

▶ **Long-range goal...**"In five years I will make partner in the specialty I like best."

▶ **Mid-term goal...**"In two years, I will be working with three clients in my chosen specialty, including two clients of my own that I've brought to the firm. I will also have published a short article in my specialty."

▶ **Immediate goal...**"By the end of the month, I will have done such good work on my current case that the partners will agree to allow me to do the oral argument...I will do extra research to gain a new assignment...and I will have joined the bar committee in my specialty."

REACHING YOUR GOALS

To plan concrete steps toward reaching your goals, you must first distinguish between *abstract/general* thinking and *practical/specific* thinking.

You also need to draw a distinction between examining the past and exploring the future. Both are important when setting your goals and solving problems.

Helpful: To represent these distinctions and clarify your thinking, take a piece of paper and draw a large circle on it.

Then draw a horizontal line across the middle of the circle. All abstract thinking and general approaches will go in the upper half of the chart. All of your thinking about practical, specific events will go in the lower half.

Next, divide the circle vertically. All thinking about the past will go on the left side of the chart, while thoughts about the future will go on the right side. *You'll be left with four quadrants—each covering a basic category of thought...*

■ Quadrant I—*Data* (lower left):
Description of the exact situation or problem you're working on.

■ Quadrant II—*Diagnosis* (upper left):
Analysis of the causes of the situation, probing what flaws in the process may be causing the problem.

■ Quadrant III—*Direction* (upper right):
One or more strategies for overcoming the problem or fixing the process.

■ Quadrant IV—*Do Next* (lower right):
Specific steps you plan to take to implement your solution.

PUTTING THE APPROACH INTO ACTION
The circle chart will help you get started on any problem without fear of getting stuck.

Begin by collecting as many facts as you can and placing them in the *data* category. Put other ideas that emerge in the *diagnosis* section...and ideas about the future in the direction section for later consideration.

When you think you've collected enough data, move on to concentrate on *diagnosis*—drawing general conclusions from your data—followed by *direction*, where you use your conclusions to shape a general strategy for the future.

Finally, when you are clear on the direction you want to take, you can tackle specific items to *do next*. If you get stuck, don't hesitate to reverse direction and return to an earlier quadrant.

> *Example: If your diagnosis seems limited, reviewing your data list may reveal some additional facts you've overlooked.*

SAMPLE PROBLEM
Let's say you and your colleagues are planning an office party. An ordinary discussion is likely to jump around, with everyone making different points at different moments in the meeting.

> *Example: "Should we invite spouses this year?"... "There were a lot of people I didn't recognize last year."... "I remember I didn't get enough to eat."*

Same discussion, using the quadrant approach...

Ann: Let's start by hearing some Quadrant I data from last year's party. For one thing, as I recall the party started at 5:00 pm and by 6:30 pm, half the people had left. Does that match up with your recollection?

Bill: Yes. What caused that? Did we run out of food or beverages?

Chris: Samantha told me she left early to meet her husband.

Dale: I heard several people say that they needed to meet spouses.

Ann: Fine, that's a Quadrant II diagnosis.

Bill: I don't think we had enough food.

Ann: That's another Quadrant II.

Chris: I was embarrassed because there were some coworkers whose names I couldn't remember. Maybe we should have name tags.

Ann: Hold on while I write down your solution in Quadrant III.

Dale: And we didn't run out of beverages. There was plenty left over.

The discussion on the circle chart...

■ Quadrant I—*Data:*
▶ **Half the guests** left early.

▶ **Some people were** embarrassed.

■ Quadrant II—*Diagnosis:*
▶ **Many people who left** early had to meet spouses.

▶ **People were embarrassed** because they didn't know guests' names.

▶ **There wasn't enough** food to eat.

■ **Quadrant III—*Direction:***

▶ **Invite spouses to the party** to limit early departures?

▶ **Give out name tags** to limit embarrassing moments?

▶ **Order more food** and serve a buffet, so guests can get refills?

As you can see, filling in the first three quadrants leads naturally to the fourth category—specific steps to take. In this case, the *do next* category may involve clearing the ideas with the full staff, assigning someone to fill out name tags, contacting a caterer, etc.

Keep Goals Visible

Look at your goals every day. Surround yourself with visual reminders. Buy a big chalkboard or a whiteboard for the wall of your office. Write the names of five clients or other goals you most want. Then list all the steps needed to achieve your goal. This will keep both the goal and the steps toward it always in your mind.

Barry Farber, president, Farber Training Systems, Inc., Livingston, NJ, quoted in *Home Office Computing.* 29160 Heather Cliff Rd., Malibu, CA 90265.

Best Friend at the Office

Your wastebasket is your best friend at the office. Work near a wastebasket to make it easy to throw things away. Get rid of anything that can be easily replaced if it is ever needed again…anything of marginal interest or value… and all for-your-information memos, summaries and forwarded documents. Create decision-making guidelines so you can throw out unneeded items as soon as they reach your desk.

Stephanie Winston, time-management consultant and author, *The Organized Executive.*

POWER DAYDREAMING

Daydreaming can boost on-the-job productivity—*if* you do it right.

How: Close your door, so you won't attract attention…put your feet up and shut your eyes …and then imagine positive scenes—anything from a tropical vacation to finishing a difficult project at work.

After five minutes: Open your eyes… stretch…and take some deep breaths. Then— get back to work gradually, by doing something relatively simple. If you are concerned that you won't know when your daydreaming time is up, set a timer for five minutes.

John Mitchell, PhD, clinical psychologist, Rochester Institute of Technology, Rochester, NY.

APPRECIATION COUNTS

Reminder: Show appreciation often. It takes only a moment to improve someone's mood and productivity. Even if there is nothing specific to praise someone for at the moment, it is worthwhile to walk over to his/her office and say how much you appreciate his overall hard work. *Bonus:* Frequent praise makes it easier for others to accept advice or coaching when needed.

Getting It Done: How to Lead When You're Not in Charge by **Roger Fisher.** Harper-Business. He is the director, Harvard Negotiation Project, Cambridge, MA.

Fostering Teamwork

Casual friends at work help foster teamwork without giving people high stakes in maintaining close relationships. If you feel that the friendship puts you or your friend in a compromised position, discuss the situation and withdraw from any possible conflicts of interest. If a friend asks a question that oversteps your sense of privacy, gracefully decline to answer. Do not misuse a business friendship for leverage. Do not impose too often on work friends or you may lose their support.

Friendshifts: The Power of Friendship and How It Shapes Our Lives by **Jan Yager, PhD.** Hannacroix Creek Books. He is a sociologist in Stamford, CT.

SECRETS OF HAPPIER COMPUTING

Be sure to do warm-up and stretching exercises before keyboarding. *Examples...*

▶ **Make a tepee with your hands** by gently pressing the fingers of each hand against each other.

▶ **Do finger curls:** Rest a hand on a table, palm up, and gently push one finger at a time toward the palm.

▶ **Rub hands together** until palms and fingers heat up, then massage the back of each hand to warm up muscles.

After starting computer use: Take frequent rest breaks to reduce strain...keep wrists in a smooth line while keyboarding...and keep elbows hanging free and fingers loose and light.

Russell Windsor, MD, associate professor of orthopedic surgery, Weill Medical College, Cornell University, New York City.

The Simple Secret of Achieving Your Goals— Focus, Just Focus

Martin G. Groder, MD, psychiatrist and business consultant in Chapel Hill, NC. He is author of *Business Games: How to Recognize the Players and Deal with Them.* Bottom Line Books.

Focusing is the process of bringing together resources to accomplish a goal. First you need a strategic plan. Then you need focus to carry yourself through each step of that plan. Focusing is most important when the task at hand is difficult, unusual and/or prolonged.

> *Example: To write a book, you focus, step by step, on gathering facts and ideas...organizing the information...writing the text...editing the text... and marketing the finished product.*

Focusing is difficult because there are so many interests clamoring for our attention. It's easy to be distracted and forget about your goals for a time. But if you don't focus and concentrate, you fritter away valuable resources.

PROBLEMS IN FOCUSING

The crucial element is having something to focus on. That something is called a goal. Without a goal, the mind wanders and becomes situation-oriented, responding to the environment rather than to an internal sense of focus. *People fail to focus because they...*

▨ Set the wrong goals.

Although many people think they have goals, they really don't.

They have not clarified the goals in a detailed, realistic way.

> *Example: The typical goal in a relationship is a happy marriage. But many people are unable to define a happy marriage.*

▨ Don't know how to reach their goals.

Their methods of attaining them often are inadequate.

Example I: A woman who wants to be happily married weds a man who has been divorced three times.

Example II: A young professional may go to work for a large Fortune 500 company, thinking he will stay there for a lifetime—only to discover later that a career-management strategy is necessary because he might have to change jobs often before retiring.

Lack interest in their goals.
People who set goals to please others don't care if they never achieve them.

> *Example: The child who goes to college only to satisfy her parents is likely to flunk out.*

Wonder if their goals are still valid.

> *Example: The middle-aged businessman who no longer focuses on wheeling and dealing may be questioning whether he wants to continue his pressured lifestyle.*

Discover that their goals are no longer attainable.

> *Example: A student going for her doctorate in English realizes that the market is glutted with college English teachers. Knowing that few jobs will be available when she graduates, she loses heart.*

IT'S NOT EASY TO FOCUS
Focusing is a problem for...

People who are anxious.
They often realize that their goals are eating up more time and energy than they are worth.

This may be true for you if you are easily distracted or you distract yourself with compulsive cleaning, phone calling, reading the newspaper,

plant watering—all symptomatic activities designed to relieve the anxiety.

Underachievers.
They don't focus because they fear the outcome will result in failure and rejection.

Paradoxically, they may also fear success and acceptance—because they think they won't always be able to live up to others' further expectations.

Remedy: Set up a counteranxiety.

> *Example: An underachiever may have more fear of missing a deadline than of succeeding. If he works on strict deadlines, he may be able to distract himself from his fear of success.*

People who are very involved with their feelings.
They need to learn how to reflect on and control their emotions.

Although feelings are important (goals are born in feelings), it takes thinking and logic to make their goals realistic.

Disenchanted people.
They refuse to compete, and they reject the entire goal-setting process.

Many such people, disillusioned with the American way of life, are still living in the 1960s. They are unhappy, but they don't know how to change without giving up their principles.

Remedy: Acknowledge that rebellion can be a trap in itself. Whether you accept or reject the American success ethic, you can still use opportunities to get what you want out of life.

Overachievers.
They can become addicted to the focusing process because it's very reinforcing.

There's such an immediate gratification in setting a strategy and then reaching a goal that they don't notice what achieving an ever-increasing set of goals will cost them.

> *Example: Joggers who set successive goals of 3 miles, 4 miles, 10 miles...until they wear themselves out.*

HOW TO STAY IN FOCUS
Soliciting feedback is the best way to find out if your goals and your strategies for reaching them

are realistic. It's important to check with people you respect as you work toward a goal.

Reason: The human capacity for self-delusion is endless. Although you may think you have clear goals and a good strategy, other people in your life may tell you that you can't get there from here.

You also need to review your goals regularly to make sure they're still in focus. As in action photography, you may be moving around a moving target—and unless you refocus continuously, you'll lose the shot.

How to Disagree Without Being Disagreeable

Suzette Haden Elgin, PhD, founder of Ozark Center for Language Studies, Box 1137, Huntsville, AR 72740, and a speaker and seminar leader. She is author of numerous books in the "Gentle Art of Verbal Self-Defense" series, including *How to Disagree Without Being Disagreeable*. John Wiley & Sons.

Disagreement is an unavoidable part of life. While at work, we have to evaluate colleagues, offer alternatives to proposals and stand up for our opinions. Outside the office, we must negotiate with spouses and deal with obnoxious strangers.

Many people dread these confrontations. When faced with potential conflicts, they keep quiet to preserve the peace...and become angry at themselves for doing so.

Or...they speak up, but in a hostile way that escalates the conflict.

It doesn't have to be this way. Whether we're receiving or delivering a negative message, we can use simple techniques to defuse hostility—making communication less stressful and more effective.

PEACEFUL CONFLICT
■ Detach yourself immediately.
To deal with conflict in a rational way, we need enough distance to evaluate the situation and determine the best possible response.

This can be difficult to do because when someone challenges, embarrasses or shouts at us, our

first instinct is to protect our self-esteem. So we lash out in an attempt to protect ourselves.

Helpful: Realize that the other person's goal was not to cause us pain. Most often, the other person was just trying to get our attention...or was reacting without taking our feelings into consideration.

Once you've reminded yourself that the other person didn't mean to do you harm, you are ready to come up with an effective response.

■ Phrase responses in neutral ways.
There are several ways to respond to a disagreeable person that won't escalate the problem.

Helpful...

▶ **Do not put extra emphasis on any of your words,** which signals your anger.

▶ **Substitute third-person language** for *I* and *you*. Instead of "You've got to start returning the files on time. It's driving everyone crazy," depersonalize and de-emotionalize the statement by saying, "When files aren't returned promptly, many people get frustrated because they can't do their work without the correct figures." (This three-part message pattern is adapted from the work of Dr. Thomas Gordon, renowned effectiveness trainer.)

By sticking to the facts and avoiding personal language, you create a sense of neutrality and control. It tends to stop an argument cold. And cutting out the "Is" and the "yous" makes the message feel less personally threatening.

Important: Make sure your statement covers the behavior you want to see changed...the effects of the current behavior...and the reasons that it needs to change.

This is very powerful when someone is trying to bait you…and you want to make a stand without getting into a fight.

▪ Avoid trigger words and phrases.
These are expressions that have hostility built into them.

They cause most listeners to brace for an attack and are guaranteed to provoke conflict. *Common triggers of hostility include…*

▶ **If you really…** *"If you really* loved me"…and *"If you really* cared about this job."

▶ **Why…?** When used with heavy emphasis, *why* implies that the other person is wrong and must justify his actions. *A more neutral way to request information is, "Tell me…"*

▶ **Managed,** as in, "I'm impressed that you managed to close that deal." It suggests that the person had major problems accomplishing the task and just barely was able to get it done.

▪ Use the Boring Baroque Response.
With this strategy, you deflect verbal attack by being elaborately and lengthily boring.

The result is that you gently talk the other person into passive behavior. Your tone of voice must be calm and neutral. If you're sarcastic and patronizing, this technique won't work.

>*Example:* Someone says to you, *"I can't believe you're eating that junk! That's disgusting! What's the matter with you?"*

Your *boring baroque response* would be, "You know, I think it is because of something that happened when I was just a little kid. We were living in Indianapolis at the time…No, wait! It couldn't have been Indianapolis, it must have been Kansas City. Because that was the year my Aunt Grace came to see us and brought her dog, and…"

By this time, even the most obnoxious attacker will have given up and gone off in search of another target.

▪ When all else fails, be honest.
Some people simply don't respond to diplomacy.

If you've repeatedly tried to get your message across in pleasant and neutral ways—without success—you may need to sit down with the person privately and state your position frankly.

Important: When you use this tactic, be sure to keep the degree of hostility in your voice as low as possible. Passion can help get your point across…hostility won't.

Lies, Lying, Liars— The Simple Giveaways

Jo-Ellan Dimitrius, PhD, one of the country's leading jury consultants, has worked with attorneys on more than 600 trials. She is founder of Dimitrius & Associates, 201 S. Lake Ave., Ste. 305, Pasadena, CA 91101, and coauthor of *Reading People: How to Understand People and Predict Their Behavior Anytime, Anyplace.* Random House.

Your ability to make sound decisions depends on the accuracy of the information that you're given.

There are proven ways to tell whether someone is being honest or dishonest with you. And—there are also steps you can take to confirm your suspicions. I have developed these through years of consulting on the selection of jurors.

SIGNS OF DISHONESTY
▪ Patterns of behavior that don't match your first impressions.
Key way to differentiate between the truth and lies—look at inconsistencies in a person's behavior.

Think about how the person you're listening to has behaved throughout your conversation.

Any abrupt changes in mood or posture can signify dishonesty.

▪ Action that is being avoided.
Sometimes what a person doesn't do speaks louder than what he or she does do.

Most people are procrastinators by nature, but in some cases, dishonest people avoid taking certain action to prevent the truth from emerging.

Self-defense: Examine the reasons why someone may be acting evasively. In most cases, once you start thinking about why someone is avoiding an action, you're on your way to unearthing the truth.

■ Vocal characteristics that deviate from a speaker's usual manner.

Change in intonation, emphasis and sentence structure can signify dishonesty.

> **Examples::** *Compare "I'd love to" (dishonest) with "Yes! I'd love to" (honest).*

Answering questions with questions, such as "Why do you ask?" can also indicate dishonesty. This strategy is used as a stalling device or to gain information so the person can have more time to think or tailor an answer.

■ Physical behavior that seems inappropriate—such as leaning into another's personal space...losing eye contact...licking one's lips...or nervous fidgeting.

These actions often signify dishonesty.

The difference between nervous behavior and dishonesty: Nervous behavior entails more than one characteristic, such as nail biting and talking fast. Dishonesty is generally associated with one abrupt characteristic that ends as soon as the lie does.

HOW TO UNCOVER THE TRUTH

If you suspect someone is being dishonest, there are ways to get the truth so you can make accurate decisions...

■ Ask a follow-up question as soon as you feel someone is being evasive.

Although you shouldn't ruin the spontaneity of the conversation by interrupting, you should try to steer it back to the topic you want to discuss.

One of the most effective ways to get the truth without trying to insult the other person is to take responsibility for the lack of communication.

> **Example:** *If you are interviewing a job candidate, confess that you don't remember if the person provided you with the information you want.*
>
> *"You may have already mentioned this to me, but I really don't remember what you said. What did you do at your last job?"*

Alternatively, acknowledge that you don't quite understand an explanation.

> **Example:** *"I don't really understand how that happened. Could you explain it to me again?"*

The second answer almost always has more detail and more explanation.

■ Steer the conversation back to safe ground.

Sometimes it's easier to reconnect on a personal level while discussing a less sensitive issue.

Then you can work forward again in the conversation.

Ask the other person an open-ended question to catch him off guard in a way that will reveal the truth.

> **Example:** *"By the way, how did you feel while you were working on that project?"*

■ Be direct if your initial follow-up doesn't work.

Sometimes, no matter what you say, you can't seem to get at the truth. In these cases, polite confrontation can be effective.

> **Example:** *You're interviewing someone who you suspect is saying the "right" things in order to get hired.*
>
> *Let the person know that you are aware of certain facts. "I couldn't help but notice that you*

said earlier you weren't pleased with the hours of your previous job. Now you're saying that you're willing to work late. What has changed between then and now?"

▨ Don't allow too much time to pass before getting a response to your follow-up.

If you want reliable answers, don't allow the person too long to ponder all possible replies.

This is especially true if the information you're seeking is sensitive.

If you want spontaneity but the question you're asking requires some amount of reflection, ask it. But after you've received the impromptu answer, then say, "Think about it some more, and we can talk again tomorrow."

▨ Trust your intuition.

If all else fails and the other person continues to lie regardless of how you rephrase questions, pay attention to your hunches and what they may be revealing to you.

Before you make a decision...

▶ **Think about what you know so far** about the person giving you the information, such as their body language or their inappropriate or their abrupt actions. Think about how the person answered questions and the intonation he used.

▶ **Pare down what you know** about the other person to the five traits that stand out.

▶ **Consider these traits in the context of your conversation.**

▶ **Make a judgment.**

Rule of thumb: If you must make a decision, do so on the safe side. Take the path least likely to have adverse consequences.

How Not to Be Fooled By a Liar

Paul Ekman, PhD, former professor of psychology at University of California Medical School, San Francisco. He is author of *Telling Lies.* W.W. Norton.

Few people do better than chance when judging whether someone is lying or telling the truth. That includes the professionals in mental health, criminal justice and journalism who have opportunities to practice their lie-detection skills every day.

The odds are worse when you deal with a person over the phone, have limited personal contact, listen to a presentation or watch a political candidate deliver a speech or participate in a debate.

Liars, or people who conceal information, often succeed because the target of their lies makes it so easy for them.

> ***Examples:*** *A manager who doesn't admit making a major hiring or firing mistake...parents who don't want to acknowledge that their teenager might be taking drugs...a wife who doesn't want to entertain suspicions that her spouse is being unfaithful.*

Unless you are prepared to deal with the truth, you are very likely to overlook the subtle signs in a person's words and voice, face and body movements that signal deception. Even after you train yourself to recognize these clues, don't be overconfident.

INEFFECTIVE LIE DETECTION

The most typical barriers to making the right judgment call...

▨ Not enough time spent with the suspected liar.

First meetings or rushed encounters are especially vulnerable to errors.

Some people are on their best behavior. They speak carefully and they suppress giveaway body activities. Others are anxious, fidgety and tongue-tied, suggesting that they are being evasive when they are not.

▧ Charm.

People who you like instinctively and want to get closer to immediately, even before you know anything about them, are much more likely to get away with lies than dour, cranky personalities.

Charmers are not necessarily more inclined to lie. You'll just have far more trouble detecting when they do.

▧ Relying on hunches or intuition about how liars act.

Most common mistake: Assuming that people who don't look you in the eye are probably lying. Other faulty stereotypes include people who fidget a lot…people who are hesitant in how they speak …or people who give roundabout answers to straight questions.

LIE-DETECTION STRATEGY

There is no universal sign of deceit—no gesture, facial expression or muscle movement that in and of itself means the person is lying. People would lie less if they thought there was such a sign.

When you suspect a person of lying, give yourself time to observe that individual face-to-face. Create situations that enable you to shift the conversation from noncritical topics about which you would not expect lies to the critical topic about which the person may be tempted to lie.

Goal: Establish a baseline in your mind of how the person talks and gestures while discussing noncritical topics. Then try to identify differences when the subject gets hot.

You are most likely to focus on the person's words and face. But these observations are not likely to provide the most powerful clues.

▧ Words.

Liars are most careful about their choice of words.

They know that they will be held more accountable for what they say than for the tone of their voice, their facial expressions or their body movements. If they have time, they fine-tune their messages. But they can be careless.

Giveaways: Significant word slips…emotional tirades—outpourings of words caused by overwhelming anger, fear or distress—that reveal more information than the liar anticipated.

▧ Faces.

A person's face is the primary site for displaying emotions.

But liars can still exert considerable control over their facial expressions—especially easy-to-identify expressions such as smiles.

Most people like to believe they can easily detect false expressions, but strong research shows they rarely can.

Lie-detection researchers have discovered that fleeting expressions, which flash on and off in less than one-quarter of a second, are often good clues to deceit—but they can usually be observed only by playing a videotape over and over again at a slow speed. *In day-to-day life, use these chief clues to detect a false expression…*

▶ **It's more evident on one side of the face than the other.** This is very subtle, but it can be detected once you train yourself to observe closely.

▶ **It lasts longer than five seconds.** Genuine expressions of delight, surprise, and other strong emotions are very short-lived.

▶ **It's not exactly synchronized with the related verbal statement.** *Example:* An angry facial expression follows a vigorous verbal denial.

RELIABLE CLUES

Pay close attention to detect some fairly reliable clues to deception in how a person speaks…

▶ **Pauses that are too long and too frequent** —especially in response to a question.

▶ **Many nonwords, such as "ah...uhh."**

▶ **Partial words,** such as "I re-really worked on that a-all afternoon."

▶ **Higher pitch to the voice**—though this is really evidence of fear or anger and not necessarily a clue to deception.

Beware: Good liars often deliberately keep their voice tones flat to disguise emotion. This unflappable style deceives many people who think it is evidence of truth telling.

Pay much closer attention to body movements than you're likely to do instinctively in most personal encounters. A liar's body leaks a great deal of information about deception because most people ignore small gestures. *Key signs are...*

Disguised gesture. *Examples:* A person's voice or face may not reveal anger, and the person may even deny being angry—while keeping a tightly clenched fist in a lap. The meaning of a two-shoulder shrug or turning the palms upward is generally clear—*I can't help it...*or *What does it matter?* But when a person makes such a gesture only partway—a quick, almost imperceptible lift of one shoulder—it can suggest fear that the lie doesn't seem to be effective.

Less use of illustrative gestures than is usual. Illustrative gestures give emphasis to a word or phrase or describe a picture in space (a spiral staircase, for instance). Once you develop a good sense of how much use a person usually makes of such gestures, it's a tip-off that he is bored...or uninterested...or sad...or uninvolved in what is being said...or is only feigning concern or enthusiasm when there is a sudden decrease in such activity.

Squirming and fidgeting are far less accurate indicators of lying than most people think. These actions are fairly easy to bring under control. And since liars know that people connect such behavior with lying, they make themselves bring it under control.

Everyone Has Intuition— How to Develop and Sharpen Yours

Laura Day, author of *Practical Intuition for Success.* Perennial. She has been teaching Practical Intuition seminars for many years.

Intuition isn't some mystical power. It is a faculty with which you're born. It's simply a process of broadening your attention in order to gather information that is not immediately obvious.

Most people get their best ideas out of the blue in flashes of insight, which they ignore or dismiss. The most successful people pay attention to their hunches. They may not act on them all, but they think them through seriously.

You tune in to this information by noticing— and then integrating—impressions that arise through your imagination, emotions and reasoning...as well as your physical senses.

With practice, you can learn to tap your own natural intuitive powers—and to benefit from the edge this provides. *To start the intuitive process...*

■ Ask questions before you act.

Instead of reacting immediately to everything you experience at work, practice asking yourself questions first.

▶ **What are the potential obstacles to my position?**

▶ **How can I develop a long-term relationship with my customers?**

▶ **Which companies would value my skills?**

▶ **What is in the way of my advancement right now?**

■ Think about the impressions—as well as the images, feelings, memories and words that come to mind.

Write them down—or use a tape recorder—to capture them as they occur to you.

Important: Don't edit your impressions. Note them all, no matter how obvious or irrelevant or distracting they may seem. Get your logical mind out of the way by speaking or writing continuously about your impressions without missing a beat.

▧ Interpret your impressions.

Intuition rarely speaks to us in direct statements, such as, "Now is the time to pitch my bright ideas at work."

After you've recorded your impressions, call on your *reasoning mind* to put them together and come to conclusions. Practice looking for patterns of positive, receptive behavior in others that signal the time is right to introduce your thoughts and launch ideas. This exercise will help develop your intuitive instincts.

▧ Verify your hunches.

Using intuition doesn't mean following your gut no matter what the consequences.

Like other information, intuition needs to be evaluated and tested.

The best decisions balance intuition, logic and emotion. If your hunch conflicts with your research and analysis—or brings up strong emotions—probe it with further questions for yourself.

KNOWING WHAT OTHERS WANT

The most basic aspect of success in business is understanding the values and needs of others and satisfying those needs. Intuition can help you uncover—and even anticipate—what others want and value. *Key:* Addressing those needs as your own so that you can use all of your senses and abilities to perceive the information that you will need.

I call this process *The I-Mode* because its elements are Intuition, Integrity and Identifying with another person.

Exercise: Think of a colleague or work-related dynamics that you would like to understand better. Allow yourself to become that person, company or situation, as though everything you think, feel or perceive is as that entity. *Now, while embodying it, ask yourself...*

- ▶ **What do I want?**
- ▶ **What do I need?**
- ▶ **What difficulties do I face now?**
- ▶ **Where are my opportunities?**
- ▶ **Who are my best resources?**
- ▶ **What is missing?**
- ▶ **What makes me say yes?**

People who try this exercise are astonished by how much they know about others—including a "hidden" sense of others that they thought they had no way of knowing. You can use a variation of this exercise whenever you need to get a quick fix on someone or something new—a new group, client, company, industry or market.

Use **I**-Mode to become your target. Pick any two of the above **I**-questions, and answer those questions from your target's point of view.

MORE GOOD INTUITIVE QUESTIONS

▧ What do I want—and have—to offer?

Each of us has a unique idea, skill, product or service to offer.

Identifying it and making it available to people who value it are what raise work from drudgery to joy. This approach also results in our best work.

Most people start by looking outward for a market, then trying to make themselves or their product fit. But true success starts with your integrity —what you love, what feeds your deepest self— and extends that knowledge outward into the world.

Exercise I: Take the questions described under **I**-Mode, and ask them of yourself...as yourself.

Exercise II: Track your interests for a few weeks. Every day, jot down what you're doing in your spare time and any ideas or actions—yours or other people's—that you find stimulating. Clip articles and pictures that attract you. Keep all the data in a large envelope.

At the end of the month, open the envelope and spread the materials out in front of you. Interpret them the way you would interpret any other intuitive impression. Assemble the information together as you would a puzzle, until the information produces a detailed, comprehensive picture of your goal. Chances are that in the process of gathering the information, you will have made significant strides toward your goal.

■ What steps should I take to reach my goals?

Working with a pen and paper, imagine yourself at the center of a map and pretend to follow different directions.

Notice what the terrain is like, who comes to mind and what actions are possible with those people.

> **Examples:** *Imagine you will teach a class with the scientist you see on TV...follow the hiker you passed on the road through the rain...take the janitor you saw at your office to lunch.*

Use I-Mode to find out what the people are focusing on, where they're going and whether their needs coincide with yours. Notice where you end up and how long it took. Jot down these impressions as points on your map. Afterward, interpret your impressions. Then use similar questions to create a tentative action plan for your own goals.

> **Examples:** *I need to become more educated about how and why this product works...I should be prepared for unexpected shifts in the business climate...I'll look for ways to get the entire support staff behind this idea.*

Don't get locked into one goal. If you proceed intuitively, your goals and action plans will change...just as you, your business and the market grow and change.

Do these exercises every few months. This flexibility can make you even more successful.

Not All Stress Is Bad

Good stress can improve performance and reduce turnover. *Examples:* Tight deadlines and challenging work with clear goals and rewards. The more stress of this type employees experience, the less likely they are to look for a new job. *Contrast:* Bad stress is "hindrance-related" and interferes with accomplishment. Causes include office politics and corporate bureaucracy.

Study of 1,800 executives conducted by Cornell University and Ray & Berndtson Inc., an international executive recruiting firm, 301 Commerce, Suite 2300, Fort Worth, TX 76102.

How Not to Get Hurt By What You Don't Know

Martin Groder, MD, Chapel Hill, NC, psychiatrist and business consultant. He is author of *Business Games: How to Recognize the Players and Deal with Them.* Bottom Line Books.

There's a lot to know in today's world—new information...expanding technology... whole areas of expertise that never existed before.

No one can know everything, and what you don't know won't necessarily hurt you—as long as you *know* that you don't know it.

> **Example:** *If you're aware that you can't change a tire, you won't get in trouble when you get a flat—because you'll call for assistance instead.*

PRAISE VERSUS CRITICISM

Praising a person for a job well done is a powerful way to build the person's morale and confidence. But too many business owners and managers mix praise with criticism—turning an intended compliment into a put-down that incites resentment. *Example:* "You did a good job here. Now, if you can only get better at...." It is also a mistake to add an attempted humorous "zinger" to a compliment. *Example:* "You did a fine job on that project, and finished on time for once, too!" *Best:* Deliver praise straight, by itself, for best effect. Save criticism and humor for other occasions.

Dennis E. Murphy, publisher, *Managing People at Work*, 210 Commerce Blvd., Round Rock, TX 78664.

What poses the biggest threat to us are the things we think we know but actually don't know. In this state of denial, we become like the person with computer problems who pops it open and causes all kinds of damage trying to fix it. This type of thinking is the source of business blunders, poor management and personal strife.

The wise person is the one who knows his/her limitations and has a healthy respect for the extent of his ignorance.

WHAT YOU DON'T KNOW AT WORK

Most people try to do a good job on the basis of what they think they know, seeking out information that they lack.

But today's world has become so complex that few people know much at all outside of their limited area of expertise. Technical tasks, analysis, business operations, require detailed know-how possessed only by those who do them.

This means that managers are faced with the task of supervising and evaluating people who are doing mysterious things for mysterious reasons.

Managers try to correct "problems" in systems whose mechanics, principles and purposes they don't understand.

Today's manager is often in the position of a person who not only can't ride a bicycle but doesn't even know how a bicycle is supposed to ride.

Trap: If you think you know more than you do about the work your employees do, your direction, criticism and supervision will be worse than ineffective. Systems will be "fixed" when they aren't broken, and real problems will go uncorrected.

Technical workers will feel misunderstood. You'll become frustrated and anxious, and suffer from feelings of incompetence.

What doesn't help: Groups of managers who get together to decide how their employees should do their jobs, creating synergistic ignorance.

They spend hours at meetings where they encourage one another to believe they know things they don't. They also develop plans that have nothing

LESSONS IN BODY LANGUAGE

Nonverbal communication can be as powerful as words...

▶ **See whether someone's body language is open or closed.** An open person tends to keep arms unfolded, turn toward you while talking and keep his/her hands in sight.

▶ **If a person is engaged in a talk, he tends to move closer.**

▶ **A person who agrees with you will tend to mimic your own body position while talking.**

Impact: Openness plus engagement and common behavior usually add up to agreement. If any quality is missing, the person may have reservations that you should explore.

Nick Morgan, editor, *Harvard Management Communication Letter,* 60 Harvard Way, Boston 02163.

to do with authentic goals and the problems that get in the way.

ESCAPE FROM IGNORANCE

Our most important step is accepting the extent and depth of our ignorance, and realizing that it is nothing to be ashamed of or defensive about.

We're all in the same position. With so much developing on so many fronts—so much new information and so many new ways to use it—the amount we don't know is expanding exponentially.

We wake up more ignorant every day, and we will for the rest of our lives. Better get used to it.

The good news: There are people around you who know more than you do. This is an age of specialists and subspecialists—people who spend time and energy mastering every area that is dark to you. Learn from them.

LEARNING TO KNOW MORE

◼ Make smart workers your teachers.

Not only will this put you in a better position to evaluate what is being done and avoid unnecessary efforts, but it will also raise workers' self-esteem and create fine working relationships.

◼ Assume you know absolutely nothing about the process, mechanism or operation at hand...and don't be afraid to ask the most simple-minded questions.

Get a working model of the worker's area of expertise...how does he/she know when things are functioning properly and when they have gone wrong? How does he troubleshoot?

◼ Stop talking—and listen, until you get a sense of what questions to ask.

What most annoys specialists in any area are outsiders who invariably ask the same questions, assuming they know something and are unaware of how stupid they sound.

Better: Take the position of an absolute beginner.

◼ Seek honest feedback.

Your best friend may tell you when you're misinformed, but it is unlikely that people who work for you will.

For good reason—the bearer of an unflattering truth is vulnerable to retaliation.

Helpful: Create a climate in which everyone feels safe giving feedback. Make it clear that you know there are things you don't know and need to find out what they are.

◼ Play a supportive role.

A single individual is as limited and powerless as a single cell.

But when a team of experts band together, they become a multicellular organism, a highly intelligent entity that can accomplish wonderful things.

As a manager, you bring expertise in coordinating efforts, resolving conflicts, acquiring the resources that your employees need. The more you know about what each member of the team actually does, the better you can help the whole operation function smoothly.

OVERCOMING PERSONAL IGNORANCE

The same principles do apply in interpersonal relationships inside and outside the office, where conflicts and bad feelings tend to arise when people don't know the effect they have on others but think they do.

EMPLOYEES WHO PLAY TOGETHER WORK BETTER TOGETHER

Voluntary recreational activities engaged in by employees outside of work help build relationships and teamwork far beyond what will ever be possible in an office setting. Such outside competitive games are a good outlet for stress from office conflicts. *Important:* Voluntary activities must be truly voluntary. "Compulsory voluntary" activities that employees are pressured into joining can produce destructive resentment. Don't hold lack of participation against anybody.

John Mariotti, president, The Enterprise Group, management consultants, 717 Brixworth Blvd., Knoxville, TN 37922.

Example: You think you're communicating concern and sympathy, but others experience you as intrusive. Or you're sure your spouse accepts your need to put in long hours at the office, but he/she actually resents your absence.

Solution: Don't assume you know other people's thoughts, feelings and reactions. Seek feedback. When you explain something, make sure you're understood. Be open to the honest feelings of others.

What you don't know about yourself can be far more enlightening than you imagine, too. When we feel confused or unhappy, we often have no idea why.

Helpful: Journaling—writing freely and at length to explore your feelings more deeply. Journaling also helps you discover parts of yourself that were hidden.

You may not find immediate answers to personal dilemmas and tough decisions. But you will learn more clearly what the problems are and what steps must be taken to resolve them.

The Work-vs.-Home Stress Cycle

The work-vs-home stress cycle can undermine employee productivity as many workers take job problems home and personal ones to work—becoming increasingly stressed in both locations. *To help break the cycle:* Give employees flexibility whenever possible—some extra time off to handle stress at home can bring increased workplace productivity. When employees have temporary home or family problems, managers should listen sympathetically and supportively—offering to help the employees or making suggestions when appropriate.

Charlene Bell, PhD, psychologist and business consultant, Des Moines, quoted in *Smart Workplace Practices,* 520 S. Pierce, Mason City, IA 50401.

Defusing Workplace Conflicts

Quickly defuse workplace conflicts that have the potential to become violent. If one team member feels threatened by another, investigate the situation promptly and keep the employees working apart while doing so. If there is any evidence backing up the person who feels threatened, immediately send the suspected aggressor home and start a formal investigation. This would be indicated if, for instance, other team members agreed that one person was intimidating another—even though they did not know exactly how or to what extent.

Mike Clark-Madison, editor, *Managing People at Work,* 2055 W. Army Trail Rd., Ste. 100, Addison, IL 60101.

Team Goals

Incorporate team goals into personnel performance requirements. *Aim:* To be sure employees make teamwork a top priority while trying to do their own best jobs as individuals. First have a team identify its overall goals. Then have each employee come up with ways he or she will contribute to the team's efforts. Make the employees' planned contributions part of their individual performance plans. *Also helpful:* Use peer review to measure each employee's skill at working with other team members to fulfill common goals.

Dennis E. Murphy, publisher, *Managing People at Work,* 210 Commerce Blvd., Round Rock, TX 78664.

TO BEAT PROCRASTINATION, FACE IT SQUARELY

Ask what your real reason is for not getting started. Write it down or tape yourself stating it. That alone may break the bottleneck so you can start. *Also helpful:* Do small tasks in real time—for instance, take phone calls when they come in instead of letting phone messages pile up. Think of three to five easy things you could do to get involved in a project, and start doing them—immediately. Arrange your desk for productivity by keeping the work area itself clear, with supplies on a credenza behind you.

Jeff Davidson, MBA, CMC, speaker, Chapel Hill, NC, and author of *The Complete Idiot's Guide to Reaching Your Goal.* Alpha Books.

PRAISE IS MOST POWERFUL WHEN GIVEN IN PUBLIC

Kind words from the boss received in private are nice, but public praise carries far more impact. Best of all is praise that is given in front of the boss's own superiors. *Payoff for both:* The employee gets a motivational lift...and the boss will receive greater loyalty from the employee who feels more appreciated.

Dennis E. Murphy, publisher, *Managing People at Work,* 210 Commerce Blvd., Round Rock, TX 78664.

Getting Feedback

To get office feedback regularly, ask supervisors and coworkers indirectly. *Example:* "I know no one is perfect—what do you think I could do better?" Ask open-ended questions—not narrow, fact-oriented ones. Establish a baseline for people with whom you work—if a boss usually calls your work good, you have probably done especially well if he or she calls a project terrific. Try finding a third party to get you information. *Example:* Someone with the same rank as your boss, who can obtain information and pass it on to you.

Nella Barkley, president, Crystal-Barkley Corp., career counselors, New York.

Worry Produces More Worry

There are only two things to worry about—things you cannot change and things you can change. If you can't change something, make a decision not to let it have a negative effect on you. *Examples:* Bad weather, heavy traffic. If you can change something, focus on what you can do. Taking action uses time and effort effectively. Worrying fritters away both.

Terry Hampton, West Plains, Missouri–based coauthor of *99 Ways to Be Happier Every Day.* Pelican.

Pessimism Is Hazardous to Your Health

Pessimism is hazardous to your health, says a study that analyzed data going back more than 70 years. In the 1930s and 1940s, participants in an ongoing lifestyle study were asked their views on life. As the participants went through life, those whose answers identified them as pessimists—more males fell into this category than females—were more likely to die from accidents, violence or suicide than those with more cheerful, optimistic outlooks. *Theory:* Pessimists may have poor problem-solving skills, more social difficulties and participate in more high-risk activities.

Christopher Peterson, PhD, professor of psychology, University of Michigan, Ann Arbor. His analysis of participants in the Terman Life-Cycle Study was published in *Psychological Science.*

Reinterpreting Your Worst Failures

Reinterpret your worst failures in light of your current life. Make a list of the 10 biggest failures in your life—and what they led to. See failures as rearrangements of your plans, not true failures. Look at what you learned or gained from each and how each led you to where you are now. Then forgive yourself for the failures.

Suzanne Falter-Barns, lecturer and consultant on inspiration and creativity, Essex, NY, and author of *How Much Joy Can You Stand?* Publishing Group West.

ALWAYS QUIT WITH CLASS

When telling your boss you are leaving, dress as you would for an interview. Do not speak ill of anyone. Show your value by completing all projects. Keep your resignation impersonal. Don't discuss where you're going. Clean out your desk after hours to avoid distracting your coworkers.

Marilyn Moats Kennedy, publisher, *Kennedy's Career Strategist,* 1150 Wilmette Ave., Wilmette, IL 60091.

STRESS CONTROL

Require employees in high-stress jobs to take periodic vacations. Individuals in high-pressure occupations need periodic vacations to remain fresh on the job. But they also are the people least likely to schedule a vacation, because they always feel they have so much to do. *Best:* Require them to take vacations—immediately, if signs of burnout or deteriorating job performance appear. A well-deserved vacation can rejuvenate an overstressed employee. *Also:* Tell employees who take man-dated vacations to leave their cell phones and laptop computers in the office, and not to call in. Assure that they get the real break from work that they need.

Mark Goulston, MD, psychiatrist, business-relations specialist, marketing consultant and sales trainer, Santa Monica, CA. He is author of *Get Out of Your Own Way: Overcoming Self-Defeating Behavior.* Perigee Books.

GIVE YOURSELF TIME ALONE REGULARLY

Everyone needs it—some need it more than others. Taking time off from your spouse does not mean rejecting him or her. Rather, you're giving yourself time for reflection, daydreaming, rest and self-healing. *Caution:* This time is not enough to strengthen a relationship. You must find projects to do together.

Lonnie Barbach, PhD, psychotherapist, department of psychiatry, University of California Medical School, San Francisco, and coauthor of *Going the Distance: Finding and Keeping Lifelong Love.* Plume.

REDUCING ABSENTEEISM

Reduce absenteeism by including it in performance reviews. Know just how often an employee was absent, and mention it as a percentage of all work days—comparing it with a standard. Write up all unexcused absences, even when employees are otherwise fine. This creates a paper trail for frequently absent employees while making it clear that everyone is treated the same way. When employees return to work, ask tactful, forward-looking questions focusing on what can be done to prevent future absences.

Morey Stettner, editor, *Working Smart,* 1750 Old Meadow Rd., Suite 302, McLean, VA 22102.

Big Help in Getting Things Done Right

Paul D. Tieger and **Barbara Barron-Tieger,** consultants in West Hartford, CT, have helped organizations work with personality types for more than 15 years. They are authors of *The Art of Speed Reading People.* Little, Brown & Company.

Treating others as you would like to be treated isn't the most effective way to deal with them. It only works with people who are similar to you.

Problem: The words and gestures that would win you over might antagonize someone else.

You'll be much more successful if you can quickly "read" people's words and actions and change your approach to fit their personalities.

MODIFY YOUR STYLE

Some people think if they adapt their behavior to suit other people, they aren't being true to themselves...or they simply don't want to bother.

But modifying your style benefits you. Whether you're dealing with a boss, coworker, customer or your child's teacher, you're more likely to get what you want if you communicate in a way that makes the other person receptive.

A good way to read people's key personality characteristics is to think in terms of four dimensions. You can learn to recognize where a person falls within these four dimensions and choose the most effective way to deal with that person.

INTROVERSION/EXTROVERSION

This quality has to do with how people get energized—from interacting with others...or by being by themselves.

Clues: Extroverts are easy to recognize. They talk a lot, think out loud and are animated when they're around other people. Introverts are calmer, speak more slowly and think before they speak.

To reach an Extrovert: Don't just let him talk —voice your opinions...keep the conversation moving...cover many topics—Extroverts get bored quickly.

To reach an Introvert: Ask for her thoughts— Introverts don't volunteer them. Listen carefully

…resist the urge to finish an Introvert's sentences …discuss one thing at a time…if possible, make your points in writing…and give her time to reflect on them.

SENSING/INTUITION

This refers to the kind of *information* we focus on. Sensing types prefer concrete facts…Intuitives are more concerned with the underlying meaning and implications of those facts.

Clues: Sensors are direct and to the point. They keep their sentences short, with each thought following systematically from the last one. They use a lot of facts and details when they talk. They remember the past with amazing accuracy.

Intuitives speak in longer, more complicated sentences. They are not linear thinkers—their thoughts jump around. They're more likely to use analogies and metaphors than facts. They talk about global issues…the big picture…the future.

To reach a Sensor: Present your information methodically, step by step. Come armed with facts and examples—how much will the project cost… how long will it take…who will carry out each task? Emphasize practical applications.

To reach an Intuitive: Talk about possibilities rather than details…use metaphors…brainstorm …emphasize the implications. What could this project mean for your company? Your industry?

THINKING/FEELING

This quality reflects how we make decisions. Thinking types do prefer logic and impersonal analysis. Feeling types are driven more by their emotions and personal values.

Clues: Thinkers assert themselves easily. They come across as objective and detached—even blunt. It's hard to offend them. Many Thinking types have a habit of numbering the points they make ("There are two things wrong with this idea—first…second…"). They enjoy a good argument.

Feelers have obvious emotional ups and downs. They are diplomatic, avoid conflict and are quick to compliment others. Feelers tend to reveal a lot about their personal lives—by keeping family pictures on their desks and talking about what they like to do after hours. They also use a lot of "value" words, such as *wonderful, terrible, beautiful* and *ugly*.

To reach a Thinker: Make sure your argument makes logical sense…appeal to his sense of fairness…stress consequences.

> **Example:** *If you need time off to visit a sick relative, don't talk about how important the person was to you while you were growing up. Instead, explain how your work will get done while you're away—and how much more productive you'll be once you've taken care of this situation.*

To reach a Feeler: Start by finding points of agreement…express appreciation…discuss "people" concerns.

JUDGING/PERCEIVING

This dimension has to do with how people structure their daily lives.

Judging types tend to be highly organized, formal and time-conscious.

Perceivers are typically more casual, spontaneous, unconventional—and disorganized.

Clues: Judgers tend to be right on time for their appointments, have a "take-charge" attitude, complete one project before starting another, move quickly and purposefully, have tidy work and living spaces and like rules and systems.

Perceivers may procrastinate, are more playful, move at a slower pace, enjoy starting projects more than finishing them, use "qualifiers" when they speak ("The best I can tell…," "I could be wrong, but…"), and keep gathering information and changing their plans.

To reach a Judger: Be punctual…be efficient and well-prepared—don't waste time…be definitive, not tentative…stick to existing plans.

To reach a Perceiver: Expect lots of questions, and welcome them…encourage the person to explore options…be willing to change plans.

Super Relaxation Treat— A Hammock

Even if you cannot hang one between trees, you can buy a hammock stand and set it up anywhere. Hammocks are most often made of cotton rope—better hammocks use a heavier gauge and are more tightly woven. Stands can be made of wood or tubular steel. Wood has nice curves and lots of attraction…metal is strong and more economical. Wheel kits are available for some stands so hammocks can be moved easily around the yard.

Mark Williams, owner, Williams Patio Furniture, Highland Park, Il.

Heart and Stroke Advisory

Chapter 11

Smart Heart Strategies— Best Ways to Beat Heart Disease

The fast-growing mountain of studies and media reports on heart disease prevention and treatments is difficult for most people to absorb. And making matters more complicated, the data on the disease are often contradictory from one study to the next.

Dr. William Castelli, one of the country's leading experts on heart disease, explains the best ways to prevent heart disease...

What is the best way to determine one's risk for heart disease? Risk is largely dependent on certain critical factors. *Important...*

■ **Total cholesterol and high-density lipoprotein (HDL) cholesterol levels.** These figures report the percentage of fatty deposits in your blood.

Your heart attack risk increases 2% for every 1% increase in total cholesterol. Total cholesterol should be lower than 150. If it is higher, the ratio of total cholesterol to HDL should be no more than four.

HDL is a form of cholesterol that's good for you. It removes cholesterol from deposits to be excreted by the liver. Low-density lipoprotein (LDL) is the "bad" cholesterol that clogs arteries. LDL should be lower than 130—or lower than 70 in people with vascular problems.

■ **Triglycerides are the most common form of fat in the human body.**

Recently identified as independent risk factors for heart disease, triglycerides tend to increase when

William Castelli, MD, medical director of Framingham Cardiovascular Institute and former director of the famed Framingham Heart Study. He taught epidemiology and prevention of atherosclerotic disease for more than 20 years at Harvard Medical School, Boston University School of Medicine and University of Massachusetts School of Medicine. He is author of *The New Good Fat Bad Fat.* Perseus Publishing.

we eat too much saturated fat and cholesterol. Triglycerides can be a problem, even when cholesterol levels are normal.

■ Syndrome X.

Elevated triglycerides have been linked to Syndrome X.

Symptoms include extra weight around the middle, low HDL, increased insulin resistance (usually a blood sugar over 100) and hypertension. Left unchecked, Syndrome X usually leads to coronary artery disease.

Ideal: Triglyceride level no higher than 150—or 100 if you have heart problems.

■ Blood pressure.

Although hypertension has been commonly linked with heart disease, the Framingham Heart Study demonstrated that almost half of all strokes occur in people with seemingly normal blood pressure.

Ideal: Most experts now agree that blood pressure should be slightly below 120/80.

■ Blood sugar level.

Beyond its contribution to Syndrome X, blood sugar level is a risk factor that most people do not consider.

Ideal: Blood sugar level that is lower than 100. Higher levels increase your risk of diabetes and heart disease.

■ Idleness greatly increases the odds for higher cholesterol and lower HDL levels.

Data show that HDL levels can be boosted by as much as 20% if you exercise for 30 minutes, six times a week.

Additional benefits of regular exercise include lowered blood pressure and weight reduction.

How important is family history as a heart disease risk factor? Indeed, it is very important. However, by controlling your numbers and exercising regularly, the genes you inherit play a much smaller role in heart disease. That's especially true since advances in medicine have given us strategies to effectively control inherited cholesterol and triglyceride problems.

Which is more troublesome—the level of saturated fat in foods or the level of cholesterol? If you watch the level of fat in the foods you eat, saturated fat is more important than cholesterol—but both need to be watched.

Ideal: Create a daily fat *budget* and stick to it. To keep your cholesterol and triglyceride levels within healthy limits, eat no more than 20 grams (g) of saturated fat...and 65 g of total fat—daily. *Helpful...*

▶ **Stick to whole grains**—such as oats, brown rice and whole wheat.

▶ **Eat at least seven or eight servings of fruits and raw or steamed vegetables daily,** with an emphasis on dark-green and yellow types, such as broccoli, spinach and squash.

▶ **Avoid eating too much animal fat,** found in red meat and dairy products. Also avoid oils like coconut oil and corn oil.

If your cholesterol, triglyceride, blood pressure or blood sugar levels are too high, eat no more than 10 to 15 g of saturated fat and 50 g of total fat daily.

▶ **Avoid hydrogenated oils, too.** Their processing creates by-products called *trans-fatty acids*, which raise levels of bad (or LDL) cholesterol.

Examples: Margarine in which the first ingredient listed is something other than water...and products that contain vegetable shortening.

Also, don't be fooled by the words *no cholesterol* or *cholesterol-free* on food boxes. Cholesterol is found only in animal fats. But these products often contain high amounts of saturated fat from vegetable oils.

Should I take aspirin daily if I'm not at risk for heart disease? Yes—but always check with your doctor first. By thinning your blood, aspirin helps lower the risk of small blood clots forming inside clogged arteries.

It's a good idea to take one 81-milligram (mg), enteric-coated aspirin tablet daily if you are a man age 50 or older...or a postmenopausal woman.

Take one aspirin tablet daily *regardless of your age*, if your numbers are above normal...or you've had a heart attack...or you're overweight...or you smoke. To help prevent stomach upset, I recommend taking the aspirin halfway through any meal.

Do alcohol-free wine and grape juice provide the same heart-protective benefits as wine? We have no conclusive evidence at this time. We do know, however, that *one 4-ounce glass* of red or white wine per day can help lower your risk of heart attack. Whiskey and beer are similarly effective.

Important: Three drinks per day *increases* cancer and *total* death rates.

Which vitamin supplements are the most beneficial for preventing heart disease? The most promising data we have are for vitamin E, which has been shown to reduce heart attacks by 77%. Since it is difficult to obtain ample amounts of vitamin E in the diet without adding too much fat, I advocate the addition of 400 international units (IU) of d-alpha-tocopherol E daily.

Smaller studies have shown that 500 to 1,000 mg of vitamin C...and 200 micrograms (mcg) of selenium also offer some protection. All three are antioxidants—compounds that appear to protect cells and LDL cholesterol from attack and oxidation by unbalanced free radical molecules. This oxidation can lead to a buildup of plaque, clogging arteries.

It's also a good idea to add a B-complex supplement to combat high levels of *homocysteines*—amino acids that can block the main coronary arteries leading to the heart.

Caution: Niacin (500 mg daily) also lowers cholesterol. Niacin can cause flushing, tingling and itching. These symptoms generally disappear within a few days, but they can return if you don't take it every day at the same time or in the same dose.

Vitamin supplements do not replace a plentiful variety of fruits, vegetables and whole grains each day.

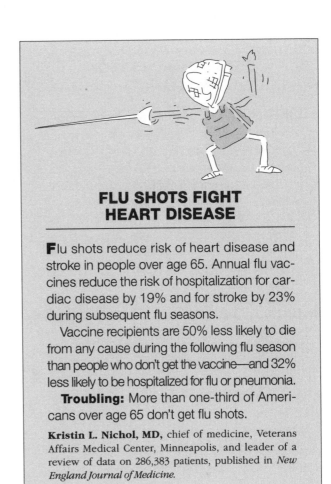

FLU SHOTS FIGHT HEART DISEASE

Flu shots reduce risk of heart disease and stroke in people over age 65. Annual flu vaccines reduce the risk of hospitalization for cardiac disease by 19% and for stroke by 23% during subsequent flu seasons.

Vaccine recipients are 50% less likely to die from any cause during the following flu season than people who don't get the vaccine—and 32% less likely to be hospitalized for flu or pneumonia.

Troubling: More than one-third of Americans over age 65 don't get flu shots.

Kristin L. Nichol, MD, chief of medicine, Veterans Affairs Medical Center, Minneapolis, and leader of a review of data on 286,383 patients, published in *New England Journal of Medicine.*

"Tired Blood" Increases Risk of Heart Attack

People who are chronically exhausted face an increased risk for heart attack. As part of a recent study, blood drawn from well-rested men was compared with blood drawn from men classified as chronically tired. *Finding:* The "tired" blood contained high levels of PAI-1, a compound linked to blood clots in coronary arteries. *Self-defense:* If you're chronically tired, ask a doctor how this could best be treated. It may also be important to have your blood PAI-1 level tested.

Willem J. Kop, PhD, research assistant professor of medical and clinical psychology, Uniformed Services University of the Health Sciences, Bethesda, MD.

BEST HEART ATTACK TREATMENT

Best treatment after a mild heart attack: Conservative treatment. Doctors should use aspirin and other medications…a treadmill exercise test to check the heart under stress… and *ventriculography*—an X-ray exam of the heart. Patients treated more aggressively after a mild attack—with angioplasty, bypass surgery or other invasive techniques—are more likely to die or have a second nonfatal heart attack in the next 12 months. After that, there is no significant difference between the two groups.

William Boden, MD, professor of medicine, University of Connecticut Health Center, whose study of 920 heart attack patients was published in *The New England Journal of Medicine.*

Tomatoes and Heart Attack

In a study, eating a diet rich in the antioxidant *lycopene* cuts heart attack risk by 50%. *Best sources:* Tomato paste…ketchup…tomato sauce… canned or bottled tomato juice. Lycopene is most easily absorbed when tomatoes or tomato products are cooked—especially in a little oil. Lycopene also reduces the risk of prostate cancer.

Lenore Kohlmeier, PhD, professor of epidemiology and nutrition, School of Public Health and Medicine at the University of North Carolina, Chapel Hill.

Heart-Saving Soy

To benefit from soy's ability to lower blood cholesterol, you need soy protein combined with isoflavones, not soy protein alone.

But: Processing soy into tofu and other products may remove most of the isoflavones—substances that also fight prostate cancer.

For foods high in isoflavones, try specialty items available in health food stores.

> **Examples:** *Nutlettes cereal…Beanuts roasted soy nuts…Take Care beverage powder…Vigor Aid nutritional drink…GeniSoy soy protein bars.*

John Crouse III, MD, director of Preventive Cardiology Center, Wake Forest University School of Medicine, Winston-Salem, NC, whose study of people with elevated cholesterol was reported in *Circulation.*

Seasonal Heart Attack Risk

Heart attacks peak in mid-winter. The increase occurs throughout the US—not just where it snows. So it may not only be caused by the physical strains of dropping temperatures and snow shoveling. *Possible:* Winter illnesses, such as pneumonia and the flu, may weaken the body, making cardiac stress more likely…decreased sunlight exposure may also increase cardiac risk.

Frederick Spencer, MD, associate professor of medicine, division of cardiovascular medicine, University of Massachusetts Medical Center, Worcester, whose study of nearly 260,000 heart attack cases was published in the *Journal of the American College of Cardiology.*

Reduce Your Heart Attack Risk

If your *good* cholesterol—HDL—is low, cholesterol-lowering drugs such as *lovastatin* (Mevacor) may ward off a heart attack even though your *total* cholesterol is OK. Participants in a recent study had below-average HDLs (less than 50) and an average total cholesterol of 221 (about the US average). Lovastatin treatment reduced heart attack risk by 40% in men age 45 and older...and in women 55 and older.

Antonio M. Gotto, MD, dean, Cornell University Medical College, New York, and senior author of a study published in the *Journal of the American Medical Association.*

Syndrome X

Gerald M. Reaven, MD, professor of medicine at Stanford University School of Medicine in Stanford, CA. He is coauthor of *Syndrome X: Overcoming the Silent Killer That Can Give You a Heart Attack.* Simon & Schuster.

I t's well known that a high cholesterol level—especially a high level of LDL (bad) cholesterol—is a major risk factor for heart attacks. Now, another risk factor is finally getting the attention it deserves as a major contributor to heart disease. That factor is insulin resistance.

Insulin—produced by the pancreas—is the hormone that ushers blood sugar (glucose) into cells. Cells can become resistant to insulin's action. When they do, the pancreas pumps out more insulin in an attempt to "force" sugar into the cells.

Excess insulin directly damages coronary arteries. It also triggers an array of metabolic abnormalities that contribute to the development of artery-clogging fatty plaques and to blood clots.

Together these abnormalities are called "syndrome X." Syndrome X affects 70 million Americans. *Symptoms include...*

▶ **Excess fibrinogen,** a substance that promotes blood clots.

▶ **Excess plasminogen activator inhibitor-1** (PAI-1), a substance that slows clot breakdown.

▶ **High levels of triglycerides,** the body's main fat-storage particles.

▶ **Low levels of HDL (good) cholesterol,** which sweeps fat out of arteries.

Many people with syndrome X also have high blood pressure. And they're likely to have glucose intolerance—a condition characterized by slightly elevated blood sugar levels.

Important: Glucose intolerance is *not* diabetes. But up to 5% of people with syndrome X go on to develop type-2 diabetes annually. That's the form that occurs when the body becomes insensitive to the effects of insulin, driving up blood sugar levels.

DIAGNOSING SYNDROME X

The results of five simple tests point to a diagnosis of syndrome X. The risk for a heart attack rises with each out-of-bounds test score.

▶ **Fasting triglyceride level** above 200 milligrams per deciliter (mg/dl).

▶ **Fasting HDL level** under 35 mg/dl.

▶ **Blood pressure** higher than 145/90.

▶ **Being overweight** by 15 pounds or more.

▶ **Fasting blood sugar level** higher than 110 mg/dl...or a level higher than 140 two hours after drinking a glucose solution.

FIGHTING SYNDROME X

■ **Eat the right diet.**

Americans are besieged by a glut of high-concept diets, all of them purporting to be the best for weight loss and health.

The American Heart Association diet counsels cutting down on fat and boosting consumption of carbohydrates. *The Zone* diet advises boosting protein intake and lowering fat.

These diets may work for people who don't have syndrome X. But protein and carbohydrates stimulate insulin production—which is dangerous for people with the syndrome.

The Atkins diet counsels consumption of few carbohydrates and as much fat as desired. But that diet is too high in artery-clogging saturated fat.

The ideal diet to combat syndrome X contains 45% of calories from carbohydrates…15% from protein…and 40% from fat.

Key: Emphasize beneficial mono- and polyunsaturated fats. These should supply 30% to 35% of the diet. Only 5% to 10% should come from saturated fats.

Good sources of healthful fats include avocados…fatty fish (such as sea bass, trout, sole and salmon)…natural peanut butter…nuts and seeds …canola, corn, olive, safflower, peanut, soybean, sesame and sunflower oils.

▨ Lose weight.
Shedding pounds improves insulin resistance.

Study: Insulin resistance declined an average of 40% in overweight individuals who lost 20 pounds.

▨ Exercise.
People who exercise daily use insulin 25% more efficiently than those who do not exercise.

Forty-five minutes of aerobic exercise a day is ideal.

▨ Stop smoking.
Smoking promotes insulin resistance.

MEDICATION
If lifestyle changes alone don't overcome syndrome X, medication can help….

▨ Triglyceride-lowering medication.
Three drugs can lower triglyceride levels.

These drugs also lower PAI-1 levels and raise HDL cholesterol.

One of them—nicotinic acid—has the added benefit of lowering LDL cholesterol. A common side effect of nicotinic acid is facial flushing.

Self-defense: To minimize flushing from nicotinic acid, increase the dose gradually.

Two other effective drugs are *gemfibrozil* (Lopid) and *fenofibrate* (Tricor). In rare cases, however, they can cause liver damage.

Self-defense: Talk to your doctor about testing your liver function periodically.

▨ Blood pressure medication.
Fifty percent of people with high blood pressure have syndrome X.

But some blood pressure drugs can actually worsen the condition.

Talk to your doctor about the potential risks of high-dose diuretics and beta-blockers if you have syndrome X.

▨ Diabetes medication.
Because syndrome X is caused by insulin resistance, it's logical to ask whether *thiazolidinediones* —drugs that increase insulin sensitivity— might be helpful. Such drugs are currently used to treat type-2 diabetes.

Ongoing research will determine if thiazolidinediones improve syndrome X. Until the studies are completed, these drugs should *not* be used to treat the condition.

Heart Attack Symptoms… Gender Differences

Lynn Smaha, MD, PhD, past president, American Heart Association, Dallas.

What are considered the classic signs of a heart attack are actually the symptoms experienced by men. Unfortunately, heart attacks in women are often undiagnosed—and untreated—because the signs of heart trouble are different. It is important to know the symptoms for each gender.

▨ For women…
▶ **Chest, stomach or abdominal pain** that does not necessarily feel acute or crushing.

▶ **Nausea or dizziness.**

► **Shortness of breath.**

► **Heart palpitations.**

► **Fatigue.**

► **General feeling of weakness.**

■ **For men...**

► **Uncomfortable pressure, fullness, squeezing or pain in the center of the chest** that lasts more than a few minutes or quickly fades in and out.

► **Pain that radiates to shoulders, neck, arms or jaw.**

► **Any of the above symptoms accompanied by lightheadedness, sweating, nausea or shortness of breath.**

Important: Whether man or woman, if you are having any of the above symptoms, immediately chew a full-strength (325 milligram) aspirin and get to the hospital as soon as possible.

ANOTHER BENEFIT OF FRIENDSHIP

Heart disease risk increases in socially isolated men.

Background: Studies have linked social relationships to better health and lower mortality rates from heart disease. In a new study of blood samples taken from men in their 70s, those with less social interaction had higher levels of C-reactive protein and other components linked to inflammation, an established risk factor for heart disease.

Theory: Social isolation may lead to negative behaviors, such as physical inactivity and smoking, which contribute to heart disease.

Eric Loucks, PhD, instructor and research fellow, department of society, human development and health, Harvard School of Public Health, Boston.

My Approach to High Blood Pressure

Timothy McCall, MD, a Boston internist, medical editor of *Yoga Journal* and author of *Examining Your Doctor: A Patient's Guide to Avoiding Harmful Medical Care*. Citadel Press.

Elevated blood pressure (hypertension) rarely causes symptoms. But it does raise the risk for serious complications like heart attacks, strokes and kidney failure.

Much can be done to prevent and treat hypertension. Unfortunately, one-third of the 50 million Americans who have the condition don't know it, and only one-quarter of those who know they have it have their pressure under control.

It's a good idea to get your blood pressure (BP) measured once a year. More frequent checks are worthwhile if hypertension runs in your family or if you have other risk factors for heart disease, such as smoking or diabetes.

Until recently, people were diagnosed with hypertension only if their readings were consistently above 140/90. But mounting evidence suggests that the risk for complications rises when readings are consistently 120/80 or above. Elevations of either systolic pressure (the top number) or diastolic pressure (the bottom number) raise the risk.

That said, if your blood pressure isn't sky-high— say 180/110—there is generally no rush to start drug treatment. Nondrug approaches may bring your readings down without exposing you to drug side effects, such as fatigue and sexual dysfunction. They may even eliminate the need for drug therapy.

▧ Lose weight.

Blood pressure often starts to rise in middle age, when people start putting on pounds.

Recent evidence suggests that even minimal weight loss—as little as one pound a year—can significantly reduce blood pressure and the risk for complications. The key is to maintain the loss.

A diet rich in fruits and vegetables, low-fat or nonfat dairy products and high-fiber foods, such as whole grains and legumes, helps keep weight off.

Such a diet is also a great source of the vitamins and minerals that are known to reduce blood pressure. These include potassium, magnesium, calcium and vitamin C. You could try getting these vitamins and minerals from supplements, but the evidence is stronger for the benefit of deriving them from foods.

▧ Stay active.

Exercise is a key factor in maintaining weight loss. It also has a direct effect on blood pressure.

I recommend aerobic activities like swimming, brisk walking and biking. But even tai chi—an ancient Chinese system of low-intensity movements —has a salutary effect. Weight training with light weights also works.

▧ Change pressure-boosting habits.

Stop smoking, limit alcohol consumption to one to two drinks a day and limit caffeinated beverages.

Some people with hypertension are sensitive to salt, so it's worth avoiding salty foods, such as canned soups. Use the saltshaker sparingly, too.

▧ Reduce psychological stress.

Stress and life satisfaction are big factors that can affect blood pressure.

Proven stress reduction measures include yoga, meditation and even owning a pet. Make time in your life for friends and family and for meaningful activities that enhance your sense of life's value.

If six to 12 months of these nondrug approaches fail to lower your blood pressure sufficiently, you may need medication. Diuretics, such as *hydrochlorothiazide* (HCTZ), and beta-blockers, such as *metoprolol* (Lopressor), seem to provide the greatest benefit. Diuretics, in particular, are inexpensive and well-tolerated—and underprescribed by physicians, largely due to the heavy marketing of more expensive drugs.

Even if you take blood pressure medication, it still pays to use nondrug measures to help keep pressure down. If you can lower your weight and stress levels, for example, your doctor might be able to prescribe a lower dose of medication—and someday, perhaps, take you off the drugs completely.

The Surprising Link Between High Blood Pressure and Hidden Emotions

Samuel J. Mann, MD, associate professor of clinical medicine at the Hypertension Center of Weill Medical College of Cornell University and New York Presbyterian Hospital, both in New York. He is author of *Healing Hypertension: A Revolutionary New Approach.* John Wiley & Sons.

When doctors diagnose and treat high blood pressure, they usually look at risk factors such as obesity and a family history of hypertension.

Emotions also play a role in hypertension—but not many doctors take emotions into account. For this reason, many patients are receiving suboptimal treatment.

TRANSIENT EMOTIONS

It's widely assumed that people who often feel tense tend to develop hypertension. Research does *not* support this belief.

Everyday anger and anxiety clearly cause *transient* increases in blood pressure. However, these brief increases have not been linked to the development of sustained high blood pressure—the kind that increases the risk for stroke and heart attack.

Hidden emotions may be an important factor for more than one in four people who develop hypertension.

What exactly are hidden emotions? They are not the feelings you consciously "hold in"—for example, when you're angry but choose not to yell at your boss.

Hidden emotions are the ones you're not even aware of. Because they're never examined or dealt with, they persist for years. And they can have a profound effect on blood pressure.

Studies suggest that people who are outwardly placid are three times more likely to have high blood pressure than people who are more outwardly emotional.

Hidden emotions are often a consequence of major emotional trauma—the loss of a loved one, physical abuse, etc.—that occurred long ago.

Most people who endure such events acknowledge their emotional pain. But some individuals insist that they don't have any feelings connected with these events.

These people do have feelings, of course. It's just that the feelings remain buried and may ultimately manifest themselves in physical ways.

CLUES TO HIDDEN EMOTIONS

Are hidden emotions contributing to your hypertension? Or is your hypertension a hereditary condition that has little to do with emotions?

There are many clues that can help you answer these questions. *Start by reflecting on your emotional history...*

▶ **Were you raised in a family that didn't discuss feelings?**

▶ **Do you tend to be unemotional** even in situations that cause other people to feel hurt or angry?

▶ **Have you gone through an event that most people would consider traumatic**—yet brushed it off as not having affected you?

Friends and family members may be able to provide clues to your emotional status. In many cases, others are more aware of our sadness, anger or tension than we ourselves are.

Your medical history can also provide clues. *Hidden emotions may play a role if you answer "yes" to one or more of these questions...*

▶ **Did your hypertension begin abruptly** rather than over a period of years?

▶ **Is your hypertension severe and unresponsive to blood pressure medication?**

▶ **Are you thin and lacking in a family history of hypertension?**

▶ **Do you have other possibly emotion-related conditions,** such as insomnia, migraines, asthma, nightmares or chronic pain?

TREATING HYPERTENSION

Lifestyle changes, including adopting a low-fat diet that's rich in fruits and vegetables...exercising regularly…cutting back on your consumption of alcohol…and in some cases, cutting back on your salt intake can help reduce the need for blood pressure medication.

Mind/body approaches—such as relaxation and biofeedback—can reduce emotional stress. However, studies show that they do not have any sustained effect on blood pressure.

For many hypertensives, simply becoming more aware of their long-hidden emotions can make a big difference.

Once hidden feelings are brought out into the open and discussed with individuals you trust, blood pressure can fall substantially.

There are effective tools to help you do this…

■ **Psychotherapy.** Therapy focused on hidden emotions can help the process of opening up to them.

■ **Support groups.** The atmosphere of mutual trust and safety that exists in a good group makes it easier to open up to painful feelings.

Contact hospitals or counseling centers to find out about support groups near you.

CHOOSING MEDICATION WISELY

If your blood pressure remains elevated despite lifestyle changes and/or emotional exploration, medication will be necessary.

Your doctor is likely to recommend drugs if your systolic blood pressure (the top number) remains above 140—particularly if you have other risk factors for cardiovascular disease, such as being a smoker or having high cholesterol or diabetes.

There are now dozens of antihypertensive drugs on the market. Doctors tend to choose a drug they think will work best—then switch the patient to another drug if there's no response after a few weeks.

But by considering whether hidden emotions are involved, your doctor can often reduce the guesswork, matching the drug to the cause…

▶ **Diuretics, ACE inhibitors and angiotensin antagonists** are good choices for people whose hypertension is hereditary rather than based on emotion.

▶ **Beta-blockers and alpha-blockers** are usually better for people whose high blood pressure is emotion-based.

High Blood Pressure And Sex

Men with hypertension sometimes have sexual problems due to medication. A change in the medication may improve these problems. *Women:* A study of premenopausal women showed those with high blood pressure had lower levels of lubrication and orgasm than healthy women. This was not related to medications. *Important:* Anyone with high blood pressure who is having sexual difficulties should see a physician.

Laurie Duncan, MD, preventive cardiology fellow, Mary Imogene Bassett Research Institute, Cooperstown, NY.

Potassium Lowers Blood Pressure

Adding potassium to the diet will lower blood pressure in some people. *Best:* A total of four or five potassium-rich foods daily. *Including:* Baked potatoes with skin…bananas…cantaloupe…orange juice…raw or cooked spinach.

Robert Hackman, PhD, research nutritionist, department of nutrition, University of California at Davis.

Folic Acid—Good for You

Folic acid isn't the only B vitamin that benefits the heart. Vitamin B-6 does, too. *Recent finding:* Women who consumed the most folic acid had a 31% lower risk for heart attack than those who consumed the least. The women who consumed the most B-6 cut their heart attack risk by 33%. Those who consumed high levels of both vitamins reduced their overall risk by 45%. Good sources of B-6 include wheat germ, yellow-fin tuna and potatoes.

Eric B. Rimm, ScD, associate professor of epidemiology and nutrition, Harvard School of Public Health, Boston. His 14-year study of more than 80,000 women was published in *The Journal of the American Medical Association*, 515 N. State St., Chicago 60610.

Safer Heart Surgery

Open-heart surgery patients who are given the drug *amiodarone* (Cordarone) face a dramatically reduced risk for *atrial fibrillation* (AF).

Ordinarily, this potentially dangerous heart rhythm abnormality strikes up to 40% of heart surgery patients after surgery.

Recent finding: Only 25% of patients given amiodarone prior to surgery experienced AF.

If you're facing heart surgery, ask your doctor about taking amiodarone.

Emile G. Daoud, MD, cardiologist, Riverside Methodist Hospital, Columbus, OH. His study of 124 open-heart surgery patients was published in *The New England Journal of Medicine*, 10 Shattuck St., Boston 02115.

BE CAREFUL DURING SNOW SEASON

A heart attack after shoveling snow is 53 times more likely to occur in someone who is out of shape. Snow shoveling causes blood circulation changes that stress the heart. Physically active people can handle the changes much better than people who are usually inactive. *Shoveling self-defense:* Wait at least one or two hours after waking up to start shoveling—blood is more likely to clot shortly after you wake up. Walk or stretch for 5 to 15 minutes before starting to shovel. Use a small, light shovel blade so you lift lighter loads.

Murray Mittleman, MD, DPH, associate professor of medicine, Beth Israel Deaconess Medical Center, Boston, whose study was published in *The New England Journal of Medicine*, 10 Shattuck St., Boston 02115.

Tea—A Treat for Your Heart

People who don't already drink tea may want to start. Having one or more cups of black tea per day cuts heart attack risk by half, report researchers at Boston's Brigham & Women's Hospital. *Theory:* Tea is rich in *flavonoids*, compounds that block blood clots and lower cholesterol levels.

Bypass Surgery Revolution

Duke University researchers say they've been able to make living arteries in the lab. Their feat was done with pig cells. If it works with human cells, doctors could begin using manmade arteries in bypass surgery. Right now, bypass surgery involves replacing diseased arteries with up to 24 inches of a vein surgically "harvested" from the patient's own body.

Exercise for Health

How hard you exercise may matter more for cardiovascular health than how much. In a study of recreational runners, only levels of HDL—"good" cholesterol—were found to respond better to distance than speed. The intensity of exercise reduces blood pressure, total cholesterol and body fat more than the amount.

Paul Williams, PhD, life sciences division, Lawrence Berkeley Laboratory, Berkeley, CA, whose study was published in the *Archives of Internal Medicine*.

WHERE TO FIND (AND AVOID) BAD CHOLESTEROL

The worst cholesterol of all seems to be the kind found in hamburgers and other fried and processed foods. It is *oxidized* cholesterol, which increases the speed at which fatty plaque builds up in the arteries that feed the heart. Oxidized cholesterol is created when cholesterol is heated or dried. It may occur in fried, processed and cooked foods that contain animal fat.

Ilona Staprans, PhD, associate research professor at VA Medical Center and University of California at San Francisco. Her laboratory study of rabbits was published in *Arteriosclerosis, Thrombosis and Vascular Biology*.

SIMPLE WAYS TO LOWER CHOLESTEROL

There are nondrug ways to lower your cholesterol level. *Worth discussing with your physician...*

▶ **Garlic:** One clove of fresh garlic daily—or a 900-mg capsule of garlic—can lower cholesterol by 9% and triglycerides by 17%.

▶ **Psyllium**—the bulking agent—can reduce cholesterol by 6% to 10%.

▶ **Oat bran:** A bowl daily can lower cholesterol by 6%...a fat substitute—*Oat Trim*—can lower LDL (*bad* cholesterol) by 6% to 16%.

▶ **Diet** combined with exercise is the best approach. A 20%-fat, low-calorie diet—1,200 calories per day for women and 1,500 per day for men—combined with a daily 30-minute walk can reduce cholesterol by 20% and triglycerides by 30%.

▶ **Niacin:** 500 mg three times a day can reduce cholesterol by 15% to 30% and triglycerides by up to 15%. The brand *Niaspan* is effective taken once a day. Have your doctor do liver function tests before taking niacin. Don't take it if you have arthritis, diabetes or gout or have had stomach ulcers in the past year.

Mary McGowan, MD, director, Cholesterol Management Center, New England Heart Institute, Manchester, NH, and author of *Heart Fitness for Life: The Essential Guide for Preventing and Reversing Heart Disease*. Oxford University Press.

Psyllium Helps Lower Cholesterol

The bulking agent psyllium lowered total cholesterol by 5% in people who drank water mixed with one heaping teaspoon of psyllium twice a day. It reduced *LDL*—"bad" cholesterol—by 7%.

Consider taking psyllium one hour before meals twice daily. Cholesterol reduction should occur in three to four weeks.

James Anderson, MD, professor of medicine and clinical nutrition, University of Kentucky at Lexington, whose study of high-cholesterol patients was published in the *Archives of Internal Medicine*.

Drug Helps Cholesterol Levels Even in Healthy People

Cholesterol-lowering drugs cut heart attack risk—even for people with average cholesterol levels. In a recent study, more than 6,500 healthy individuals with average cholesterol readings of about 220 were given either the drug Mevacor or a placebo. Those who were given Mevacor had a 36% lower rate of heart attacks.

Antonio Gotto, MD, dean and professor of medicine, Cornell University Medical College, New York.

Benefits of Alcohol

Alcohol cuts the cardiac risk for men who have already survived one heart attack. Men who consume about one alcoholic drink per day after a heart attack may cut their risk of another attack by up to 30%. Stroke victims may get a similar benefit. *Caution:* Discuss any therapeutic alcohol consumption with your doctor. Consuming too much alcohol has significant risks.

Michael Gaziano, MD, director, Massachusetts Veterans Epidemiology Research and Information Center, Boston, whose study of almost 6,000 heart attack or stroke victims was reported at a conference of the American Heart Association.

Heart Doctor's Stop-Smoking Plan

▶ **Write down the day you will quit**—between two and four weeks from the day you decide—and keep the date in sight.

▶ **Pick a nonworking day to quit**—to limit stress.

▶ **For seven days, record every cigarette smoked.** Number each cigarette, and write when you smoked it and why.

▶ **See which cigarettes you smoked from habit and boredom, and drop them first.** Work toward dropping the harder ones.

▶ **Start walking or bike riding regularly.** Fight smoking urges by brushing your hair or playing with a rubber band.

▶ **Take it one day at a time**—most withdrawal symptoms end within four weeks.

Heart Fitness for Life: The Essential Guide to Preventing and Reversing Heart Disease by **Mary McGowan, MD,** director, Cholesterol Management Center, New England Heart Institute, Manchester, NH. Oxford University Press.

AID TO QUITTING SMOKING

Smokers find it easier to quit when they take *nortriptyline* (Pamelor). When 25 to 75 milligrams (mg) per day of this prescription antidepressant was added to a standard behavioral smoking cessation program, the quit-rate at six months was 14%, compared with only 3% for those who got the standard program only. The nortriptyline group also reported less anxiety, anger and irritability. Side effects of the drug include dry mouth and taste disturbances.

Allan V. Prochazka, MD, MSc, assistant professor of research of ambulatory care, Veterans Affairs Medical Center, Denver. His study of 214 smokers 18 to 70 years of age was published in the *Archives of Internal Medicine,* 515 N. State St., Chicago 60610.

TO QUIT SMOKING...

Change routines to quit smoking. If you smoke while driving to work, get to work a different way—in a car pool or by public transportation.

If you smoke before or after drinking coffee, switch to tea.

If you associate smoking a cigarette with the end of a meal, leave the table right after finishing the food, brush your teeth and take a quick walk.

If you smoke while drinking an alcoholic beverage, give up alcohol until you become a nonsmoker.

If you smoke while watching TV, turn off the set for a few weeks and start a hobby that requires you to work with your hands.

Heart Fitness for Life: The Essential Guide to Preventing and Reversing Heart Disease by **Mary McGowan, MD,** director, Cholesterol Management Center, New England Heart Institute, Manchester, NH. Oxford University Press.

Stroke Self-Defense— Up-to-the-Minute Advice From the Stanford University Stroke Center

Gregory W. Albers, MD, director of the stroke center at Stanford University Medical Center in Palo Alto, CA, and professor of neurology at Stanford University Medical School in Stanford, CA.

Stroke is the number-three killer of Americans —after heart disease and cancer. It's the number-one cause of disability.

Not everyone can recognize the symptoms of a stroke. That's tragic, since the ability to recognize the symptoms—and get immediate treatment— often means the difference between health and severe disability.

BLOCKAGES AND BLEEDING

Stroke occurs when blood circulation in the brain is interrupted. *This happens in one of two ways...*

▶ **In an *ischemic* stroke,** blood vessels are blocked by a blood clot or fatty deposits (plaques) that form along artery walls. Eighty-five percent of strokes are ischemic.

▶ **In a *hemorrhagic* stroke,** a blood vessel bursts, resulting in bleeding into the brain. Fifteen percent of strokes are hemorrhagic.

Without oxygen-rich blood, brain cells quickly die. The symptoms of stroke depend on the type of stroke...and which portion of the brain is affected. Hemorrhagic stroke often causes a severe headache. But ischemic stroke is usually painless.

Since they feel no pain, many people who have an ischemic stroke fail to realize that they are in jeopardy. As a result, they wait precious minutes or hours before getting medical attention.

The key to recognizing either kind of stroke is to watch for the telltale symptoms...

▶ **Sudden weakness, numbness or heaviness of an arm or leg or in the face.** Typically, only one side of the body is affected.

▶ **Difficulty speaking or difficulty understanding speech.** This can include slurred speech, speaking gibberish or being unable to talk.

▶ **Sudden loss of vision in one eye.**

▶ **Double vision.**

▶ **Sudden dizziness,** difficulty walking or an unsteady gait.

If you observe any of these symptoms—in yourself or someone else—call 911 at once. Do not call your doctor or your HMO. That wastes precious time.

RISK FACTORS
High blood pressure.
Hypertension is the biggest risk factor for both kinds of stroke.

The higher your pressure, the greater the stress on your blood vessels—and the greater your risk for stroke.

Have your blood pressure checked at least once a year. It should be below 120/80.

Mild hypertension can often be controlled simply by exercising, losing weight, cutting back on alcohol and salty foods and boosting your intake of fruits, vegetables and dairy foods.

If your blood pressure remains above 140/90 after three months of lifestyle modification—or if your pressure is initially above 150/90—you may need to take blood pressure medication.

High cholesterol.

Too much cholesterol in the bloodstream causes *atherosclerosis.* That's the process in which fatty deposits form in the arteries.

Have your cholesterol levels checked at least once a year. Total cholesterol should be below 200, and LDL (bad) cholesterol below 120.

The first approach to lowering elevated cholesterol levels is usually exercise coupled with a low-fat, high-fiber diet.

If your LDL level remains higher than 130 after several months of regular exercise and an appropriate diet, your doctor may recommend a statin medication, such as *pravastatin* (Pravachol).

Statins have proven highly effective at preventing stroke among people with high cholesterol or heart disease.

Irregular heartbeat.

A type of irregular heartbeat known as *atrial fibrillation* can trigger the formation of blood clots in the heart.

If these clots travel via the bloodstream to the brain, they can cause an ischemic stroke.

To give yourself a crude test for atrial fibrillation, feel your pulse by pressing your index finger lightly on the inside of your wrist on the thumb side.

If you detect unsteadiness in your pulse, ask your doctor to check it. If you do have atrial fibrillation, your doctor may prescribe *warfarin* (Coumadin). This prescription anticoagulant has been shown to reduce the risk for stroke.

High levels of *homocysteine.*

Having too much of this amino acid in your blood increases your risk for both stroke and heart attack.

Diabetes.

Poorly controlled diabetes can lead to blood vessel damage.

If you have diabetes, be sure to follow your doctor's instructions for keeping glucose under control.

Smoking.

Nicotine promotes atherosclerosis.

If you smoke, quitting reduces your stroke risk significantly. In fact, five years after quitting, smokers' stroke risk is similar to that of nonsmokers.

Heavy drinking.

Have no more than two drinks a day. More than that, and your stroke risk rises.

Sedentary lifestyle.

Exercise helps keep blood pressure under control and arteries elastic.

It also raises levels of HDL (good) cholesterol, reducing the risk for cardiovascular trouble.

Aim for 30 to 60 minutes of aerobic exercise, three or four times weekly.

EARLY WARNING

In many cases, an ischemic stroke is preceded by one or more "mini-strokes."

Just like full-fledged strokes, these *transient ischemic attacks* (TIAs) stem from a blocked blood vessel. But with a TIA, symptoms disappear within 20 minutes or so—because the artery becomes unblocked.

There's no easy way to tell the difference between a stroke and a TIA, so it's essential to get immediate medical attention.

Many TIAs can be traced to a blockage in one of the blood vessels in the neck—the carotid or vertebral arteries.

Doctors can check the extent of the blockage via ultrasound or *angiography*, a technique in which a dye injected into the bloodstream highlights blood vessels in an X ray.

If the carotids are more than 60% blocked, it's often appropriate to undergo carotid *endarterectomy*, a surgical procedure in which the blockage is scraped away.

This procedure is relatively safe, and it reduces the risk for stroke by roughly 50% in appropriately selected patients.

STATE-OF-THE-ART TREATMENT

For some people who are having an ischemic stroke, a powerful drug called *tissue plasminogen activator* (tPA) can be used to dissolve the clot.

tPA is remarkably effective at preventing disability—*if it's administered within three hours of the onset of symptoms.*

DON'T RISK A STROKE

People with high blood pressure who stop taking their medication more than double their risk of stroke. The increased risk of stroke is even higher for those who also smoke or are under age 55.

Amanda Thrift, PhD, research fellow, department of neurology, Austin and Repatriation Medical Centre, Heidelberg, Victoria, Australia, whose study was published in *Hypertension.*

Blood Thinner Savvy

A cetaminophen warning for people taking the blood-thinner warfarin: Warfarin (Coumadin) is a medication used to lower the risk of stroke. Its effects are increased by continuous doses of acetaminophen—the active ingredient in Tylenol and certain other pain relievers—and together, warfarin and acetaminophen can lead to hemorrhage. *Self-defense:* If you are taking warfarin, consult your doctor before using acetaminophen.

Elaine Hylek, MD, physician, department of medicine, Massachusetts General Hospital, Boston.

MEDICATION ALERT

Take medications that cause lower blood pressure in the *morning* if your doctor says you can. *Reason:* If the drugs are taken at night, when blood pressure normally drops, the additional medication-induced drop can trigger serious eye problems. *Among the drugs that lower blood pressure:* Some prostate drugs…Hytrin …beta-blockers, calcium channel blockers, ACE inhibitors and other antihypertensive drugs.

Sohan Singh Hayreh, MD, PhD, professor emeritus of ophthalmology, University of Iowa College of Medicine, Iowa City, whose study was published in the *American Journal of Ophthalmology.*

Conquering Chronic Ailments

Chapter 12

Managing Chronic Pain With Wonderful Treatments

Pain that persists beyond the normal period of healing is known as chronic pain. What starts out as a simple mishap or injury may leave behind pain that ultimately permeates every aspect of a person's life.

Fortunately, advances in pain research have led to innovative treatment solutions.

CAUSES OF CHRONIC PAIN

▨ Inactive pain-suppressing chemicals.

When you mistakenly touch a hot stove, you immediately pull back your hand.

In that split second, pain receptors in your hand send a quick message to your brain about the pain's location and why you're experiencing pain.

This pain "news network" acts to sound a general alarm, controlling reflexes and breathing. It even blocks other pain messages by using the body's own protective pain-suppressing chemicals—called opioids. The family of opioids, including *enkephalins* and *endorphins*, reside in the brain.

▨ Injury to nerves.

Called neuropathic pain, this type of chronic pain occurs when nerve signals anywhere along the route to or from the brain are disrupted.

It's a problem of "disease of the messenger." In other forms of chronic pain, the messenger works and the *body* is the problem.

Researchers believe that in chronic-pain sufferers, continual pain may lead to long-term changes in the nervous system that can make patients sensitive to even the gentlest touch.

TREATMENTS

▨ Lower-back pain.

More than 95% of back pain is temporary and goes away by itself within five days with simple

Peter Clarke, PhD, professor of preventive medicine and director of the Center for Health and Medical Communication at the University of Southern California School of Medicine in Los Angeles. He is coauthor of *Surviving Modern Medicine: How to Get the Best from Doctors, Family & Friends.* Rutgers University Press.

steps, such as limiting pain-evoking activity and taking over-the-counter analgesics.

Early on, it may not even matter if the patient received treatment from a doctor. Too much rest can actually be bad. If the pain is severe or doesn't get better soon, seek medical attention.

The most frequent reason for chronic back pain is muscle spasm. But we sometimes worry that it's something more serious—perhaps the vertebrae… spinal disks…or other nerves that come out of the spinal cord through the spine.

We also have to worry about other causes that have nothing to do with the spine—such as muscles, ligaments or other joints—that can masquerade as back pain. And back surgery that corrects a problem may not eliminate the pain. *Treatments…*

Nerve blocks, or injections of anti-inflammatory or anesthetic drugs, play two key roles in treating chronic lower-back pain.

▶ **By numbing discreet areas of the back,** they allow doctors to isolate the pain.

▶ **They deliver potent medications** to the area of pain to alleviate symptoms.

Drugs that treat seizures in the heart and brain are now being used to treat chronic pain due to nerve injury, or neuropathic pain, which can include lower-back pain.

> ***Examples:*** *Anticonvulsants such as gabapentin (Neurontin), or heart medications such as mexiletine (Mexitil).*

Overfiring and misfiring of nerve signals are similar to the excessive brain charges found in epileptic seizures. So, quieting nerve signals at the area of pain may help restore balance in the nervous system.

Spinal cord stimulators are electric filaments that are implanted under the skin near the spinal cord.

They transmit small shocks in varying frequencies to the spinal cord in order to interrupt and block nerve-cell signals.

In other words, they trick nerve cells into believing there is no pain. Early successes have been observed, and experts are cautious but optimistic about their long-term effectiveness.

Chronic neck pain is closely related to lower-back pain, as both areas are linked to the spinal cord.

The treatments for both lower-back pain and neck pain are similar, if not identical.

Chronic, recurrent headaches affect roughly 40 million Americans.

This area of pain management presents one of the largest challenges. *Treatments…*

▶ **Sumatriptan** (Imitrex) is one of the most innovative treatments for stopping chronic migraines.

The drug works by stimulating certain chemical receptors (*serotonin*) in the brain, which scientists believe are an integral part of the body's pain-controlling pathway. The newest form of sumatriptan is a nasal spray. Many drugs similar to sumatriptan are also now available.

Other serotonin stimulators, such as antidepressants, are often used in treating headaches and other types of chronic pain.

▶ **Nerve blocks** are also effective for certain types of chronic headaches. One type in particular, *occipital neuralgia*, occurs in the back of the neck and over the back of the head. It appears to respond to local injections of either anesthetics or anti-inflammatories.

Arthritis is considered a chronic form of acute pain—ongoing pain that changes as tissue changes.

Osteoarthritis is the inflammation and degeneration of bone and tissues around the bones. In rheumatoid arthritis, the body attacks joint cartilage.

Combined, these forms of arthritis affect about 20 million Americans. Treatment can focus either on slowing down the disease or treating the symptoms. Arthritis is traditionally treated with anti-inflammatory medications—in particular prescription-strength NSAIDs (nonsteroidal anti-inflammatory drugs), which include, but may be more potent than, the ibuprofen sold over the counter.

While effective, these medications can cause troublesome—and sometimes serious—side effects. *Treatments ...*

▶ **Drugs that block the substances** involved in launching the immune response and inflammation of rheumatoid arthritis.

▶ **COX-2 inhibitors,** which function like regular ibuprofen—but the part that causes side effects is extracted. COX-2 inhibitors inhibit the enzyme that is responsible for pain at the site of injury but, unlike other anti-inflammatory drugs, avoid blocking the other enzyme that protects the stomach lining and helps the kidneys function.

These innovative drugs may deliver pain relief without the harsh side effects of current treatments.

Many other new drugs and formulation of older pain drugs are on the horizon. Also, there are non-drug approaches, such as physical therapy, acupuncture and biofeedback, which are commonly used, either alone or in combination with drugs.

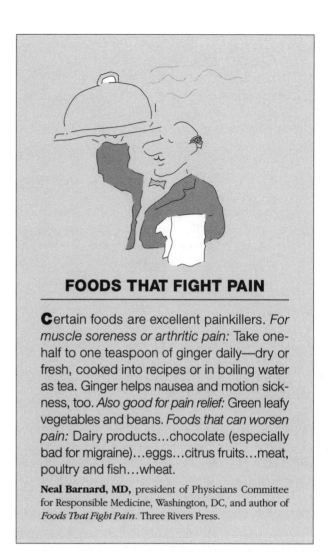

FOODS THAT FIGHT PAIN

Certain foods are excellent painkillers. *For muscle soreness or arthritic pain:* Take one-half to one teaspoon of ginger daily—dry or fresh, cooked into recipes or in boiling water as tea. Ginger helps nausea and motion sickness, too. *Also good for pain relief:* Green leafy vegetables and beans. *Foods that can worsen pain:* Dairy products...chocolate (especially bad for migraine)...eggs...citrus fruits...meat, poultry and fish...wheat.

Neal Barnard, MD, president of Physicians Committee for Responsible Medicine, Washington, DC, and author of *Foods That Fight Pain.* Three Rivers Press.

Instant Allergy Aid

People with life-threatening allergies should ask their physicians if they need EpiPen injection kits. The kits contain syringes of epinephrine for emergency use. *Important:* After using the kit, go to the emergency room. A second reaction follows the first apparent recovery in 25% to 30% of cases. If you have an EpiPen kit, call your pharmacy to confirm that it was not recalled for inadequate potency.

Hugh A. Sampson, MD, chief of pediatric allergy and immunology at Mount Sinai Medical Center, New York City.

FOOD ALLERGY STRATEGY

Fiery spices can make food allergies flare up. In a recent study, spices like paprika and chili pepper were shown to interact with the lining of the digestive tract. This may make it easier for allergens in other foods to pass into the body. *Example:* People allergic to milk may normally be able to consume small amounts without a reaction. But if they eat food seasoned with paprika or chili pepper, the barriers that would keep the allergens out may open temporarily—and the allergy flares up.

Joanne Lupton, PhD, professor of nutrition, Texas A&M University, College Station.

Allergy Fixes

In spite of what some might think, allergy shots are no quick fix. It usually takes several months for shots to begin working—and they do not work at all in some people. *Situations in which shots can be particularly effective:* Allergy to bee, wasp, yellow jacket or hornet stings…seasonal pollen allergy…well-documented sensitivity to dust mites or cat dander. Results are much less predictable with sensitivity to dog dander or for mold allergy.

Harold Nelson, MD, professor of medicine, National Jewish Center for Immunology and Respiratory Medicine, Denver.

Outsmart Your Allergies

Art Ulene, MD, author of *How to Outsmart Your Allergies,* in collaboration with the Asthma and Allergy Foundation of America.

There is no cure for allergies. But there is also no reason to suffer from them. The most effective way to avoid allergy-related health problems is to reduce your exposure to allergens, including such triggers as pollen, animal dander, dust mites and molds.

Develop a personal action plan to outsmart your allergies. *Here are a few suggestions…*

AT HOME

► **Vacuum your carpets often.** Better yet, remove wall-to-wall carpeting in rooms where you spend a lot of time.

► **Bag your stuffed animals,** and keep them in the freezer during the day to kill dust mites.

► **Run your stove fan while cooking** to lower humidity and remove fumes and smells.

► **Use your central air-conditioning** or a dehumidifier to keep indoor humidity below 50%. Mold-prone rooms—such as the kitchen, bathroom and basement—need to be well ventilated.

► **Wash the walls of your bathrooms,** the basement and other mildew-prone areas with a mixture of one part bleach to 10 parts water. Use paint that blocks mold formation.

► **Consider giving your cat away** and replacing it with a hairless, dander-free pet such as an iguana or a turtle.

► **Prune trees and bushes regularly** to reduce heavy vegetation around the house. Wear wraparound sunglasses to minimize pollen contact with your eyes.

► **Replace down, feather and foam pillows** with fiberfill products.

AWAY FROM HOME

► **Plan vacations during high-pollen seasons in your home area.** *Helpful resource:* The National Allergy Bureau has a free information packet that includes a pollen calendar for major cities in the US, 800-976-5536.

▶ **Keep car windows closed,** and put your air conditioner on "recirculate."

▶ **Request a nonsmoking room at hotels,** and make sure that it is air-conditioned.

▶ **Airline travel** presents problems of its own. You can't control the air you breathe, but your doctor may have suggestions for medications that can keep your reaction to onboard allergens to a minimum.

AT WORK AND IN SCHOOL

▶ **Remove potted plants from work areas.** Soggy plant soil encourages mold.

▶ **Make sure that office ventilation and heating systems have clean filters** and are functioning well. This can help minimize your exposure to allergens.

▶ **Check out your child's school for allergy triggers,** such as animals in the classroom, roaches in lockers and dust mites in preschool and kindergarten floor rugs.

PREVENT ASTHMA ATTACKS

Once-a-day asthma pills help prevent attacks and simplify chronic treatment. These prescription drugs, called *antileukotrienes*, are designed to control asthma by preventing attacks. Patients still need inhalers or other medicines in case of acute episodes and for long-term asthma control.

Richard Martin, MD, head of the pulmonary division, National Jewish Medical and Research Center, Denver.

ARTHRITIS FOOD CURES

Both osteoarthritis and rheumatoid arthritis cause painful inflammation that usually gets worse with age. Proper food choices can help reduce this pain—without the side effects caused by some painkillers.

Best food: Fatty fish (salmon, mackerel, sardines, etc.). The omega-3 fatty acids in fish counter the effects of *prostaglandins*, chemicals that promote inflammation. Eat three or more fish meals weekly. If you are pregnant, ask your doctor whether you should eat fish.

Also helpful: Brazil nuts. They contain selenium, a trace mineral that may reduce arthritis symptoms. One Brazil nut supplies the recommended daily intake of 70 micrograms (mcg).

Approximately 20% of osteoarthritis and rheumatoid arthritis cases are linked to food allergies. Common offenders include soy, coffee, eggs, milk, corn, wheat, potatoes, beef, pork and shellfish (especially shrimp).

I advise patients with severe arthritis to stop eating these foods, one at a time, to see if symptoms improve.

Isadore Rosenfeld, MD, the Rossi Distinguished Professor of Clinical Medicine at Weill Medical College of Cornell University in New York City. He is the author of nine books, including *Doctor, What Should I Eat?* (Warner). His newest book is *Dr. Isadore Rosenfeld's Breakthrough Health* (Rodale).

Diabetics in Control

People with diabetes enjoy big improvements in well-being with even tiny improvements in control of their blood-sugar levels. Yet among doctors who care for diabetics, only one-third of the patients followed the best practices designed to keep blood sugar under control. *Example:* A simple blood test—HbA1c monitoring—can help patients greatly improve their blood-sugar levels by giving them a "snapshot" of how well they have managed their blood sugar over time.

George C. Halvorson, president and chief executive officer, Health Partners, Inc., a Minneapolis-based health plan.

Heartburn Alert

Over-the-counter antacids can mask serious illness. Because antacids are so effective at curbing heartburn, some people who use them regularly go for years without being checked by a doctor. *Recent study:* When heartburn sufferers were examined, 57% were found to have hiatal hernia, a condition in which the stomach intrudes into the chest cavity. Almost half had damage to the lining of the esophagus (*esophagitis*). Six percent had Barrett esophagus, which can lead to throat cancer. *Self-defense:* See a doctor if you take antacids more than three times a week.

Malcolm Robinson, MD, professor of medicine, University of Oklahoma Health Sciences Center, Oklahoma City. His study of 155 chronic heartburn sufferers was published in the *Archives of Internal Medicine.* 515 N. State St., Chicago 60610.

SEVERE HEARTBURN HELP

The acid-suppressing drug *omeprazole* (Prilosec) can be just as effective as surgery at controlling severe heartburn—also known as *gastroesophageal reflux disease* (GERD).

Recent study: GERD patients who received omeprazole did just as well as similar patients who underwent *fundoplication.* That's the surgical procedure commonly used to treat GERD.

Lars Lundell, MD, PhD, professor of surgery, Sahlgrens University Hospital, Gothenburg, Sweden. His study of 310 GERD patients was presented at a Digestive Disease Week meeting.

VICTORY OVER VARICOSE VEINS

Varicose veins are inherited. Genetics is a big reason varicose veins develop—but even people prone to them can control their severity. *Important:* Maintain ideal weight—extra weight puts more pressure on veins. And...exercise legs regularly to keep blood vessels healthy. *Helpful:* Stair climbing...and/or running. When you must sit or stand in one place for a long time, flex feet and legs periodically so that blood does not pool in your legs.

Dee Anna Glaser, MD, assistant professor of dermatology and internal medicine, St. Louis University School of Medicine.

Combat Swollen Legs

Leg swelling and achiness caused by varicose veins can often be controlled without surgery. *Key:* Circulation-boosting exercise, such as a daily 30-minute walk...or a five-minute walk once an hour for those who sit or stand for long periods of time. *Also helpful:* Elevating the legs for 20 minutes, three times a day...sleeping with a pillow under the calves...wearing compression stockings.

Judith A. Koperski, MD, assistant clinical professor of dermatology, University of California, San Diego, School of Medicine.

Treat Ulcers and Live Longer

Ulcer sufferers live longer when they get effective treatment. In a study of peptic ulcer sufferers 40 to 44 years of age, life span was up to 2.3 years longer in those who got treated than in those who went untreated. Treatment helps prevent potentially life-threatening conditions that can arise from ulcers. *Good news:* Antibiotics can cure most peptic ulcers.

John M. Inadomi, MD, assistant professor of medicine, University of New Mexico, Albuquerque. His study was published in *The American Journal of Gastroenterology.* 600 S. 42 St., Omaha, NE 68198.

Effective Treatment for Hepatitis C Patients

Hepatitis C patients fare much better when they take the antiviral drug *ribavirin* (Virazole) along with the standard drug *interferon alpha* (Intron A). The drug combo is two to three times more effective than interferon alone at eliminating signs of virus in the bloodstream. About four million Americans have hepatitis C, a chronic liver infection that can lead to cirrhosis, which in turn may necessitate liver transplantation.

John G. McHutchison, MD, director, gastroenterology and hepatology research, Duke Clinical Research Institute, Durham, NC. His 48-week study of 912 hepatitis C patients was published in *The New England Journal of Medicine*. 10 Shattuck St., Boston 02115.

WHY TIMING IS EVERYTHING

The time of day that you take certain medications can affect how well they work. *Examples of chronobiology:* Asthma attacks are most likely at 4 am...hay fever worsens at 6 am...heart attacks are most common between 7 am and 11 am—the hours when blood pressure peaks ...stomach acid peaks around 10 pm. If you notice symptoms appearing at certain times, talk to your doctor about changing your dosage schedule, so that the maximum amount of a drug is delivered when it is most needed.

Michael Smolensky, PhD, director, Hermann Center for Chronobiology and Chronotherapeutics, University of Texas–Houston.

How to Win the Dandruff War

Richard Berger, MD, clinical professor of dermatology at the Robert Wood Johnson Medical School of the University of Medicine and Dentistry of New Jersey, New Brunswick.

Dandruff can't be cured—but some ways of controlling it are better than others. Dandruff exists because our skin constantly sheds its outer layer of cells. New cells form underneath, and old cells flake off. This becomes a concern when the flakes are abundant and obvious...and they are accompanied by an itchy scalp. Then it's called dandruff.

Dandruff's causes: Yeasts that normally occur in the skin and overactive oil glands. A smaller percentage of cases are the result of an inflammatory form of psoriasis—the ailment that causes red, scaly patches to develop on the skin.

Dandruff isn't contagious. It is aggravated when scratching causes a bacterial infection.

DANDRUFF TREATMENT

Some people with dandruff mistakenly shampoo less often—or use milder shampoos if they see dandruff.

Better: An over-the-counter dandruff shampoo containing zinc pyrithione or selenium sulfide.

The secret to controlling dandruff is shampooing correctly.

▶ **Lather up,** and leave the shampoo on for two minutes.

▶ **Rinse**—and lather again, leaving medicated shampoo on for at least another four minutes.

▶ **Shampoo this way two or three times a week.** You can use regular shampoo in between.

Tar-based shampoos are good for stubborn dandruff caused by psoriasis. But they smell bad, leave stains in light-colored hair and cause sensitivity to the sun.

Over-the-counter hydrocortisone scalp solutions can reduce the inflammation or rash-like feeling on your scalp. You apply this solution, and leave it on. It can be used daily or twice a day in addition to the dandruff shampoo.

Great News for Hemorrhoid Sufferers

Stephen Gorfine, MD, associate clinical professor of surgery at Mount Sinai School of Medicine and a colon and rectal surgeon in private practice, New York.

Hemorrhoid trouble typically begins when specialized (hemorrhoidal) veins within the rectum become enlarged, eventually prolapsing into the anal canal.

The condition is not dangerous. But as anyone who has ever had hemorrhoids knows all too well, it can be extremely painful.

Psychological stress seems to play a role in hemorrhoids. So does constipation. Straining to defecate puts pressure on hemorrhoidal veins, which causes them to prolapse.

Over time, the prolapsed hemorrhoidal veins and surrounding tissue can become so enlarged that they hang outside the anus. At first this occurs only during bowel movements—the tissue retracts once stool has passed. Eventually, the tissue hangs outside the body at all times.

In rare cases, the pressure of the anal musculature cuts off the blood supply to the prolapsed tissue. Without prompt medical attention, such a "strangulated" hemorrhoid can lead to gangrene. This condition usually calls for emergency surgery.

MILD HEMORRHOIDS

The first symptom is typically bleeding from the rectum during bowel movements. Of course, rectal bleeding can also be symptomatic of colon cancer.

If you notice rectal bleeding: Do not assume that you simply have hemorrhoids. Consult your doctor, who will probably recommend flexible sigmoidoscopy or colonoscopy to check your colon for cancer or precancerous polyps.

To minimize discomfort during flare-ups, your doctor will probably recommend the following...

■ Drink more water.
Six to eight glasses a day help keep the stool soft, which helps prevent constipation.

■ Get more dietary fiber.
The average American consumes 19 grams of fiber a day.

To avoid constipation, you need at least 25 and preferably 30 grams a day.

As you may know, the best sources of fiber are grains, fruits and vegetables. Start by adding one fiber-rich food to every meal.

> ***Examples:*** *A bran muffin with breakfast...an apple or a handful of prunes as a midmorning snack...spinach salad with lunch...lima beans or broccoli at dinner.*

Also helpful: Metamucil and similar fiber supplements.

■ Don't dally on the toilet.
Sitting on the toilet for longer than 10 minutes at a time causes blood to pool in the hemorrhoidal veins.

This stretches the supporting tissues, encouraging further prolapse and more severe symptoms.

If nothing happens after 10 minutes, try again later.

Many hemorrhoid sufferers find they are more comfortable on the toilet if they rest their feet on a stool—so they can assume a semi-squatting position.

■ Take hot baths.
You can buy a plastic tub that attaches to the toilet, but a bathtub works fine.

Stay in the tub for five minutes three or four times a day.

■ Sit on a cushion.
Donut-shaped cushions are *not* recommended.

They place *more* pressure on hemorrhoids, causing them to prolapse even further. Better to stick with a soft foam or feather pillow.

Important: Each of these measures is also helpful for treating anal fissures—tears in the lining of the anus. If sharp pain continues even after a bowel movement—and you don't feel a lump in your rectum—you probably have a fissure.

Some patients swear by over-the-counter hemorrhoid remedies, such as Preparation H and Anusol. However, there is no proof of their effectiveness.

INTERMEDIATE MEASURES

Many people with more severe hemorrhoids opt for one of the minimally invasive treatments that are available.

The four procedures in widespread use seem to be equally effective…

■ Rubber-band ligation.

A tiny rubber band is wrapped around excess hemorrhoidal tissue, cutting off its blood supply.

The tissue shrivels and sloughs off, often within 10 days.

■ Ablation.

Excess hemorrhoidal tissue is destroyed with infrared light, low-voltage electric current or a laser beam.

■ Sclerosing injections.

Tissue is destroyed by injecting it with phenol or another irritant solution.

HEMORRHOIDECTOMY

This old-fashioned outpatient procedure involves cutting off enlarged hemorrhoidal tissue and then stitching things back up.

It takes about 45 minutes and involves a painful one- to two-week recovery.

Hemorrhoidectomy is appropriate only for people with extensive hemorrhoids who want to take care of everything with a single treatment.

It's also the treatment of choice for hemorrhoid sufferers who want to minimize the risk for recurrence. Of those who undergo hemorrhoidectomy, just one in 20 experiences a recurrence of hemorrhoids.

EMERGING TREATMENTS

Long used to treat heart pain (angina pectoris), the muscle relaxant *nitroglycerin* may soon become the treatment of choice for hemorrhoids.

Nitroglycerin is of proven effectiveness in treating anal fissures, and it appears to relieve pain following hemorrhoidectomy. Its effectiveness against hemorrhoids is still under study.

The FDA has not yet approved the rectal use of nitroglycerin, although some doctors have already begun to prescribe it for hemorrhoid sufferers.

Such "off-label" use of nitroglycerin is tricky. The available forms of nitroglycerin are too strong for anal use, and headache is a common side effect.

Another emerging treatment for hemorrhoids and fissures is injections of *BoTox,* the same purified bacterial toxin that's used to treat wrinkles and crossed eyes (strabismus).

BoTox has certain drawbacks. Many patients find the injections painful. And if the doctor injects too much BoTox, the patient may temporarily lose control of his anal sphincter. That means fecal incontinence, which is often an extremely unpleasant condition.

At Last…Good News About Irritable Bowel Syndrome

Gerard Guillory, MD, clinical professor of medicine at the University of Colorado Health Sciences Center in Denver and an internist in private practice in Aurora, CO. He is author of *IBS: A Doctor's Plan for Chronic Digestive Troubles.* Hartley & Marks. He maintains the Web site *www.ibsinformation.com.*

Thirty million Americans have irritable bowel syndrome (IBS). The condition is characterized by bloating…abdominal pain…urgent need to defecate…mucus in the stool…and episodes of diarrhea or constipation—or alternating bouts of both.

Only a few years ago, IBS sufferers awaiting diagnosis endured months of fear as doctors first ruled out other conditions like cancer and Crohn's disease.

When these patients finally got their diagnosis, all too often doctors told them that the ailment was "all in their head"—due simply to stress or emotional problems.

Today, IBS is usually diagnosed after just one doctor's visit. Patients have more treatment options …and no longer have to endure put-downs from skeptical doctors.

DIAGNOSING IBS

IBS experts now agree on a set of criteria to diagnose the condition without first excluding many other possibilities. *These criteria include…*

▶ **Presence of abdominal pain** and at least two of the following symptoms for at least 12 weeks in the preceding year…

▷ Unusually frequent or sporadic defecation during periods of abdominal pain.

▷ Unusually hard—or soft—stools during periods of abdominal pain.

▷ Relief of abdominal pain with defecation.

▶ **Absence of the following: Fever, weight loss, abdominal pain at night, blood in the stool or anemia.** These signs and symptoms are suggestive of another diagnosis, such as colon cancer or Crohn's disease.

WHAT CAUSES IBS?

Research shows that certain nerves in the colons of IBS sufferers are overreactive. These are the nerves that control sensation (what is felt in the colon) and motility (how colon muscles move).

Result: Mild stimuli that would not bother most people cause the colon to spasm. These stimuli include the pressure of intestinal gas…colon contractions triggered by eating (*peristalsis*)…and psychological stress.

GETTING RELIEF

Self-help strategies can be remarkably effective in easing IBS symptoms…

■ Prevent excess gas.

People with IBS are intolerant of even normal amounts of intestinal gas.

To minimize it…

▶ **Avoid gum and candy.** They stimulate salivation, which increases the number of swallows. With each swallow, a little air goes into the intestine.

▶ **Eat slowly.** Quick eaters gulp their food… and swallow more air.

▶ **Avoid carbonated drinks.**

■ Avoid trigger foods.

IBS symptoms often occur after consumption of sugary and/or fatty foods.

Undigested sugar ferments in the colon, causing more gas. Fat causes the body to release *cholecystokinin,* a hormone that stimulates colon contractions.

Other common food triggers are caffeine, nicotine and alcohol. *Monosodium glutamate* (MSG) and *aspartame* (NutraSweet) can also trigger IBS symptoms.

Sources of MSG include commercially prepared soups, bouillon, low-fat salad dressings and most restaurant foods.

Products that contain aspartame or MSG must say so on the labels.

To identify triggers: Keep a "look-back" diary. After every IBS attack, jot down a list of all the foods you consumed in the previous 12 hours. You should spot patterns that point to foods you should avoid.

■ Get more fiber.

Fiber helps IBS sufferers who are constipated or whose constipation alternates with diarrhea.

It's not helpful for diarrhea-predominant IBS.

Gradually add fiber-rich foods such as fruits, vegetables and whole grains to your diet. Add foods one at a time to make sure they're not trigger foods.

Another option: Use psyllium seed supplements such as Konsyl or synthetic fiber supplements such as FiberCon. Take them at mealtime so they mix with foods. This produces a soft stool that is easy to pass. Avoid supplements that contain sugar or aspartame.

▓ Reduce stress.
Eliminate as many stressors as you can…and increase your use of stress-reduction techniques.

Good ones include exercise and yoga.

MEDICATION
If self-help strategies fail to alleviate symptoms, medications may help.

Historically, doctors have treated IBS using muscle relaxants, antidiarrhea drugs and antidepressants.

Conquering Incontinence… Surprisingly, It's Very Common—Good News: A Drug-Free Approach Is Often All That's Needed

Mary Dierich, RN, adjunct instructor, School of Nursing at the University of Minnesota in Minneapolis. She is coauthor of *Overcoming Incontinence: A Straightforward Guide to Your Options.* John Wiley & Sons.

Urinary incontinence—leakage of urine—is a mainstay of TV and magazine ads. But the condition is rarely discussed where it ought to be—in doctors' offices.

At least 30% of the estimated 17 million Americans who have incontinence—two-thirds of whom are women—fail to bring it up with their physicians.

Many are silent because they believe incontinence is an inevitable part of aging…and that it's incurable.

They're wrong on both counts.

Incontinence has many causes besides aging. These include vaginal and urinary tract infections …constipation…medication side effects…childbirth …prostate disease…and neurological conditions.

Good news: Regardless of the cause, incontinence can usually be ameliorated.

TYPES OF INCONTINENCE
There are three kinds of urinary incontinence…

▶ **Stress incontinence**—leakage that occurs with activity.

This is most commonly caused by weakness of the pelvic floor muscles that support the bladder and control the urinary sphincter. That's the muscle at the base of the bladder that controls urine flow.

▶ **Urge incontinence**—a sudden and uncontrollable need to urinate. Common causes of urge incontinence include bladder infection, medication and neurological disease.

▶ **Overflow incontinence**—leakage from an overly full bladder. It is common in men with enlarged prostates.

Other causes include blockage of the urethra or inability of the bladder to contract efficiently.

HELPFUL MEDICATIONS
Many incontinence medications are now available. *These include medications that…*

…reduce bladder contraction.

…increase muscle tone of the urinary sphincter.

…alleviate blockage of the urethra.

Medications are often recommended as the first line of defense against incontinence. Drug therapy can be effective for the condition and is relatively inexpensive.

Trap: The medications can cause side effects, including heart palpitations, high blood pressure, dizziness, dry mouth and constipation. And using medications doesn't usually correct the *cause* of the problem—such as pelvic floor muscle weakness.

By contrast, individuals who are willing to go a nonmedical route can usually correct the problem's cause, not merely treat its symptoms.

SELF-HELP STRATEGIES

Nonmedical approaches do require commitment and follow-through—sometimes for a lifetime. *Five self-help strategies can be remarkably effective...*

▶ **Avoid irritants that trigger bladder contraction.** These include caffeine, aspartame (NutraSweet) and alcohol.

▶ **Drink plenty of water.** Consume at least six eight-ounce glasses daily. This dilutes urine so it won't irritate the bladder.

▶ **Boost consumption of fruits and vegetables.** Five servings daily help prevent constipation, a potential trigger of stress and urge incontinence.

▶ **Avoid sleep medications.** Even over-the-counter sleeping aids induce sleep so deep that the signal to get up and urinate can be missed.

▶ **Do Kegel exercises.** These exercises work for stress and urge incontinence. Effective for men and women, they strengthen the pelvic floor muscles.

What to do: Two to three times daily, contract the muscles used to hold back intestinal gas and urine flow. To begin, do five contractions at a time while lying down. Hold each contraction for five seconds. Relax for 20 seconds after each contraction. Gradually work up to a total of 40 contractions daily, holding each for 10 seconds.

Once perfected, Kegels can be performed standing or sitting.

Some people have trouble doing Kegels. *If you do, ask your doctor about trying...*

■ **Biofeedback.**
A sensor placed in the vagina or rectum monitors pelvic floor muscle contractions.

A computer analyzes the contractions and points out problems. Biofeedback typically requires about five sessions—at home or at an incontinence specialist's office—to learn how to correct the errors and do Kegels reliably.

■ **Pelvic muscle stimulation.**
Pelvic muscles are stimulated by a device briefly inserted into the vagina or rectum.

Equipment is used in medical offices or at home. Treatment typically takes at least three months. After it's completed, the muscles are strong enough to do Kegels effectively.

Eyes, Ears, Mouth and Throat

Chapter 13

The "Big Three" Eye Diseases Are Easy to Avoid

As we reach our sixties and beyond, our eyes become increasingly vulnerable to three vision-robbing disorders…

■ Macular degeneration.
The leading cause of blindness in older people, this disorder destroys cells in the retina.

■ Cataracts.
A gradual clouding over of the lenses within the eyes causes light sensitivity and blurry vision.

■ Glaucoma.
Rising pressure in the eye damages the optic nerves, causing tunnel vision.

Lifestyle plays a major role in determining who develops these problems…and who does not. *Here's how to minimize your risk…*

■ Eat at least five servings of fruits and vegetables a day.
Antioxidants found in plant foods help deactivate cell-damaging compounds known as *free radicals*.

Free radicals are associated with every major eye disease.

Carrots, squash, broccoli and red onions contain the antioxidant *beta-carotene*.

Spinach, collard greens, celery, corn, green beans, kiwi fruit and red grapes contain the antioxidants *lutein* and *zeaxanthin*.

Asparagus, garlic and onions are rich in sulfur, which the body uses to make a key antioxidant known as *glutathione*.

■ Eat less sugar.
Too much sugar leads to *hyperinsulinemia,* a condition in which the pancreas secretes abnormally high amounts of insulin.

Marc R. Rose, MD, an ophthalmologist in private practice in Los Angeles. He and Michael Rose, MD, are the authors of *Save Your Sight!* Warner Books.

Hyperinsulinemia is associated with all three eye diseases, as well as diabetes, high blood pressure and cancer.

To keep insulin levels in check, you must limit your intake of sugary desserts and other sweets—but that's not all. Substitute brown rice for white rice, and eat sprouted grain breads instead of ordinary flour-containing bread.

Emphasize nutritious sources of protein, such as tofu...and salmon, cod, sardines and other deep-water fish.

■ Get enough essential fatty acids.

Cold-water fish are good sources of omega-3 and omega-6 fatty acids, which help curb the body's inflammatory response.

Ordinarily, this process helps heal injured cells. But when it gets out of hand, pressure builds inside the eyes. This can lead to glaucoma.

For maximum benefit, eat cold-water fish three times a week. If you don't like fish, get fatty acids by eating ground flaxseed instead. One to three tablespoons a day—sprinkled on cereal or salads—is fine.

■ Take a daily vitamin supplement.

It should include...

▶ **B-complex.** Vitamins B-6, B-12 and folic acid help neutralize homocysteine, a toxic by-product of cellular metabolism.

▶ **Chromium.** This trace mineral helps stabilize blood sugar levels, preventing hyperinsulinemia.

▶ **Vanadyl sulfate.** Works like chromium to stabilize blood sugar.

▶ **Zinc.** Zinc deficiency is now thought to contribute to macular degeneration.

Supplements specially formulated for the eyes can also be helpful. Sold in health-food stores, these usually contain lutein, zeaxanthin, bilberry extract (to strengthen capillaries in the eye) and vitamin C.

■ Drink at least 6 eight-ounce glasses of water a day.

Some researchers believe that chronic dehydration contributes to degenerative diseases, including those that affect the eyes.

■ Wear wraparound sunglasses.

If you're out in the sun for more than 10 minutes—or at midday for any length of time—wear wraparound sunglasses.

These should block 100% of ultraviolet A and B light. Too much sunlight contributes to macular degeneration and cataracts.

Trap: Not all sunglasses labeled "UV-blocking" really are. Play it safe by buying your sunglasses from an optometrist or ophthalmologist you trust.

If you wear prescription glasses, have wraparound sunglasses made up in your prescription...or wear plastic eye protectors over your regular glasses. These protectors are sold at drugstores for about $10.

■ Don't smoke.

Smoking is known to increase the risk for cataracts, macular degeneration and glaucoma.

■ Use medication with caution.

Some prescription drugs can cause eye damage.

Be especially careful about...

▶ **Aspirin, ibuprofen and acetaminophen.** These anti-inflammatory drugs can cause dry eyes and corneal deposits. There's even evidence that they can cause delicate vessels in the eyes to hemorrhage.

▶ **Corticosteroids**. Use of *prednisone* (Deltasone) and similar drugs has been linked with cataracts and glaucoma.

▶ **Photosensitizing drugs.** Certain antibiotics, diuretics and antiarrhythmic drugs make eyes sensitive to sunlight, raising the risk for retinal damage.

If you take any of these drugs on a regular basis, ask your doctor about their possible effects on your eyes. Your doctor may be able to recommend a safer alternative.

■ Get regular screenings.

Everyone age 40 or older should see an ophthal-mologist or optometrist for an eye exam at least every two years (annually if you take drugs that can affect the eyes or if there is a family history of eye disease).

Important: Testing blood glucose levels is a standard part of a yearly physical. If you have a family history of diabetes or hypoglycemia, your glucose levels should be tested twice a year after the age of 40.

Ask your doctor for the fasting blood sugar and fasting insulin tests rather than a simple blood glucose test.

■ Always wear protective sports goggles or glasses while playing racquetball, baseball, etc....and using power tools.

ADJUSTING TO NEW GLASSES

Adjusting to new glasses may require 7 to 10 days—even with just a small prescription change or change in frame size. During this period, keep notes about symptoms such as discomfort or blurred vision. If problems continue after 10 days, consult your optometrist or ophthalmologist.

John Amos, OD, chair, Clinical Care Center, American Optometric Association, 243 N. Lindbergh Blvd., St. Louis 63141.

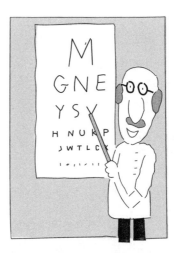

Asthma-Steroid-Cataract Connection

To decrease the risk of cataracts—an occasional side effect of the inhaled corticosteroids used to treat severe asthma—you can attach a spacer device to the inhaler. Spacers are portable holding chambers that help keep the steroid spray out of the user's eyes and mouth—and inhaled particles go only to the lungs. The brand *Inspirease* is particularly good for children. *Also*—rinse your mouth after using an inhaler. Asthmatics *and* nonasthmatics can reduce their risk of developing cataracts by avoiding strong sunlight...not smoking...eating more fruits and vegetables...and taking daily doses of 250 milligrams (mg) to 500 mg of vitamin C and 400 IU (international units) of vitamin E. Consult your physician about alternatives to inhaled—*or oral*— corticosteroids.

Teresa Corcoran, MD, an internist and pediatrician on staff at Cambridge Hospital in Cambridge, MA.

Better Cataract Surgery

If you need surgery on both eyes, have the surgeries done within three months—or less —of one another. This short time span reduces the complications of adjusting to different vision in both eyes.

Melvin Schrier, OD, vision consultant in Rancho Palos Verdes, CA.

MINIMIZING UNDER-EYE CIRCLES

Dark shadows under eyes are usually inherited traits—they are not caused by lack of sleep. But additional sleep can minimize them by making your eyes look brighter, so the circles are less noticeable. The circles become more evident as people age and their skin thins. *Helpful for women:* Avoid lower-lid eye makeup—it may call attention to the circles. A concealer slightly lighter than your foundation may minimize the circles. *Also:* Plastic surgery of the lower lid can make the skin appear tighter.

Mary Ellen Brademas, MD, clinical professor of dermatology, New York University Medical Center, NY.

BEST WAY TO CLEAR RED EYES

Use cool compresses or artificial tears, such as *Viva* drops or *HypoTears*. If redness persists or is around the iris, see your doctor. Avoid daily use of eyedrops. They can mask potential eye problems. *Also:* Be cautious of eye decongestants. Using this type of product regularly can create a rebound effect leading to swollen eyelids and conjunctivitis.

Melvin Schrier, OD, vision consultant, Rancho Palos Verdes, CA.

Eyesight Can Be Protected By Taking Vitamin and Mineral Supplements

R*ecent finding:* People who took 500 mg of vitamin C, 400 international units (IU) of vitamin E, 25,000 IU of beta carotene and 80 mg of zinc had a 25% lower risk for age-related macular degeneration (AMD) than people who did not take these supplements. AMD is a leading cause of blindness. *If you are age 55 or older:* See your eye doctor to determine your risk of developing AMD and whether taking these vitamins and minerals might be beneficial for you.

Emily Chew, MD, deputy director of epidemiology and clinical research, National Eye Institute, Bethesda, MD.

Eyedrop Magic

B*est way to apply eyedrops:* Wash hands. Tilt head back. With an index finger, pull the lower eyelid away from the eye to form a pouch. Drop the medicine into the pouch. Close the eye gently, and keep it closed for one to two minutes. *Do not blink.* Never let the tip of an eyedrop applicator touch the eye or any other surface.

The USP Guide to Heart Medicines, the US Pharmacopeia Expert Advisory Panel on Cardiovascular and Renal Drugs. Avon.

Dry Eye Relief

Open clogged oil glands by holding a warm, wet washcloth on closed eyelids for 5 to 10 minutes, several times a day. Wear protective eyewear during outdoor sports to shield eyes from wind. Point car vents away from eyes...and heating and cooling ducts away from areas where you spend a lot of time. Blink often when concentrating on work or watching a TV or computer screen. Keep air moist indoors during heating season. If dry eyes persist, see an ophthalmologist.

Eric Donnenfeld, MD, codirector, cornea department, North Shore University Hospital, Manhasset, NY.

Relief for Ear Disorder

One common ear disorder responds better to the cancer drug *methotrexate* (MTX) than to steroids. An autoimmune disorder of the inner ear, Ménière's disease causes vertigo, temporary deafness and buzzing or ringing in the ears (tinnitus). Doctors typically prescribe *prednisone* (Deltasone) or another steroid, but those drugs can cause weight gain and other side effects. *Recent finding:* Among Ménière's patients treated with MTX, vertigo disappeared in 77%, hearing improved in 28% and tinnitus improved in 65%. The minor side effects that occurred stopped when the patients stopped taking MTX.

Aristides Sismanis, MD, chairman of otolaryngology, Medical College of Virginia at Virginia Commonwealth University, Richmond. His study of 18 Ménière's patients was presented at a meeting of the American Laryngological, Rhinological and Otological Society.

Childhood Ear Infections

The incidence of childhood ear infections has increased dramatically—44% over a seven-year period. *Probable reasons:* The growth in the number of children attending day care and the increased prevalence of allergies among kids. Research has also shown that children who get their first ear infection before their first birthday are twice as likely to get infections again as children whose first occurrence comes later.

Bruce Lanphear, MD, associate professor of pediatrics, Children's Hospital Medical Center, Cincinnati, whose analysis was published in *Pediatrics.*

Know How to Detect An Ear Infection In Your Child

High-tech devices to check for kids' ear infections shouldn't replace a trip to the doctor. Home otoscopes, a new middle-ear monitor, and other do-it-yourself instruments are touted as simple—though often expensive—screening tools. But because small children have narrow, angular ear canals, it is difficult to check the eardrum—and earwax may further block the view. *Best:* Instead of using an instrument to indicate the need for a doctor, rely on the child's symptoms—including fussiness, loss of appetite and fever, especially following a cold.

Cheston Berlin, MD, professor of pediatrics at Penn State College of Medicine, Children's Hospital, Hershey, PA.

Infant Hearing Test Alert

All infants should have their hearing checked within one month of birth—and the sooner, the better. The earlier any hearing problems are detected, the more likely children will develop full speech and language skills. If your state does not mandate hearing tests for newborns—only about one-third do—ask your pediatrician to make sure your baby gets the *Auditory Brainstem Response Test* (ABR) or the *Otoacoustic Emissions Test* (OET). *At greatest risk:* Premature infants…those who weighed less than about 3.5 pounds at birth or who have blood or kidney problems.

Charles Berlin, PhD, former director of Kresge Hearing Research Laboratory, department of otolaryngology, head and neck surgery, Louisiana State University, New Orleans.

FIGHT MOUTH BACTERIA

Rinse your mouth with water after eating to help neutralize decay-causing acids…and cut bacteria levels by one third. You can also neutralize acids and reduce bacteria levels by chewing sugarless gum.

Academy of General Dentistry.

Protect Yourself from Gum Disease

Robert J. Genco, DDS, PhD, professor and chair of oral biology and director of the periodontal disease research center at the State University of New York in Buffalo.

Four out of five American adults have some form of periodontal (gum) disease—from swollen gums to bleeding gums to loose teeth.

The damage isn't limited to the mouth. Gum disease contributes to heart disease and can cause trouble for diabetics and pregnant women, recent studies show.

HOW GUM DISEASE DEVELOPS

Gum disease is caused by bacteria that breed in plaque. That's the substance formed by food debris that accumulates around the gum line.

If it's not removed by brushing, plaque eventually turns into tartar (*calculus*). Tartar roughens tooth surfaces, making plaque adhere even more tightly to teeth.

Toxins produced by the bacteria in plaque inflame gums, making them red, swollen and prone to bleeding. This condition is called *gingivitis*.

Unless inflammation is arrested, gums eventually pull away from teeth. Bacteria then collect in the resulting pockets, further promoting tissue destruction.

Over time, the infection and inflammation destroy bone and tissue. Teeth then loosen and fall out.

Although gum disease usually has obvious symptoms, it can lurk in the mouth even if gums don't bleed. *Among the lesser-known warning signs:* Persistent bad breath…a change in the way teeth fit together when they bite…a change in the fit of partial dentures.

Anyone can develop gum disease. But some factors put people at special risk. These include smoking, diabetes, stress and low bone density.

THE THREATS TO YOUR HEALTH

Severe gum disease (periodontitis) poses serious health risks…

▓ Heart disease.

People with periodontitis have nearly twice the risk of having a fatal heart attack as do those without the disease.

However, recent studies suggest that the milder form of gum disease—gingivitis—is *not* associated with heart disease.

How does gum disease harm the heart? The same bacteria that cause gum disease may also raise heart attack risk by provoking a barrage of inflammatory substances that exacerbate coronary artery plaques. They're the sticky deposits that clog blood vessels and lead to heart attack.

▓ Diabetes.

Diabetics are more likely to develop gum disease.

And, for unknown reasons, diabetics with gum disease have more trouble controlling their blood sugar than do other diabetics. The more severe the gum disease, the worse their blood sugar control.

▓ Pregnancy.

Pregnant women with periodontitis are at risk for delivering low-birthweight, premature babies.

REVERSING GUM DISEASE

The same oral hygiene regimen that prevents gum disease can reverse it if it's caught early.

▓ Brushing.

Twice a day, brush gently for three minutes with a soft-bristled brush.

Don't brush side-to-side or in circles. Hold the brush at a 45-degree angle to the gums and sweep from the gum line to the tip of the tooth. Brush the back of each tooth, too.

What about the special grips and bristles common in toothbrushes nowadays? They're frills. Use them if they make brushing more enjoyable. But they're no more effective than straight-handled, straight-bristled versions.

Electric toothbrushes are not necessarily better than manual ones. But they can be useful for people who have difficulty brushing properly because of arthritis or other conditions.

The newest devices—sonic toothbrushes—use sound waves to dislodge plaque and debris. These brushes can help with plaque removal. But good flossers do just as well with old-fashioned manual toothbrushes as with sonic ones.

▓ Flossing.

Floss at least once daily.

Guide the floss between each set of adjacent teeth in sequence, so you don't miss any. Slide the floss gently down the side of one tooth, then up the side of the other.

Caution: Never drag the floss into your gums.

Some flosses are waxed or Teflon-coated. Some are flavored. Some are thin filaments. Others are broad ribbons or tapes. None is inherently better than the others. Use the type you prefer.

To make sure you remove all plaque and debris between teeth, add at least one of these strategies to your flossing routine...

▶ **Use a rubber-tipped stimulator** or an interproximal brush—a tiny flexible brush perched atop a metal wand. The brush is useful for people with spaces between their teeth. Insert the brush or stimulator between teeth at the gum line and move gently back and forth.

▶ **Try an irrigator** such as a Water Pik. The stream of water dislodges debris caught between teeth.

▓ Mouthwash.

Some mouthwashes have been proven to fight gingivitis.

Look for the American Dental Association seal of approval.

▓ See your dentist.

Even if you're doing everything right, regular dental checkups and professional cleanings are essential.

Twice-yearly cleanings suffice for most people. But some need more frequent attention, no matter how scrupulous their home regimen.

Ask your dentist what schedule is right for you. Make sure he or she examines your mouth for signs of bone loss at every visit.

FIGHTING ADVANCED DISEASE

Periodontitis is most often treated with root "scaling" and "planing." Scaling removes plaque and tartar below the gum line at the tooth's root. Planing smooths the root to keep plaque from accumulating along rough surfaces.

In especially severe cases, surgery is needed to cut away detached gum tissue and regenerate bone.

Treatment for periodontitis usually includes antibiotics. New strategies have been developed to deliver antibiotics and germicides directly to gum tissue. These include a gel that hardens in the gum pocket …and a tiny chip that's inserted into the pocket.

HAVE A TOOTHACHE?

Transient tooth pain generally isn't a problem. But see your dentist right away for tooth pain that comes on spontaneously and lingers… is triggered by hot, cold or sweets *and* lasts 10 seconds or more…wakes you up in the middle of the night.

These symptoms suggest that you have a deep cavity or nerve damage.

Aspirin or ibuprofen (Advil) can help alleviate the pain. Do *not* place the pill directly on the gum. That could "burn" the tissue.

Alan Winter, DDS, periodontist and partner, Park Avenue Periodontal Associates, 532 Park Ave., New York City 10021.

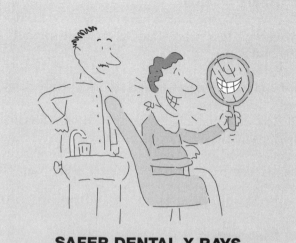

SAFER DENTAL X RAYS

Check the equipment and patient protection used by your dentist. The equipment should have a long lead-lined rectangular tube pointed at the cheek—not a short, pointed plastic cone. Patients should wear a lead apron and collar. *Also:* Ask how the machine's radiation dose is monitored. The dentist and assistants should promptly explain what they do. *Plus:* Ask if the dentist uses Ektaspeed X-ray film, also called E film. It reduces the extent of patient exposure to radiation—but only about 20% of dentists use it.

Take This Book to the Dentist with You by **Charles Inlander,** president, People's Medical Society, Allentown, PA.

Help for Sensitive Teeth

If you have sensitive teeth and use a special desensitizing toothpaste—such as *Aquafresh Sensitive* or *Sensodyne*—see your dentist if your teeth are still painful after about one month of use. *Reason:* To make certain you don't have decay, a cracked tooth or other problems. If serious causes are ruled out, your dentist may suggest sealants, bonded resins or other treatment.

Alan Winter, DDS, periodontist and partner, Park Avenue Periodontal Associates, 532 Park Ave., New York City 10021.

Dental Infection Linked to Stroke

People who have frequent dental infections—and other chronic infections, particularly bronchitis—are more likely than others to suffer a stroke. *Possible reason:* Infections may activate coagulation or make it easier for fatty plaque to build up in arteries—a precursor of stroke. *Self-defense:* Clear up dental and other infections as quickly as possible.

Armin Grau, MD, neurology department, University of Heidelberg, Germany, whose study of 166 stroke victims was published in the American Heart Association journal, *Stroke.*

Asthma Can Lead to Dental Problems

Adults and children with asthma have difficulty moving air in and out of their lungs, so they tend to breathe more through their mouths. This practice—combined with oral inhalers—can significantly increase the risk for gum disease. *Bottom line:* Asthmatics should visit their dentist at least every three months for a cleaning. They should also consider using a supplemental fluoride rinse or gel to fight plaque buildup and cavities.

John M. Coke, DDS, associate professor of diagnostic and hospital dentistry, University of Alabama School of Dentistry, Birmingham.

FEAR OF DENTISTS

Fear of dentists is treatable through talk. Most dentists today are taught to communicate with patients and help them handle fear. If your dentist seems unsympathetic, find one who relates to your concerns. If your main concern is pain, ask the dentist about pain-relief options. *Example:* Some people do better with a local anesthetic that does not contain *epinephrine*—a compound that can cause the heart to race, making some people feel panicky.

Louis Siegelman, DDS, director of dental anesthesiology, Lutheran Medical Center, Brooklyn, NY and a dentist in private practice in New York.

Dentures Can Be Dangerous

Dentures account for 6% of all cases of foreign object ingestion. Because of their large size and sharp edges, dentures are more likely than other foreign objects to puncture the esophagus. *Self-defense:* Make sure dentures are in good shape and are not too loose. Don't sleep with your dentures in.

Ricardo Gotti, MD, staff, gastrointestinal endoscopy unit, Posadas Hospital, Buenos Aires.

Chewing Ice Can Lead to Tooth Decay

Abrupt temperature changes that occur as tooth enamel meets ice—in combination with ice's hard texture—can cause tiny fractures in the tooth surface. Bacteria can then make their way into the tooth interior through these cracks.

Manuel Cordero, DDS, a dentist in private practice in Sewell, NJ, and a spokesperson for the Academy of General Dentistry, Chicago.

HERBS CAN AFFECT DENTAL HEALTH

Let your dentist know about any herbal remedies you take so that he or she can consider possible side effects. *Example:* Ginkgo biloba may cause bleeding gums or make existing gum disease worse.

Andrew Rubman, ND, associate professor of clinical medicine, Lane College of Integrative Medicine, Orlando, FL, and medical director, Southbury Clinic for Traditional Medicines, Southbury, CT.

Combat Garlic Breath

For sweeter breath after eating garlic, try chewing fresh parsley…fennel…or citrus peel. *Also:* You can use BreathAsure tablets, available at drugstores.

Alan Winter, DDS, periodontist and partner, Park Avenue Periodontal Associates, 532 Park Ave., New York City 10021.

Bottled-Water Fluoride Trap

Few bottled waters contain adequate levels of fluoride—an important element in fighting tooth decay. People who drink only or mostly bottled water—or who live in a municipality that does not have the recommended level of fluoride in the water supply—may end up with dental problems. Children are at especially high risk. *Self-defense:* Discuss the fluoride levels of your drinking water source with your dentist and ask about fluoride mouth rinses or tablets. Also look for bottled waters with fluoride—some brands now add it. And be sure to use a toothpaste with fluoride regularly.

Steve Levy, DDS, Preventative & Community Dentistry, University of Iowa College of Dentistry, Iowa City.

Vocal Cord Repair

Voices lost to vocal-cord injury can now be restored almost to their original sound.

Doctors surgically implant a newly developed ceramic device that supports the damaged cord so it can function properly.

Patients who undergo the 30-minute procedure rave that their voices sound just the way they used to. Previously, restored voices tended to sound breathy and hoarse.

Charles Cummings, MD, chair, department of otolaryngology, Johns Hopkins University School of Medicine, Baltimore.

HERBAL TEA MAY ERODE TOOTH ENAMEL

Many coffee drinkers are turning to tea for its antioxidant potential. But acids in fruit teas and lemon-flavored iced teas can erode enamel, due to their high content of fruit acids. In one study, chamomile was the only tea that did not erode enamel. The researchers did not study the increasingly popular green tea or the effect of adding milk to tea.

Smart idea: Drinking tea through a straw could potentially reduce the risk for erosion.

Jeremy Rees, PhD, senior lecturer, division of restorative dentistry, University of Bristol Dental School, Bristol, England. His study was published in *Journal of Dentistry,* Langford Lane, Kidlington, Oxford OX5 1GB.

For Women Only

Chapter 14

Disease and Gender

Many diseases have different symptoms—and require different treatment—in women and in men. *Example:* Women who have heart disease may show such atypical symptoms as chest, back and arm pain not brought on by exertion. *Problem:* Many doctors are not as familiar as they should be with women's special health needs. Patients should choose doctors—either female or male—who show awareness of their particular issues. *Questions to ask:* Has the physician taken a professional course like the American Medical Women's Association Advanced Curriculum? Does the physician routinely perform comprehensive exams that include pelvic and breast exams?

Lila Wallis, MD, clinical professor of medicine, Cornell University Medical College, NY.

How to Fight PMS

Premenstrual syndrome (PMS) symptoms can be improved with lifestyle changes—aerobic exercise, such as brisk walking or cycling...stress reduction through relaxation techniques...reducing caffeine and salt intake...and taking daily multivitamins. Special PMS clinics may be helpful if run by responsible doctors who offer counseling, understand psychological and medical aspects of PMS, and tailor treatment to each patient.

JoAnn Manson, MD, professor of epidemiology, Brigham & Women's Hospital and Harvard Medical School, Boston.

Solving an Embarrassing Problem

About 17 million people in the US have overactive bladders. Most are women. The prescription drug *tolterodine tartrate*, sold as *Detrol*, helps control urinary urgency, frequent urination and urinary incontinence in people with overactive bladders. Clinical trials report fewer significant side effects than with other drugs currently used.

Alan Wein, MD, professor and chairman, division of urology, Hospital of the University of Pennsylvania, Philadelphia.

Danger in Ignoring the Calls of Nature

*S*hort-term danger in ignoring the calls of nature: Urinary leakage and constipation. *Long-term*: Bladder infections, especially in women, and nerve damage. Although nerve damage is rare, it may occur if over many years you make it a habit to hold back urinary flow. *Bottom line:* Do not wait to relieve yourself until you feel extreme discomfort or pain.

Ingrid Nygaard, MD, professor of obstetrics and gynecology, University of Iowa, Iowa City.

BREAST IMPLANT RISKS

Risks of *saline* breast implants: Infection and complications of anesthesia, as with any surgery...scar tissue that can harden breasts ...rupture or deflation of implants, requiring additional surgery to replace them. Implants can also interfere with mammography. Despite risks, breast enlargements are becoming more popular.

Scott Spear, MD, professor and chief of plastic surgery, Georgetown University, Washington, DC.

Protect Yourself Against Breast Cancer

*S*imple lifestyle changes may lower breast cancer risk.

▓ **Limit alcohol consumption,** which has been linked to increased breast cancer risk.

Restricting intake to no more than two to three drinks a week will minimize risk.

▓ **Keep weight in check.**
Fifteen to 20 extra pounds or more gained throughout adulthood increases postmenopausal risk.

▓ **Eat five servings per day of fruit and vegetables.**
These contain cancer-fighting antioxidants and phytochemicals.

▓ **Exercise regularly.**
Some studies suggest physical activity favorably affects levels of beneficial hormones.

These measures all have plenty of other health benefits, too, and are worthwhile for everyone.

JoAnn Manson, MD, professor of epidemiology, Brigham & Women's Hospital and Harvard Medical School, Boston.

Mammogram Alert

*A*woman who receives a mammogram every year for a decade has a 50-50 chance of getting a false-positive result. These false alarms are caught only after the woman has been called back for further tests—which can be a frightening experience. Women under 50 years of age have the highest rate of false alarms. *Needed:* Better understanding—and better patient counseling to explain the possibility of false-positive test results.

Joann Elmore, MD, University of Washington School of Medicine, Seattle, whose study of 2,400 women was published in *The New England Journal of Medicine*.

Do Breast Self-Exams Two Ways

Do breast self-exams two ways—lying down and standing up. Lying on your back forces breast tissue to expand, thus allowing the entire breast tissue to be examined. Standing lets breast tissue be examined from a different angle. *Important:* Inspect breasts visually as well as with fingers. Do self-exams right after a menstrual period, when hormone levels are low and breasts are the least tender and lumpy.

Cristina Matera, MD, assistant professor of clinical obstetrics and gynecology, Columbia–Presbyterian Medical Center, NY.

BETTER BREAST EXAM

Women with dense breasts should consider having an ultrasound—in addition to a mammogram—to detect breast cancer. When 2,600 women with dense breasts underwent follow-up ultrasounds, 250 were found to have solid masses not seen in mammography. Ten of these turned out to be very small early-stage cancers. The only way to tell whether a woman has dense breasts is with mammograms—size and firmness have nothing to do with it.

Thomas Kolb, MD, assistant clinical professor of radiology, Columbia–Presbyterian Medical Center, NY, whose study of more than 8,000 women is ongoing.

BREAST CANCER NEWS

In a recent study of 37,000 women, the drug tamoxifen was shown to significantly reduce the risk of a recurrence of breast cancer—and the risk of developing the condition in the other breast. Tamoxifen also reduces the chance of developing breast cancer in the first place.

However...researchers caution that the drug increases the risk of uterine cancer and blood clots. It should be used only in select groups of women with a high risk of breast cancer.

JoAnn Manson, MD, professor of epidemiology, Brigham & Women's Hospital and Harvard Medical School, Boston.

Mastectomy Trap

Breast cancer patients sometimes undergo mastectomy (breast removal) needlessly. *Reason:* Not all doctors follow national guidelines for treating the disease. More than half of women with stage one or stage two breast cancer undergo mastectomy. Yet 75% of these women are eligible for lumpectomy, a less invasive procedure in which only cancerous tissue is removed. *Lesson:* Breast cancer patients who are told they need a mastectomy should ask their doctor to explain why.

Monica Morrow, MD, professor of surgical oncology, Northwestern University Medical School, Chicago.

Scarless Mastectomy

Instead of making the incision across the breast, the surgeon makes it around the nipple. Once breast tissue is removed, nearby tissue is used to rebuild the breast.

Among women who had this procedure, 40% rated the results as excellent, 37% as good and 23% as fair.

Catch: Only women who have sufficient "donor tissue"—from a fatty lower abdomen, for instance—are candidates for scarless mastectomy.

David Hidalgo, MD, former chief of plastic surgery, Memorial–Sloan Kettering Cancer Center, New York. His study of 30 mastectomy patients was presented at a meeting of the American Society of Plastic and Reconstructive Surgeons. He is now in private practice in New York City.

What You Need to Know If You Were a Premature Baby

Women who were born prematurely are more likely to have premature babies themselves. A woman who was born before 37 weeks of gestation is significantly more likely to have a premature baby herself than a woman who was born at full term. Prebirth counseling may help women to be more aware of the risk and better prepared to cope with a premature infant.

T. Flint Porter, MD, perinatologist, maternal-fetal medicine, department of obstetrics/gynecology, University of Utah, Salt Lake City, whose study was published in *Obstetrics and Gynecology.*

For Even Healthier Pregnancies

If you are planning to become pregnant, find out your ideal weight from your doctor and then try to stay near it—that may make it easier to conceive. Do *not* diet excessively.

■ Before you conceive...

You and your partner should meet with your physician to discuss your medical histories and backgrounds—including immunizations...genetic disorders...family history...and other factors that could help or harm a pregnancy.

Eat a healthy diet with lots of roughage.

Folic acid: Make sure you get 1 mg of folic acid a day—which will usually require a prescription from your doctor. Folic acid can also be taken as part of a pregnancy multivitamin.

■ During pregnancy...

Once you are no longer nauseated, eat at least one serving of protein—meat, fish or cheese—a day.

Portions should be about the size of a pack of playing cards.

Avoid raw meat or fish—and also avoid handling cat litter because of the danger of toxoplasmosis.

Jonathan Scher, MD, gynecologist/obstetrician in private practice, Scarsdale, NY.

AMNIOCENTESIS ALTERNATIVE

Amniocentesis does not increase the risk of birth defects or miscarriage when performed after 15 weeks of pregnancy. *However:* Amniocentesis earlier in pregnancy leads to a small increase in the rate of miscarriage and a large increase in the number of babies born with clubfoot, a limb deformity. *Safer alternative:* Chorionic Villus Sampling (CVS), in which a small amount of tissue from the developing placenta is removed for testing. Studies have shown that CVS is unlikely to cause deformities when performed at least 10 weeks into a pregnancy.

R. Douglas Wilson, MD, associate professor of obstetrics and gynecology, University of British Columbia, Vancouver, whose study of more than 4,000 pregnancies was published in *The Lancet.*

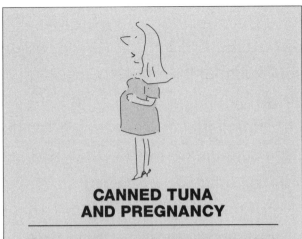

CANNED TUNA AND PREGNANCY

Avoid canned tuna while pregnant, and serve children younger than school-age no more than one tuna sandwich (6 oz.) per week. *Problem:* Mercury present in some tuna can interfere with the development of fetuses and very young children. While canned tuna is generally considered safe, there is—as yet—no agreement on how much people can eat or feed to children. These recommendations are designed for maximum safety as research continues.

Caroline Smith DeWaal, JD, director of food safety, Center for Science in the Public Interest, Washington, DC.

Douching Is Dangerous

Women who douche frequently and then become pregnant are more likely to give birth prematurely. So suggests preliminary research conducted at the University of Rochester School of Medicine in Rochester, New York. It is best not to douche, says the lead researcher. If you insist, avoid douching during the middle of the menstrual cycle. *Science News.*

Don't Touch It

Pregnant women shouldn't touch the antibaldness drug *finasteride* (Propecia)—literally. Women who handle crushed or broken finasteride pills can absorb the drug through their skin. It can cause birth defects in the unborn child.

Merck & Co.

How Much Weight Gain Is Healthy?

Weight gain during pregnancy should be 15 to 25 pounds for women with normal body-mass index. This is less than the 25-to-35-pound gain often recommended to avoid premature or low-birth-weight babies. Recent studies show gains of more than 25 pounds are no better for babies—and are more likely to stay on the mothers after the birth. Women who are underweight or overweight when they become pregnant may need more—or less—weight gain. Consult your obstetrician.

Denice Feig, MD, assistant professor, department of medicine, University of Toronto, whose review of weight-gain studies was published in *The Lancet.*

TIMING MATTERS

Conception can result from intercourse several days *before* a woman ovulates. *Reason:* Sperm remain active for two to four days.

Owen K. Davis, MD, associate director, The Center for Reproductive Medicine & Infertility, NY.

Stronger Sexual Desire

Women's sexual desire may grow stronger following hysterectomy—that was the surprising conclusion of a study of 1,000 women. Researchers discovered that after surgery, 15% more of the women desired sex at least once a week, 12% more made love at least five times a month and 9% more experienced orgasms. Only 5% felt the quality of their sex life had deteriorated.

Kristen H. Kjerulff, PhD, associate professor of epidemiology, University of Maryland School of Medicine, Baltimore.

Very Personal

Pornography *does* turn on women, just as it stimulates men. Both males and females show significant increases in the sex hormone testosterone after watching a pornographic film. Men's testosterone tends to increase more, but the increase in women is also substantial. The more testosterone a woman produces during her monthly cycle, the more sexually active she tends to be.

Study by researchers at the Ludwig Boltzmann Institute for Urban Ethology, Vienna, Austria, of the response of 10 men and 10 women to a 15-minute sex film, reported in *New Scientist.*

Very, Very Personal

Vaginal burning during sex is most often caused by lack of lubrication. *Helpful:* Engage in more foreplay, so the tissues become fully moistened. *Also:* Try using a lubricant, such as K-Y Jelly or Astroglide. Stinging or burning can also be caused by a vaginal infection or vulvodynia, conditions that require a doctor's care. See your doctor if you experience bleeding, malodorous discharge, urinary frequency, urgency or burning...or pelvic pain. Any symptoms that do not resolve or improve after a few days or with the use of a lubricant deserve medical attention.

Gloria Bachmann, MD, professor of obstetrics and gynecology, Robert Wood Johnson Medical School, and director, Women's Health Institute, Robert Wood Johnson University Hospital, New Brunswick, NJ.

CONDOM RISK

Caution: Unlubricated condoms significantly increase the risk of a woman developing a first-time urinary-tract infection. The problem is 30 times more likely.

Betsy Foxman, PhD, professor, department of epidemiology, University of Michigan School of Public Health, Ann Arbor, whose study was published in *Epidemiology.*

FACTS ABOUT IUD USE

New IUDs are safe, effective contraceptives for women in mutually monogamous relationships. The most commonly used IUD in the US —the Copper T380A—is associated with a 1% or less risk of pregnancy. This is comparable to the pill in reliability, without having to take a pill every day. There is little chance of pelvic infection—as with some older IUDs—if inserted properly by a physician and if the woman is at low risk for sexually transmitted diseases (STDs). Among the women who shouldn't use them—those whose sexual habits put them at risk for STDs...those who have uterine fibroids or have had recent pelvic inflammatory disease...or women who are allergic to copper.

Roberto Rivera, MD, director of international research ethics, Family Health International, a reproductive-health organization in Research Triangle Park, NC.

Discharge Dilemma

O diferous vaginal discharge can be normal after sex—but may indicate infection if it occurs at other times. The presence of discharge usually points to an overgrowth of bacteria, called *bacterial vaginosis*. This can be cured with a gel, cream or oral antibiotics. Women sometimes assume that all discharges are yeast infections and treat them as such. That approach is worse than useless. It can let microorganisms spread to the uterus and fallopian tubes, which can cause infertility or preterm birth.

James McGregor, MD, professor of obstetrics and gynecology, University of Colorado Health Sciences Center, Denver.

Viagra Alert

V *iagra's downside for women:* Increased likelihood of a condition usually called honeymoon cystitis. It produces frequent, urgent, burning urination and usually occurs after extended sexual activity. Cystitis is becoming more common among women ages 55 to 75 whose husbands have taken Viagra to overcome impotence. *Self-defense:* Drink extra liquids, and urinate before and after sex. If the condition persists, see your doctor. Antibiotics may be required to treat cystitis.

Henry M. Patton, MD, internist in private practice in Covington, GA.

Chest Pain in Women Is Often Misdiagnosed

M any doctors are quick to ascribe chest pain to heart disease. But often the real cause is mus-

cle soreness caused by bad posture, overuse, etc. Typically, chest pain that flares up with exercise is associated with heart disease. Muscle-related chest pain typically does not flare up with exercise...but does flare up when the arms are raised overhead (to wash the hair, for example). *Good news:* Muscle-related chest pain can be controlled with stretching, acupressure and hot packs. But discuss the matter with a doctor.

Ronald S. Baigrie, MD, staff cardiologist, Sudbury Regional Hospital, Sudbury, Canada. His study of 50 women with chest pain was presented at a meeting of the Canadian Cardiovascular Society.

Is Hormone-Replacement Therapy Good for Older Women?

Steven R. Goldstein, MD, professor of obstetrics and gynecology at New York University School of Medicine. He is also codirector of bone densitometry and director of gynecologic ultrasound at New York University Medical Center, New York City. He is coauthor of *The Estrogen Alternative.* Putnam.

M enopause is the period in a woman's life when estrogen levels plummet and menstrual periods stop entirely.

Before menopause, a woman enters a four- to 10-year phase during which she stops ovulating, but continues to produce estrogen.

Called *perimenopause*, this phase of life is often marked by irregular bleeding and the onset of subtle psychological problems, such as moodiness, memory loss and/or anxiety.

Once menopause begins, many women experience hot flashes, night sweats, vaginal dryness and other obvious symptoms.

Even in the absence of these symptoms, however, the body is undergoing dramatic physiological changes. Bones weaken. Cholesterol levels rise.

Over a period of years, these changes can lead to osteoporosis and heart attack.

HORMONE REPLACEMENT THERAPY

The goal of hormone-replacement therapy (HRT) is to replace the estrogen that the body no longer makes. HRT—taken as pills or absorbed from adhesive skin patches—is good at controlling menopausal symptoms such as night sweats, hot flashes, vaginal dryness, insomnia, mood swings and diminished libido. It also helps prevent osteoporosis, lowers the risk of colon cancer, reduces cholesterol levels and keeps skin smooth and supple.

Despite the benefits, estrogen raises the risk of breast, ovarian and uterine cancer. Recent evidence from a major randomized controlled study, called The Women's Health Initiative, suggests that the combination of estrogen and progestin increases the risk of heart disease. This contradicts previous studies. The Women's Health Initiative also found that HRT raises the incidence of strokes and blood clots in the lungs.

SERMS

New "designer" hormones known as *selective estrogen receptor modulators* (SERMs) seem to provide the benefits of HRT without the health risks.

Like estrogen, SERMs protect the bones and keep cholesterol levels low. Unlike estrogen, SERMs do not promote uterine cancer. And they actually *lower* breast cancer risk.

Several SERMs have been approved by the FDA —*ralosifene* (Evista), *tamoxifen* (Nolvadex) and *toremifene* (Fareston). *Droloxifene* and others are currently being studied.

QUESTIONS TO CONSIDER

For some women, the benefits of HRT or raloxifene therapy clearly outweigh the drawbacks. But it can be hard to determine which approach to take, and some women should forgo hormone therapy altogether. *Pondering these questions can help you make this decision…*

■ Do you suffer from deep vein thrombosis, clotting problems or liver disease?

If so, you may not be a candidate for HRT or raloxifene.

Either can trigger clots…and can be detrimental to a liver that's already weakened by disease.

■ Have you stopped having menstrual periods?

If you have any sign of a menstrual period—even if bleeding is irregular—you're not yet menopausal and, therefore, not yet a candidate for HRT or raloxifene.

■ If you are menopausal, do you have obvious symptoms?

If so, HRT can help keep these symptoms in check.

Raloxifene does not curb menopausal symptoms. In fact, it can make hot flashes worse.

■ What is your personal risk for breast cancer?

The average woman has a 4% chance of dying of breast cancer. HRT raises that risk to about 5.5%.

Women who are at high risk for breast cancer can safely go on HRT for the few months that menopausal symptoms are most troublesome…and then switch to raloxifene.

Raloxifene is a better choice for asymptomatic women who are at high risk for breast cancer.

■ What is your personal risk for osteoporosis?

Every woman should be sure to get a baseline bone-density test at age 50.

If the test indicates that your bones are weak, either HRT or raloxifene can be helpful in preventing further bone loss.

Important: The risks of osteoporosis and breast cancer rise with age. For this reason, raloxifene can bring important health benefits even to women who don't start taking it until they're well into menopause.

GOING "NATURAL"

There is no meaningful difference between the effects of black cohosh, soy, or wild yam root and other natural menopause remedies and estrogen or raloxifene. All are metabolized in the liver into the same basic molecules. The health benefits they bring—as well as the side effects and risks—are essentially the same.

The main difference is that "natural" products are unregulated. Dose strength varies widely among brands—even among different pills in the same bottle.

If you get your estrogen at the health-food store without a prescription, make sure your doctor monitors you for side effects.

Certain Foods Worsen Menopause

Depending on your symptoms, there are specific foods to avoid. If you suffer from…

■ **Hot flashes:** Avoid caffeinated beverages, such as coffee, tea and cola …alcohol…spicy foods…and hot drinks.

■ **Nausea:** Avoid fatty, greasy foods, including junk foods, rich sauces and high-fat cheese.

■ **Mood swings:** Eat regularly throughout the day. Have a snack when you are hungry…and don't skip meals.

■ **Calcium loss:** Avoid diets that are high in protein and sodium. Cut back on processed foods, salty snack foods and prepared mixes.

■ **Headaches:** Stay away from red wine and beer. Also avoid coffee and chocolate, although caffeine may help alleviate a headache, depending on the individual.

Suzanne Havala Hobbs, DrPH, RD, adjunct assistant professor, School of Public Health, University of North Carolina, Chapel Hill.

Did You Know…

Few women are capable of multiple orgasms. So those women who do not experience multiple orgasms should not feel frustrated or inadequate. *Reason:* During arousal and climax, many women have a surge of *prolactin*. This hormone acts as an automatic "shut-off switch" for sexual desire immediately after orgasm. Chronic prolactin elevation is known to reduce libido.

Michael S. Exton, PhD, senior research fellow, Institute of Medical Psychology, University of Essen, Germany.

HRT ALTERNATIVE

Women concerned about the side effects associated with hormone-replacement therapy should talk with their doctors about the drug *Evista*. Evista, or *raloxifene,* is aimed at offering some of estrogen's benefits—such as more bone mass while avoiding its tendency to increase the risk of breast cancer and heart disease.

Nananda Col, MD, Decisions Research Group, Department of Radiology, Brigham & Women's Hospital, Boston, and author of *A Woman Doctor's Guide to Hormone Therapy.* Chandler House Press.

HRT OPTIONS

Antidepressants soothe hot flashes without hormones. In recent tests on menopausal women, two common medicines—Prozac and Effexor—reduced hot flashes by 50% or more. Ask your doctor if they are worthwhile for you.

Charles L. Loprinzi, MD, professor of medical oncology, Mayo Clinic, Rochester, Minnesota, and leader of a study of fluoxetine in 81 women with a history of breast cancer, published in *Journal of Clinical Oncology.*

Viagra for Women

Although more commonly prescribed for men, *sildenafil* (Viagra) has been shown to help postmenopausal women who suffer from sexual arousal problems, including lack of genital sensation and lubrication.

Possible side effects: Facial flushing, headache and nausea.

Caution: Anyone taking nitrates (e.g., for angina or heart failure) should not take Viagra. Ask your doctor if Viagra treatment is right for you.

Jennifer R. Berman, MD, director, Female Sexual Medical Center, University of California, Los Angeles, and leader of a study of 202 postmenopausal women, reported in *The Journal of Urology.*

For Men Only

Chapter 15

Ease Urinary Problems

Urinary problems in men can be eased with *botulinum toxin* (BoTox). In a preliminary study, four men who had trouble urinating as a result of prostate inflammation were given injections of BoTox into the urinary sphincter—the muscle that controls the flow of urine. After four weeks, three of the men noted striking improvements in their ability to urinate. A muscle paralyzer, BoTox has been used to treat a range of conditions, from constipation to facial wrinkles.

Giorgio Maria, MD, assistant professor of surgery, Catholic University of Rome. His one-year study was published in *The Lancet*.

Hypertension Side Effect

Urinary problems in men often go hand in hand with high blood pressure. In a recent study, 22% of men with high blood pressure had urinary urgency and/or pain. Only 13% of men with normal blood pressure had urinary problems.

Glen McWilliams, MD, chief resident, department of urology, Columbia–Presbyterian Medical Center, NY.

Smoking Lowers Sperm Quality

In a recent study, men who smoked an average of 42 cigarettes a day for at least the past three years produced less active, less resilient sperm than did lifelong nonsmokers.

Panayiotis Zavos, PhD, professor, reproductive physiology–andrology, University of Kentucky, and codirector, Kentucky Center for Reproductive Medicine, Lexington.

Smoking Hurts Men's Sex Drives

Men who smoke report having sex only half as often as nonsmokers...and report less satisfaction with their sex lives. Also, sperm cells from men who smoke are of lower quality than those of nonsmokers.

Study of 290 couples being evaluated for infertility, led by **Panayiotis Zavos, PhD,** University of Kentucky and Kentucky Center for Reproductive Medicine, Lexington.

Facts About Impotence

A man may be impotent even if he has spontaneous nighttime erections. Impotence means failure to have erections when desired...not failure to have them at all. If erections occur during sleep, impotence most likely has a psychological origin. *Another impotence myth:* Failure to perform every time means a man is impotent or about to become impotent. *Reality:* It is common and normal for men to be unable to have erections occasionally.

Isadore Rosenfeld, MD, Rossi Distinguished Professor of Clinical Medicine, New York Hospital–Cornell Medical Center, NY.

Cure Impotence the Natural Way

Natural alternatives to Viagra, Levitra and Cialis for treating impotence: Extracts of ginkgo leaves or ginseng root. They are available at drugstores and health food stores. Consult your physician before trying either remedy. These are the dosages

I would discuss. *Ginkgo:* 40 milligram (mg) extract, three times a day. Don't use it if you take aspirin or blood thinners. *Ginseng:* 100 mg to 200 mg extract daily. Men using ginseng should have their blood pressure monitored regularly. Don't use it if you drink caffeinated beverages regularly or take other stimulants. And be patient—it may take several months to see results.

Adriane Fugh-Berman, MD, a medical researcher based in Washington, DC, and author of *Alternative Medicine: What Works.* Williams & Wilkins.

What to Do About Penile Injury

Penile fracture is the most common severe injury to the penis. Pain is intense. The penis turns purple and swells. The injury almost always occurs during intercourse, when the penis can be jammed against the woman's pelvic bone or another hard surface. *Self-defense:* Be careful when changing positions and when the woman is on top. If penile fracture occurs, get to an emergency room immediately. Penile fracture needs to be repaired surgically. If it's improperly repaired, penile deformity or impotence may result.

Tom F. Lue, MD, professor of urology, University of California, San Francisco, School of Medicine.

Bald Again?

People using the popular anti-baldness drugs *Propecia* and *Rogaine* will lose their new hair—but not what they already had—if they stop taking the medication. The loss of the new hair takes three to 12 months.

Neal Schultz, MD, dermatologist in private practice, 1130 Park Ave., New York City 10128.

HOW TO WIN THE BALDNESS WARS

Medications: The prescription drug *Propecia* (available in pill form) and the drug *Rogaine* (available as an over-the-counter lotion) take at least four to six months to produce significant results. *Cost:* About $40 for one month's supply of either drug. *Caution:* The new hair is lost if treatment is stopped. Consult your physician about possible side effects.

Hair transplants: Instead of transplanting small plugs of hair, surgeons now insert one hair at a time, producing better cosmetic results. *Cost:* Up to $15,000 for a complete scalp.

Scalp reduction: When bald skin from the middle of the head is removed, hair-bearing scalp from the sides can be put in its place. *Cost:* Up to $15,000.

Neal Schultz, MD, a dermatologist in private practice, 1130 Park Ave., New York City 10128.

Shrewder Shaving

If you use razor blades, wait two minutes after applying shaving foam, cream or gel to give the product time to work into your beard.

▶ **To minimize irritation,** shave no more than twice over any area. Shave *with* the grain first—and then *against* the grain.

▶ **Best for sensitive skin:** Shave at the end of a shower while you are still in the shower stall, and use shaving gel. Avoid shaving just before exercising—perspiration irritates newly shaved skin.

▶ **Shave only once a day, if possible.** If you must shave twice, switch to an electric shaver to lower the chance of irritation. Some men get the best results by alternating between an electric razor and wet shaving.

Neal Schultz, MD, a dermatologist in private practice, 1130 Park Ave., New York City 10128.

Updating Your Appearance

New hair-transplant procedures—mini- and micro-grafts—give a more natural look than older techniques. The risk is minimal as long as anti-bacterial ointments are used to prevent infection. *Cost:* About $2,000 to $8,000. *Also very popular for men:* Liposuction—surgical fat removal—to eliminate double chins, "love handles" and other bulges. *Cost:* $1,500—and up. Using local instead of general anesthesia greatly reduces both the risks and postsurgical "downtime" of liposuction. More men are turning to cosmetic surgery to stay competitive in the youth-oriented workplace.

Bruce Katz, MD, a dermatologist and director, Juva Skin and Laser Center, New York.

WALK TO LENGTHEN YOUR LIFE

Men who walked more than two miles a day were almost half as likely to have died during a 12-year period as men who walked less than one mile a day. The earlier you establish a walking habit, the more you reduce your risk of cancer and heart disease later in life.

Robert Abbott, PhD, professor of biostatistics, University of Virginia School of Medicine, Charlottesville, whose study was published in *The New England Journal of Medicine*.

SAFER BICYCLING FOR MEN

Avoid long periods on bicycle seats. This can cause crotch injuries and impotence. *Self-defense:* Level the saddle or point the nose slightly downward. Lower the seat so knees are slightly bent when feet are at the bottom of each stroke. Avoid aero bars—handlebar extensions favored by triathletes—because they encourage riding on the nose of the saddle. Try a different, wider style of saddle. Stand up and pedal every 10 minutes. When riding over bumps, rise out of the saddle.

Irwin Goldstein, MD, professor of urology, Boston University Medical Center, Boston.

Blood Test for Prostate Cancer

A new prostate-cancer blood test may lower the need for biopsies—and the anxiety of men whose *prostate-specific antigen* (PSA) test is positive. Doctors know the PSA test shows high levels in many men who do not have prostate cancer. Until now, the only way to be *sure* has been a prostate biopsy. *Much better:* The new test measures both total PSA and the percentage of blood PSA that is free—not bound to other proteins. Free PSA is considered a much better indicator of possible cancer than total PSA.

Robert Flanigan, MD, professor and chairman of urology, Loyola University Medical Center, Maywood, IL, whose study of 773 men was published in the *Journal of the American Medical Association.*

Fight Prostate Cancer

F ight prostate cancer with aged garlic tablets. The tablets, sold in health food stores as *Kyolic,* contain antioxidants that have slowed cell growth in the laboratory. Animal-model results suggest that four tablets a day may be effective in slowing the development of prostate cancer in men. Consult your physician before using.

John Pinto, PhD, clinical nutrition research unit, Institute for Cancer Prevention, Valhalla, NY.

Help for Enlarged Prostate

A bout 80% of men get enlarged prostates after age 50. *Benign prostatic hyperplasia* (BPH) is uncomfortable and can be dangerous if it stops urine flow. *Helpful for men with BPH:* Eliminate caffeine and alcohol…avoid over-the-counter antihistamines and decongestants…maintain regular bowel movements…empty the bladder before going to sleep.

Patrick Walsh, MD, director, department of urology, Johns Hopkins Medical Institutions, Baltimore.

Prostate Problems

A popular prostate remedy can mask other serious health problems. Frequent urination and other symptoms of *benign prostatic hyperplasia* (BPH) can often be relieved by the herb saw palmetto. But those same symptoms can also be caused by prostate cancer, prostate infection or kidney disease. *Trap:* Many men start using saw palmetto to control symptoms without first being screened for these more serious ailments. *Self-defense:* See your doctor first to rule out dangerous conditions before starting saw palmetto.

Glenn Gerber, MD, associate professor of urology, University of Chicago Pritzker School of Medicine.

BEST TREATMENT FOR PROSTATE CANCER

Surgery remains the best treatment *for larger, more aggressive prostate cancers.* A recent study compared surgery, implantation of radioactive seeds and external beam radiation. For men with smaller or less aggressive prostate cancer, these three treatments were equally effective—regardless of the patient's age. That may make radiation the most desirable choice in such cases.

Anthony D'Amico, MD, PhD, radiation oncologist, Brigham & Women's Hospital, Boston. He is a professor of radiation oncology at Harvard Medical School. His study of almost 2,000 patients was published in *The Journal of the American Medical Association.*

New Aid for Prostate Surgery

A sensing device—called CaverMap—may help the surgeon prevent impotence from nerves that are cut during prostate surgery. *How it works:* The closer the scalpel gets to a nerve, the faster the machine beeps a warning. *Caution:* The device is not a replacement for a surgeon highly skilled at prostate surgery.

Michael Manyak, MD, chairman of urology, George Washington University Medical Center, Washington, DC.

Blood in Semen

Blood in semen is rarely a sign of disease—particularly in younger men. It is usually caused by harmless bleeding from tiny blood vessels in the seminal vesicles. Older men taking blood-thinning medicine are more likely to find blood in their semen. Have your doctor check the condition. In rare cases, it may indicate urologic disease.

Patrick C. Walsh, MD, director, department of urology, Johns Hopkins Medical Institutions, Baltimore.

WHAT YOU NEED TO KNOW ABOUT SELENIUM

Taking selenium to protect against prostate cancer can be dangerous. While one Harvard study found that daily selenium supplements may result in a reduced risk of advanced prostate cancer, the study failed to look at the incidence of other kinds of cancer. It also did not look at the overall death and illness rates. *Also:* There is little evidence that Americans are deficient in selenium. Excessive supplemental doses can lead to nausea, abdominal pain, diarrhea, fatigue and even death.

The late Victor Herbert, MD.

Men Are More Casual About Medical Care

Men are more likely than women to forgo receiving medical care.

Only 60% of American men have had a medical checkup within the past year—76% of women have. Eight percent of American men have not had a checkup for more than 10 years.

Men 18 to 34 years of age are the least likely group to get checkups.

Jim Daniels, Opinion Research International, Princeton, NJ.

Risky Surgery

Penile enlargement surgery can be very dangerous. It can lead to erectile dysfunction, scarring, infection and numbness or irritation...and it does not produce good cosmetic results. *How it's done:* The penis is lengthened by surgically detaching the ligaments that attach it to the pelvis...girth is added by injecting fat or wrapping grafts of fat around the penis. The Society for the Study of Impotence has issued a statement against penile enlargement. Urologists do not commonly perform it.

Arthur L. Burnett, MD, professor of urology, Johns Hopkins Hospital, Baltimore.

Relationship Secrets
Chapter 16

How to Keep Your Marriage Happy And Stop Troubles Before They Start

Traditional marriage counseling focuses on repairing long-standing problems. Most troubled couples wait an average of six years before they seek help. A new approach is to teach relationship skills early, before negative habits become entrenched and destructive. At the Seattle Marital and Family Institute, we have studied hundreds of couples to see what leads some to happiness and others to break up. Based on our research, we have developed numerous techniques to strengthen marriages and help spouses deal with conflict.

MARRIAGE EDUCATION

▓ Balanced marital ecology.
Critical to any marriage is having a healthy ratio of positive and negative emotions toward each other.

We have found that the ideal ratio is five times as many positive feelings as negative ones.

This ratio of positive to negative feelings not only nurtures your relationship but also builds up your emotional reserves when arguments and ill feelings strike—as they do in any close relationship.

Important: Don't expect to eliminate all negative emotions toward your spouse. Couples need to air and resolve disagreements. Most stable couples see their conflicts not as divisive but as shared and strengthening experiences.

Some negativity may also help keep sexual passion alive as couples first withdraw and then renew their affection.

▓ Accentuate the positive.
To keep your own positive ratio high, don't allow everyday tasks and commitments to crowd out thoughtfulness, affection and closeness.

John Gottman, PhD, professor of psychology at the University of Washington in Seattle and codirector of the Gottman Institute, Box 15644, Seattle 98115. He is author of *Why Marriages Succeed or Fail … and How You Can Make Yours Last.* Simon & Schuster.

Give thoughtful compliments...call each other during the day just to check in...and share private time together.

Consciously appreciating your spouse's good qualities also helps you maintain the vital positive–negative ratio when negativity appears. *Helpful...*

▶ **List your partner's positive contributions** to your life together. Think about how much harder life would be without those contributions. When you find yourself mentally criticizing your mate, "interrupt" your thinking with positive items from the list.

▶ **Dispel negative feelings after a disagreement** by looking through vacation picture albums or remembering your best times together ...even reading old love letters.

▶ **See the relationship as half-full rather than as half-empty** to defuse potentially irritating situations.

> *Example: If your partner leaves dirty dishes in the sink for several nights in a row, don't blow up. Think of all the other things he or she does to help the house run smoothly.*

■ Complain without being critical.
Voicing grievances is healthy and positive in a marriage. Attacking your spouse's character is not.

Important: Criticism may often begin with the word *you*, as in, "You're too irresponsible to call when you're going to be late."

Blaming and accusing can lead to anger and resentment.

Better: Complaints that begin with the word *I* and deal strictly with the specific behavior you would like changed. Addressing an issue rather than a character flaw allows room for discussion.

> *Example: "I wish you had let me know you wouldn't be home on time."*

Contempt, which goes way beyond criticism to insults, name-calling, hostile humor and mockery, *must be completely banned* from all discussions with your spouse.

You can guard against the temptation to voice contempt by not seeing arguments as a way to retaliate or exhibit moral superiority.

Instead of criticism, contempt and kitchen-sinking—dragging a multitude of grievances into an argument—I advocate gentle confrontation.

This involves emphasizing that you love your spouse and that your complaint concerns behavior he can, indeed, change. You can also say that you are bringing up the issue only to strengthen your relationship.

■ Structure your arguments.
When arguments intensify, both spouses may experience *emotional flooding*—sharply elevated heart rate and blood pressure...and increased adrenaline secretion.

All stimulate a reaction called *fight-or-flight*—an attack or a defensive withdrawal. That is always fatal to mutual understanding or problem solving.

Helpful: Put a 15-minute limit on arguments. If either of you feels emotionally flooded, call a 20-minute time-out.

Since continued negative thoughts and feelings of revenge will only reinforce flooding, we stress self-soothing during the time-out.

> *Example: Say to yourself, "We have a good marriage," or "We still love each other."*

When both of you are calm, continue the discussion for another 15 minutes.

■ Communicate nondefensively.
When you react defensively, you unintentionally sidetrack arguments rather than resolve them.

In addition, the stonewalling defense of silence and withdrawal usually leads the blocked spouse to attack harder in hopes of getting through.

Instead, use these two strategies—*nondefensive speech*, and, what we call, *validating.*

▶ **Nondefensive speech** cools down the argument and helps both parties feel more positive. Even if you can't give sincere praise and admiration, really listening signals that you understand your partner's feelings, even if you don't share them.

Example: *"That's a good point."*

▶ **Validating**—or verbally empathizing with your spouse's emotions and/or viewpoint—encourages discussion, openness and sharing. The nonvalidating statement, "You always ignore me when you come home from work," separates you further. The validating approach, "I understand you're tired after work, but I would still like to feel you're happy to see me," helps bring you together.

ARGUING AND ILLNESS

Newly married women had hormone fluctuations dramatic enough to weaken their immune systems in the hours following a marital spat. *Theory:* Women get more frustrated than men when they fight because men tend to tune them out. And the more the women stewed, the weaker their immune defenses became.

Janice Kiecolt-Glaser, PhD, professor, and **Ronald Glaser, PhD,** director, Behavioral Medicine Research Institute, Ohio State College of Medicine, Columbus. Their study was published in *Psychosomatic Medicine.*

The Dangers of Winning Too Often

Having to be right all the time is a barrier to personal and professional success. When you feel the need to show you are right, ask yourself if winning is important enough to risk hurting others—and being resented. When it is important to prove you are right, do it without making others feel wrong. Be sure to recognize and acknowledge the value of others' opinions. *Bottom line:* Being wrong sometimes does not make you less worthy—it makes you more human and approachable.

Get Out of Your Own Way: Overcoming Self-Defeating Behavior by **Mark Goulston, MD,** assistant clinical professor, Neuropsychiatric Institute, University of California, Los Angeles. Perigee.

Don't Forget Your Spouse

Treat your spouse like a client. You would not neglect an important client over time and expect the client to continue giving you business. And you cannot reduce the time you give your spouse over the years without risking serious damage to your relationship. You must make romance as high a priority as keeping your best clients. Without those clients, your business goes bankrupt. Without a firm, constantly strengthened emotional foundation, your marriage can go bankrupt, too.

Honey, I Want to Start My Own Business by **Azriela Jaffe,** founder, The Critical Link, consulting firm for individuals and couples in business, Lancaster, PA. Diane Publishing Company.

Marriages Do Survive Affairs

Couples therapy is almost always useful. The therapist helps the couple analyze how the affair happened—making sure neither partner bears all the blame. Couples learn that regaining trust will take a great deal of time, so they do not expect a rapid resumption of intimacy. The person who had the affair learns how to handle his or her partner's outbursts of anger and periods of depression. *Good news:* Most couples who receive help after an affair stay together.

K. Daniel O'Leary, PhD, professor of psychology, State University of New York at Stony Brook, whose research survey was published in the *Journal of Sex & Marital Therapy.*

Jealousy... Causes and Cures

Ayala Malach Pines, PhD, professor of psychology at the School of Management at Ben Gurion University in Israel. She is author of *Romantic Jealousy: Causes, Symptoms, Cures.* Routledge.

Jealousy is one of our strongest—and also one of our strangest—emotions. It tears some couples and friends apart while, oddly, drawing others closer together.

No matter how solid and enduring your personal relationships, they are all vulnerable to feelings of jealousy. How deeply you are affected by jealousy and whether you can respond rationally to what you're feeling depend on how quickly you can step back and evaluate your emotions.

JEALOUSY VS. ENVY

We feel jealous when we perceive an external threat to a relationship that is important to us. The relationship's importance may be due to either an emotional or a sexual bond...or the self-esteem or social prestige that we get from it.

When we become jealous, a physical reaction commonly follows. Your knees may shake...your heart may pound. The cascade of emotions that follows can take the form of rage, fear, sadness or embarrassment.

Many people confuse jealousy and envy, but the two are very different.

Jealousy always involves three people—the two people who have the relationship and the outsider who threatens the bond.

Envy involves just two people. One person covets what another person has...wealth...good looks... an adoring spouse, etc.

Envy also has an "evil" connotation that jealousy does not have. We may feel ashamed when we feel envy. We recognize that it's unfair to want what someone else has.

However, we frequently feel justified in feeling jealous. Our turf has been challenged, and we feel that our emotional reaction is the proper response.

WHY WE FEEL JEALOUS

Freud and many modern psychologists and psychoanalysts say jealousy has its roots in our childhood. They say that when children are at the Oedipal stage, around age two, they're "in love" with the parent of the opposite sex, but face a bigger, stronger rival—the other parent.

When we grow up, any "triangular" relationship reawakens the powerful and painful emotions we experienced during our childhood.

Darwin and the evolutionists go back in time even further to find jealousy's roots. They propose that it evolved to advance the survival of the species. Warding off threats to your relationship helps ensure that your genes will be passed along to the next generation. They point out that animals display jealous behavior, too.

MEN, WOMEN AND JEALOUSY

Men and women feel jealousy with equal frequency and intensity. It is usually triggered by similar situations, but there are differences.

In men, jealous passions are often provoked by sexual infidelity. Women become most jealous at signs that their partner is emotionally involved with someone else.

Individuals vary widely in how readily and strongly their jealousy is aroused. Almost anyone would become jealous if their mate were sexually unfaithful. But when a partner is emotionally involved with someone else, some take it in stride while others find it catastrophic. *Examples...*

Would it make you jealous to see your mate...

▶ **Laughing with a stranger at a party?**

▶ **Attending an out-of-town conference with a coworker of the opposite sex?**

▶ **Glancing with obvious appreciation at an attractive person at the next table?**

In extreme cases, jealous fantasies are aroused by the slightest clues—a phone call returned two hours late or a fond greeting.

The key to an overly strong jealousy response may be hidden in early life. *Examples...*

▶ **A child who was unloved or neglected by parents** often becomes an adult who is never convinced of his spouse's affection.

▶ **People with older brothers** tend to be more prone to jealousy.

▶ **A parent's sexual infidelity** can leave a life-long legacy of jealousy.

WHEN JEALOUSY IS A PROBLEM

Most of the time, jealousy is an occasional event that causes some distress but no real harm. It even can have some positive effects. *Examples...*

▶ **When your relationship feels threatened,** you may stop taking your partner for granted, which is often the cause of "couple burnout."

▶ **A jealous episode turns up the emotional heat** and rekindles passion.

But when jealousy is ongoing and disproportionate, it means real suffering and can ultimately undermine the relationship. Even the most faithful of partners may be worn down and driven away by constant suspicion.

If you realize that you are excessively jealous, turn your attention away from your partner and toward yourself. *Questions to ask yourself...*

▶ **What exactly am I feeling?** Is it rage? Fear of loss or abandonment? Embarrassment?

▶ **Are my feelings truly relevant to the present situation?** Or are they emotional baggage from childhood? Did I feel less than special as a child? Did I witness a parent's infidelity? Do I harbor doubts about my own worthiness and attractiveness?

When people make the distinction between the current triggers of jealousy and its roots in early life, they are often amazed to see how much easier their emotions are to handle. The pain may still be there, but they don't feel they have to act on it by showing jealousy.

It also helps to talk about your emotions with your partner. Share your discovery that your jealousy has its origins in your childhood, but that it is still painful and you would appreciate your partner's help.

This kind of discussion clears the air and enables partners to reassure each other. Together, you can agree on mutually acceptable ways for your partner to allay your jealousy.

> ***Example:*** *"When you're talking to others at a party, it would be nice if you would periodically come over and sit with me...or even introduce me to them as your partner."*

It also may be helpful to try "relabeling" what you're feeling. Rather than thinking of jealousy as "painful," perhaps you can relabel it as "exciting" or "provocative," even an "aphrodisiac."

Instead of brooding, "With all those beautiful people around him, what if—" substitute, "but he is mine and is loyal to me."

IF YOUR PARTNER IS JEALOUS OF YOU

A frank, open discussion about what triggers his jealousy and what reasonable things you can do to minimize it may be helpful.

Effective approach: Change the dynamics of your relationship. If you are the nonjealous member of the couple, start behaving as if you were jealous. Call your partner six times a day…ask detailed questions about his every move. The jealous partner usually loves the attention…calms down…and feels more secure.

Above all—avoid blaming, and remember to take responsibility. Jealousy is a problem that must be solved together.

All About Time Alone to Understand Ourselves

Ester Schaler Buchholz, PhD, professor of applied psychology at New York University. She is a clinical psychologist, psychoanalyst and codirector of training at the Institute for Child Adolescent and Family Studies in New York. Dr. Buchholz is author of *The Call of Solitude: Alonetime in a World of Attachment.* Simon & Schuster.

In this age of cell phones, E-mail and faxes, some people are constantly communicating with others to keep up with all that they need to know.

But we also need time alone—to really know ourselves, understand how we think and feel and where we want to go.

WHY SOLITUDE IS IMPORTANT

Alonetime can give you the opportunity to sort things out and to relax both intellectually and emotionally.

Time alone restores your integrity, allowing you to think about the beliefs and values that matter most. It forces your creative side to flourish, as ideas and solutions emerge that were buried by the daily rush. Despite all of these benefits, many people are still afraid of solitude.

Our extroverted society encourages communication, not introspection. But the need to pull away from other people is as universal as the urge to connect.

> **Example:** *Child-development researchers have found that even babies signal a desire to retreat from contact when they're overstimulated—by squirming or turning away from their caregivers.*

Alonetime renews our energy and feeds our curiosity, so when we resume our interactions with others, we have the insight and courage to begin to take new risks.

WHEN TO FIND TIME ALONE

Your irritability level is a good way to tell whether you need alonetime.

> **Example:** *If you're arguing more than usual with your spouse, there may be nothing wrong with the relationship—you may simply need some brief, self-restoring time apart.*

Rather than waiting until you have a whole day or week free, think of alonetime as part of your everyday life. Walking in a park…sitting in a room listening to music…soaking in the bathtub…even focusing on your breathing for 10 minutes are all good ways to pull back from the excessive activity and tension of the day.

Magic words: A good way to announce your need for solitude without making other people feel rejected is to say, "I'm really looking forward to spending time with you, but first let me unwind for a half hour." The more experience that you have with alonetime, the more easily you'll be able to feel this sense of solitude even when you're surrounded by people.

Some people get a lot out of writing in a journal. It's a very effective way to get started. Others use the time for contemplation.

If you're often distracted or preoccupied, simply paying attention to your surroundings can be very refreshing. So can pursuing any absorbing activity on your own, such as reading or painting. Some people are restored by gazing idly into space, free of any demands.

If you aren't used to being alone, you might feel a little bored at first. Stay with it. After a few minutes without the usual external stimulation, you'll start getting in touch with resources that you had forgotten you had…and you'll feel both energized and relieved.

COUPLES' COMMUNICATION STYLES

Men usually like to talk side-to-side…women, face-to-face. So a man may want to discuss important subjects while driving in a car, while a woman may prefer to wait until they get where they are going. Women should not be put off by men who tend to move away from face-to-face conversation—and each sex should be aware of the other's preference.

The First Five Minutes: How to Make a Great First Impression in Any Business Situation by **Mary Mitchell,** president, Uncommon Courtesies, business-communication consultants, Philadelphia. John Wiley & Sons.

SEXUAL MYTHS

Myth: Sex is wonderful if you love your partner. *Reality:* Good sex is learned. Love can be a strong foundation, but good sex also requires learning what pleases your partner and increases his or her desire and passion. *Myth:* Male and female sexuality are the same. *Reality:* Men and women experience sex differently. Women's responses vary widely. Partners need to identify their own sexual feelings and discuss them. *Myth:* Good sex is spontaneous. *Reality:* Sex that is planned into busy lives can be just as enjoyable as spontaneous sex.

A Woman's Guide to Overcoming Sexual Fear & Pain by **Marc Agronin, MD,** assistant professor of psychiatry, University of Miami School of Medicine, New Harbinger Publications.

Think Ahead

Better sex must start in the brain. To improve lovemaking, think about it during the day…and call your loved one to share your thoughts and get him or her thinking about it, too. *Be romantic.* The right setting—lighting, temperature, aroma, attire, flowers, etc.—sets the mood. *Progress slowly.* Don't rush to finish. Savor all of the sensations you experience.

Secrets of Better Sex by **Joel D. Block, PhD.** Prentice-Hall. He is a clinical psychologist, North Shore-Long Island Jewish Health System, New Hyde Park, NY.

Schedule Talks About Sex

Schedule talks about sex until you and your partner become comfortable talking about it without preplanning. After intimacy, try telling each other something that pleases you and something you would like to change. *Myth:* Most people are satisfied with whatever their partners do. *Reality:* Sexual likes and dislikes differ greatly because of physical and emotional variations among men and women. It is almost impossible to have a good sex life without openly discussing your preferences.

EASY ROUTE TO A BETTER SEX LIFE

Allow yourself small pleasures regularly—such as a hot bath or a movie matinee—so you and your partner can relax and enjoy sexuality. Schedule at least one hour a week just for you and your spouse. Do not watch TV at night—play a board game, read out loud or do something else that will bring you closer. Do not discuss anger-provoking issues near bedtime. If you're always too tired to make love, try setting the alarm for 90 minutes after you fall asleep or for one hour earlier in the morning and make love then. And don't worry about frequency. *Quality matters more than quantity.*

Secrets of Better Sex by **Joel D. Block, PhD.** Prentice-Hall. He is a clinical psychologist, North Shore-Long Island Jewish Health System, New Hyde Park, NY.

Greater Sex

A fulfilling sexual experience can take just a few minutes or hours—and the time that one experience lasts does not predict how long the next one will take. Research reports that cite average times are misleading. Even a person's own average time has little relevance. *Reason:* There is no normal time before climax during intercourse. And sexual interest varies from day to day...and person to person.

Al Cooper, PhD, clinical director, San Jose Marital and Sexuality Centre, San Jose, CA.

Jump-Start Your Sex Life...Naturally

Chris D. Meletis, ND, dean of clinical affairs and chief medical officer of the National College of Naturopathic Medicine in Portland, OR. He is author of *Better Sex Naturally*. HarperCollins.

Well before Viagra, Levitra and Cialis, people relied on aphrodisiacs to increase sexual desire...boost stamina...improve performance...and increase pleasure.

Many of these compounds owe their reputation to folklore, but several herbs and dietary supplements have proven to have sex-enhancing effects.

Good news: Products that improve sex naturally may be less likely to cause serious side effects than prescription drugs. Many strengthen the cardiovascular system and help regulate hormone production. That's as important for good sex as having an erection or being sufficiently lubricated.

Sex-enhancing herbs and supplements are taken daily until there's a noticeable improvement in sexual performance.

At that point, some people take a pause to see if the herbs and supplements are no longer necessary. Others continue taking the preparations indefinitely.

Important: Use herbs and supplements only under medical supervision. That way you'll be sure to get the product and dosage that's right for you.

Caution: Fresh or dried herbs differ greatly in potency from batch to batch. Use capsules or tinctures, instead. They've been standardized to contain the proper amounts of active ingredients.

For better sex, try one of the following natural enhancers. Select the one that best suits your needs. Give each preparation a few months to work. If you see no effect, try another.

GINKGO BILOBA

Ginkgo contains a variety of compounds that relax blood vessels and increase circulation to the brain and pelvic area.

For women, increased blood flow improves vaginal lubrication and sexual responsiveness.

For men, adequate blood flow is essential to achieve and sustain erections.

Typical dosage: *Capsules:* 40 milligrams (mg) to 60 mg of 24% standardized powdered extract, three to four times daily. *Tincture:* 30 drops three to four times daily.

Side effects: Ginkgo may cause dizziness, headache or heart palpitations.

Caution: Ginkgo is a blood thinner and can increase the blood-thinning effects of aspirin and *warfarin* (Coumadin). Check with your physician before using ginkgo if you're taking either medication.

MUIRA PUAMA

Also known as "potency wood," this herb contains sterols and other compounds that boost levels of testosterone, a hormone that plays a critical role in sexual desire in women as well as men.

Muira puama also contains volatile oils, including camphor and beta-carophyllene. These oils are thought to restore sex drive by stimulating nerves in the brain's pleasure center.

Typical dosage: 250 mg, three times daily in capsule form.

Side effect: Muira puama may lower blood pressure by as much as 10%. Check with your doctor before using this herb if you have low blood pressure (hypotension).

GINSENG

This herb is an "adaptogen," meaning it helps the body compensate for extended periods of stress.

Stress can be a factor that causes sexual desire and performance to plummet.

Compounds in ginseng root stimulate the adrenal glands to release substances that lower the levels of adrenaline and other stress hormones.

These compounds also improve blood flow to the penis, help the tissues use oxygen more efficiently and boost the production of testosterone in men and progesterone in women.

Typical dosage: *Capsules:* 10 mg to 50 mg, one to three times daily. *Tincture:* 30 to 60 drops every day.

Side effect: Ginseng may cause diarrhea… high blood pressure…sleeplessness.

ASHWAGANDA

A member of the pepper family, this herb contains *withanolides*, substances that increase the activity of testosterone and progesterone. Ashwaganda also relieves stress and anxiety.

Typical dosage: *Capsules:* 1,000 mg, once or twice daily. *Tincture:* 60 to 90 drops, two or three times daily.

Side effects: Because ashwaganda has anti-anxiety properties, it should not be used by anyone taking medications to treat anxiety and/or depression. The herb could intensify the drugs' actions as well as their side effects. Ashwaganda may also trigger miscarriages.

ARGININE

Taken in supplement form, this amino acid has been shown to relax smooth muscle contractions. This boosts arterial dilation, bringing more blood to the pelvic area.

The body uses arginine to produce nitric oxide, a chemical needed to achieve erections. (Sildenafil works, in part, by making nitric oxide more readily available in the body.)

Typical dosage: 1,000 mg to 2,000 mg twice daily in capsule form. Take the capsules between meals, since many foods contain *lysine*, an amino acid that counteracts arginine's effects.

Side effect: Don't take this herb if you get cold sores caused by the herpes simplex virus. Arginine stimulates viral replication.

FOR MEN ONLY

The herb *yohimbé* is used to treat impotence and low sex drive.

Yohimbé contains a compound called *yohimbine*, which helps dilate blood vessels in the penis. Most men who take yohimbé experience an increase in sexual desire within an hour.

Typical dosage: 15 mg to 25 mg daily in capsule form. Divide this into several doses throughout the day to minimize side effects. Take smaller amounts at first—5 mg or 10 mg a day—then gradually increase the amount over several weeks.

Side effects: Elevated blood pressure, nausea, racing heart and anxiety. Use yohimbé only under medical supervision.

FOR WOMEN ONLY

The herb *dong quai* contains plant sterols that help correct estrogen deficiencies.

Studies suggest that dong quai can increase sexual desire as well as the intensity of orgasms.

Typical dosage: *Capsules:* 1,000 mg, three to four times daily. *Tincture:* 45 to 60 drops, two or three times daily.

Caution: Pregnant and lactating women should not use dong quai. The herb also increases sensitivity to sunlight.

DON'T BE FOOLED BY A SEXUALLY TRANSMITTED DISEASE

If signs of a sexually transmitted disease (STD) clear up on their own, do not assume the STD is gone. Some STDs have visible signs that go away, although the disease has not. Untreated STDs can cause sterility or damage to the cardiovascular system, central nervous system or the bones. *Self-defense:* See your doctor immediately if you develop signs of an STD. *Caution:* People rarely develop immunity to STDs—most can be contracted repeatedly.

Soap, Water, and Sex: A Lively Guide to the Benefits of Sexual Hygiene and to Coping with Sexually Transmitted Diseases by **Jacob Lipman, MD,** sex-education lecturer and former internist, New Rochelle, NY. Prometheus Books.

You talkin' to us?

TALKING ABOUT SEX MAKES IT BETTER

Men and women who tell their partners about their sexual likes and dislikes report better sexual relationships—and higher overall relationship satisfaction—than those who don't discuss the subject.

E. Sandra Byers, PhD, chairperson, department of psychology, University of New Brunswick, Fredericton, Canada, whose study was published in *Journal of Sex Research.*

Love, Kindness, Compassion— And Your Health

Bernie S. Siegel, MD, one of the country's leading experts on the connection between a positive mind and a healthy body. He is founder of Exceptional Cancer Patients, 522 Jackson Park Dr., Meadville, PA 16335, which provides information and therapeutic support. He is author of several books, including *Love, Medicine and Miracles.* HarperPerennial.

Through loving, kindness and compassion, we can achieve a harmony within ourselves and with the rest of the world. Achieving this state of inner peace requires a positive mental outlook on life as well as a respect for ourselves and for others.

Studies have shown that achieving a state of emotional tranquillity has the power to heal. Reaching this state prevents negative thinking from clouding good judgment and allows us to concentrate on what is important in life. Emotional tranquillity also frees our healing systems to better care for our bodies.

To improve your outlook on life and improve your healing process...

■ Love yourself—and everyone who you meet.

A characteristic of people who have achieved peace of mind is a love of self. Without love, feelings of loneliness, despair and hopelessness dominate, and we can't reach our potential as human beings. Accepting and loving ourselves allows us to reach out and love others.

Loving others is a profound way to add love to our lives—and, equally important, make anger, hostility and stress disappear. Loving not only brightens each day and makes you feel good about yourself, it also makes others naturally want to return that love to you.

We can choose our responses to everything in life. Make a conscious effort to feel love toward yourself and everyone you meet. Think of yourself as an actor or athlete who is rehearsing or practicing this skill. When you feel love, you allow joy and a sense of fulfillment into your life—and into others' lives as well.

■ Teach yourself to forgive.

Becoming angry at ourselves and at others is part of human nature. But staying angry and wallowing in self-righteous outrage takes a great toll on our mental and physiological health.

Verbal and physical anger increase your pulse rates and blood pressure—as well as stress your immune system. Nursing any type of resentment undermines your ability to find inner peace for yourself.

Concentrate on seeing the internal good that exists in everyone.

Forgive others for their actions, no matter how strongly you feel that you have been wronged. Make an effort to communicate with these people and to understand their behavior. Mastering your response to them is one way to let go of your anger and resentment.

This doesn't mean you shouldn't release negative emotions. But you should express your feelings appropriately—in a journal, through painting, in therapy—without directing those feelings toward others, unless you have been treated disrespectfully.

It's also important to acknowledge your own weaknesses continually and to view them as opportunities for growth and learning.

This self-recognition produces humility, and it makes it easier to accept and forgive the weaknesses of others. And when people feel your true forgiveness, they'll be much, much less likely to wrong you again.

■ Embrace morality.

Forgiving others requires knowing the difference between right and wrong. Most people know it's important to do the right thing, as well as what the right thing is.

This is especially true in our business dealings with others, when power, money and position play major roles. But without morality, we can never experience real peace.

Still, the lines between right and wrong are easily blurred in modern society, resulting in actions that aren't true to our real values.

Use your mind as a "remote control" to decide which of life's channels you are going to tune into.

Decide which important messages you are going to transmit to the outside world through your behavior.

Use a thorough examination of yourself at the end of each day to assess how you may have wronged others and, in doing so, wronged yourself. Whatever is troubling you, or whatever wrong you've done, you need to repair it.

Example: *If you've hurt someone's feelings today, apologize.*

■ Recognize the value of silence.

We're all so accustomed to the hustle-bustle of modern life that it's easy to forget the beauty and importance of being still and quiet.

However, it is only in times of quiet meditation, when the intellectual mind is replaced by the inner voices of your body and spirit, when life's toughest problems can be solved—and healing and peace can be achieved.

Schedule a regular time each day to be silent, so that your unconscious mind can be awakened.

Take 15 minutes in the morning, or use your breaks at work to be alone with yourself. Gaze out the window, or lie down, close your eyes and concentrate on your breathing and bodily sensations. Make arrangements with your family or colleagues not to disturb you.

While this daily healing interval can take many forms, its result is the same—answers to problems and difficult situations, and a more balanced body.

■ Help someone who needs support.

People who volunteer their time live longer—and happier—lives.

Acting "from the heart" and contributing our own uniqueness to the world brings fulfillment, joy and purpose. It also validates our self-worth as well as that of others.

By simply responding to the needs of others, you allow love into your life and influence a positive change in everyone you encounter and help.

Making and Keeping Good Friendships

Letty Cottin Pogrebin, author of several books, including *Getting Over Getting Older.* Berkley. She was a founding editor of *Ms.* magazine and president of the Authors Guild.

Let's be friends sounds easy, but from the nursery to the nursing home, we all work hard to make, keep and enjoy our friendships.

The role friends play in our lives is always changing, depending on age, gender, marital status, cultural background, health, time commitments and competing priorities.

MAKING NEW FRIENDS

Old friends can keep you well grounded. New friends keep you young. *If you haven't made three or four new friends during the past year, ask yourself if you've been too...*

▶ **Self-involved**—boring, overbearing, uninterested in others.

▶ **Out of balance**—a loner, a workaholic or a socially challenged person.

▶ **Lazy**—cultivating and maintaining friendship takes work.

▶ **Time-crunched**—who isn't?

▶ **Confused**—finding it difficult to manage it all?

Here are ways to improve the quality and quantity of your relationships…

Schedule friends on your calendar.
Just as you would business appointments or romantic dates, set aside one evening a week to spend with a new friend, or one Saturday once a month if that's all you can manage. Make that time sacred. Don't cancel at the last minute or let other demands impinge.

Be proactive.
If you're unsatisfied with your current friendships or feel that you've outgrown old friends, go out and recruit new ones.

To meet folks beyond your job and neighborhood, enroll in an evening course, go to a yoga retreat or sign up for a political campaign, chess club or wine-tasting event. Before long, you'll have many new friends.

Take the initiative.
Transforming acquaintances into friends can be as easy as including them in whatever you wanted to do anyway.

▶ **Suggest a potluck at your place** or dim sum at a Chinese restaurant.

▶ **Offer an extra ticket for a ball game** or the theatre.

▶ **Get your families together** for a trip to the aquarium.

▶ **Meet for a morning jog** or tennis.

▶ **Take a serendipitous journey** to a farmers' market, antiques fair, beach—anywhere activity and conversation can be seamlessly combined.

Practice listening.
Ask new friends two questions about themselves for every sentence you utter about yourself—and don't use their replies as an invitation to circle back to yourself.

Assess before you invest.
Adding someone new to a busy life represents an investment of time, energy and spirit—three things that are in short supply for most of us.

Questions to ask…

▶ **Are you always eager to see this person**… or do you sometimes get together out of obligation or social climbing?

▶ **Do you respect him?** Do you care about his well-being?

▶ **Are you interested in her mind,** experiences, problems?

Open up.
Once you've "fallen in like," it's impossible to achieve true intimacy without exposing your inner self. The ground rules of friendship assume that the two of you will share feelings, exchange personal histories and current dilemmas, confide your private needs and deepest fears. Yet some people—usually men—consider it a sign of weakness to admit their worries.

Rule of thumb: If you have a big problem—say your wife has cancer or your husband lost his job—and you aren't willing to unburden yourself to your friend, there's something missing in the friendship…or in you.

MAINTAINING FRIENDSHIPS IN AN OVERPROGRAMMED LIFE

Stay connected.
Regular contact is friendship's rock-bottom prerequisite. Make it your business to pick up the phone or send an E-mail, if only to say, "I'm swamped, but I miss you."

Inquire about the outcome of your friend's unfinished business. "Did that deal ever come through?"…"What happened with your daughter's medical school applications?"…"How was your trip to Bali?"

Return a friend's call within 24 hours. If you haven't heard from someone in a while, contact him. Plan a future get-together, even if it's months in advance.

▣ "Face time" matters.
How can you make time to see friends in your busy life?

Give up TV.

▣ Strive for symmetry.
Ideally, what differentiates friendship from most other relationships—parent/child…teacher/student… boss/worker—is its absolute equality. Back off and stop martyring yourself if you feel taken advantage of, especially after you've made yourself vulnerable by baring your soul while your friend is still a closed book…or if you've been doing most of the giving.

Or begin exercising your "taker's rights." When you're miserable, call and say, "I need to talk." Moving to a new apartment? Ask for help.

Whatever you want, ask for it, directly and without manipulation. You will discover once and for all if you've been driving down a one-way street.

FRIENDSHIP'S TOP FIVE PITFALLS

▶ **Don't have sex with your friends.** People think they can cross that line and return to the status quo if things don't work out. But more often than not, things don't work out and everything turns sour or awkward. Ask yourself if it's worth risking a beautiful friendship for a flash-in-the-pan affair.

▶ **Don't travel together unless you're totally compatible.** If he's an Oscar and you're a Felix, or she's Type A and you're laid back, or they're night people and you're up at dawn, those differences—sure to get magnified on the road—can ruin both the vacation and the friendship. Instead, go your separate ways and compare snapshots later.

▶ **Don't be a knee-jerk truth-teller.** Okay, so you hate her new haircut and his mate is an idiot. Honesty isn't always the best policy if the truth is too painful or destroys the friendship.

▶ **Don't double date.** If your best friend marries someone you or your spouse can't stand, just meet your friend for lunch. Forcing the issue is futile.

▶ **Don't ever betray a confidence.** Not even if you can trade the information for profit…or get a laugh…or make yourself look good. Betrayal is friendship's kiss of death, and anyone who does it is a snake.

DON'T MISS CREATIVE MOMENTS

Boost your creativity by taking advantage of the creative peaks we all have just before falling asleep—and also right after waking up. *How:* Keep a pen and paper by your bedside to jot down ideas and solutions that come to you during these times.

Arnon Dreyfuss, MD, former editor, *TopHealth,* wellness newsletter for employees, Box 381116, Birmingham, AL 35238.

Tish Baldridge Makes Super-Successful Socializing Very Simple

Letitia Baldridge, who served as the late Jacqueline Kennedy's White House chief of staff. She is author of numerous books on manners, including *In the Kennedy Style.* Bantam Dell.

Feeling comfortable while socializing takes time and practice. *My secrets for becoming the social magnet of any party...*

BEING POSITIVE PAYS

If you go in thinking you're going to have a terrible time, you will. Before you walk into a roomful of strangers, look in a mirror and smile. Take some deep breaths. Tell yourself you are as good and as smart as anybody in there.

Go over to the most agreeable-looking group of people. Wait until there's a break in the conversation and say, "My name is Joe Smith. I don't know anybody here. You all look like you're having such a good time, I thought you wouldn't mind if I joined you." They will take care of you. It always works.

MAKE EYE CONTACT

Don't think about what you're going to say next. When you think, you look down and away. Listen, instead. Making eye contact will be a natural reaction. If you look in people's eyes when they are talking, they will be much more responsive and enthusiastic. Making eye contact will also keep you from thinking while they're talking, so you can really listen to what they are saying.

LEARN TO DISCUSS ANYTHING

Instead of spending so much time on your exercise equipment, exercise your brain. If you read the newspaper, you will pick up many kinds of things—somber, glamorous and funny. It will make you a good conversationalist.

If people ask about your work and you don't want to discuss it, don't dismiss the question. Answer briefly and politely. Learn to talk about your company in a short, complimentary manner. Then change the subject. Say, "I'd really like to know what you think about..."

DON'T DRAG OUT STORIES

Don't use clichés in conversation. Don't use technical jargon. If people's eyes glaze over, you've become a bore. Instead, draw information out of people. Ask questions, but don't be overbearing.

DETONATING BORES

If you must socialize with boring people, invite an interesting close friend along. Explain the situation in advance. Ask for their help. If you're trapped by a bore at a party, glance at your watch, then say that you must make a phone call right away and excuse yourself. Then go make a call to anybody.

ENTERTAINING WHEN YOU'RE BUSY

Throw small dinners. I invite eight or 10 people. I give up one hour a night for three nights before the party and prepare the bar, food and decor. Use the same menu often so you can do it without thinking—pasta and a great salad, peppermint ice cream and chocolate sauce. Or buy prepared food.

To keep up with hard-to-reach people, ask to take them out to dinner on a *Sunday* night. Or invite them for Sunday lunch...but don't let them take up your whole day. I always say "I'm working all weekend. Come at 12:30, and I hope you'll leave by 2:30"—and I laugh. Nobody minds. They know I'm serious. At 2:30, if no one has left, stand up and say, "Hasn't this been great?" Don't forget to laugh again.

The Healthy, Safe Child

Chapter 17

What All Parents Need to Know About Their Children's Health Care

*D*espite a seemingly endless array of childhood ailments, concerned parents often find themselves seeking answers to the same basic questions about their children's health…

◼ How can I find a good doctor to care for my child?

While a pediatrician is the most obvious choice, family practitioners and internists often make equally good doctors for children.

Carefully interview different types of doctors, then pick one that meets your requirements…one with a pleasant, caring attitude…a willingness to talk directly with your child as well as with you…a clean, orderly office…and a good system for fielding after-hours phone calls. Make sure your child gets along with the doctor and that the doctor accepts your health insurance plan.

Caution: If the doctor belongs to a group practice, ask that you be allowed to make appointments specifically with that doctor.

Ask if the doctor can provide you and your child with videotapes, pamphlets and other educational materials regarding specific health issues. They're a big help when illness strikes—or during puberty.

◼ Does my child need an X ray?

In addition to being expensive, X rays, CT scans, magnetic resonance imaging and other diagnostic tests are typically frightening to children, risky and unnecessary.

They should be administered only if their findings will have a direct bearing on your child's treatment. If your child has a cough, for example, a chest X ray is generally unnecessary—unless the doctor has reason to suspect a serious lung ailment. Before agreeing to any test, question the doctor thoroughly to make sure it is necessary. *Key questions…*

Charles B. Inlander, president of People's Medical Society, Box 868, Allentown, PA 18102, the nation's largest consumer health advocacy organization. He is coauthor of several books on medical topics, including *Take This Book to the Pediatrician with You.* People's Medical Society.

▶ **What's the name of the test?**

▶ **Why is it necessary?**

▶ **What will it reveal that you don't already know?**

▶ **What will happen if the test is not performed?**

▶ **What are the possible side effects?**

▶ **Is a less invasive test available?**

▶ **Will the test results change your method of treatment?**

■ Are childhood immunizations safe?
Most states require that all children be immunized against eight diseases—diphtheria, pertussis (whooping cough), tetanus, measles, mumps, rubella (German measles), poliomyelitis and Haemophilus influenza type B (bacterial meningitis).

These vaccinations are typically administered between the ages of two months and 16 years. They are generally quite safe.

Exception: Pertussis. Half of all children who receive this five-dose vaccine develop fever, and, in rare cases, children have developed mental retardation or another permanent disability. However, because pertussis is such a serious disease, it is still prudent to have your child immunized.

To minimize risk: Insist that your child receive the recently approved *acellular* pertussis vaccine. It's less likely to cause dangerous reactions than the old vaccine, which remains in use.

The pertussis vaccine should never be given to any child who is over age six, who has a fever or has already had pertussis. Any child who experiences fever, shock, persistent crying, convulsions or neurological problems after the first pertussis shot should not receive any of the additional pertussis boosters.

■ My child has recurrent throat infections. Should his tonsils be removed?
Tonsillectomy is neither necessary nor particularly effective at curing recurrent ear or throat infections, even though doctors often urge surgery.

When tonsillectomy is appropriate: Only if the tonsils become so swollen that they interfere with the child's breathing, or if lab tests indicate the presence of abscesses behind the tonsils. In all other cases, it's best to treat such infections with antibiotics.

■ What about chronic ear infections?
Ear infections (otitis media) are common among children of smokers.

If you smoke—stop. New mothers should avoid bottle-feeding their children. Recent research suggests that breast-feeding helps prevent earaches. Beyond this, there's no real consensus on treatment.

The American Academy of Pediatrics believes observation can sometimes be an alternative to oral antibiotics such as amoxicillin.

The surgical insertion of drainage tubes through the child's eardrums (tympanostomy) can cause serious complications, including severe infections and hearing loss.

Conservative approach—to discuss with your doctor: At the first sign of pain, give your child acetaminophen (Tylenol) or another nonaspirin painkiller. *Also helpful:* A heating pad held against the ear.

■ Do children's hospitals offer better pediatric care than general hospitals?
Many parents seem to think so.

In most cases, however, the standard of care in children's hospitals is no better than that in general hospitals with good pediatric sections. If your child requires inpatient surgery, pick a hospital that performs that surgery on a routine basis.

■ My teenager's doctor refuses to give me details of my teen's medical care. What can I do?
Parents sometimes fail to realize that all doctor-patient relationships are private.

When your children are very young, of course, you are by necessity intimately involved in all aspects of their medical care. As children approach puberty, however, they may wish to keep some aspects of their medical care private. Parents should respect that right.

Medication Mistakes That Parents Make...But Could Prevent

Jill Baren, MD, assistant professor of emergency medicine and pediatrics at the University of Pennsylvania School of Medicine, Philadelphia. She is a contributor to the book *Now I Know Better: Kids Tell Kids About Safety.* Millbrook Press.

Despite the best of intentions, many parents improperly medicate their children when their kids are sick. *Here are the top medication mistakes to avoid...*

Giving too much medicine.

Many parents worry that their child isn't getting sufficient amounts of medication.

Examples: A toddler dribbles a liquid medication when taking it...or has the flu and throws it up within an hour of taking the medication.

Danger: Giving extra doses can cause health complications. Just a few extra doses of over-the-counter pain relievers over several days can cause potential liver or kidney damage.

Safety first: Call your pediatrician and ask before giving another dose. With some medicines, an extra dose can be dangerous.

Forgetting to carefully read the package's label.

Many parents rely on memory or a quick read when giving familiar medicines to their children.

That can lead to dosage and timing errors.

Example: The pain reliever Tylenol comes in two formulations for children—an infant liquid that is highly concentrated...and a children's liquid that is less potent.

Many parents, believing that the formulas are the same, continue using the infant formula—in larger doses—on older children.

Danger: They don't realize that they're actually giving their child two to three times more medicine when they use the infant formula rather than the child's formula.

Safety first: Use only age-appropriate medications. Don't substitute formulations.

Beware: Pediatric doses are based on weight rather than age—and kids grow rapidly. It's important to factor in the child's current weight when figuring out the dose.

Not using proper measuring devices.

A recent Egleston Children's Hospital (Atlanta) study found that fewer than half of parents measure out the correct doses of nonprescription medications for their children.

Danger: Many parents use a kitchen spoon to give medicine. But these spoons vary substantially in size and the amount of medicine they hold.

Safety first: Only use the measuring devices—spoons, droppers or cups—that come with drugs. Or buy specially calibrated devices at your pharmacy.

Not following dosing instructions.

Some drugs need to be given with certain foods or beverages.

Examples: Ibuprofen should typically be given with food or milk to prevent an upset stomach. Milk can make tetracycline antibiotics less effective.

Safety first: A glass of water is the best beverage to give with all medications. It's the least likely to interact with any drug...and it will aid drug absorption.

Not finishing a prescription medication.

Many parents believe that once a child is feeling better, it's not necessary to continue giving medication.

They figure it's better to save remaining medicine for some future need—rather than waste it. But not finishing the full course can be very dangerous.

Example: If a child is prescribed an antibiotic to treat an ear infection, stopping the medication after a few days because the child no longer has ear pain could lead to residual infection.

■ Giving prescription medications to other patients.
This is a double error.

You haven't given the full course of medicine to the person who needed it originally. And the person who gets the medicine from you may not need it.

> *Example: If you give your daughter your son's antibiotic for a sore throat, she may not get the right medicine to cure her infection. She may not even have a bacterial illness that requires medicine. Or she may be allergic to the medicine.*

■ Using multisymptom cold and flu products.
Many cold and flu products treat all symptoms of a particular illness.

But your child may not have all of the symptoms, so you may be giving more medicine than needed and causing unnecessary side effects.

Safety first: Buy only single-symptom products to relieve specific symptoms.

> *Example: If your child has a cold that is causing congestion and a hacking cough, give him a decongestant to unstuff the nose and a cough suppressant.*
>
> *By doing this, you'll forgo the antihistamine (for sneezing) and the pain reliever (for reducing a fever) found in multisymptom products.*

STORAGE STRATEGIES

▶ **Ask your pharmacist or doctor for storage instructions.** Medicines that aren't stored in the correct manner generally lose their potency and become ineffective—or even dangerous.

> *Example: Many antibiotics must be stored in the refrigerator.*

▶ **Don't keep any unsealed medications in the bathroom.** Humidity can cause pills to disintegrate.

▶ **Don't store different types of medication in the same bottle.** For convenience sake, many adults deposit a variety of medications in one bottle to make it easier to carry the medicine around with them.

However, if curious children get into the bottle, it will be difficult to tell what they've taken and how to treat them.

▶ **Never give expired medication.** Medications that are past their prime can be ineffective or even poisonous.

Always look for expiration dates on bottles before purchasing or using a medication.

ZINC NOT FOR COLDS

Zinc does not help kids' colds. Zinc lozenges are effective at treating colds in at least some adults. But in a recent study, a lower-dose zinc lozenge had no effect on the duration of kids' colds or the severity of their cold symptoms.

Michael L. Macknin, MD, chairman, general pediatrics, The Cleveland Clinic Foundation, whose study was published in *The Journal of the American Medical Association.*

Children and Medicine

Use medicines formulated specifically for children—or, if that's not possible, an adult medicine with dosing recommendations for children. *Also:* If your child is taking more than one medicine at a time, note the ingredients to avoid a potential overdose. *Helpful:* Since children's dosages are sometimes based on weight, keep an accurate household scale in your home.

Harry Lubell, MD, director of pediatrics, Phelps Memorial Hospital, Sleepy Hollow, NY.

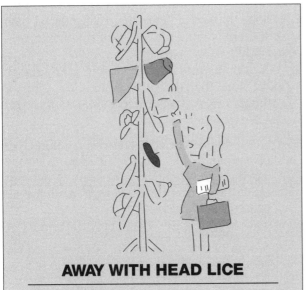

AWAY WITH HEAD LICE

To prevent head lice: Discourage children from sharing things that come in contact with the head, such as hats, coats, towels, scarves, brushes, combs or athletic headgear—helmets, swimming caps. Do not put your head on pillows or backs of seats in movies. On trains or airplanes, bring your own pillow. Lice can live two days in settings like those without a human host. *Good news:* Lice cannot fly or jump from person to person. And they cannot infest dogs or cats—they require human hosts.

Barbara Bilek, MA, director, division of family health, Greenwich Department of Health, Greenwich, CT.

Beware of Alcohol in Alcohol-Free Products

Alcohol may be in alcohol-free products. Propylene glycol, a form of alcohol used to prevent active ingredients from settling to the bottom of a liquid, is used in many drugs sold as *alcohol-free.*

This includes medicines for children. The compound can cause some of the same problems as common forms of alcohol—such as liver problems and mild inebriation. *Self-defense:* Read labels carefully.

Kenneth McMartin, PhD, a professor in the department of pharmacology, Louisiana State University Medical Center, Shreveport.

Infant Drug Allergies Are Uncommon...

There is no strong evidence that allergies to penicillin or other drugs run in families. *How to tell if a baby is allergic:* Allergic reactions do not usually develop during the first round of medication. If a widespread rash develops when the infant gets the drug again—or within a few days after medication is stopped—alert your pediatrician immediately. Unfortunately, there is no way to test for such an allergy in advance. *Beware:* People who are allergic to drugs are often allergic to insect stings—and vice versa.

Martha V. White, MD, pediatric allergy and asthma specialist, Institute for Asthma and Allergy, Washington Hospital Center, Washington, DC.

Children and Their Summer Ailments— How to Avoid Trouble

Jill Baren, MD, assistant professor of emergency medicine and pediatrics at the University of Pennsylvania School of Medicine, Philadelphia. She is a contributor to the book *Now I Know Better: Kids Tell Kids About Safety.* Millbrook Press.

Be adequately prepared and equipped for children's injuries—which are so widespread in summer. Knowing what to do and having the right supplies are especially important when you're away from home and can't get to a doctor immediately.

INSECT STINGS AND BITES
For insect bites and stings that result in minor swelling and itching...

▶ **Place ice or an instant cold pack on the bite or sting.** If the area around the sting begins to swell, give children oral *diphen-hydramine* (Benadryl), according to the instructions on the package.

▶ **Apply an anti-itching preparation,** such as hydrocortisone.

WOUNDS

Puncture wounds, splinters and abrasions are a special problem because of children's tendency to go barefoot. *Procedures...*

▶ **Clean the wound and surrounding area gently** with plenty of soap and running water.

▶ **For bleeding, elevate the affected part, and apply direct pressure** with a clean gauze dressing for 10 minutes. Apply an antibacterial cream, such as polysporin, to prevent infection.

▶ **Cover the area with a clean, dry bandage.**

SPLINTERS

Any foreign body that remains embedded in the skin can cause an infection. *Procedures...*

▶ **Clean a pair of pointed tweezers with an alcohol wipe...**or hold the tweezers under scalding hot, running water for a minute. Don't hold tweezers over a match to sterilize.

▶ **Use your thumb and forefinger** to gently squeeze and raise the skin segment to stabilize it. Then grasp the base of the splinter with the tweezers and pull in one movement. Cover the area with a bandage or gauze.

▶ **Attempt removal only if the splinter is near the skin surface.** Picking at it can cause infection.

▶ **Don't soak the area**—that can cause a wood splinter to expand and make removal more difficult.

▶ **If removal is impossible,** cover the area with a soft gauze bandage to avoid infection. A thick pad can also help weight-bearing areas, such as the bottoms of feet. See your doctor immediately.

EAR INFECTIONS

▶ **Middle-ear infections are triggered by colds and congestion.** They are typically accompanied by fever, vomiting and imbalance. If you suspect a middle-ear infection, you need to see a doctor for a prescription for antibiotics.

▶ **Outer-ear infections.** "Swimmer's ear" affects people who swim a lot. Swimmer's ear can be confirmed by gently tugging on your child's earlobe. If the child experiences significant pain or if there is drainage or a foul smell, infection is likely.

If you suspect swimmer's ear, you need to make sure that moisture from showering or bathing doesn't reach the ear canal before you can see a doctor.

▷ Use lambswool or cotton with a thin layer of petroleum jelly to plug the entrance to the canal during showering or bathing. Do not push the plug into the ear canal, as it may cause complications.

▷ An analgesic pain reliever, such as ibuprofen or acetaminophen, is often used for general discomfort.

SUNBURN

To prevent burns, apply sunscreen with SPF of at least 15 *before* children go outdoors. Reapply after swimming or perspiring.

Treatment: Cool oatmeal baths and aloe vera gel can help soothe the burn and provide relief. An analgesic medication with anti-inflammatory properties, such as ibuprofen, may also help.

Hearing Loss and Kids

More than seven million US children ages six to 19 have at least slight hearing loss. The problem may interfere with speech and learning ability, but it often goes undetected. *Reason:* It may not be picked up by routine screenings that do not test specifically for sensitivity to high- and low-frequency sounds. *Helpful:* When your child's hearing is tested, be sure both high and low frequencies are used.

Amanda Sue Niskar, RN, nurse epidemiologist, Centers for Disease Control and Prevention, Atlanta, whose six-year study of more than 6,000 children was published in *The Journal of the American Medical Association.*

Baby's Birth Weight Linked to Cancer Risk

A newborn infant's birth weight may affect her risk of breast cancer later in life. The less a female infant weighs at birth, the lower her risk. *Unknown:* Whether low-weight infant boys face a lower cancer risk.

Karin B. Michels, ScD, epidemiologist, Harvard School of Public Health, Boston.

Secondhand Smoke And Children

I n a recent study, children who already had high cholesterol and were exposed to passive smoke had HDL ("good") cholesterol levels an average of 10% lower than children whose parents or other household members did not smoke.

Ellis Neufeld, MD, associate chief, clinical hematology division, Children's Hospital, Boston, whose study of 103 children was published in *Circulation*.

DANGERS OF NEWBORN GOING HOME TOO SOON

Newborns discharged from the hospital before they are three days old are twice as likely to be readmitted—most often for jaundice—than infants kept longer. *Important:* Infants discharged before three days should be checked by a physician or nurse within two or three days of coming home.

M. Jeffrey Maisels, MD, chairman, department of pediatrics, William Beaumont Hospital, Royal Oak, MI, whose study was published in *Pediatrics*.

FEVER MEDICATION ALERT

Children with fever often go undermedicated. In a study of kids with high fever, 55% had been given too small a dose of *acetaminophen* (Tylenol) or *ibuprofen* (Advil).

Doctors may be misinforming parents about correct dosages...or parents may be unable to read labels correctly or are so fearful of giving their children an overdose that they wind up giving a dose that's too small to be effective. Be sure to follow dosage guidelines printed on the package label.

Mara McErlean, MD, chair, emergency medicine, Albany Medical College, Albany, NY. Her study of 140 children was presented at a meeting of the American College of Emergency Physicians.

Be Wary of Home Drug-Abuse Tests

H ome-administered tests for drug abuse are unlikely to help concerned parents. Parents often begin to suspect involvement with drugs when they notice drastic negative changes in a child's behavior and personality. Because drug use usually reflects a poor relationship with parents, insisting on a drug test at home may further damage the relationship. *Instead:* Ask the family or school doctor to check for drug abuse discreetly during a routine physical exam.

Kevin Leman, PhD, Tucson-based family psychologist and author of *Making Children Mind Without Losing Yours.* Revell Publishing.

Beware of Nuts For Children

Nuts are the greatest choking danger for children—more than four times as danger-ous as any other food. *Other foods that can cause choking:* chunks of meat, chicken parts, seeds, carrots, hot dogs, sausage, fish bones, apples, hard candy. More than three-fourths of choking injuries requiring hospitalization involve children under age four.

James S. Reilly, MD, chairman, department of surgery, Alfred I. duPont Hospital for Children, Wilmington, DE.

EATING TOGETHER MAKES HEALTHIER KIDS

Family mealtimes help kids adjust. Eating reg-ularly with a parent helps children become well-adjusted, drug-free teenagers and young adults. *Also:* One study found that frequent family din-ners during childhood reduce the risk of alco-holism in later life.

Blake Sperry Bowden, PhD, senior psychology fellow, Center for Developmental Disorders at Cincinnati Chil-dren's Hospital Medical Center.

Children Who Eat Breakfast Regularly Do Better in School

They think faster and more clearly, solve class-room problems more easily and are less fidgety and disruptive. Children who skip breakfast are less able to select the information they need to solve school problems. Their emotional stability suf-fers…they're less attentive…and their ability to recall and use new information is lessened. *Helpful:* Chil-dren are more likely to eat breakfast if someone—a sibling or a parent—eats with them.

J. Michael Murphy, EdD, staff psychologist, Massachusetts General Hospital, and assistant professor of psychology, Harvard Medical School, both in Boston.

GETTING KIDS TO EAT HEALTHIER

To get kids to eat more fiber, add bran flakes or another high-fiber cereal to a favorite low-fiber kind—or alternate between high- and low-fiber brands.

Sandwiches: Use one slice of white bread and one slice of whole-grain.

Snacks: Make trail mix from raisins…nuts…and high-fiber cereal. Instead of juice, offer canned fruit—without added sugar.

To figure out how many grams of fiber a child needs daily, add five to his or her age.

Lynn Hoggard, MS, RD, health team nutritionist, WRAL-TV, Raleigh, NC.

Girls Thrive from Sports

Benefits of sports for teen girls extend well beyond exercise and physical fitness. Teenage girls who play sports tend to start sexual activity later…and are less than half as likely to get pregnant during the teenage years as girls not involved in sports. *Possible reason:* They have higher self-esteem and are more confident making sexual choices that further long-range goals. *But:* Teenage boys who participate in sports do not show a significant change in sexual behavior.

Don Sabo, PhD, project director, Women's Sports Foundation Teen Pregnancy Study, East Meadow, NY.

Safer Environment For Little Ones

Pretend to be your child's size once a month. Look at the world from his or her level, and you will more easily see potential dangers around the house. Doing this every month will keep you aware of your child's changing size—and alert you to new dangers.

Joel Fein, MD, attending emergency department physician, Children's Hospital, Philadelphia.

Guidelines for Swings

Limit a baby's swing time to one-half hour per session. Do not use an infant swing until the baby is at least six weeks old. Be sure the swing has secure restraining straps, smooth edges and surfaces, and sturdy construction. Avoid swings that hang in doorways or contain small parts. Never leave a swinging infant alone.

Parenting, 1325 Avenue of the Americas, New York City 10019.

Know Your Child's Caregiver

Talk regularly with your child's caregiver—and not just about your child. Get to know the caregiver—the more interest you show, the more valued the caregiver will feel and the better your relationship will be. *Helpful:* Be open-minded about your caregiver's suggestions and observations—she spends a lot of time each day with your child and likely has valuable ideas. If you have a concern involving her, set up a time to talk so she won't feel caught off guard.

Barbara Willer, PhD, director of public affairs, National Association for the Education of Young Children, Washington, DC, quoted in *American Baby,* 249 W. 17 St., New York City 10011.

BUY CHILDREN FEWER TOYS

Have them rely more on their own resourcefulness for entertainment—or on toys that invite creativity instead of requiring specific types of play. The best toys are ones kids make themselves. The best commercial toys can be used in lots of ways to encourage a child's imagination—building sets, clay, crayons.

Why You Should Not Use Baby Walkers

Beware: Baby walkers delay infant development rather than accelerating it. *Reason:* Walkers keep babies from seeing their legs and lower bodies, hampering their physical development. *Recent study:* Babies who did not use walkers sat at five months, crawled at six months and began to walk at 11 months. Those who used walkers that fully obstructed their view of the lower body sat and crawled at seven months and walked at one year. *Also:* In mental development, babies who used walkers lagged behind other babies.

A. Carol Siegel, PhD, postdoctoral fellow, Case Western Reserve University, Cleveland. Her unpublished study of 109 infants six to 15 months of age was reported in *The New York Times.*

Why Some Toys Are Better than Stuffed Toys

Stuffed animals are not good toys for babies younger than nine months. Stuffed animals can collect dust, aggravate allergies, shed hair and stuffing, and lose plastic eyes or noses that could then be swallowed. *Better for very young children:* Push toys…busy boxes with switches and levers to push and noises to make…sturdy picture books—the pictures may be meaningless to young children, but they enjoy moving the pages back and forth.

Complete Book of Baby & Child Care by **Paul Reisser, MD.** Tyndale House. He practices family medicine in Thousand Oaks, CA.

Perils of Drawstrings

Most children's clothing made since 1994 eliminates drawstrings in hoods and necks. The strings can seriously injure children by getting caught on slides or handrails or in school-bus doors. *Self-defense if you have older clothing with drawstrings:* Replace hood and neck drawstrings with snaps, buttons or Velcro. Make sure a drawstring at the bottom or waist of a jacket hangs no more than three inches on either side. If necessary, shorten the drawstring by sewing it to the middle of the back of the garment.

Ken Giles, US Consumer Product Safety Commission, Washington, DC.

SAFER BABY BATHING

Infant bathtub seats are not safety equipment. Drownings have actually increased since the seats became widely used. *Reason:* A caregiver leaves a child alone in the tub, believing the seat guarantees safety. But the seat can easily tip over, and an infant can drown in only a few inches of water. *Self-defense:* Never leave a baby unattended in a bath. Use infant seats correctly—to hold the baby upright and free an adult's hands for washing.

Renae Rauchschwalbe, compliance officer, US Consumer Product Safety Commission, Washington, DC.

For Safer Kids in These Scary Times

Bethany Kandel, New York mother of two children and author of *The Expert Parent: Everything You Need to Know from All the Experts in the Know.* Pocket Books.

Keeping your children safe while you are on vacation, at home or at a store, requires a bit of advance planning. *What you can do now to avoid trouble later…*

TRAVEL
Before leaving on a trip, be sure you take along…

▶ **Your medical insurance card.**

▶ **Children's acetaminophen** (Tylenol).

▶ **Adhesive bandages.**

▶ **Sunscreen and insect repellent.**

▶ **Electric-outlet covers and electrical tape** to cover outlets and tape down lamp or TV wires if you are traveling with toddlers.

▶ **A copy of any prescription your child uses regularly.**

▶ **Phone numbers for your pediatrician and pharmacy**—in case you need information about your child's medications.

▶ **When you arrive at your hotel, look up—and jot down—the numbers for the local Poison Control Center and a 24-hour pharmacy...**and find out the location of the nearest emergency medical facility.

BABY-SITTER OR CAREGIVER

▶ **Leave a phone number where you can be reached**—as well as a phone number for a friend, a relative or a neighbor.

▶ **Next to the phone, put the numbers for police, fire department, poison control, ambulance, pediatrician and dentist.** Use large letters.

▶ **Write your address and clear directions that your sitter can give out over the phone** describing how to locate your house.

▶ **Show the number of a local taxi service,** in case your sitter needs to take your child to the hospital. Include the name of, and directions to, the nearest hospital.

▶ **Prepare and sign a consent form authorizing emergency treatment for your child** by an emergency-room doctor if you are not present.

CRIME PREVENTION

▶ **Help children memorize their full name, address, phone number and how to call 911** in an emergency.

▶ **Teach kids how to get help.** Point out safe people (store clerk, policeman, firefighter)...and safe havens (library, a friend's house) in your neighborhood.

▶ **Engage in what-if role-playing games** to rehearse situations that might arise and how to handle them.

Example: "What if a stranger said I told him or her to pick you up from school?"

▶ **Establish a family code word.** Tell your children not to go off with anyone who doesn't know the secret word.

▶ **Don't display children's names on clothing or book bags.**

A Loving Touch...

A loving touch fights kids' ills. A parent's massage of an infant or a toddler for 15 to 20 minutes per night just before bedtime helps...*asthma*—improving peak air flow and lung function...*juvenile diabetes*—children comply better with medication and food regimens...*skin rashes*—reduced redness and scaling of skin...*sleep problems*—effective against stress-related insomnia.

Tiffany Field, PhD, director, Touch Research Institute, University of Miami School of Medicine.

TEACH CAUTION, NOT FEAR

Teach caution, not fear, by encouraging children to follow their gut feelings if they are uncomfortable when an adult or older child asks them to do something. *Key:* Letting kids know they can always tell you about the problem. *Trap:* Some children say they cannot tell their parents about a problem because the children were not supposed to be in the place where the problem happened. *Needed:* Mutual trust to let you and the child focus on the bigger problem and ignore the smaller one.

Jane Conoley, PhD, dean of education, Texas A&M University, College Station.

Miami School of Medicine.

Often-Overlooked Childproofing

Put a thick, soft rug under a baby's crib in case he or she climbs out—and falls...glue small blocks of cork to the lower edge of the lid of a piano or chest so kids' fingers are not caught if the lid slams down...drape a thick towel over the top of a door so children cannot close it...install window guards—put a screw into the inside frame to prevent the bottom from opening.

Denise and Alan Fields, consumer writers, Boulder, CO, and authors of *Baby Bargains.* Windsor Peak Press.

Babies Love Books

Make books a part of bedtime rituals when children are as young as six months. Start with picture books that are very short, have simple pictures and use simple sentences and rhymes. Concentrate on naming and describing the pictures for very young children. Read the same book several times—babies love repetition. Let the baby hold the book and turn the pages. Make the whole experience fun. Quit when the child gets tired.

Kathryn Fletcher, PhD, assistant professor of psychology, Ball State University, Muncie, IN.

MORE FUN READING WITH YOUNG KIDS

▶ **Just talk about the pictures in a book.** Skip over plots and the books' text if children are not ready for them.
▶ **You don't have to read the whole book.** Let your child's interest level guide you.
▶ **Read things you enjoy yourself.** If you are not having fun, neither will your child.
▶ **Try adding movement or touching.** *Example:* Bounce your child on your knee when the book says a pony trots.
▶ **Keep favorite books with you in a diaper bag,** purse or glove compartment—to read when waiting at a restaurant or a doctor's office.

Nancy Hall, contributing editor, *Parents,* 375 Lexington Ave., New York City 10017.

Parenting Know-How

Chapter 18

How to Deliver a Baby If You Have To

While you probably won't ever have to deliver a baby, you never know. *The first step:* Call 911 immediately. Emergency service dispatchers are trained to talk you through the delivery process if there is no time to get to the hospital. They will also send an ambulance.

If you do not have access to a phone, or if there is no time, here are the basics…

▪ Have the woman lie down on the floor.
That's better than a bed or couch—slippery newborns may fall off beds.

Make the woman comfortable on the carpet, towels or blankets or in the car's backseat. Use pillows if you have them.

Your job is to create a clean area. If you are outside, use coats, jackets or seat covers.

▪ Help the woman control her breathing.
She should be comforted and assured that help is on the way and that you're in control.

Urge her not to hyperventilate—rapidly breathing in and out—so that she is able to save her energy. Deep breathing is not helpful in relieving discomfort or stress. Also, don't give her anything to drink, not even ice or water. She could choke.

Better: Give her a lollipop or a moist washcloth to suck on.

▪ Do you see the baby's head?
If so, this is called crowning.

Get ready to hold the head gently as the baby emerges naturally.

Your job is to support the baby's head and guide the rest of the baby out, which could take a few seconds or a few minutes.

Don't pull the baby. It will come out naturally as the mother tightens her muscles and pushes.

▪ Once the baby's head is popping through, cradle it gently.
Use a clean cloth moistened with lukewarm water to wipe its face.

Elaine Josephson, MD, FACEP, attending emergency physician at St. Luke's–Roosevelt Hospital Center in New York City.

Then clean out the mouth and nose gently, so the baby can breathe. Be careful not to poke your fingers around in the baby's mouth.

■ As the mother tightens her muscles to push, guide the baby out.

Don't be alarmed if the mother's tissue tears and bleeds.

WHEN THE BABY IS OUT
■ Keep the newborn warm.
Wrap the baby in a blanket, towel or coat.

Dry the baby, and rub its back gently to stimulate crying.

■ Observe the umbilical cord.
The umbilical cord will still be attached.

If emergency services are on the way, keep the baby right next to the mother, cord intact.

If that's impossible because you're far from medical services, tie the cord off in two places—a few inches apart—with string, floss or other sturdy thread. Cut the cord between the two tied-off areas carefully with a knife that is sterile.

Important: Leave a part of the umbilical cord attached to the baby. The hospital will need it to get blood typing for further care.

SECRETS TO BETTER PARENTING

Praise a child realistically and specifically. *Example*: "Sharing your toys with your sister was a very nice thing to do." *Carefully listen* to what the child has to say. *Be willing to show weaknesses* in front of your children so they know that everyone has some weaknesses. *Read, read, read*.

Sheila Littauer, EdD, learning disabilities teacher/consultant, River Vale, NJ.

What Parents Need to Know About Children's Nutrition Now

William V. Tamborlane, MD, professor of pediatrics and chief of pediatric endocrinology at Yale University School of Medicine, New Haven, CT. He is editor of *The Yale Guide to Children's Nutrition*. Yale University Press.

Modern living creates special challenges for busy parents who are concerned about their children's food choices and eating habits.

Here are the major nutrition questions that parents are facing today...

■ What can parents do to get children to eat a good breakfast when they say they're not hungry in the morning?
Some children aren't hungry when they first wake up. Their appetites surface around midmorning.

Don't insist that children eat breakfast before they leave the house. It's a losing battle. Instead, pack snacks for them to eat in the car or on the bus on their way to school or at around 9 am or 10 am.

A low-fat granola bar and a juice box is an excellent morning snack. So is cheese with crackers and a piece of fruit.

■ Should parents of picky eaters let their kids eat what they want and hope they'll get the nutrition they need?
There's no need to micromanage your child's eating.

All children have an internal food regulator that tells them what and when to eat. Much of our appetite is actually genetically programmed and operates on a subconscious level.

I wouldn't worry if a child's appetite seems small or if the child insists on eating the same foods over and over again. Such food fads will change or disappear over time.

Even though there may be day-to-day variations in food intake, almost all kids, left to their own devices, will satisfy their nutritional needs over the course of a few days to a week. Research also indicates that children's day-to-day variations in appetite probably relate to their calorie expenditures the day before. If they were very active yesterday, they're likely to be ravenous today.

My best advice: Stock your kitchen with a variety of nutritious foods...provide balanced meals...and let your children eat as they desire. Forcing them to eat foods they don't like only makes them more resistant.

What can I do when children object to eating vegetables?
Substitute fruit, or try giving them more selections from the grain, cereal, rice and pasta group.

This will provide some of the minerals, trace nutrients and fiber they are missing by not eating vegetables.

I still suggest, however, that you offer children vegetables at most meals—especially in combination with foods they like. You could also offer raw instead of cooked vegetables with or without sauces. Or simply the one favorite vegetable they will eat over and over again.

Example: My teenage son only eats salad, so we make sure to have that with dinner every night.

How many sweets a day should I allow my child?
Don't exclude cookies or candy from a child's diet.

But—don't use them as a reward for good behavior. Those rules only make these "forbidden" foods more attractive.

The goal is to make sweets a small but acceptable part of a total diet. I think a few cookies a day to satisfy the sweet tooth is fine. Also encourage your children to get more physical activity. Have them get out and play...ride bikes...jump rope...hike...or play team sports.

An active lifestyle helps children manage their weight and increases the chance that they'll be hungry come dinnertime.

You, too, should get into the habit of exercise if you don't already work out. You have a wonderful opportunity to help your youngsters learn good eating and exercise habits by setting a good example.

Do children need a daily multivitamin supplement?
For children who eat varied and balanced diets, vitamin supplements are not necessary.

However, if children are finicky eaters or they won't eat breakfast, it won't do them any harm to give them a multivitamin/mineral supplement.

Any of the leading brands of children's vitamins is fine, but be sure the supplement you choose contains iron and calcium. These are two minerals in which children's diets may be deficient.

Give the supplement at breakfast or dinner. Food helps the body to better absorb vitamins and minerals.

How Busy Parents Can Make More Time for Parenting

Nancy Samalin, founder and director of Parent Guidance Workshops, 180 Riverside Dr., New York 10024. She is author of several parenting books, including *Loving Your Child Is Not Enough: Positive Discipline That Works.* Penguin.

Too many parents say they have too much to do and too little time in which to do it all. Most time crunches are self-created. You alone have the power to lighten up and spend more time with your kids. Parents in my workshop tell me that it is well worth the effort.

Here are the strategies that parents I know have adopted to make more time for parenting...

DECIDE WHAT'S IMPORTANT

People are always saying to me, "I have to get better organized," as if that were the solution to finding more time to spend with their children.

Time management is certainly helpful, but it involves much more than rearranging the items on your "to do" list. Maybe your list is just too long.

Remember that "busyness" is not in itself a virtue. You may find ways to spend time and save time, but for what?

The key to time management is to rediscover what matters most and relinquish some of the "shoulds" that may be cluttering up your days.

Helpful: Try making a list of everything you do in the course of a day. Then take your list and divide it into three categories—*musts...shoulds...* and *pleasures.*

After you review the categories, try to think of ways you can organize the musts, cut down on the *shoulds* and increase the *pleasures* that relate to your children.

PRACTICE FAMILY SHARING

The best way to make your children feel important and included in your life is to involve them in the activity of being a family. Kids often feel proud and important when they are allowed to be useful.

> ***Examples***: *If you're preparing dinner, let your child set the table. When you're doing the laundry, ask him to separate the light clothes from the dark ones. When gardening, show her how to plant seeds or use a rake.*

These tasks may take a little longer, but the time will be well spent in building a bond between you and your child.

LIMIT THE WORK YOU DO AT HOME

I realize it's not always possible, but try to separate your work life from your home life.

Work activity is often discouraging for kids, who wait eagerly for mom or dad to arrive home only to have them both disappear from view to continue working through the evening.

Helpful: Work on office projects in the living room while your child practices the piano. Or wait until your kids go to bed to do your work.

CREATE TIME FOR KIDS

Children cherish special time alone with a parent. These memories are happy ones because they recall times when a parent was totally in the moment and solely focused on being with the child, one on one.

Helpful: When you're really squeezed for time, try to find ways to carve out small moments with your kids.

> ***Examples:*** *A mother in my workshop makes it a point to take a 20-minute walk with her seven-year-old daughter every evening after dinner—weather permitting. Another parent has a 10-minute evening ritual that begins with her saying to her five-year-old, "Tell me four things that were funny today." An artist I know spends a half hour every night drawing with his son. Together, they choose their favorites to put up on the door.*

It's easy to tell children, "I love you," but it's the actual time that we spend focused on them alone that makes them feel important and worthwhile.

QUALITY TIME COUNTS

Keep quality time uncomplicated. To a child, quality time is simply time with a parent. It need not be planned. Just be sure to interact with your children at their level—listening, comforting or laughing with them. Make family time spontaneous and easy—have a picnic, visit a park or play a board game. Build activities around common interests...teach kids that every activity may not be equally enjoyable to everyone.

The Working Parents Help Book by **Susan Crites Price and Tom Price.** Peterson's. They are syndicated columnists focusing on parenting issues, Washington, DC.

Work Time, Play Time

For better work at home—*with a child around:* near your work area, set up your child's workplace. Include a craft desk with toilet-paper rolls, stickers, crayons, paper, glue, tape and similar items. *Schedule:* Set a timer for work time. While the timer runs, focus on work and have your child do the same. When the timer goes off, reset it for play time—and focus totally on your child. When the timer goes off again, return to work and reset it for the next playtime break. Decide how long to set the timer based on your child's age.

Sherri Breetzke, president, The Creativity Zone, quoted in *Our Place*, Box 500164, Austin, TX 78750.

Five Alternatives to Criticizing Your Children—Better for All

Nancy Samalin, founder and director of Parent Guidance Workshops, 180 Riverside Dr., New York 10024. She is author of several parenting books, including the classic *Loving Your Child Is Not Enough: Positive Discipline That Works.* Penguin.

Many parents assume that criticism is the only way to correct a child's undesirable traits. But instead of motivating kids to change, critical words usually backfire and undermine our efforts to improve behavior.

WORDS THAT STING

Children take a parent's criticism personally and feel attacked by someone whose admiration they dearly desire. Criticism can make children feel inept and lower their self-confidence. Criticism also can put children on the defensive, so we shouldn't be surprised if our words elicit back talk, hostility or disobedience.

Helpful: Recall your own parents' criticism of you. Remember how their fault-finding felt? Their words probably didn't encourage you to change and may have made you resentful.

To help kids improve their behavior, we need to drop critical remarks and replace them with positive teaching techniques. *Five alternatives to criticism...*

■ Describe what needs to be done.

When children make mistakes—and they inevitably do—respond by focusing your response on the problem rather than on your children.

> **Example:** *If kids spill cereal, try not to react with the impulsive, "How can you be so careless? Why don't you ever watch what you're doing?"*

Instead of attacking your children's sloppiness, address what they have to do to solve the problem. "The cereal needs to be swept up. Here's the broom."

A calm, impersonal statement about the situation is more effective than pointing out a child's shortcomings.

> **Example:** *"Damp towels won't dry when left in a heap on the bathroom floor" is more likely to get children to hang them up than a comment like "You're such slobs. Who do you think I am, your personal maid?"*

■ Let your children suffer the minor consequences of undesirable behavior.

Kids learn much more from their mistakes when parents don't bail them out too fast.

When children break a favorite toy, let them do without it rather than rushing to fix it for them. Or have them at least start to save their allowance for a new one.

When children frequently lose their possessions, don't be too quick to replace them. If your child loses his lunch box, suggest using a paper bag.

When children forget their homework, their teachers usually can enforce the consequences better than you can.

■ Treat mistakes as the beginning of a learning curve, not the end of the world.

When kids are having difficulty, we often jump in to criticize their mistakes and show them how to correct them.

But our intervention can undermine their self-confidence and rob them of opportunities to discover their own solutions.

Example: A friend's son was finishing a wood-working project and couldn't get the paint smooth enough. My friend took the brush from his hand and said, "No, no, that's not right. You're leaving brush marks. Let me show you how to do it the right way."

The parent finished the painting, and the child walked away totally discouraged. If the dad had permitted his son to learn by finishing the job himself, his child would have gained experience and a sense of completion—more important than any smooth surface.

When children argue—which is an unavoidable part of any sibling relationship—let them negotiate their own solutions rather than leaping into the fray with criticism or ready-made answers.

Unless siblings are physically harming each other, it's better to stay out of the middle and enable them to find their own way to solve their problems.

■ Offer motivating statements when kids are struggling.

When children are frustrated or in a tough spot, don't blame them for getting into that situation in the first place.

Example: If we say, "You should have listened to me. If you had started that paper earlier, you wouldn't be in this fix," we are apt to discourage rather than to motivate our kids.

Better: Avoid telling children what's wrong with them. Encouraging remarks are much more helpful in boosting children's confidence.

Don't say, "Come on, it's easy" whenever children are struggling. Such comments, even though well-meaning, make them feel more inept. Instead, try saying, "That's not easy, is it? But I bet you can handle it."

Example: The 10-year-old daughter of an acquaintance was struggling to learn her part for a class play. Her parents offered to listen to her practice her lines and reinforced her efforts with, "Those are difficult words to pronounce...It's hard to remember when your next line comes in...It's quite a challenge to learn this part, but I can see you're really working at it."

■ Express praise and appreciation.

Once you have curbed critical remarks and substituted the suggested alternatives, add the two most important ingredients—praise and appreciation.

This will inspire good behavior and help children feel capable and competent.

Children shouldn't have to earn all As on report cards to win praise. We can find many opportunities every day to recognize a job well done, a kindness shown or a pitfall avoided. Emphasize effort rather than outcome.

Sometimes it's difficult to notice these little achievements, but you can start by looking for one positive aspect of your child's behavior each day and expressing your appreciation.

Example: Another parent broke the habit of nagging her son for leaving his toys strewn around the living room by noticing a rare occasion when the boy put away his building set without having to be reminded. "Good job. Now you'll know where to find all those pieces when you want to build another fort. And I appreciate how much neater this room looks."

Praise works best when it is specific and directed at an effort.

General statements like "You're such a good girl" are vague, but "You were so kind to Grandma when you helped find her glasses" is more precise and effective in helping your child to be more thoughtful.

The Effects of Family Conflict

Family conflict can affect some children's brains. Stress triggers the release of cortisol—and chronic high levels of cortisol affect the hippocampus, a part of the brain that is important for learning and memory. *Also:* Family conflict may impair growth.

Scott Montgomery, PhD, research fellow in medical epidemiology, Royal Free Hospital School of Medicine, London, whose study of more than 6,500 children was published in the *Archives of Disease in Childhood.*

PRAISE WITHOUT THE PRESSURE

Praising children effectively gives them values to live by as adults. But well-meaning praise can impose pressures. *Examples:* Calling kids *perfect, brilliant, gorgeous* or *extraordinary* can backfire by giving them unreasonable expectations as teenagers and adults. *Better:* Words that motivate without pressuring—*good thinking, hard-working, smart, talented, persevering* and *attractive.*

Why Bright Kids Get Poor Grades and What You Can Do About It by **Sylvia Rimm, PhD.** Three Rivers Press. She is director, Family Achievement Center, MetroHealth Medical Center, Cleveland.

PHONE SAVVY

Teach kids to use the phone in case of emergencies. Children should learn their phone numbers—including the area code—as soon as they become verbal. They should know it is all right to dial 0 or 911 in an emergency, even before calling home or anyone else. Teach them how to dial from various phones—home, pay, hotel and business. Tell them to dial 911 and leave the phone off the hook if they are in danger—since emergency operators can trace the call rapidly.

Raising Safe Kids in an Unsafe World by **Jan Wagner,** founder, SAFE-T-CHILD, Austin, TX. HarperCollins.

Better Ways to Disagree In Front of the Children

When parents disagree politely, adolescents and young adults benefit mentally and emotionally. Effective communication among parents and offspring as well as between husbands and wives without the offspring present was associated with young adult adjustment. When parents criticize each other harshly, children are more likely to develop social and psychological problems such as anxiety, nervousness and substance abuse.

Clifford Notarius, PhD, professor of psychology, Catholic University, Washington, DC, and author of a three-year study of 54 families.

Much Better Parenting—Made Simple-ish

John Gottman, PhD, professor emeritus of psychology at University of Washington in Seattle and cofounder of the Gottman Institute. He is author of *The Heart of Parenting: How to Raise an Emotionally Intelligent Child.* Simon & Schuster.

Many parents think of their children's intelligence in terms of academic achievement. While grades are important, so is a child's emotional intelligence—the ability to understand feelings and express those feelings appropriately.

Children's emotional intelligence is critical because their ability to navigate the world of emotions determines success in all relationships with family, classmates and teachers—and later in adult life.

After conducting two 10-year studies of more than 120 families, I've concluded that there are five significant steps that parents can use to coach children to be more emotionally intelligent...

Recognize your child's emotions.
Many parents are keen observers of their children's behavior, but they don't always detect the emotions that are behind the behavior.

Example: If a child is scribbling on the walls or grabbing toys from another child, it's natural to focus on curbing the misbehavior.

But look as closely at the why as the what. Why is the child upset? Why is he angry?

Even when no misbehavior is involved, it's important to notice low-intensity emotions—such as sadness when a toy breaks—before they escalate into problems.

Helpful: To become more attuned to a child's feelings, parents need to be more aware of their own emotions first.

Think about how you handle worry...sadness...anger...and fear.

Are you temperamentally intense—or more easygoing? As you think about, and become more aware of, your emotional reactions, you'll be better able to decode your child's feelings and behavior.

Consider your child's emotions as opportunities for intimacy and teaching.
View a child's negative emotions as a chance to bond and teach, and you can turn negative situations into positive interactions.

By viewing behavior differently, children's anger, sadness and fear become more than just a reflection on you and your parenting style.

Helpful: When children are upset, comfort them and listen...and talk about how they feel rather than immediately moving to discipline them. This type of reaction lets children know they are understood, loved and valued.

Like coaching an athletic skill, our concern gives children a chance to practice how to express emotions and solve problems each time an occasion arises.

Listen carefully.
Listening means more than passively collecting information through your ears.

It means tuning in to the child's current emotions by paying attention to his body language and facial expressions as well as to his words.

Then you're ready to see the situation from his perspective, and you can reflect his emotions back to him in soothing, noncritical words.

Example: At first, your responses may be a brief "Ummm,"..."Okay," or "I see." But as you draw out your children, you can better assess their emotional situations.

You can also acknowledge their feelings by giving those feelings their proper names—"Sounds like you're anxious about..." or "You seem to be a little timid. Why?"

This part of emotional coaching shows your children that it is acceptable to feel the way they do...that you're interested enough to listen patiently...and that you believe they are able to cope.

By listening carefully, you also have refrained from jumping in with a ready-made solution. You haven't minimized or contradicted your children's genuine feelings by saying, "Don't feel bad. It will be all right if you..."

Instead, you have given your children a chance to express their emotions and, in the process, to search for their own solutions to the problems they face.

■ Help your children find words to name their emotions.
Words have power.

When you help your children label their feelings, you give them some control of those feelings.

Naming emotions helps a child transform a scary or vague feeling into something real that can be defined and is normal.

> *Example: To a young child, jealousy may be an indistinct, unpleasant feeling. The child knows he doesn't like the fact that other children are being called on in school. But he hasn't yet reached the developmental milestone of abstract thinking, so he cannot identify his uncomfortable feeling.*

If we use the term *jealousy* to name it, he learns that the amorphous feeling he has whenever other children are given special attention in class is acceptable. The feeling has a name. Other people know about it, and it's fine to feel that way.

Simply naming emotions will have a calming effect on children when they're upset.

By knowing and using the names of their feelings, they can learn to soothe themselves. Kids who learn this early in life are more likely to concentrate better, achieve more in school, enjoy good health and have better relationships with their peers.

Remember that children, like adults, experience mixed emotions. Children, however, don't know that unless we teach them.

> *Example: A child who is about to go off to camp may feel both proud of his independence and fearful that he'll be homesick. Parents can guide him by exploring his range of emotions and reassuring him that it's normal to feel two or more emotions at the same time.*

■ Set limits on behavior as you explore strategies to solve problems.
If the emotion of the moment is anger and the accompanying behavior is bopping a sibling on the head with a ball, you need to let the angry child know that hitting is absolutely unacceptable, but feeling angry is acceptable.

Strategy: You might say, "Hitting isn't allowed," as you remove the child from the sibling. "I see you're pretty angry at Johnny, but you cannot hit people. Can you tell me why you're so mad at him? Maybe you would like to draw an angry picture to show me how you feel?"

Help your children try to find their own method of expressing emotions in acceptable ways.

How Not to Spoil Your Children

Nancy Samalin, founder and director of Parent Guidance Workshops, 180 Riverside Dr., New York City 10024. She is author of several books on parenting, including her classic *Loving Your Child Is Not Enough: Positive Discipline That Works.* Penguin.

In this age of abundance, many parents don't know how to give their kids what they want without spoiling them.

Without knowing it, well-meaning moms and dads fall into what I call the *Happiness Trap.* They simply can't bear to see their children sad or disappointed in any way—so they give them everything they ask or plead for.

How to establish limits so children are less likely to become spoiled…

■ Make sure *no* means *no*.
When you say no, does it sound more like *maybe*?

If you're at all ambivalent, kids easily pick up on it. They recognize the signs that you don't want to make them unhappy. They sense it when you're uncomfortable saying no to them.

When you don't send a clear message, you encourage pleading, whining, wheedling and even tantrums.

Expect your kids to test you. That's their way of finding out if you really mean what you say.

Act secure about saying no when you have to. Changing your no to a yes might make your child happy for the moment, but it's a short-lived happiness and the stakes will only get raised the next time you say no.

Recognize manipulation, and don't give in to it.
Be aware if you've established patterns with your children that allow them to manipulate you.

If children know a public tantrum will get you to change your mind, they will do it. Make it clear that you won't be manipulated in that manner.

> **Example:** *If you're in a public place, say, "Stop now or we'll have to leave"—then do it. If you're at home, say, "Please go to your room until you've calmed down," or just, "I'm sorry you're upset, but I'm not going to change my mind."*

Don't be afraid of negative feelings.
One of the sure signs that you've fallen into the *Happiness Trap* is that you can't stand to see your children expressing unhappiness or complaining.

Helpful: Let your child know that it is acceptable to feel and express negative emotions. Acknowledge his feelings, but let him know that you're going to stick to your decision.

> **Example:** *Instead of saying, "There's no reason to cry," you might say, "I know how much you were looking forward to going to the amusement park. Of course you're disappointed. But I can't let you go while you have a cold."*

Expressing empathy doesn't mean that you agree with what your children want or feel. It just means that you are not judging or criticizing them for having those feelings.

Focus on needs, not wants.
Kids are not always able to make the distinction between what they want and what they need.

Parents have to do it for them, even if it makes children momentarily unhappy.

Of course, it can feel uncomfortable to deny children their desires. Don't expect them to give you a big hug and say, "Oh, thank you, Mom, for not buying me that skateboard."

But disappointed children are not necessarily unloved children. Also, realize that a child isn't necessarily happier when he gets everything he wants. In fact, children feel much more secure when the boundaries are clear and you are firm about your decisions.

Helpful: Just because your child expresses a desire, it doesn't mean you have to respond immediately. Sometimes it's more effective to say, "Let me think about it and get back to you later." And do get back to him. However, you may sometimes be surprised to find that by the time you're ready to discuss it, your child won't be so interested anymore.

Be a parent, not a friend.
Sometimes parents who grew up in strict households want their kids to be raised in more open and flexible environments.

There's nothing wrong with that. The problem arises when you try to be your child's friend rather than his parent.

> **Example:** *You refuse to let your child go biking after school because you think he's too young to be out unsupervised. He's furious with you and yells, "I hate you. You're not my friend."*

This kind of statement can really hurt or anger a parent—especially if you're not clear that your role is to sometimes be unpopular with your kids.

Instead of feeling guilty or caving in, you might say, "I'm sorry you feel that way, and I hope you change your mind—but the answer is still no."

Teach your child that sometimes other people come first.
I firmly believe that only by taking care of your own needs can you truly model respect for others.

The best way to teach children not to be self-centered is to show them that you were not put on the earth to cater only to them.

Common example: *Many children interrupt parents when they're talking on the phone with mundane requests designed to get attention.*

Instead of immediately putting down the phone or hanging up to deal with a child's nonemergency request, it's a good time to establish that your needs are separate. You might turn to your child and say briefly, "I'm on the phone. I'll listen to you as soon as I'm finished." Then return to your call.

No parent falls deliberately into the *Happiness Trap.* Usually, the motivation is intense feelings of love and caring. That's what makes it so difficult to avoid.

The *Happiness Trap* becomes easier to avoid when we learn to get rid of our own guilt, to recognize the difference between needs and wants and to believe that the happiest child is the one who is given both love—*and limits.*

Truth...Consequences... And Your Kids

Nancy Samalin, founder and director of Parent Guidance Workshops, 180 Riverside Dr., New York City 10024. She is author of several books on parenting, including *Loving Each One Best: A Caring and Practical Approach to Raising Siblings.* Bantam Books.

Almost all of the parents I know feel very strongly that their children should always tell the truth.

A big part of the parents' concern is practical, of course. Parents need to have reliable information, especially about safety issues, such as knowing where their kids are going and who will be there.

But most parents I know also consider the truth to be an important value. They know that people who are honest inspire trust and confidence in others.

Here's how to help establish and nurture a healthy foundation for honesty in your home...

■ **Create a truthful environment.**
The best way to teach honesty is to set a good example.

Children will not respect the truth if they see that there are times when you are deliberately deceitful.

Many adults feel it is acceptable to tell white lies when situations warrant it. But they don't always see the negative impact that even a fib can have on children. *Examples...*

▶ **A man I know still remembers how he cringed when his father secured a cheaper bus ticket** for him by telling the driver that he was five when he was really six.

▶ **A woman remembers how her mother used to drive very fast...**but whenever she was stopped by a police officer, she always denied that she was speeding.

These adults found it easier to justify lying when they were kids by thinking of their own parents' examples. As kids, they couldn't differentiate between degrees of dishonesty. There was the truth...and there were the lies...and the subtleties were lost on them.

Important: Don't lie in front of your children—even when you think the situation warrants a half-truth. Instead of begging off from a social situation by pretending to be sick, simply say, "I don't feel up to it" or "This isn't a good time for me."

■ **Don't overreact to small lies.**
Most kids tell small lies to avoid getting punished or incurring a parent's wrath.

This is normal, self-protective behavior.

If you catch your children in a "Yes-I-washed-my-hands" type of lie, resist launching into a tirade. Instead, calmly remind them that the truth is a

value in your household and that you expect them to be honest.

Remember to focus on the incident of dishonesty, and don't come to broad conclusions about your child's personality. When parents feel their trust has been violated, they often become angry and run the risk of making children feel that they are habitual liars with serious character flaws.

Example: If your child assures you that he has finished his homework and you later find out he only did part of it, don't immediately conclude that he is incapable of telling the truth.

Better: Instead of making a blanket accusation such as, "You're a liar!," it's better to say, "When I ask you a question, I'm upset if I can't count on you to tell me the whole truth." This approach is more likely to open the door for a fearless and truthful dialogue.

■ Teach tact along with truth.
Teach your children that being honest does not mean they have to always say exactly what's on their minds—especially if those thoughts would hurt someone's feelings.

Kindness and sensitivity to others are important values, too.

Example: You wouldn't want your child to turn down a play date by saying, "I don't want to come to your house because I don't like you"—even if that is the honest response.

The goal is to be honest without being insulting or mean. This is a difficult concept for young children since they tend to blurt out their feelings without being aware of how other people feel.

It takes time to teach children to be diplomatic.
Helpful: Encourage your children to think of responses that are truthful but that also protect other people's feelings.

Example: If grandma sends your daughter a sweater for her birthday instead of the doll she

had really hoped to get, help your daughter to write a gracious thank-you note that expresses her appreciation for her grandmother's thoughtfulness and generosity.

■ Don't punish honesty.
While telling the truth sometimes means facing up to unpleasant consequences, you need to make it safe and comfortable for children to tell the truth.

Let children know you'll respect them for being honest.

Helpful: Always make a point of acknowledging when your child is truthful about something that was difficult for him to admit to you. That doesn't mean you have to let him off the hook, but your praise for his honesty or his difficult admission will make a positive impact.

If a negative consequence is in order, make sure children understand that the penalty was for violating the rules of the house, not for telling the truth.

Example: If your child owns up to breaking your favorite vase, you might say, "I realize that it took a lot of courage for you to tell me what you did— especially since you know how strongly I feel about your not playing ball in the living room. And—I truly appreciate your honesty. However, we agreed that I would take away your ball if you played with it in the house."

■ Don't use entrapment.
One of the best ways to encourage lying is to entrap children.

I call it asking "Fifth Amendment" questions— you already know the answer, but you ask the question anyway, which encourages a child to lie. Nobody—neither adults nor children—wants to be put in such a miserable position.

Example: If you see cookie crumbs on your child's mouth, don't ask, "Did you take a cookie?" If he is like most kids, he'll deny it. Instead of putting him on the defensive, simply state the rule— "The cookies are not to be eaten before dinner."

Understand that sometimes it is easier for a child to tell a lie. Helping your child to become truthful is a process that requires your patience and understanding.

Teens and Emotions

Teens' brains process emotions differently from adults' brains. When dealing with emotions, teenagers' brains show high levels of activity in a region involved in instinctual responses—what many call "gut instinct." Adults dealing with emotions show more activity in a brain area associated with rational thinking. This may explain why teens cannot clearly understand the consequences of their behavior, but adults can.

Deborah Yurgelun-Todd, PhD, director of neuropsychology and cognitive neuroimaging, McLean Hospital Brain Imaging Center, Belmont, MA.

Best Ways to Relate to Troublesome Teenagers

Lawrence Bauman, PhD, a psychotherapist in New York and director of inpatient services at South Beach Psychiatric Center in Staten Island, NY. He is author of *The Nine Most Troublesome Teenage Problems and How to Solve Them.* Carol Publishing Group.

The challenges of dealing with troublesome teenagers are not easy. But—there are solutions to many of these problems.

Here are some of the most common problems faced by parents of teens…and how to solve them…

■ **Teens who don't take responsibility.**
Chores that have not been done, incomplete homework and expensive sports equipment left lying outside are familiar issues to parents of teens.

To the parent, irresponsible behavior points to a troubled future. Teens, meanwhile, are neglecting responsibilities, such as taking out the garbage, because they are concentrating on new ones—particularly changed expectations at school, a new peer group or dating.

Helpful: Expectations and rules are important, but parents also must understand the world in which teens live. It is understandable that teens—with their heads full of music, complex relationships and clothes—forget things.

Still, it is not in your best interest or theirs if you are always the one to remember things for them. Step back…allow teens to be responsible for their own behavior…and let them face the consequences of their own irresponsible behavior when it occurs.

In some situations, you may have to change their responsibilities.

> *Example: If your teen never seems to clean his room, try changing the responsibility to better fit his capabilities. Instead of insisting that he clean his room every day, ask that he do it once a week. The teen is more likely to be able to comply with this rule.*

Trap: Reminding teenagers when they forget something sends the message that it is your responsibility to do the remembering for them. Of course, you should provide guidance and support when necessary. But the responsibility for their actions ultimately must rest with them.

Helpful: Let your teen know that household responsibilities are a two-way street. What would it be like if mom or dad cooked dinner whenever they felt like it…or her allowance was given on an unset schedule? Living together means agreeing to share responsibilities. If not, the family system starts to break down. Explain this to your teen.

■ **Teens who always act bored.**
Our children have come to think that they must be stimulated all the time.

They think something is wrong if their lives do not keep up with what they see on TV and in the movies. But teens need to learn how to amuse themselves when their peers are not around.

> **Examples:** *Suggest that your teen look over a collection, or give him a good book to read. He may roll his eyes at first, but the fifth or sixth time you suggest an activity, he may actually jump in and try it.*

Trap: Trying to occupy teens yourself is just another way of saying that all stimulation has to be externally generated. Your teen needs to learn how to amuse herself. If left to her own resources, eventually she will find things to do on her own.

■ Teens who lie.

Lying really upsets parents because they see it as the ultimate betrayal.

A teen, however, views a lie differently.

To a teen, a lie may be a way of avoiding trouble (*What my parents don't know can't hurt me*)...or it can be a way of asserting independence (*There's no reason why they need to know about my report card*).

Better: Look at the issue your teen lied about. You cannot deal with the lie without dealing with the circumstance that led him to lie. Is your teen afraid of punishment? Is your rule too harsh? It may be best to change a rule that isn't crucial to your teen's safety.

Is he afraid he will be criticized? Afraid to share something with you because he knows how you will react?

If you can prove to your teen that you are more interested in helping him resolve the underlying problem than in the lie itself, you may be able to get him to open up next time and talk to you truthfully.

Keep in mind that a conversation brought about by an instance of lying should occur in a calm, private atmosphere (without other siblings present) and be nonaccusatory.

Trap: Harsh punishments and inflexible rules may make lying more prevalent rather than less. When there is no room to negotiate, teens are more likely to lie.

Parents need to realize that lying is not a "federal case" and that most teens will do it because they are young and inexperienced, and the lies seem like the easiest way to cope with problems in their lives.

■ Teens who are doing badly in school.

By the age of 12 or 13, your child is facing a new world at school, one that is more demanding academically and socially.

In some cases, this change may result in a dip in grades.

Talk to your teen first. Find out what she thinks happened in class. Did she hand in all homework assignments, study for tests and quizzes, etc.?

If necessary, visit the school and speak to her teachers whenever an unsatisfactory report comes in. But do not go in angry over the fact that your teen has been criticized. Usually, such negative reports are based in truth.

Understand that your teen probably has not consciously neglected schoolwork. There are just so many other things on a teen's mind that academics can take a temporary nosedive.

In some cases, it's enough that you have noticed the trend and have had a friendly talk with your teen. In other cases, however, this is not enough to get a child back on track. Look at the *underlying* cause of school problems...

▶ **Is there something in the child's life** that may have caused her grades to drop?

▶ **Is there a learning disability?**

▶ **Are there problems with friends?**

A teen may react by "giving up" at school if there are large nonschool problems to deal with, such as a divorce.

Trap: Having expectations that are too high may actually cause a child to underachieve. Teens may decide to punish an overly demanding parent, or they may rebel by performing below their real potential.

■ Teens with whom it is difficult to communicate.

Teens who perhaps once hung on your every word now act with great annoyance when you have something to say.

They let you know in no uncertain terms that they're not listening or don't want to talk about it.

A parent who is suddenly cut off from what used to be pleasant and open conversation with a child is going to feel hurt—and react accordingly. Parents sometimes also worry that this inability to communicate means the child is becoming a moody social misfit—or worse.

In many cases, the truth is that teens just don't want to share their thoughts with an adult.

Helpful: Understand that teens may not want to talk about what they did with their friends because then the experience won't really belong to them anymore.

Instead, work on being a good listener. This means asking fewer questions and giving a lot less unsolicited advice.

TROUBLE WITH TEENAGERS CAN BE AVOIDED

Don't argue with teenagers unless the issue involves safety or values. For advice to be effective with teenagers, it must be selective. If you see behavior that you don't like, don't make an issue of it unless it is dangerous or hurtful or will make a real difference to their lives over time. *Examples:* Telling you where they are if they stay out late at night is not negotiable— but don't make a fuss about eating habits… clothes…hairstyles…or messy rooms.

Nancy Samalin, founder and director of Parent Guidance Workshops, 180 Riverside Dr., New York City 10024. She is author of several books on parenting, including *Loving Each One Best: A Caring and Practical Approach to Raising Siblings.* Bantam Books.

For You and Your Children Of All Ages—Happiness And Inner Peace

Wayne Dyer, PhD, psychologist and lecturer in Maui, HI. He is author of numerous books, including *Manifest Your Destiny* (HarperTorch), and *What Do You Really Want for Your Children?* (Quill).

When I ask parents today what they want most for their children, I find their first wish is not wealth or fame…but happiness and inner peace.

So why don't parents spend more time teaching children about happiness and serenity? Because many parents aren't sure exactly how to help their children enjoy life spiritually.

Here's how I teach my eight children to enjoy life…and how you can cultivate these qualities in your own children…

POSITIVE SELF-IMAGE

Our impression of ourselves is the single most telling factor in determining our ultimate success and happiness.

While many people believe talent, opportunity, IQ and a positive outlook are the barometers for determining one's potential for success and happiness, these factors are all secondary to possessing a healthy, positive self-image.

Once you have developed a strong self-portrait, the opinions of others will never immobilize you or cause you to doubt yourself.

The same principle works for children. A child's self-image is a direct result of the verbal and physical reinforcements he receives from his parents every day. Each reinforcement forms a mini "self-picture."

Important: Praise your children for their positive behavior, and don't react only to their negative behavior. Regardless of their behavior, tell them you love them every day. Show them that they are lovable by hugging them, kissing them and demonstrating that they are terrific.

Beware: Watch for negative messages that your children send to themselves. Whenever you hear them say, I'm stupid...I'm too fat...or I can't ride a two-wheeler, you are hearing a signal to help them raise their self-esteem.

RISK-TAKING

The wonderful part about risk-taking is that it makes life much more exciting, interesting and rewarding. One wonderful characteristic in children is that they are natural risk-takers.

Yet too often, our own irrational fears and constant warnings inhibit our children's natural tendencies, causing them to grow up clinging only to the safe and familiar.

Another main inhibitor to risk-taking is *fear of failure*. Too many of us see failure as something to be avoided, and, as a result, we embrace only those tasks that are easy. *Helpful...*

■ Whenever possible, get out of your children's way and let them experiment.

Sure, they might get some bumps and bruises, but as long as what they're doing is not truly dangerous, those bumps and bruises will teach them what to do and what not to do.

> **Example:** *When you see your young child pouring milk into a glass, your inclination might be to say every two seconds, Be careful.*

Better: Remain quietly watchful, and be ready to step in only if necessary. If the milk spills, forget about it. Make your child feel that such mistakes are not cause for alarm or hysteria.

■ Allow your children to fail—even fail a lot.
That's the way we learn.

Actually, I believe there is no such thing as failure. Everything we do produces a result. It's only what we do with those results that matters.

> **Example:** *The same year that Babe Ruth hit 60 home runs, he struck out more times than anybody else.*

If you want your children to hit home runs, you must be willing to let them strike out.

FREEDOM FROM ANXIETY

Children are raised in an environment of social anxiety. This anxiety takes a tremendous toll on their self-confidence.

In reality, there's no such thing as anxiety. There are only people who think anxious thoughts—people who succumb to pressure and stress.

The more your child is able to be contemplative and peaceful, the less likely he will become unnecessarily anxious.

Helpful: Provide your children with opportunities to learn about inner serenity. *Examples...*

▶ **Take a yoga class together.** Children as young as age eight enjoy yoga.

▶ **Practice meditating together with an instructional** audio- or videotape.

▶ **Learn about self-hypnosis,** and practice those techniques.

▶ **Listen to peaceful music.**

A child who knows how to rest her mind stands a better chance of handling the busy pace of life.

SELF-RELIANCE

Once children learn to trust their instincts and judgment, they will have the confidence to solve problems and reach their goals in their own way.

When they become self-reliant, they will be less likely to doubt their abilities when others express negative opinions. The sense of achievement that results will be most rewarding.

Let your children know it is impossible to please everyone all of the time or even any one person all of the time. When they feel bad about something someone else does or thinks, be sympathetic but always bring it back to what they think and feel about themselves.

Example: Your young daughter comes home crying because another girl called her names. Instead of chastising the girl, tell your daughter, "I know you are hurt right now because of what that girl said to you. But don't you think you are making her opinion of you more important than your own opinion of yourself? Even if she thinks you're stupid, does that mean you really are?"

Teach your children not to blame others for anything. It's a very strong inclination in all of us to place responsibility for how we are doing or what we're feeling on someone or something outside of ourselves. But whenever we do that, our self-reliance is eroded.

APPRECIATION

Being appreciative of what we already have is what I call the ability to celebrate the present moments of our lives.

Helpful: To teach children to appreciate what they have, expose them to others who are not as fortunate. Such experiences can come from looking at pictures in newspapers and magazines—or by volunteering time or donating money to good causes.

Example: When Hurricane Andrew came through south Florida in 1992 and destroyed many of the areas near Miami, my wife, children and I helped an organization pass out food to children who were made homeless.

How One Top Debating Coach Motivates Kids to Study... And You Can, Too

Linda M. Collier, JD, a lawyer and associate professor of communication studies at the University of Missouri–Kansas City. For more than 15 years, she has been director of debate at the university, where she has coached students to several national championships. She also runs a consulting firm that offers seminars on helping students achieve peak performance.

When the University of Missouri–Kansas City won the national collegiate debate team championship in March, the team beat out many prestigious universities—including Harvard, Northwestern and Cornell. Part of their success was the result of the motivational strategies their coach used to help them excel far beyond what they believed they could achieve.

Linda Collier, the debate team's coach, suggests how parents can adapt her motivational strategies to help their children reach their potential. *Here's her advice...*

■ Break tradition when helping kids memorize information.
Students are easily bored by the rote practice that is necessary to help them remember critical information.

While memorizing and repeating information isn't the only way to absorb knowledge, it is an essential first step. But no one said memorizing had to be dull.

Helpful: Improve students' self-discipline by injecting creative diversions into their routines. Even the tiniest departure from the norm will animate the dull process of repetition and satisfy their need for autonomy.

Example: During the final week of the summer, I hold a rigorous preseason minicamp at the university for the debate team. Getting the team to practice their enunciating skills is particularly difficult at that time of year.

To make the exercise more interesting, I ask the debaters to put a pencil in their clenched jaws and talk to each other for several minutes.

Use your imagination to come up with ways to make rote tasks more fun and applicable. One way is to show kids how the skills and information that they're learning apply directly to the real world.

■ Don't dwell on setbacks.

Defeat can be devastating for students—but only if they're allowed to dwell on it.

Better: After a setback or disappointment, such as a poor grade or a loss on a sports team, tell them they have only 30 seconds to be upset about it. Then encourage them to look forward, and focus their energies on the next challenge.

By setting a 30-second grieving limit, poor performances become temporary setbacks rather than permanent conditions. If students continue to be upset, I focus on specific small goals to give them increased confidence.

Important: The 30-second rule applies to you, too. Release your frustration and disappointment for a finite period, then take a proactive approach to any problem or setback.

■ Try to be your children's learning coach instead of their parent.

Parents tend to take their children's imperfections and failures personally.

When a child forgets his or her homework or does not achieve a top grade, parents often assume the worst about the child's future, and they let the child know it. They also feel they've failed their child by not staying more involved.

But presenting such doomsday scenarios only stifles motivation.

Better: A good learning coach treats students as responsible individuals who are capable of making their own choices. The coach's role is to advise team members on how to make better choices, not to do the work for them or bully them into working harder.

Good coaches also make team members realize they must accept responsibility for the consequences of their actions and for what they achieve.

Example: *We were debating in the championship round at a tournament in Florida several years ago. I told my team that they were going to have to make a radical change in their strategy—which involved the way they answered a particular argument—if they wanted to beat their competition. They chose not to adapt because they had gotten all the way to the finals by doing it their way. Rather than rant and rave about the likely outcome, I simply told them what I thought and left them alone to make their own decision.*

They didn't change, and they lost that particular debate—but they learned on their own that they had to think ahead.

■ Don't let fear rule students.

The biggest reason children lack self-motivation is fear of failure and embarrassment.

It becomes easier and safer for them not to try very hard or take chances. It's far better for parents to teach kids strategies to help them deal with their fears. *Steps to take…*

▶ **Demystify any process.** Parents worry that talking about a new challenge will just intimidate children. In fact, it's just the opposite. The more information children have about what's going to happen, the more familiar it seems. Don't be reluctant to examine both the best- and worst-case scenarios.

Example: *In preparation for the debate that would decide the national champion, I had my team sit in the actual room and the actual chairs where the contest was to be held. You might think* *this would intimidate or paralyze them. Instead, they were told to discuss each phase of the debate and what could go wrong. Being there served as a release valve for their anxiety. And...it worked.*

▶ **Encourage personal rituals that help concentration.** Professional athletes often visualize winning before a big match. It's just as important for kids to relax and reassure themselves.

Example: *Before one tournament, one of my debaters dressed so quickly, he forgot to put on his belt. He won every match that weekend. For the rest of the season, before each debate he would go in the bathroom and remove his belt. If it were just a good-luck ritual, I would have discouraged it. But I recognized that this time gave him the few minutes he needed to be alone with his thoughts and mentally prepare himself.*

▶ **Set small, incremental goals that are clear and achievable.** As homework, I ask my first-year debaters to stand up and read out loud for 10 minutes before bedtime each night. That way they can hear their own voices and ease into public speaking. Children are largely motivated in the present. Telling children that they must study so they can get into a good college rarely works.

Better strategy: Just as trophies are tangible evidence of a debater's success, they can provide a motivation and a measure of success for younger people, too.

■ **Solve the right motivational problems.**
If children have trouble focusing on homework, it may not be enough to give them a quiet part of the house and good lighting.

Maybe your child is afraid of looking foolish in front of his classmates. Maybe he's more interested in a different, equally appropriate project. Listen for what children need before you decide how to help them.

Important: When your children are trying their hardest, tolerate good-faith failure. You must balance your own aspirations for your kids with what they can realistically do. Don't push kids to learn. Create the right environment, and they'll learn on their own.

How to Help Your Child Have a Constructive Summer

Terri Thompson, director of the Knight–Bagehot Fellowship in Economics and Business Journalism at the Columbia University Graduate School of Journalism, New York.

Running a summer business teaches kids fiscal and personal responsibility. *Here's advice you can give your children...*

■ **Assess the neighborhood's needs.**
Consider running a play group if you live in a suburb full of kids.

If you live in an apartment building with lots of older folks, a personalized grocery-shopping service might be ideal.

■ **Size up the competition.**
If your child is going to set up a cookie-making business, check out the local bakeries.

How much do they charge? What's the going rate for baby-sitters? How much do lawn-care people get? Your child will probably have to undercut them to build his or her business.

Important: Don't set a price so high that only your child's grandparents and next-door neighbors will pay it.

■ **Write a business plan.**
Your child should outline a clear statement of what she intends to accomplish—her goal, what her costs will be, what she'll charge and what profits to expect.

By writing down a simple business plan, she'll learn how realistic her goals are.

▦ Establish an appealing business concept.

This can be as simple as naming the business—"Jim's Total Grassroots Lawn-Care Service."

Rather than mowing lawns, he'll also bag the clippings, trim the flower beds and zap the crabgrass clumps with weed killer.

▦ Keep track of every penny that's earned and spent.

Your child should not buy anything that doesn't produce money—customized T-shirts or fancy stationery, for example.

A *good* use of money would be to print up posters or flyers—advertising that brings in customers.

GREAT KID-RUN BUSINESSES TO START NOW
▦ House-sitting.

During summer lots of people need someone to tend their primary residences—water the plants, feed the pets, pick up the mail and turn on the lights at night.

▦ Pet pampering.

Offer a package of all the things that dog and cat owners often neglect—give their pets weekly flea baths, brush them regularly, inspect them for ticks, teach them new tricks or take their picture.

▦ Flower power.

Find a flower wholesaler or grow your own, and provide a weekly fresh flowers home-delivery service.

▦ Desktop publisher.

Buy some affordable software that will allow you to print out computer-generated greeting cards, customized calendars, stationery, flyers, banners and yard-sale signs on the family computer.

Put together a sample portfolio and go door-to-door.

▦ Summer school.

Set up a daily play group with a twist—nature walks, exercises, finger painting, handicrafts, escorted trips to the movies.

Parents need help during the summer, and kids can multiply ordinary baby-sitting earnings by taking care of half a dozen kids at a time.

Parenting Positively: John Gray's Best Advice on Raising Happy Children

John Gray, PhD, author of numerous books, including *Men Are from Mars, Women Are from Venus* and *Children Are from Heaven.* HarperCollins. An internationally recognized expert in the fields of communication, relationships and personal growth, he has been conducting seminars in major cities for more than 20 years.

What's the best way to be a good parent—beyond simply loving your children? Being authoritarian leaves children unable to say no to anyone—including peers who may lead them astray. Being too permissive makes them self-centered and demanding.

The best way to raise happy, disciplined kids is to practice what I call *positive parenting*. The necessary skills are easy to learn, and they work right away. *Secrets of positive parents…*

UNDERSTAND EACH CHILD'S TEMPERAMENT

When a parent says that one child is a dream and another is a terror, what he or she really means is that the dream child is *similar* to him. If a child's temperament is like yours, you instinctively give him the kind of nurturing he needs.

If his personality differs from yours, your intuitive response is likely to create resistance rather than cooperation.

Once you understand a temperament, you can use the most effective approach. *Four basic temperaments...*

■ **Sensitive children** feel disappointment and distress more acutely than others.

They need empathy and validation. A parent should never try to cheer up a sensitive child—he won't cooperate until he feels fully heard.

> **Example:** *"I know you're mad about not getting a cookie right now. I promise that if you eat a good dinner, you'll get a cookie."*

■ **Active children** like to do things...and they want to see results.

They are not concerned with emotional responses to situations. Without structure, rules and responsibility, they get out of control.

> **Example:** *If several children are playing on the swing set, give the active child the job of making sure everyone gets equal time.*

■ **Responsive children** will seek more stimulation than other kids do.

They're impulsive and tend to lose interest in an activity before finishing it. The best way to get cooperation from these kids is to distract them.

> **Example:** *If a responsive child skins his knee and cries, don't talk about how bad he feels. Sing to him...or tell a story about the next fun activity— We'll go to the park and feed the ducks, and we'll have lots of fun.*

■ **Receptive children** are often anxious about change.

They need rhythm to feel secure—consistent bedtimes, mealtimes, playtimes, etc. Don't push receptive kids to participate in new activities. Let them watch first. Once they understand the situation, they'll step in.

AIM FOR COOPERATION... NOT OBEDIENCE

Children need a strong sense of self and values to deal with peer pressures. Teach them discipline and a sense of self by inviting their cooperation. Do not try to control them. This does not mean letting your kids run wild. It means treating them respectfully. Instead of *ordering* your child to do something, make a friendly request.

> **Example:** *"Would you please clean your room now?" (Not "Clean your room.")*

MOTIVATE WITH REWARD... NOT PUNISHMENT

Children—like adults—don't respond well to threats. They just dig in their heels. Promising a reward for good behavior works better than threatening to punish bad behavior.

Important: A reward is not the same as a bribe. Don't offer money or presents to get a child to do what he is actually supposed to do. Instead, offer valuable intangibles.

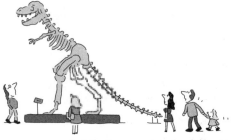

For a younger child, the most valuable reward is time with you. For a teenager, it may be a later curfew, car privileges or some other symbol of freedom.

Phrase requests in positive ways—showing positive consequences—by saying, "If you do...," rather than, "If you don't...."

> **Example:** *Instead of "If you don't brush your teeth, I won't read you a story," say, "If you brush your teeth now, there'll be time for three stories."*

ASSERT YOUR LEADERSHIP

Sometimes nurturing a child's unique temperament and offering positive rewards aren't enough to get him to cooperate. When that happens, switch to command statements. A command statement is a brief expression of what you want and expect—without arguing, lecturing or getting emotional.

Repeat the statement calmly and as often as necessary. This gives the child a chance to express his resistance…and to find out that you won't give in to it. *Example…*

You: I want you to put away your bicycle now.
Child: I don't feel like it.
You: I want you to put away your bicycle now.
Child: I didn't put it there. Somebody else did.
You: I want you to put away your bicycle now.
Child: Why do I have to?
You: Because I want you to do it now.
Child: I don't want to!
You: I want you to put away your bicycle now.
Child (sulkily): OK.
You: Thank you. I appreciate it.

Thank your child once he cooperates—even if he does so with a poor attitude. Lecturing him for putting up a fight effectively eliminates any reward for surrendering. He'll be even more resistant next time.

Surprisingly, command statements work faster than arguing or yelling—and they are easier on everyone's nerves. At first, you may feel awkward repeating the same statement over and over. But once you've used the technique a few times—and your kids realize you're serious about it—you'll be amazed at how cooperative they become.

COMMUNICATE ACCEPTANCE

Positive parents help kids grow up confident and compassionate by letting them know they're accepted. Parents communicate this acceptance in words—and demonstrate it in their behavior. *The five most powerful messages of acceptance…*

▶ **It's OK to be different.**

▶ **It's OK to make mistakes.**

▶ **It's OK to express emotions** that are negative.

▶ **It's OK to want more** (but you don't always get it).

▶ **It's OK to say no** (but remember Mom and Dad are the bosses).

How to Help Your Kids Build the Right Kind of Friendships with the Right Kinds of Kids

Nancy Samalin, founder and director of Parent Guidance Workshops, 180 Riverside Dr., New York City 10024. She is author of several books on parenting including *Loving Each One Best: A Caring and Practical Approach to Raising Siblings.* Bantam Books.

Parents have much more influence than they think over their children's choice of friends.

But in our attempt to protect our children, it is important to recognize that peer relationships are vital to children's development. It's the arena in which they learn to make decisions, to lead or follow, to become considerate and loyal and to recover from mistakes.

How to have a positive influence over your children's choice of friends…

■ Deemphasize popularity.

Many parents unwittingly push kids to make friends.

They fret if their children aren't invited to every birthday party. They are devastated whenever their kids are rejected by the "in" crowd.

But when you push for more popularity, your children get the message there is something wrong with them.

Encourage quality over quantity. The number of friends your children have is less important than if they have one or two good friends. And if you emphasize popularity or being part of the clique, your children may become followers who go along blindly with the crowd.

If children are left out—or picked on by their peer group—help them recognize that it is not necessarily their fault. Instead, reassure them that it is normal, though painful, to be "in" one week and "out" the next.

I've found that these popularity contests are more upsetting to parents than to kids. Most kids are more resilient than we give them credit for. Try to ride the waves of friendship fads, remembering that kids are fickle and peer groups are constantly in a state of flux.

■ Don't interfere without good reason.
Unless your children's friends are leading them into potentially hazardous situations, resist meddling in their relationships.

If you suspect that risky behavior is involved, remind your children about your clear, firm rules.

> *Example: When my kids wanted to go along with peer pressure, a phrase we used was, "Safety is a nonnegotiable issue in this family."*

Otherwise, allow children opportunities to negotiate their own issues and differences. Kids need time among themselves to learn how to develop their own rules, to share and take turns, to play fair and square, to recover from bruised egos.

Certainly there are times and places for adult supervision, but try to intervene selectively.

■ Listen to your child.
The stronger children's self-confidence, the better they'll be able to resist negative influences of peers.

Help strengthen children's egos by listening attentively when they're having trouble with friends.

Don't jump right in with ready-made solutions or criticism. Invite children to tell you what happened before you overreact...and listen. They're not likely to open up if you go through the roof.

> *Example: Your son comes home in tears because his friends ridiculed him for backing out of a scheme to shoplift.*
>
> *Don't immediately yell, "You're not spending time with those kids ever again." Instead, listen to his anguish about being ridiculed. Encourage him to talk about his feelings, and praise him for being strong and taking an unpopular stand.*
>
> *You might say, "I know that was tough. It took a lot of courage not to go along with the guys. I'm wondering, though, if these are kids you really enjoy being with."*

Try to determine whether your child is afraid of being left out. If that's the problem, help build up his self-confidence by praising him when he shows independent thinking.

■ Encourage individuality.
Keep in mind that you and your child have different tastes and opinions.

He may be attracted to people to whom you don't relate at all, just as you and he probably don't share the same tastes in food, music or movies.

Try to respect your children's differences even when you don't like the friends they keep.

Helpful: Encourage children to make choices and solve problems...ask their opinions about people you meet, TV shows and articles and books you read together.

When your child mentions a new best friend, don't grill him with lots of intrusive questions. Withhold your judgment.

Even if you don't like his choice of friends, don't automatically denigrate him, especially without any evidence of harmful behavior.

■ Encourage children to stick up for themselves.
Help your children practice this skill by allowing them to disagree with you in reasonable ways.

That doesn't mean tolerating sassy backtalk or outright defiance, but it does mean supporting their self-expression.

> *Example: When your daughter insists that she must have a pair of expensive sneakers because all her friends are wearing them...or when she begs you to let her stay out with peers past her curfew...give her a chance to express her reasons for asking.*

You don't have to agree, but show respect for her opinions. You might say, "Well, I'm ready to listen—try to convince me..." or "Let me hear your point of view..."

Even if you disagree with her, you are giving her opportunities to think for herself and evaluate her options.

If you decide that your child should not stay out past her curfew or that you cannot afford to buy her those expensive sneakers, reassure her that she can still be part of the group.

Point out that the other kids still invite her to play basketball in her old sneakers or that she'll be able to go off with her friends on other excursions—even though she must be home by 9 pm on this particular night.

By supporting children in voicing and defending their opinions, you help them practice a skill that they can also use with their peers.

They will become more confident about saying no the next time friends try to lead them toward misbehavior or toward values that are unacceptable to you.

Lessons from A Teacher of the Year

Philip Bigler, who teaches 11th-grade history and humanities at Thomas Jefferson High School for Science and Technology in Alexandria, VA. In 1998, he was named Teacher of the Year, a national award sponsored by the Council of Chief State School Officers and Scholastic Inc. Mr. Bigler has won numerous teaching awards and written several books, including *Hostile Fire: The Life and Death of First Lt. Sharon Lane.* Vandamere Press.

The great challenge for any parents is to help their kids do the best they can in school. **Key:** How well children do in school determines so much of their futures—college versus high school...good schools versus bad.

Mr. Bigler, national Teacher of the Year, has lots of ideas about what parents can do to excite their children about school and learning.

Here are his award-winning motivational suggestions...

■ Promote a culture of reading at home.
Reading is the gateway to all knowledge and it's fundamental to academic excellence and ideas.

Computers are wonderful tools, but they cannot replace books. Reading stimulates the imagination and encourages creative thinking.

Helpful: Read with your children, and discuss the books and articles in the car...while walking to school...and at the dinner table.

It's also important to set aside time for reading and make sure children view this time as a joy, not as a chore or a punishment.

One way to turn reading into a pleasurable event is to take children to libraries and bookstores once a week. Give them an allowance, and let them choose the books they want without questioning what they've chosen.

Important: Don't insist that children always read "educational" material. When I was a kid, I read the Hardy Boys mysteries all the time, and I think that's where my lifelong love of reading started. I still set aside one hour to read each night before bed.

■ Stimulate your children's curiosity.
Children need to be encouraged to ask "Why?" when they don't understand something.

Learning is a constant process, and children think the process is over once they have an answer. They need to be taught to probe and push for more answers.

Helpful: When children ask "Why?" don't turn them off or respond with pat answers. Even when you know the answer, it is more stimulating to ask, "What do you think? Why do you think that's so?" Or, "I'm not sure, let's look it up."

Your questions will show them that wondering "why" is an important part of learning.

Aim: To spark their curiosity in a spontaneous way so that it becomes fun—not a lesson or lecture.

> **Examples:** *Make up trivia games that you both can play regularly, even when you're on the run…help kids become active participants in the learning process by giving them chances to experiment around the house with measuring, cooking, fixing and other activities that require finding and using information.*

Know what's going on in school.

Attend school events, send notes to teachers at the opening of the school year to express your availability to them, and ask if you may phone them whenever you have questions or concerns.

Also, get involved with your kids in detailed descriptions of what they're studying in school.

Helpful: Encourage teachers and schools to print out an informational sheet to tell parents what children are studying week to week.

I have a Web page that the parents of my students can access to see what the class assignments are—and when they are due. More and more teachers I know are doing this now.

It's also important to become involved in school activities. Even if you can attend only a few events, your presence shows your children that you're interested in their school life and value its importance.

Establish a sense of ethics in children.

It's critical that parents have the courage to say "No" when children's interests are in conflict with what is acceptable.

As your children get older, continue to uphold firm, clear limits but gradually give them more opportunities to make choices and live with the consequences.

It is easier to establish these standards in first- and second-graders than in preteens. However, there are ways to encourage preteens to adhere to standards of behavior.

> **Examples:** *In school, we teach students to say "Thank you" and write thank-you letters to speakers who visit.*

> *We teach a sense of helping others through a strong mentoring program in which better students tutor others. We teach them stories of justice. We try to teach kids that there is right and wrong.*

Celebrate the thinking process, not just the ability to retain information.

Inquisitive, active learners have social skills that have been nurtured by parents and teachers.

Those skills include listening, thinking, sharing information and clearly expressing themselves.

Helpful: If your child is not a particularly good listener, get down to his or her eye level, touch his shoulder and look him in the eye before speaking. When he talks to you, give him your full attention.

Listening to children closely gives them practice in expressing themselves. Whenever they come home with a problem, don't hand them a solution. Ask them to tell you more about it.

Let them explain and talk through possible solutions—this is an important exercise for problem-solving. Such social skills are the underpinning for success in school and in life.

REDUCE HOMEWORK BATTLES

Set a schedule to make sure that homework will be done by a reasonable hour. Most children need time to unwind after school—so build that time in. Kids also have trouble concentrating when they are hungry. If homework is done before dinner, give your child a healthy snack. Younger children are less able to sit still for long periods than older ones—so divide their work into small sessions.

How to Help Your Child with Homework by the late **Marguerite Cogorno Radencich, PhD.** Free Spirit Publishing.

Unraveling Problems At School

If a young child dislikes school, spend several hours—at different times and on different days—observing the classroom and talking at home about what might be bothering your child. Try having the child draw a picture of the classroom for clues to what the trouble might be. Common problems and their solutions: *Trouble with transitions and limits*—find ways at home to help your child get used to changing activities and waiting his turn. *Personality conflict with teacher*—try filling in the teacher on your child's likes and dislikes to find some common ground. Separation anxiety—try reminding her of after-school plans and putting loving notes in her book bag.

Fred Provenzano, PhD, psychologist in private practice specializing in family and school issues, and former clinical instructor at University of Washington, Seattle.

Getting Along With Your 20 Year-Olds

Lois Leiderman Davitz, PhD, and **Joel Davitz, PhD,** Somers, New York–based psychologists and authors of many books and articles on family relationships, the latest being *Getting Along (Almost) with Your Adult Children: A Decade-by Decade Guide* (Sorin). They have been married for almost 60 years and have two adult sons.

Having a child turn 21 provides parents with a lovely feeling of accomplishment. But, as they quickly find out, parenting never ends.

The purpose now, though isn't to rear your children and instill values in them. After all, you can no longer tell your child what to do. Nor should you try. Your task is to foster and reinforce a loving relationship between you. Wrong turns, at this point, have bigger stakes attached—they can result in bad feelings that carry over for years. How to be sure this doesn't happen in your family...

DEALING WITH 20-SOMETHINGS

Twenty-somethings aren't really selfish. It's just that they are busy trying out who they are and they aren't terribly interested in what's up with you. The major task they face in this decade is to establish a strong identity in the world of adults. Their idea of being an adult, though, doesn't jibe much with yours—responsibility and a forward career track are not what they are cultivating, thank-you, even though they may worry about it. Don't take it personally that they don't want to be like you. It simply reflects their need to declare their own identity—and it isn't going to be conservative and stodgy like yours.

What you need: Patience...lots of it. One day your son informs you that he plans to get his PhD in philosophy, a few months later he's going to be a rock singer. Count on a number of surprising turn-arounds before your 20-something finds what he really wants to do.

Helpful: Understand that you don't take up much room in your 20-something's life. While he/she might be willing to spend time with you occasionally, don't expect to be pals as you may have been before. Your kids will give you snippets of information, seldom the full story. And they don't want your advice unless they specifically ask.

Don't get sucked into fearing that your child's far-out ideas will become lifelong paths. You don't want to overreact—the worst thing you can do with your kids now. Be empathetic and give praise whenever you have the chance—these are hard years for your kids. Keep any criticism and opinions to yourself as your kids struggle to find their way.

Safe at Home

Chapter 19

How to Protect Your Family Against Food-Borne Bacteria

Despite recent concern over the pesticide residues on produce, the most serious threat from the foods we eat continues to come from bacteria.

Most cases of food-borne illness resolve on their own after a few days. But E. coli and certain other especially virulent bacteria can be deadly.

At special risk: People under age five or over age 80...pregnant women...individuals with AIDS, Hodgkin lymphoma, leukemia or another immune system disease...chemotherapy patients...transplant recipients...and people who take antacids on

David Acheson, MD, chief medical officer, Office of Science, Center for Food Safety and Applied Nutrition, Food and Drug Administration, Washington, DC, and director of the Food Safety Initiative at New England Medical Center in Boston. He is coauthor of *Safe Eating: Protect Yourself and Your Family Against Deadly Bacteria.* Dell.

a regular basis. Reduced stomach acid means a more hospitable environment for bacteria.

Bacteria cannot be completely eliminated from the foods we eat. *But by avoiding these eight common mistakes when handling and preparing foods, the risk can be minimized...*

Mistake: Not washing fruits and vegetables. Thoroughly rinsing raw produce in cold water protects you not only against bacteria, but also against pesticide residues. Most pesticides are water-soluble.

How long should produce be washed? A few seconds helps a bit, but a full minute is better. That's especially true if you're preparing food for someone at risk for food-borne illness.

Be sure to wash the *entire* fruit or vegetable, including the end opposite the stem. That's a favorite hiding place of bacteria.

Washing is unnecessary for bananas and other fruits that are peeled before being eaten—unless you slice them with the skin intact.

Berries—especially raspberries and strawberries—require special care. Before rinsing them, soak them in a bowl of cold water for five minutes.

Also: Be sure to wash fruit before leaving it out in a bowl. Otherwise, people are likely to grab something and assume that it's already been washed.

Caution: Organic produce needs rinsing, too. True, organic produce contains no pesticide residues. But because manure is often used in organic farming, the bacterial risk may actually be greater with organic produce than with ordinary produce.

Mistake: Mishandling meat and poultry. The juices that collect inside plastic-wrapped packages of meat and poultry often contain high levels of disease-causing bacteria.

If you find that a package is leaking when you arrive home, carefully pour the juices down the drain.

Once you've gotten rid of the juices, promptly cook the meat or transfer it to a plastic container for refrigeration.

Carefully mop up any spilled juice with a dilute bleach solution and paper towels. Then wash your hands in warm, soapy water.

Good news: Any bacteria present in meat or poultry can be killed by cooking it at 325° F until no pink remains.

Mistake: Refrigerating fresh meat, poultry and fish in close proximity to produce. To keep uncooked meat, fish and poultry from spreading bacteria to produce, designate one compartment of your refrigerator "meat" and another "produce."

Caution: Frozen meat, fish or poultry should never be defrosted at room temperature. Let it thaw gradually in the refrigerator...or quickly in the microwave.

Leftovers should be covered when refrigerated, although the covering need not be airtight.

Mistake: Eating raw oysters, clams or other shellfish. During summer months, a majority of Gulf oysters carry traces of *Vibrios*, a family of bacteria that can cause a nasty gastrointestinal infection.

Mistake: Drinking unpasteurized apple juice or cider. These beverages are often contaminated with *Listeria monocytogenes* or another bacterium.

It's safest to buy only pasteurized juice or cider and to keep it refrigerated at all times. Discard it as soon as it reaches the "use by" date printed on the container.

People with reduced immunity should avoid unpasteurized dairy products, too.

Mistake: Leaving cooked foods out at room temperature for extended periods. If you cook a meal and then let it sit at room temperature for two hours or more, you're providing an ideal environment for bacterial growth.

Bacteria thrive at temperatures between 40° and 140° F.

For absolute safety, keep cooked foods at a temperature of at least 140° F while waiting to serve them. Use an electric warming plate or a sterno can...or just keep the food in the oven on low heat.

Mistake: Eating raw eggs. Since eggs are occasionally contaminated with salmonella, they should be eaten only after being cooked to the point where the yolks are no longer runny.

Cooked eggs should be eaten as soon as possible…and left out at room temperature for no more than two hours.

Mistake: Not washing your hands and cooking utensils often enough. Always wash your hands in warm, soapy water before and after handling produce…and before and after handling meat, poultry, eggs or seafood.

Wash any utensils with which these foods come in contact…and any countertops, cutting boards or surfaces the foods have touched.

Since sponges quickly become reservoirs for bacterial infection, it's best to stick with paper towels.

If you insist on using a sponge, clean it after each use with warm, soapy water. Once a day, sterilize it by dousing it with boiling water or a mild bleach solution…or microwaving it on high for one minute.

Handle Food with Care

The leading cause of food-borne illness is not salmonella. It is a bacterium found in poultry called *Campylobacter*. This organism causes four million infections in the US every year. It is little known because it does not cause large outbreaks. Usually only three or fewer people get sick at a time, and they recover within one week with no special treatment. *Self-defense:* Carefully follow safe handling and cooking practices.

Kaye Wachsmuth, retired deputy administrator, office of public health and science, Food Safety and Inspection Service, US Department of Agriculture, Washington, DC.

MAIL-ORDER MEDICINE SELF-DEFENSE

Be sure medication does not sit in your mailbox during hot weather.

Temperatures of the boxes in which medicine is shipped can easily rise above 100°— possibly affecting some medications.

Compare the date on the package with the date you received it—medicine should not take more than four days to reach you. Inspect medicine promptly—if it seems discolored or damaged, call the pharmacy.

Ask your doctor or pharmacist if a particular drug is very heat-sensitive. If it is, consider buying it locally during hot weather.

Claudia Okeke, PhD, researcher, US Pharmacopeia, Rockville, MD.

Safe Food-Storage Guidelines

Eggs usually stay fresh for three weeks after the date of purchase—do not store on the refrigerator door. *Yogurt* stays fresh two weeks past the date of purchase if unopened. *Hard cheese* stays fresh for six months if unopened—two to three weeks if opened. *Mayonnaise* stays fresh for two months after the jar is opened if refrigerated. *Freshly sliced lunch meats* like ham, turkey and roast beef should be eaten in three to five days.

Bessie Berry, manager, USDA Meat & Poultry Hotline, provides information on safe food handling and food labeling, Washington, DC, 888-674-6854.

Safer Homes

Make sure your home is easy to spot in case police or emergency medical service personnel are called for an emergency. Mark your house with large, reflective numbers and/or paint your house number on the curb with fluorescent paint. Trim any foliage that might obscure your address. Turn on all of the lights—including your porch light. Have someone stand out front to wave down the ambulance.

Peter Canning, EMT–P (emergency medical technician–paramedic) in Hartford, CT. He is author of *Paramedic: On the Front Lines of Medicine.* Fawcett Ivy.

Frozen Lock Trick

Thaw a frozen door lock by heating the key with a match or a cigarette lighter. Use pliers to hold the key. If close to an electrical outlet at home, aim a handheld hair dryer at the frozen lock. Or spray lock de-icer into the key opening. *To prevent locks from freezing:* Periodically lubricate locks with an approved lock lubricant.

The Family Handyman Simple Car Care & Repair by **Gary Havens,** editor, *The Family Handyman.* Reader's Digest.

How to Handle Dangerous Cords

Worst electrical danger to kids age 12 or younger: *Electrical cords.* Cords are more than twice as likely to cause injury as outlets. *Trap:* Young children bite them. The danger increases as cords age, wear or become damaged. *Self-defense:* Actively search for and throw out old, frayed or damaged cords. Carefully supervise young children around wires. Teach older children how to use electrical appliances and cords safely.

Rob Sheridan, MD, assistant chief of staff, Shriners Burn Hospital, Boston, whose study of electrical injuries was published in the *Archives of Pediatric and Adolescent Medicine.*

WASH THAT SPONGE

Loofah sponges can harbor skin-irritating bacteria. If you use one or any other natural sponge, be sure to disinfect it occasionally. One minute in diluted bleach works well.

Soap Traps

Antibacterial soap traps: They generally cost more than regular soap…kill beneficial bacteria that protect against germs…and can chafe sensitive skin. They are ineffective against viruses. *Best:* Thoroughly scrub hands with regular soap and tepid water for about 30 seconds.

Gary Noskin, MD, associate professor of medicine, Division of Infectious Diseases, Northwestern University Medical School, Chicago.

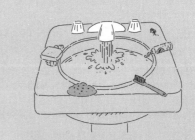

ANTIBACTERIAL AID

Antibacterial cleaners do not take the place of soap and water. Vigorous scrubbing followed by drying with a clean towel remains the most effective way of getting hands clean. But antibacterial products can be helpful when water is not available. *Example:* After eating a fast-food lunch in the car or after changing a baby's diaper at a place where washing up is not practical.

Michael Parry, MD, director of infectious diseases, Stamford Hospital, Stamford, CT.

SAFER SUMMER COOKOUTS

Buy perishable foods last when shopping—and put them away first. If food is frozen, defrost food in the refrigerator, not on a counter. Wash hands well with soap and hot water when handling raw food. Cook hamburger until the center is brown and juices run clear. Do not baste meat with its marinade. Do not taste food until it is thoroughly cooked. Wash all produce—even if it has a peel or rind you throw away.

Julie Miller Jones, PhD, professor of nutrition, College of St. Catherine, St. Paul, MN, and author of *Food Safety.* Eagan Press.

What You Need to Know About Gas Ranges

Gas cooking may play a role in childhood asthma, hay fever and eczema. In a study, these conditions were far more prevalent among children who lived in homes with gas ranges than in homes with electric ranges. Affected children who live in homes with gas ranges should be kept out of the kitchen during meal preparation. If this strategy fails, it may be necessary to switch to an electric range.

Torsten Schäfer, MD, MPH, research assistant, department of dermatology and allergy, Munich Technical University, Munich, Germany. His study of 4,000 German children was presented at a meeting of the World Congress of Health and the Urban Environment in Madrid.

Important Fact About Residential Fires

Seven out of 10 residential fire deaths occur in homes without a working smoke detector. Eighty-eight percent of the homes in a survey had a detector, but in 23% of these detectors the batteries were missing or dead.

Ruth A. Shults, MPH, epidemiologist, National Center for Injury Prevention and Control, Atlanta. Her study of smoke detectors was published in the *American Journal of Preventive Medicine,* 5500 Campanile Dr., San Diego 92182.

Fireplace Safety

For added fireplace safety in a new, tightly constructed home that has gas heat and gas hot water, open a window a crack while burning a fire. If no window is open, the air going up the fireplace flue can create negative pressure inside the house compared to the air outdoors—causing outside air to be pulled down the flue of the furnace or water heater. This is known as *backdrafting* and can prevent dangerous carbon monoxide from venting safely. Opening a window slightly helps the fireplace draw better, reducing the danger.

Stephen Elder, home inspector and home-repair columnist, Pittsboro, NC.

CHECK FOR CARBON MONOXIDE

Beware: Many carbon monoxide (CO) detectors often remain silent, even when CO levels are high. *Self-defense:* Have your furnace and heating ducts inspected annually...and install a CO detector bearing the Underwriters Laboratories label. *Good news:* New alarm standards should result in better detectors.

Ken Giles, US Consumer Product Safety Commission, Washington, DC.

How to Protect Your Home From Liability Risks

William E. Bailey, an insurance-law attorney and liability-policy specialist in private practice in Boston.

As a home owner, you are liable if guests are accidentally injured on your property. *How to improve the safety of guests and reduce your liability risk...*

ACTIVE KIDS

When you invite young children to your house, assume they will be running around. You are liable if a child is injured on your property or by items left on your property.

Safer: As guests arrive, tell them where children may play and the areas that are off-limits. Ask all adults to keep an eye on kids and alert you if children are behaving recklessly.

While it is essential to make it impossible for children to access hazards on your property—such as equipment, tools or a swimming pool—make sure there are activities to keep children busy and away from trouble.

Better: Appoint several guests to take turns keeping children together and safe.

INTOXICATION

At summer parties, people tend to drink more beer and wine than they should.

You may be liable if you didn't try to stop an intoxicated guest from driving and he or she is involved in an accident.

Safer: Publicly urge all guests to refrain from drinking too much. In cases where a guest has had too much, publicly insist that the guest be driven

home by another guest. If the guest refuses, call a taxi, or have the guest stay over.

PETS THAT BITE

You are liable if your pet bites or scratches a guest. If your pet might be trouble in any way, especially with children, put it in a room or bring it to a kennel for the day. Also make sure all guests are clear on what they may and may not do with your pets.

TAINTED FOOD

Hot temperatures accelerate the growth of bacteria in food and on the surfaces it touches.

Basics: Keep food wrapped and in the refrigerator until ready to be cooked or served. Always clean your grill before cooking a new meal. Clean cutting boards especially well, too. Never serve rare meat—it might contain illness-causing E. coli bacteria.

PROTECTION

An "umbrella personal liability policy" can protect you from a lawsuit that could devastate your assets and income.

How it works: Umbrella insurance kicks in after the liability coverage from other policies is consumed. Most people buy umbrella coverage from the agent who handles their homeowner's and/or auto insurance policies.

Consult your agent to determine the amount of coverage that is best for you.

Most agents recommend coverage of $1 million or more. To obtain the lowest annual price, ask for price quotes from several providers.

Annual premiums: Prices should run $150 and up for a $1 million policy...$250 and up for a $2 million policy...and up to $500 for a $5 million policy.

Cleaning Strategies to Simplify Your Life

Louise Rafkin, who has cleaned houses in the Cape Cod area for many years. She is author of *Other People's Dirt: A Housekeeper's Curious Adventures.* Plume.

▓ Vacuum—don't dust.

Dusting just moves dirt around.

Better: Buy the best vacuum you can with a variety of dusting nozzles that have horsehair bristles.

My favorite: The Miele Blue Moon by Best Vacuum, Inc., with an 1,100-watt motor and a HEPA Active Filter. 888-205-3228.

KITCHEN

▓ Clean the microwave.

Spray the inside with a cleanser such as Simple Green (available in most hardware stores) or another nontoxic, all-purpose cleanser that breaks up grease and food particles easily.

Then wipe with a rag.

To remove smells such as burnt popcorn from the microwave, use a saucer of water and a few tablespoons of red or white vinegar. Set the time for about one minute—or wait until the mixture splatters—and wipe down with a rag.

▓ Mop with an easy-to-use, dense sponge mop.

The less you bend, the easier it feels to clean.

▓ Use a soapy toothbrush instead of a sponge or rag for hard-to-reach areas, such as the knobs on the stove.

Other great places to use a toothbrush: The rubber gasket seal on the refrigerator door, the number buttons on the telephone, the hinges on the toilet seat lid and the ridge where the kitchen sink attaches to the countertop.

BATHROOM

▓ Cleaner shower tiles.

Spray paper towels with a heavy-duty tub-and-tile cleanser.

Tamp the soaked towels onto the dry shower wall for 15 minutes. They will loosen dirt and scum and whiten grout between tiles. Wipe and rinse thoroughly.

▓ Clean fixtures with a polish, such as Star Brite Marine Polish or Flitz, to make them shine.

Available at most hardware stores.

TALKING TAPE MEASURE

Measure windows, doors, etc....then record their dimensions using the built-in voice recorder. Just press the button to play back. Measures up to 25 feet...records up to 20 seconds.

Zircon, 1580 Dell Ave., Campbell, CA 95008. 800-245-9265. Item #554298.

Best Home Water Filters...They're Very Important Now

Richard P. Maas, PhD, professor of environmental studies at University of North Carolina, Asheville. He is codirector of the university's Environmental Quality Institute, a leading center for research on tap-water purity.

With regular news reports about water contamination—even in the best communities—more and more people are turning to home water filters to protect their families' health.

DETERMINE YOUR NEEDS

To choose the best filter for you, have your tap water tested.

Larger water utilities are now required to send an annual report to customers with the results of tests for approximately 80 different contaminants.

If you have well water—or if you don't want to wait for your water company's report—look in the *Yellow Pages* under "Water Testing" or "Laboratories—Testing." Test price depends on what contaminants you look for. The range is wide—between $17 and $800. The most likely contaminant is lead (20% of US households), which can be picked up by the household plumbing system.

Clean Water Lead Testing (828-251-6800) provides a two-sample, mail-in test (first drawn and after running water for one minute). *Warning:* Home testing kits may be unreliable.

CARAFE FILTERS

Water flows by gravity, and there's plenty of the filtering medium with which it interacts to remove lead, reduce chlorine byproducts and improve taste and smell.

Drawbacks: Slow...holds only two to three quarts...filters must be changed often, generally every 50 to 100 gallons, depending on the level of contaminants in the water.

Top carafe filter: Pur Pitcher CR-800. Half-gallon pitcher uses carbon and an active agent to improve water taste while reducing levels of lead, chlorine, copper and zinc. Safety gauge indicates when filter needs replacing. *Replacement filters:* 800-787-5463.

FAUCET-MOUNTED

Inexpensive (less than $100)...easy to install and change filters.

Drawbacks: Units are small, and water pressure forces water through the filter too quickly to thoroughly remove all impurities.

Top faucet filter: Pur Plus FM-9000. Removes microorganisms, such as giardia and cryptosporidium, as well as contaminants, including lead, chlorine and mercury. Automatic shut-off stops water flow when filter needs replacing. Filters last for 100 gallons. 800-787-5463.

UNDER-SINK FILTER

Contains a reservoir so water has more time to pass through the filtering mechanism...long-lasting filters.

Drawbacks: Costs $100 or more...may require a plumber for installation.

WHOLE-HOUSE FILTER

For homes on well water and not connected to a municipal water system.

Contains sophisticated filtering material tailored to meet the home's specific needs—removes hardness...neutralizes water...removes bacteria. Filtered water is supplied to the whole house, including taps, showers and washing machine.

Drawbacks: Expensive ($1,000 to $3,000 installed plus filtering materials)...requires monthly maintenance—changing filters and/or adding filtering materials.

There is no *best* whole-house system—it depends on your water-treatment goals. Leading manufacturers include Culligan, Flek and Hauge. The company that services your well can provide guidance following a comprehensive water test. Or look in the *Yellow Pages* under "Water Purification & Filtration Equipment."

Risks of Power Lawn Mowers

Faster than a speeding bullet—stones and other small "missiles" can be kicked up by power lawn mowers. In a recent accident, a piece of cyclone fencing pierced a major blood vessel in a four-year-old boy. *Self-defense:* Clear debris from the lawn before mowing...keep blades sharp so equipment can be used at low speed...wear protective glasses and shoes...make sure people stay at least 10 *yards* away...keep children off mowers.

Scott Zietlow, MD, associate professor of surgery at the Mayo Clinic College of Medicine in Rochester, MN.

Cat Bite Alert

About 80% of cat bites become infected—because of germs that cats carry in their mouths. Hand bites are especially dangerous. *Self-defense:* See a doctor—or go to an emergency room—as soon as possible after a cat bites you. *Interesting:* Only 5% of dog bites become infected.

Jay Siwek, MD, professor of family medicine, Georgetown University Medical Center, Washington, DC.

A PET SAFETY CONCERN

Danger: Pets ingest antifreeze—or other toxic substances such as motor oil...gasoline ...paint...paint thinner—when they step in a spill and then lick their feet. One tablespoon of antifreeze can cause irreversible kidney damage in an average-sized dog. *Extra measure of caution:* Consider buying the antifreeze Sierra, available in many hardware stores, which is less toxic to pets.

Peter Eeg, DVM, veterinarian in private practice, in Poolesville, MD.

PET FENCES

Invisible fences—to keep pets from straying—are rarely effective for long. Most animals quickly learn that the brief punishment—an electric shock or high-pitched squeal—is worth the lure of freedom. *Exception:* The fences may work for small dogs and for those with less assertive temperaments. *Also:* Such fences can make a dog neurotic and fearful if, for example, it receives a painful shock while running to greet you.

No More Myths: The Facts About Pet Care by **Stefanie Schwartz, DVM.** Grammercy Books. She is a veterinarian and pet behavior consultant, Brookline, MA.

Dog Bite Prevention

Never pet an unfamiliar animal unless the owner is there and gives permission. Allow the dog to smell your hand in a nonthreatening way first. Don't play with a dog that is eating, sleeping or nursing puppies. Dogs with something in their mouths should be left alone—even if they are usually friendly. When playing fetch, let the dog take the lead. Instead of taking a toy out of its mouth, wait for the dog to drop it.

Mark Stegelman, MD, pediatrician, Atlanta.

Better Dog Training

To train dogs more effectively: Use a "wrong-behavior signal"—a simple signal like the word *wrong*—whenever the animal behaves unacceptably. Then have a short time-out by ignoring the dog for about 15 seconds.

Gary Wilkes, animal-behavior specialist from Mesa, AZ, writing in *Dog Fancy*, Three Burroughs, Irvine, CA 92618.

HOW TO DESENSITIZE YOUR DOG TO LOUD NOISES

Desensitize dogs to loud noises by exposing them to the sounds on purpose—at low but ever-increasing volume. *Example:* Play a recording that sounds like thunder at a very low volume. As long as the dog stays calm, reinforce its behavior with toys or treats. Build volume gradually until the dog is unaffected by full-volume playback. *Helpful:* For dogs frightened by thunder—the most common noise phobia—try this technique during the winter, when natural thunderstorms are rare. This prevents real thunder from interfering with carefully planned training.

Linda Ross, DVM, associate professor, small animal medicine, Tufts University School of Veterinary Medicine, 200 Westboro Rd., North Grafton, MA 01536.

The Perils of Overpampering Your Dog

Nicholas Dodman, BVMS, director of the Animal Behavior Clinic at Tufts University School of Veterinary Medicine, North Grafton, MA, and author of *The Dog Who Loved Too Much: Tales, Treatments, and the Psychology of Dogs.* Bantam Books.

Just as giving in to your toddler's every whim can produce bad behavior, so too can giving in to your dog's.
Some of the most common errors people make in pampering their dogs…

■ **Responding to your dog's every wish.**
Certain breeds—such as rottweilers, cocker spaniels, springer spaniels, Akitas, shih tzus and chow chows—have a high proportion of dogs with dominant traits.

Such dogs tend to view overly permissive owners as weak. Instead of returning their owner's kindness, their natural instinct is to take the dominant position as "leader of the pack." The more indulgent the owner becomes, the more aggressive and willful the dog becomes.

Solution: Positively reinforce desired behaviors and ignore unwanted behaviors. Give one-word commands, such as *sit, come* or *down*, and reward timely and accurate responses with immediate praise and a brief petting under the chin and in the chest area. Avoid confrontations and rough play, both of which increase the dog's aggressiveness by making it feel challenged.

■ **Allowing a dog to become totally dependent on you.**
Dogs who begin life in a pound, puppy mill or pet store, where human contact is limited, are prone to separation anxiety.

When kindly owners adopt them, they bond so strongly that they feel sheer panic when separated from the owners. In their panic, they may refuse to eat—or may destroy their surroundings.

Solution: Build your dog's confidence in being left alone by helping it become more independent. Have it sleep in its own bed rather than with you. Teach it to lie in its bed or play with a toy when you're home rather than following you around every minute. Have it sit and stay while you move progressively farther away. Distract it with a food treat, such as a large bone, that will hold its attention before, during and after your departure.

■ Overfeeding your dog—or feeding it the wrong type of diet for its activity level.

Overweight dogs are susceptible to the same health problems as overweight humans.

Feeding a high-performance type of food to a dog with a relatively inactive lifestyle can cause it to become hyperactive and exacerbate existing behavior problems.

Solution: Consult your veterinarian for the diet that is best for your dog—taking into account its age, health history and level of exercise.

■ Allowing your dog to lead a sedentary life.

Many people feel that a walk around the block provides sufficient daily exercise for their dogs.

For optimum health, all dogs should get at least 20 to 30 minutes of aerobic exercise daily—unless there is a medical reason that prevents it. Simply putting them outside isn't enough because they won't push themselves.

Solution: If you're a runner, take your dog along. If this isn't an option, take the dog outdoors and throw a ball for it to fetch—not allowing it to rest in between throws. Keep the dog moving vigorously for at least 20 to 30 minutes.

■ Dressing your dog up in designer dog clothes.

Some clothing can be helpful to extremely thin-coated breeds when they are outdoors in the winter.

But dressing a dog because you think it is funny or cute doesn't benefit the dog in any way and only makes it feel helpless when it can't get the clothing off.

WINTER WOES FOR CITY DOGS

Winter dangers to city dogs: Ice, salt and commercial de-icers. Dogs can be poisoned when they lick ice-melting products off their feet. Ice itself can bond to the hair on dogs' feet and make them red, swollen and irritated. *Self-defense:* Keep hair between dogs' toes well groomed. Put petroleum jelly on a dog's foot pads to keep ice from sticking to the hair. Keep baby wipes by the door to wipe the dog's feet right after a walk. Consider buying dog boots for full protection—many dogs accept them if they are introduced gradually.

Minott Pruyn, DVM, Pruyn Veterinary Hospital, Missoula, MT, quoted in *Dog Fancy,* Three Burroughs, Irvine, CA 92618.

How to Know if a Puppy Is Healthy

To choose a healthy puppy, look for eyes that are clear, bright and expressive...strong, symmetrical body...ears that are clean and free of discharge or foul odor...nose that is cold and wet, but not running...pink gums and white teeth...clean, shiny fur that does not shed much when stroked...effortless, enthusiastic walking and running.

The Complete Dog Owner's Manual by **Amy Marder, VMD.** Chain Sales. She is vice president of behavioral medicine, ASPCA.

WISE WINTER HABITS FOR DOG OWNERS

▶ **Protect pets in winter:** Keep poisonous holiday plants—holly and poinsettias—out of animals' reach.

▶ **When walking your dog at night,** wear a reflector vest and keep the animal on a short leash.

▶ **Keep pets—especially older ones—indoors as much as possible** to avoid frostbite and hypothermia.

▶ **Keep towels handy** to dry pets as soon as they come back inside.

▶ **Be sure to wipe any road salt from an animal's paws,** so the salt doesn't get licked off and ingested.

▶ **Keep hair between foot pads trimmed** to avoid the formation of ice balls.

▶ **Use a sweater** to keep very young, very old, chronically ill or short-haired dogs warm when outside.

Laura Salter, VSA director, World Society for the Protection of Animals, 34 Deloss St., Framingham, MA 01702.

Pretest a Pet

Before buying a dog, call a pet-owning friend and ask if you can borrow his or her animal on a weekend "test-drive." This will give you the opportunity to learn if your family is ready for the rigors and responsibilities of dog ownership.

Ilene Raymond, freelance writer whose family decided not to buy a dog, writing in *Family Fun*, 114 Fifth Ave., New York City 10011.

Healthy Travels

Chapter 20

Travel and Your Health Insurance

Always check with your health maintenance organization (HMO) about health insurance coverage before you go away for more than a day or two.

Don't ask your doctor—call the member services department of your HMO and ask about out-of-area coverage.

Get the name of an appropriate physician at your destination and a toll-free number you can use to call your HMO directly in an emergency.

Important: Always write down *whom* you spoke to…*what* was said…and *when* you spoke.

If you are going abroad: Be prepared to pay up front—cash or credit card—for any medical services, and seek HMO reimbursement later.

Vincent Riccardi, MD, president of American Medical Consumers, a membership organization supplying information, advice and advocacy to users and providers of medical services, 5415 Briggs Ave., La Crescenta, CA 91214.

Better Fitness While Traveling

Take a jump rope…a stretchy elastic rubber band that works with resistance…and a long rubber tube with handles on each end. All are available at sports stores. *Warm-up:* Jump rope lightly in your hotel room. *Arms and shoulders:* Sit in a chair. Place one end of the band in each hand…raise hands so they are in front of your face, with arms extended…pull the band out to the sides, then  back in. *Biceps:* Stay seated…put one foot on the rubber tube…with palms up, elbows at sides, pull handles up toward shoulders. Repeat each exercise 12 to 15 times. *Legs:* Climb stairs—two at a time going up, one at a time going down.

Patrick Netter, independent sports and fitness equipment consultant, 2461 Santa Monica Blvd., Santa Monica, CA 90404.

MEDICAL TRAVEL KIT BASICS

Many drugs and medical supplies common in the US are hard to find abroad—so carry your own kit. *Include:* Bandages, gauze, first-aid tape, thermometer, topical antibiotic ointments and steroid creams, anti-inflammatory drugs such as aspirin and ibuprofen, oral decongestants, sunscreen with SPF of 15 or more and nonprescription motion-sickness and diarrheal remedies.

Gary Barnas, MD, associate professor of medicine, Medical College of Wisconsin, Milwaukee.

Which Backpack Is Right for You?

A better backpack for your back is one with an external frame. Many hikers prefer internal-frame packs, which offer more stability and freedom of movement than external-frame packs. But the construction of internal-frame packs makes you bend forward at the hips—causing some people to tire easily and suffer back strain.

Tom Shealey, editor, *Backpacker*, 33 E. Minor St., Emmaus, PA 18098.

Side Effect of Diarrhea Treatment

Antibiotics used to treat traveler's diarrhea can also cause swelling and pain in the Achilles tendon. Tendinitis has been added to the warning labels on Cipro, Floxin and other fluoroquinolone antibiotics. Contact a physician if you experience swollen tendons while taking any of these drugs.

Susan Cruzan, Food and Drug Administration, Rockville, MD.

MOUNTAIN VACATIONS

Ascend gradually to high elevations to avoid mountain sickness. The body needs a few days to get used to the lower oxygen levels at higher elevations. If you feel faint, disoriented or nauseated, try *pursed-lip breathing*—take a deep breath, and breathe out slowly through lips that are slightly parted. This will open or keep inflated more areas of your lungs. Drink plenty of fluids. Ask your doctor about taking the prescription drug Diamox (*acetazolamide*) to relieve queasiness.

Allen Cymerman, PhD, chief, Altitude Physiology and Medicine Division, US Army Research Institute of Environmental Medicine, Natick, MA.

Better Eating On the Road

At fast-food restaurants, buy a grilled chicken sandwich without mayonnaise. Avoid sauces, gravies, butter and other fatty toppings and dressings. Use mustard or salsa as condiments. Be sure to get at least half the day's food from breakfast and lunch. Eat less in restaurants—most portions are twice what you need. When going out for a big meal, eat vegetarian the rest of the day.

Georgia Kostas, RD, nutrition director of Cooper Clinic at the Cooper Aerobics Center, Dallas.

Take Care of Dental Necessities

Before going abroad, you should have a dental exam. Obtaining dental care in a foreign country can be very tricky. Have your teeth cleaned and checked for cavities...and your fillings checked for secure fit.

Tips for the Savvy Traveler by **Deborah Burns,** travel writer based in Williamstown, MA, who has circled the globe and visited every state in the US. Storey Communications.

International Travel Know-How

Stuart R. Rose, MD, director of the International Travel Clinic at Noble Hospital in Westfield, MA, and president of Travel Medicine, a travel-oriented publishing and mail-order company in Northampton, MA. He is author of *International Travel Health Guide.* Travel Medicine.

These days, travelers are vulnerable to everything from infectious diseases to terrorism, as demonstrated by the recent SARS scare.

Here are the most significant threats travelers now face—and how to guard against them on your next trip abroad...

MOTOR VEHICLE ACCIDENTS

You may be surprised to learn that infectious diseases, such as malaria, account for only 1% of deaths among international travelers. Nowadays, the biggest danger to Americans abroad is accidental injury, especially from motor vehicle accidents.

You already know how important it is to wear seat belts. *Here are some other ways to minimize your risk of being injured or killed in an accident...*

▶ **Don't drive at night in rural areas.**

▶ **Don't ride a motorcycle, moped or bicycle—** even if you feel comfortable riding one at home.

▶ **Don't accept a ride in an overcrowded bus or other vehicle.**

▶ **Bring a car seat for any infant traveling with you.**

If you hire a guide or driver, don't hesitate to tell him or her to slow down—and drive cautiously.

If you plan to rent a car, go for the biggest car you can afford. The bigger the car, the greater the protection it affords occupants in case of a collision.

Make sure you can decipher road signs and traffic patterns in the country you'll be visiting.

Helpful resource: The Association for Safe International Road Travel in Potomac, Maryland, 301-983-5252, *www.asirt.org.* This not-for-profit organization will send you a report on road safety and driving conditions in over 150 foreign countries.

FIRES AND VIOLENT CRIME

Aircraft crashes, homicides and fires—along with drownings—account for most of the other deaths among Americans abroad. One way to protect yourself from these threats is to avoid regions in which drug trafficking is a problem. *Other ways...*

▶ **Avoid small airlines or charter flights in undeveloped nations.**

▶ **Don't travel alone or outside urban areas at night.**

▶ **Don't hitchhike—or pick up hitchhikers.**

▶ **Don't sleep in a vehicle that is parked along the road.**

▶ **If possible, book your hotel room between the second and seventh floors.** That's high enough to prevent easy access by intruders... yet low enough for fire equipment to reach you.

If you're planning a trip to a region troubled by violence or political instability, contact the US State Department before your departure. Experts at the Department's Bureau of Consular Affairs can alert you to crime, terrorism or other concerns in more than 200 countries.

The Department can be reached at *http://travel. state.gov...*via telephone at 202-647-5225.

If terrorism is a concern, do not wear expensive clothing...and don't wear or carry any item with a corporate logo or another detail that marks you as an American.

LYME DISEASE

This tick-borne illness occurs throughout Canada, Europe, Asia and the US.

It's a good idea to avoid ticks if possible. This means wearing long-sleeved shirts and long pants tucked into socks whenever you venture outdoors in an area where Lyme is a problem. Light-colored clothes make it easier to spot the ticks, which are dark.

Spray clothes with the insecticide *permethrin* (Duranon). Treat exposed skin with a bug repellent containing at least 20% DEET.

Caution: If you develop symptoms of Lyme, see a doctor, who should prescribe the appropriate antibiotics right away.

Lyme symptoms include fever, headache, muscle and joint aches, swollen glands, fatigue, nausea, loss of appetite and a circular, bull's-eye shaped, pink rash at the site of the tick bite.

Good news: The same precautions used to prevent Lyme disease also reduce your risk for malaria, dengue fever and other diseases transmitted by insects.

DIARRHEA AND HEPATITIS

Traveler's diarrhea and hepatitis A—a liver disorder that causes fever, fatigue and jaundice—are common diseases in countries that have poor sanitation.

To cut your risk for both diseases: When traveling in a region where sanitation conditions are questionable, drink only commercially bottled or packaged beverages…or water that's been boiled or chemically treated. Ice cubes are usually made from tap water, so it's best to avoid them.

Eat only well-cooked foods served hot. Avoid salads. Fruits and vegetables are okay only if you can peel them yourself. Don't eat food from street vendors.

If diarrhea strikes: Begin a three-day course of *ofloxacin* (Floxin) right away. It's best to get a supply of this prescription drug before departure and take it along.

For fastest relief of diarrhea, take two tablets of *loperamide* (Imodium AD) along with the first dose of ofloxacin.

For total protection against hepatitis A, you should ask your doctor about getting the *Havrix* or VAQTA vaccine at least three weeks before your departure. This is generally a good idea for all international travelers over age two who are headed to any foreign country outside Canada, Western Europe, Australia, New Zealand or Japan.

EMERGENCY EVACUATION

If you need sophisticated medical treatment in a hurry, a travel health insurance policy that arranges and pays for an air ambulance can save your life.

Two reputable companies: International SOS Assistance—800-523-8662, *www.international sos.com*…and Worldwide Assistance Services—800-777-8710, *www.worldwideassistance.com.*

TRAVELING TRANSLATOR

This helpful gadget ectronically converts seven languages (French, German, Italian, Polish, Portuguese, Russian, Spanish) to and from English. Also converts foreign currency…measurements into metric…temperatures from Fahrenheit to Celsius. Fits in shirt pocket. Comes with batteries and case.

Travel Smart, Box 397, Dobbs Ferry, NY 10522.

HOW TO FIND A DOCTOR ABROAD

If you must seek care while abroad, insist on a doctor who speaks English. Otherwise the doctor may not understand you as you relate your medical history. *Helpful:* Call the American Embassy for a referral. The embassy keeps a list of reliable English-speaking doctors, clinics and hospitals. Ask where embassy personnel go when they get sick. Also, go to the largest private medical facility. A teaching hospital is best. You may have to wait hours for treatment at a public hospital. Be prepared to pay cash—though some large hospitals take credit cards. *Important:* Make sure medical personnel fill out your insurance forms in legible English.

Adam Stracher, MD, a faculty member in the division of international medicine and infectious diseases at Cornell University Medical College in New York, and a physician at New York Hospital's International Health Care Service.

All About Hepatitis A Vaccines

A hepatitis A vaccine gives longer-lasting protection than a shot of gamma-globulin, the traditional defense against this liver disease. The shot, made from the inactivated virus, is given four weeks before travel to regions where hepatitis A is common—including Africa, Asia (except Japan), Mediterranean countries and parts of the Caribbean. A booster shot is given six to 12 months later for long-term protection—10 or more years. Gamma-globulin is no longer available for this purpose.

William Kammerer, MD, consultant, division of executive and international medicine, Mayo Clinic, Jacksonville, FL.

Lyme Disease Self-Defense

Tuck pants into socks or boots, and tuck shirts into pants to keep out ticks ...apply insect repellents before venturing into wooded or bushy areas ...wear light-colored clothing to spot ticks easier ...wash clothing worn outdoors in hot water and dry at high temperature...clear brush and tall grass from around the house.

Allen Steere, MD, chief of rheumatology and immunology, New England Medical Center, Boston.

Protect Against Mosquito-Borne Diseases

Mosquito repellents also protect against mosquito-borne diseases like encephalitis and malaria. *Self-defense:* Use repellents containing 8% to 12% concentrations of DEET two to three times a day for children and concentrations of up to 35% only once a day for adults.

Davidson H. Hamer, MD, director, Travelers' Health Service, New England Medical Center, Boston.

Cruise Control

Plan ahead for medical emergencies on cruises. *Self-defense:* Before sailing, be sure the cruise line conforms to care guidelines from the International Council of Cruise Lines (*www.iccl.org*) and

TROPICAL TRAVEL AHEAD?

Before traveling to the tropics, consult with your physician about preventive measures for…

▶ **Malaria:** Prevalent in rural areas of Asia, Central and South America—especially dangerous in sub-Saharan Africa, even in cities. *Self-defense:* Pre-exposure drugs, such as chloroquine…DEET repellent on skin…permethrin insecticide on clothing.

▶ **Dengue fever:** Caribbean, Latin America, Southeast Asia, India, Africa. Disease has flu-like symptoms with a high fever and rash. *Self-defense:* Protect against mosquito bites—there is no vaccine.

▶ **Hepatitis A:** Risk in all underdeveloped countries. *Self-defense:* Get a hepatitis vaccine at least two weeks before travel.

▶ **Traveler's diarrhea:** High risk in all under-developed countries. *Self-defense:* Eat only well-cooked foods and drink only bottled water. Take along a standby antibiotic such as Floxin.

▶ **Other precautions:** Make sure all your routine vaccinations are up-to-date…buy a travel-insurance policy to cover emergency air ambulance evacuation.

Stuart Rose, MD, president, Travel Medicine, Inc., 351 Pleasant St., Northampton, MA 01060.

American College of Emergency Physicians (*www. acep.org*). If you have a preexisting condition, have your travel agent or the cruise line check the ability of the ship's infirmary to handle it. Find out what your insurance plan covers. If your coverage is inadequate, consider travel insurance.

Richard Coorsch, Health Insurance Association of America, 555 13th St. NW, #600 East, Washington, DC 20004.

Auto Life Saver

Always carry an object that is capable of breaking your car's window glass in case you get caught in a flash flood or drive into deep water.

Good choice: An automatic center punch, sold in any hardware store. The tool will break the glass simply by pressing the pointed end against the window. A tire iron, jack handle, heavy-duty flashlight or hammer will also do the job.

Helpful: Keep the object where it is readily accessible, such as in the glove compartment or taped under the driver's seat.

David Solomon, certified master auto technician and chairman, *Nutz & Boltz,* Box 123, Butler, MD 21023.

Reading and Riding

Forty percent of people who read while they ride in the car get carsick. *Reason:* The motion seen out of the corner of the eye confuses the brain, causing queasiness. *Helpful if you want to read and ride:* Sit in the front seat…turn away from the nearest window…shield your eyes from the view of the side window—or while facing straight ahead, hold the book up to eye level…keep your head as still as possible.

Roderic Gillilan, OD, optometrist in Eugene, OR, and spokesperson for The American Optometric Association, 243 N. Lindbergh Blvd., St. Louis, MO 63141.

Computing and Driving—No, No

Outrageous! Laptop-computer use while driving is on the rise. Some companies are actually selling hardware for mounting laptops next to the driver—or even on the steering wheel. *Bottom line:* Anything less than full-time driving is extremely dangerous.

Ricardo Martinez, MD, chairman, Safety Intelligence Systems Corp., Atlanta.

MUSIC MATTERS WHEN DRIVING

A car stereo can be very dangerous—or it can be a lifesaver. It depends on how loudly it is played. When music is played softly, reaction time is better than during silence. Drivers can brake more quickly and see items moving across their visual field slightly sooner. But when music is played loudly, drivers lose the ability to scan their environment effectively—they are much slower at spotting items coming into their peripheral vision. *Bottom line:* Keep the music level low when driving.

Helen Beh, PhD, professor of psychology, University of Sydney, Australia, whose study was reported at the Fifth European Congress of Psychology.

CHILD CAR SAFETY

Kids should never sit on pillows or cushions when riding in cars. *Reason:* If the car is hit, the child may slide out from under the seat belt.

Heather Paul, PhD, executive director, National SAFE KIDS Campaign, Washington, DC.

The Bigger the Better

Vehicle size is more important than antilock brakes or air bags when it comes to motorist safety. The bigger and heavier a car, the less likely its occupants are to be injured in a collision. *Trap:* Many people fail to consider vehicle size when shopping for a new car.

Frederick P. Rivara, MD, MPH, director, Harborview Injury Prevention and Research Center, Seattle.

Protect Your Head In the Car

Before buying a new car, check the built-in head restraints. The higher they are, the more protection they provide in a crash. When you drive, the headrest should reach as close to the top of your head as possible and touch the back of your head. *Best system:* Active head restraint/seat systems, available on some new BMWs and Saabs, which move to protect your head and neck in the event of a crash. *To protect yourself in your current car:* Adjust the headrest to make it high enough to touch the back of your head, but not your neck. Keep the seat back as close to vertical as possible. *Most at risk:* Tall people, whose heads roll back over the top of the restraints in a crash.

David Solomon, certified master auto technician and chairman, *Nutz & Boltz,*® Box 123, Butler, MD 21023.

Be Good to Your Back

Take care of your back on long car trips by using a lumbar support for your lower back. *Helpful:* Rolling up a towel and placing it in the small of your back. Stop every hour, walk around a rest area and do standing stretches to refresh back muscles. *Caution:* After a long drive, do not park and get your luggage immediately. Your back is fatigued and not ready to lift a full suitcase. Relax, walk around and wait a while before unloading your car.

Back in Shape by **Stephen Hochschuler, MD,** board-certified orthopedic surgeon specializing in spine surgery and cofounder, Texas Back Institute, Plano, TX. Houghton Mifflin.

Beat Jet Lag

Beat jet lag by adjusting eating and sleeping times to local schedules right away. If you arrive at night, go to sleep as soon as possible …if you arrive in the morning, stay awake until local bedtime. *Also:* Take a walk during daylight hours. Natural light helps your body clock adjust.

Bradley Connor, MD, medical director, Travel Health Services, 50 E. 69 St., New York City 10021.

Energy Boost

Before a meeting or other important event, take a nap for 45 minutes or less—this will make you more alert and improve your performance.

Drink caffeinated coffee 15 to 30 minutes before you need to be alert. Stay physically active—try taking a swim or brisk walk before an important event. Eat energy-boosting foods early in the day—such as poached eggs, grilled fish or low-fat cottage cheese or yogurt. Visualize alertness—using your mind can help you get through periods of tiredness.

Travel Fitness by **Bill Tulin, JD.** Human Kinetics. He is a San Francisco–based attorney, personal trainer and business executive who often flies more than 100,000 miles per year.

FLY SAFE

The safest seat on the plane is an aisle seat near an exit. The location of exits varies according to aircraft and carrier. When obtaining your advance seat assignment, ask the airline or travel agent where the exit rows are…and, if there is a last-minute equipment change, ask again.

Flying Blind, Flying Safe by **Mary Schiavo.** Harper-Collins. She is former inspector general, US Department of Transportation, and a licensed pilot.

Older and Wiser

Chapter 21

Beta-Carotene vs. Arthritis

Patients with rheumatoid arthritis have lower blood levels of beta-carotene—a powerful antioxidant. Low levels may increase the risk of contracting arthritis. *Foods with high beta-carotene levels:* Apricots...cantaloupe...carrots...pumpkin...spinach and other dark-green vegetables...and sweet potatoes.

George Comstock, MD, DrPH, professor of epidemiology, Johns Hopkins University School of Hygiene and Public Health, Baltimore, whose study of the relationship between beta-carotene levels and arthritis was published in the *Annals of the Rheumatic Diseases.*

Special "Senior" Formula Vitamins

Special "senior" formula vitamins offer little more than regular multivitamin/mineral supplements—even for those age 65 or older, we hear from Michael Hirt, MD. Formulas, such as Centrum Silver and Geritol Extend, may provide more B vitamins but hardly any additional amounts of other important vitamins and minerals, such as vitamin E and calcium. Seniors require more nutritional supplementation because of their decreased ability to absorb nutrients and their generally less nutritious diets. However, basic all-purpose multivitamins should be sufficient. They're less expensive, too.

Michael Hirt, MD, founder and medical director, Center for Integrative Medicine, Tarzana, CA.

Don't Be Deficient in B-12

Did you know that vitamin B-12 deficiency affects up to 20% of those over age 50? This is despite the fact that most people seem to be getting at least the recommended daily allowance of the vitamin (6 micrograms). As the body ages, the ability to absorb the vitamin from food declines. Deficiency can cause nerve damage, resulting in a tingling sensation, lack of balance, memory changes and disorientation. *Self-defense:* Take a daily multivitamin or eat a B-12–fortified breakfast cereal.

Robert M. Russell, MD, associate director, USDA Human Nutrition Research Center on Aging, Tufts University, Boston.

Vitamin E Slows Alzheimer's

Vitamin E slows progression of Alzheimer's disease. In a recent study, Alzheimer's patients who took 2,000 IU (international units) of the fat-soluble vitamin had marked delays in functional decline (defined as the time until "negative endpoints," such as nursing home placement or death), compared with those on a placebo. *Caution:* The usual recommended daily dosage for vitamin E is only 800 IU to 1,000 IU. Over time, high doses of vitamin E are presumed to accumulate in the body. The long-term effects of such an accumulation are unknown. Vitamin E should not be taken to prevent Alzheimer's.

Dorcas Dobie, MD, assistant professor of psychology and behavioral sciences, University of Washington, Seattle. Her study of 341 Alzheimer's patients was presented at a meeting on geriatric psychiatry sponsored by the University of San Diego.

GOOD ATTITUDE BEATS AGING

Feistiness makes dealing with aging easier. Old-fashioned psychological assertiveness can go a long way toward making it possible for people to stay mobile and take care of themselves as they age. Older people who are most likely to be self-sufficient have a commitment to independent living, a subjective belief in their own good health and a sense of mastery of life. *Bottom line:* A personal determination to stay independent can help overcome increasing physical frailty.

Elia Femia, project coordinator, Pennsylvania State University, University Park, whose study of more than 300 elderly individuals was published in the *Journal of Gerontology.*

A GOOD TRICK FOR BAD MEMORY

You can unstick your memory by distracting your brain. *Example:* If you lose your car keys, start counting by fives or saying the names of the states alphabetically. Then focus on your keys again. You should find them more easily—because your memory has continued searching for them while your conscious mind was doing something else.

Dharma Singh Khalsa, MD, president and medical director, Alzheimer's Prevention Foundation, Tucson, and author of *Brain Longevity.* Warner Books.

The Blood Pressure– Alzheimer's Connection

Untreated high blood pressure raises the risk for Alzheimer's disease. It's long been recognized that high systolic blood pressure (the upper number) raises the risk for dementia. A recent study found that the risk of developing Alzheimer's was 50% lower in individuals who were treated for their systolic hypertension than in individuals who went untreated.

Françoise Forette, MD, professor of internal medicine and geriatrics, University of Paris. Her two-year study of 2,418 elderly patients was published in *The Lancet,* 42 Bedford Sq., London WC1B 3SL.

Alzheimer's Relief

Alzheimer's patients who suffer from severe behavior problems can be calmed by using the antipsychotic drug *olanzapine* (Zyprexa). They should also suffer fewer delusions and hallucinations.

Bonus: Olanzapine is less likely than haloperidol (Haldol) and other commonly used antipsychotics to cause rigidity, tremor and restlessness. Plus, patients given olanzapine showed no deterioration in cognitive status.

Evan Collins, MD, assistant professor of psychiatry, University of Toronto Faculty of Medicine. His review of a study of 206 Alzheimer's patients was presented at a meeting of the European Federation of Neurological Societies.

How to Stop the Clock

Miriam E. Nelson, PhD, associate chief of the human physiology laboratory at Jean Mayer USDA Human Nutrition Center on Aging, Tufts University, Boston. She is author of *Strong Women Stay Young* (Bantam) and *Strong Women Stay Slim.*

Inactivity can cause men and women to lose significant amounts of muscle and bone mass by age 55. Left unchecked, this process continues well into later years, leading to frailty. That triggers imbalance, depression and an increased risk for chronic illness, particularly heart disease and diabetes.

At Tufts University, we've discovered that strength training can turn back the clock and make our bodies physically and metabolically more youthful. Moreover, initial results take only four weeks.

USE IT OR LOSE IT

The body contains more than 600 muscles. They power every move. Muscles are made up of tiny tissue bundles that are clustered into units. When these units receive nerve impulses, they release chemicals that cause the muscle fibers to contract and relax repeatedly.

The body does not maintain unused muscle. Hence, muscle wastes away. Strength training stimulates muscle cell growth and increases the production of enzymes that help store and use energy.

It also reactivates muscle units that have lain dormant because of inactivity.

> **Example:** *When NASA sent the first astronauts into space, they returned weakened, with significant drains in muscle and strength reserves. In the weightlessness of space, they weren't using their muscles. Today, exercise equipment is on every flight.*

Muscles are protected by a framework of more than 200 bones, joined by ligaments and connective tissue. Like muscle, bone is constantly undergoing repair and renewal.

Of the major factors that influence bone formation, physical impact is most important.

> **Example:** *Walking stimulates bone growth more than swimming.*

After age 35, bone mass begins to decrease. The most critical time for preventive measures is age 50 and beyond, when the rate of bone loss increases. This is especially true for women, who don't have as much of the male hormone testosterone to protect their bone and muscle reserves.

If bone loss isn't stopped, it often results in osteoporosis—the bones become very fragile and subject to fracture, even from activities like bending over.

Strength training improves bone density because the tug of muscle against bone works the same way other types of physical impact do.

Evidence: A study comparing the racket arm with the other arm of professional tennis players found that the playing arm was 15% to 20% denser.

In our study at Tufts, the strength-training group gained an average 1% of bone density in the hip and spine over one year.

Building bone and muscle also helps improve balance, which experts say starts to deteriorate in middle age.

Balance relies on an important flow of information about the body's position to the brain. This reflex can't work well unless the muscles are strong and the joints are flexible enough to respond to changes in position.

Our research demonstrated a 14% increase in balance scores among people who had one year of strength training versus an 8% decline in those who didn't.

STRENGTH-TRAINING BASICS

Strength training can be done anywhere. All it takes to see results is the proper equipment and a commitment to the program for at least four weeks.

To start, you'll need a pair of dumbbells—five pounds each for men, three pounds for women... ankle weights—the type with compartments for 20 pounds of weights...and a sturdy chair with a seat that is high enough and deep enough so that your knee joint is situated just over the edge when you sit. You can increase the weights by one or two pounds every other week as you build up your strength.

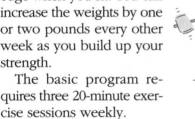

The basic program requires three 20-minute exercise sessions weekly.

■ Chair stand (warm-up).

Sit toward the front of the chair seat with feet flat on the floor, shoulder-width apart, and arms crossed against the chest.

Your fingertips should touch opposite shoulders. Keeping the back straight, lean forward slightly and stand up slowly. Pause. Slowly return to starting position. Rest and repeat eight times...for two sets.

Remember to move slowly and lean forward slightly as you start the move.

■ Overhead press.

Stand straight, arms at your sides with dumbbells in each hand.

Your palms should be facing forward, and your feet should be shoulder-width apart. Push dumbbells up until arms are overhead and extended. Make sure that the dumbbells don't move forward or out as you lift. Pause, and slowly lower to starting position. Repeat eight times...for two sets.

■ Bent-over row.

Sit forward in the chair, feet flat on the floor, shoulder-width apart, with a dumbbell in each hand.

Allow arms to hang at sides, palms facing inward. Bend slightly forward at the waist, with back straight and abdominal muscles slightly contracted, until your chest is just above your thighs.

Using shoulder and upper-back muscles, pull dumbbells straight up to your rib cage. Make sure your head, neck and back are in a straight line and your back isn't arched. At the top of the move, your elbows should point back. Pause, and slowly lower dumbbells to starting position. Repeat eight times ...for two sets.

Important: If you have osteoporosis or back problems, speak to your doctor before doing this exercise.

■ Calf raise.

Stand behind the chair with fingertips resting on the chair back.

Slowly raise yourself up on the balls of your feet, hold for three seconds. Lower heels to starting position. Pause, and repeat eight times...for two sets.

■ Knee extension with ankle weights.

Sit back in chair with feet shoulder-width apart and a towel rolled up under your knees for padding.

Toes should brush the floor. Rest hands on thighs. Slowly raise right leg until the knee is as straight as possible, with toes flexed upward. Pause, and lower leg slowly while relaxing the ankle and toes. Repeat with opposite leg. Repeat eight times with each leg...for two sets.

It's important to cool down by stretching for about five minutes after each session. Finally, remember to go slowly and breathe throughout your training.

NEW DRUG WORKS OVERTIME

The new drug *raloxifene* (Evista)—used by postmenopausal women to reduce osteoporosis risk—also lowers some risk factors for heart disease. Like estrogen *raloxifene* protects the bones and keeps cholesterol levels low. Unlike estrogen, *raloxifene* does not promote uterine cancer. And it actually *lowers* breast cancer risk.

Brian Walsh, MD, director, Menopause Center, Brigham and Women's Hospital, Boston, whose study was published in the *Journal of the American Medical Association.*

KEEP BONES STRONG

Vitamin D deficiency is widespread, even among people who think they are getting enough. *Latest guidelines to keep bones strong:* 200 IU (international units) daily for people under age 50...400 IU, if between ages 50 and 70...600 IU, if over age 70. *How to get enough:* Take a multivitamin...get into the sun two or three times a week for five to 10 minutes, avoiding overexposure...drink plenty of milk.

Michael Holick, MD, PhD, professor of endocrinology at Boston University School of Medicine and a leading expert in vitamin D and osteoporosis.

Osteoporosis— Not for Women Only

Osteoporosis affects men, too. It is usually thought of as a women's disease—but one-third of men will be affected by age 75. *Self-defense:* Calcium and vitamin D reduce the risk of fractures in men as well as women. All adults over age 50 should consume 1,200 mg of calcium and 400 to 800 IU (international inits) of vitamin D per day.

Bess Dawson-Hughes, MD, professor of medicine and chief of the Calcium and Bone Metabolism Laboratory, Tufts University, Boston.

Easy Bone Test

Osteoporosis test is noninvasive and gives results in minutes. The patient slides a foot into a small machine, which uses ultrasound—not X rays—to determine bone density. The test has been approved by the Food and Drug Administration.

Sandra Raymond, executive director, National Osteoporosis Foundation, 1150 17 St. NW, Suite 500, Washington, DC 20036.

Hip Fracture— Effective Avoidance Strategies for This Devastating Injury

Steven R. Cummings, MD, associate chair for clinical research and professor of medicine and epidemiology and biostatistics at the University of California San Francisco School of Medicine. For more information on hip fracture, contact the National Osteoporosis Foundation, Dept. MQ, Box 96616, Washington, DC 20077, or *www.nof.org.*

Each year, about 250,000 Americans—mostly older people suffering from osteoporosis—break their hip.

For most of these unfortunate individuals, hip fracture causes a lasting loss of mobility—and independence. One in five hip-fracture sufferers die within the next 12 months—often as a direct result of infection, cardiovascular trouble or another problem arising from the fracture.

PREVENTING FALLS

Because many falls that result in hip fracture are caused by poor vision, it's essential that older adults have a comprehensive eye exam at least once every two years.

Other ways to reduce your risk of falling…

▓ Eliminate hazards in your home.
Make sure that all areas of your home are well-lit. Tack down carpet edges.

Install handrails in tubs and showers and along all stairways.

Nonslip mats inside tubs—and on the floor *beside* tubs—are important, too.

Keep items on shelves in the kitchen and elsewhere within reach. If you have to stand on a chair or a stepladder to reach something, consider storing it at a lower height…or get a grasping tool.

▓ Exercise regularly.
Whether it's playing tennis, running or walking—or shopping, gardening or doing housework—regular exercise slows the insidious loss of muscle and bone that is associated with aging.

Exercise also helps maintain your sense of balance. Poor balance is a factor in many falls.

▓ Drink alcohol in moderation.
In the past, doctors have warned people at risk for hip fracture about drinking.

Regular alcohol consumption does seem to cause a slight decline in bone density. But recent studies have found that having two or three drinks a day actually cuts hip fracture risk by 30%.

The reason for this reduced risk, doctors theorize, is that drinking boosts estrogen levels (in men as well as in women). Estrogen is known to boost bone mass.

▓ Watch out for drugs that impair balance.
These include certain sedatives, sleeping pills and antidepressants.

▓ Avoid dizziness.
Transient low blood pressure caused by abruptly standing after you've been sitting or lying down can cause dizziness.

If you tend to become dizzy upon standing, make it a point to get up very slowly.

▓ Avoid high heels.

▓ If a cane or walker has been prescribed for you, use it at all times.
Whether or not you use an assistive device, always be especially careful when walking in icy or rainy conditions.

PROPER NUTRITION

Bone strength depends in large part on adequate consumption of calcium and vitamin D. Adults need 1,200 mg of calcium per day. That's the equivalent of three 8-ounce servings of milk.

Unfortunately, the average American gets only 700 mg of calcium a day. Depending on their dietary intake most postmenopausal women should take a daily supplement containing 500 mg of calcium carbonate or calcium citrate.

Taken along with vitamin D supplements (400 international units a day), calcium supplements can reduce hip fracture risk by up to 50%.

New finding: Vitamin K—a nutrient better known for its role in blood clotting—may also play a key role in preventing osteoporosis and hip fracture.

In a recent study, hip fracture was 30% less common among women whose diets were high in vitamin K than in women whose diets were low in K.

Sources of vitamin K: Broccoli, lettuce, spinach and kale.

BONE-DENSITY TESTING

Bone-density testing is recommended for all women at age 65, as well as for all women age 50 or older who have one or more of the risk factors for osteoporosis.

Some women may benefit by having a second test in three to five years if the result of the first test is borderline for osteoporosis.

Osteoporosis risk factors…

▶ **Weighing less than 125 pounds.** Low body weight is often associated with weak bones.

▶ **Being a cigarette smoker.** Smoking weakens the bones.

▶ **Having a parent who had a hip fracture.** In many cases, hip fracture runs in families.

▶ **Suffering a bone fracture after age 45.** That suggests that the bones are already weak.

Men, too, are at risk for osteoporosis and hip fracture. But the age at which men should begin getting bone-density testing hasn't yet been determined.

Bone density can now be measured via a number of different devices…and at a number of sites on the body, including the finger, knee and spine.

But the best way to gauge your risk for hip fracture is with a *dual-energy X ray* (DXA) of the hip. If DXA indicates that you have osteoporosis, ask your doctor about getting treatment.

TREATMENT FOR OSTEOPOROSIS

Hormone-replacement therapy (HRT) has long been prescribed for postmenopausal women as a way to guard against osteoporosis. But recent research suggests that HRT's effect on bone loss isn't as great as once believed and HRT increases the risk of heart disease, breast cancer and stroke.

For this reason, any woman at risk for hip fracture should ask her doctor about taking *alendronate* (Fosamax) instead.

In patients who are at very high risk for hip fracture, alendronate is often teamed with *calcitonin* (Miacalcin). This bone-strengthening hormone—available as an injection or nasal spray—appears to help prevent hip fracture.

The "designer estrogen" *raloxifene* (Evista) also appears to reduce the risk for hip fracture. Unlike estrogen, however, it does not boost the risk for uterine cancer, heart disease, breast cancer and stroke.

A Blood Test Not to Miss

Everyone over age 50 should have a fecal occult-blood test every year. The test, which detects minute traces of blood in the stool, screens for the possibility of colorectal cancer. It is safe, painless and noninvasive…and can detect the presence of a potentially fatal cancer while it can still be treated.

Robert Fletcher, MD, professor of ambulatory care and prevention at Harvard Medical School and Harvard Pilgrim Health Care, Boston.

CARBONATED WATER— NOT A PROBLEM

Seltzer is fine for bones—despite rumors that the carbonation removes calcium from them. Some carbonated waters even contain significant amounts of calcium. Check the label on the bottle. *Caution:* People taking the drug Fosamax for osteoporosis should not take it with carbonated water—the carbonation will make the drug ineffective. The medicine should be taken with plain water. It is okay for Fosamax users to drink carbonated beverages several hours before or after taking the medicine.

John Bilezikian, MD, director, Metabolic Bone Diseases Program, Columbia–Presbyterian Medical Center, New York City.

Important Cancer Test After 50

Colorectal screening is vastly underused. It shouldn't be, because colorectal cancer is the second leading cause of US cancer deaths. But fewer than half of adults over age 50 have annual stool blood screenings—and only 38% have ever had a *sigmoidoscopy* procedure, which doctors recommend every five years beginning at age 50.

Nancy C. Lee, MD, associate director for science, division of cancer prevention and control, National Center for Chronic Disease Prevention and Health Promotion, Atlanta.

MEDICATION AND YOUR AGING PARENT

Older people who are treated by several different types of doctors run the risk of over-medication or drug interactions. Protect your parents by telling each doctor involved in their care about all medicines prescribed by all doctors. *Helpful:* Put all medicines used—including over-the-counter ones—in a brown bag and take them to your parent's next doctor appointment, or to a pharmacist, for review. Be sure all prescriptions are filled at a single pharmacy—computer programs can track medications and alert you to possible interactions.

Joy Loverde, founder and president, Silvercare Productions, eldercare consultants, Chicago. She is author of *The Complete Eldercare Planner.* Hyperion.

Best Ways to Prevent Colon Cancer

Samuel Meyers, MD, clinical professor of medicine at Mount Sinai School of Medicine, New York City. He is coauthor of the medical textbook *Bockus Gastroenterology.* W.B. Saunders.

If someone told you that a 20-minute medical test literally could save your life, wouldn't it be foolish to refuse it? Unfortunately, millions of Americans are doing just that when they fail to get periodic colon cancer screening.

Result: Each year, up to 57,000 Americans die unnecessarily from the disease.

Here's what you must know to protect yourself against colon cancer...

SCREENING WORKS

Almost all malignancies of the large intestine and rectum start out as *premalignant polyps,* flat or mushroom-shaped growths that are harmless but may become cancerous. If a polyp is detected and removed, cancer will not develop. That's why screening—regular exams to detect polyps or cancer in its earliest stages—is crucial.

The most recent screening guidelines, published by the US Multisociety Task Force on Colorectal Cancer in February 2003, recommend screening for all men and women beginning at age 50. If you have already had surgery for polyps or colon cancer—or if you have inflammatory bowel disease, such as ulcerative colitis or Crohn's disease—your risk for colon cancer is increased and you should have colonoscopy on a schedule determined by your doctor.*

*People with a close relative (parent, sibling or child) who has had colon cancer or polyps should start regular screening with colonoscopy at age 40 (or five years earlier than the youngest diagnosis in the family). If you have two close relatives with the disease, have a colonoscopy every five years. If three relatives, you should have genetic counseling and possibly start colonoscopy screening at age 25 or younger.

SCREENING OPTIONS

■ Colonoscopy every 10 years.

This screening test is the most accurate and has been shown to prevent 85% to 90% of colon malignancies. Many health insurance plans now pay for screening colonoscopy, as does Medicare. Without health insurance, the procedure costs about $3,000.

Unfortunately, colonoscopy has a reputation for being embarrassing and painful. Both criticisms are overblown. Most patients say colonoscopy is not nearly as bad as they had expected.

What's involved: While you are sedated, a flexible, one-half-inch diameter tube that employs digital video optics is threaded through the anus and passed through the large intestine, enabling the doctor to see your entire colon lining on a video monitor. The procedure itself usually takes no more than 20 minutes.

Many people find the preparation, which involves laxatives to empty the bowel, much more unpleasant than the colonoscopy itself.

Until recently, the standard bowel preparation method involved drinking four liters of a bad-tasting colon-cleansing solution, such as *Golytely*, the night before. *Newer products now make the process less unpleasant...*

▶ **Phospho-soda** also tastes bad, but you only take several tablespoons dissolved in liquid the night before and the morning of the procedure.

Helpful: While you can mix it with any clear liquid, most patients prefer to mix it in ginger ale to make it more palatable.

▶ **Visicol** contains the same ingredient but is in tablet form. Instead of downing a liquid solution, you swallow a total of 40 tablets in multiple doses.

Helpful: Whatever bowel prep method you use, consume at least three eight-ounce glasses of fluid the night before to prevent dehydration. You can drink any liquid, but Gatorade, which contains electrolytes, is preferred.

▶ **Sigmoidoscopy every five years.** This test is less invasive than colonoscopy and requires less preparation (an enema the night before and the morning of the procedure) and no sedation. Because the procedure is less thorough than colonoscopy, it identifies only 50% of colon malignancies.

What's involved: The same flexible tube that is used in a colonoscopy is passed through the lowest third of the large intestine (sigmoid colon), where half of all tumors occur.

Sigmoidoscopy appeals to people who don't want to be sedated. The procedure, which costs about $400, is also less expensive than colonoscopy.

Important: On a subsequent day, you should return to take a barium enema, followed by an x ray, to view the remaining two-thirds of the colon. A barium X ray costs about $500.

Although sigmoidoscopy combined with a barium X ray screens the entire colon, it is still less accurate than colonoscopy.

▶ **Fecal occult blood test once a year.** People who don't want to undergo colonoscopy or sigmoidoscopy can opt for this test. It is the least accurate screening option and only reduces colon cancer rates by one-third.

Typical cost: $5.

What's involved: A chemical applied to stool samples detects traces of blood, which would suggest the presence of polyps or tumors. No preparation is required, but you must avoid certain foods (such as red meats and broccoli) for three days and medications (such as aspirin) for a week before to ensure accuracy. Since the test detects blood, taking aspirin, which can cause internal bleeding, could trigger a false positive.

Some people find the procedure unpleasant because it involves smearing small bits of your own stool on specially treated cardboard. If blood is detected, you'll need to have a colonoscopy.

NEW TEST

Virtual colonoscopy uses computed tomography (CT) to provide detailed radiographic pictures of the colon. It is relatively noninvasive, requires no sedation and can be done at your radiologist's office. It does require the same kind of preparation as colonoscopy.

This test is less accurate than conventional colonoscopy—it detects 75% to 80% of polyps larger than one centimeter, but just 40% to 50% of smaller ones. Health insurers will *not* pay for it.

Typical cost: $900.

It may be a good option for people with heart or lung disease, for whom sedation can be risky.

No More Facial Wrinkles

Neal Schultz, MD, a dermatologist in private practice, 1130 Park Ave., New York 10128.

Facial wrinkles are caused by a variety of factors, including heredity, excessive sun exposure and smoking. There are several different ways to have the wrinkles removed or minimized at a dermatologist's office.

LASER SKIN RESURFACING

This is suitable for treating lines and wrinkles of all depths. It is performed under local anesthesia. *Cost:* $1,500 to $5,000.*

How it works: A computer-controlled laser beam vaporizes the skin of the wrinkled area to a flat or almost flat surface. The surgeon using this technique halts the process when the lines disappear. Healing takes seven to 10 days. It is more rapid than dermabrasion and deep chemical peeling.

Laser skin resurfacing is much more precise and accurate than other techniques—with less chance of scarring.

Follow-up: Usually there is no pain shortly after the procedure. During the first seven to 10 days of healing, the skin is bright red. After this period, the skin is pink—but the color fades over the ensuing weeks and months and is easily concealed with makeup.

While a significant part of the improvement in the wrinkles is visible one to two months after the procedure, improvement continues for six to 12 months after the procedure as new skin grows.

*All prices are estimates and vary by geographic region.

ANTI-AGING CREAMS THAT WORK

Creams containing alpha-hydroxy acids (AHAs) are the first over-the-counter anti-aging preparations that really work. Derived from natural sources including sugar cane, grapes and milk, AHAs act as exfoliants, encouraging new cell growth, fading discoloration and reducing or eliminating fine lines. There are now dozens of AHA creams on the market, each with its own special acid (lactic, citric, etc.). All work equally well. Just be sure the label specifies an AHA concentration of 10% or so. That's the minimum strength capable of really smoothing the skin. AHA creams yield noticeable results only after several months of daily use—so you must be patient.

Gerald Imber, MD, clinical assistant professor of surgery at New York Hospital–Cornell Medical Center and a plastic surgeon in private practice, New York.

Important: During healing (until the pink color fades), it is essential to avoid the sun because sun exposure can cause the skin to heal with uneven color and cause serious damage.

SKIN PEELS

▓ Dermabrasion.

The top layers of the skin are "sanded" off with a rapidly rotating wire brush.

The treated area heals as new skin grows in.

This process removes wrinkles of all depths and can be done under local or general anesthesia. The procedure takes about one hour.

Results are less predictable than with laser resurfacing—except when performed by surgeons with exceptional experience. Some pain is experienced in the first few days after the procedure.

The skin that was removed grows back in one to two weeks, and your face's pinkness will disappear in about two to three months. The sun must be avoided during this time. *Cost:* $3,000 to $5,000.

▓ Deep peels are done with an acid.

The acid peels away the skin until the wrinkles flatten out. These peels are suitable for mild to moderately deep wrinkles. The skin that was removed grows back in seven to 10 days. Your skin's pinkness will fade over a period of two to three months. Here, too, avoid the sun.

Results of this type of peel are less predictable than with laser resurfacing because the depth of penetration of the acid solution is more difficult to control. There is also a greater risk of scarring and loss of color. *Cost:* $300 to $2,000.

▓ Glycolic and beta-peels.

The acid is painlessly applied for several minutes and then removed.

These need to be repeated 6 to 10 times. The peels have little effect on wrinkles and are more suitable for treating uneven skin texture and skin tone. *Cost:* $150 to $250.

COLLAGEN INJECTIONS

Collagen injections fill out the wrinkles instead of burning or scraping them away. This is better for people with dark skin for whom the pinkness of

raw skin would be more obvious and in whom there is a greater chance of discoloration from laser peels and dermabrasion. A six-week skin test is required to determine if there is an allergic reaction.

Drawback: The injected collagen lasts only a few months before wrinkles begin to re-emerge. As a result, injections need to be repeated on a regular basis. *Cost:* $350 to $2,000, depending on how much collagen is needed.

Grandparent Savvy I

S taying close to grandchildren can make it possible for you to help them through difficult times as they get older. Have one-on-one time with each grandchild starting when he or she is very young. Then talk will flow naturally as he gets older.

Important: Stay in touch when grandchildren become teenagers. They often need someone other than friends to talk to. Keep a grandchild's confidence unless you feel his parents must know. Then tell him how you feel—and offer to be present when he and his parents discuss the matter.

Lillian Carson, DSW, psychotherapist and author of *The Essential Grandparent.* Health Communications.

Grandparent Savvy II

T ravel with grandchildren may require special documentation. Many countries require specific forms for minors traveling alone, with only one parent or with an adult who is not a parent. Check the rules before you go.

Christopher Lamora, press officer, Bureau of Consular Affairs, US Department of State, Washington, DC.

ELDERLY HEART ATTACK PATIENTS

Elderly heart attack patients often fail to get clot-busting medication or angioplasty. This is true even though these treatments are known to *double* their chances of surviving for at least one year after the attack. *Reason:* Doctors are often reluctant to administer clot-busting drugs to elderly patients because they fear—wrongly—that they'll trigger a stroke. In heart attack patients over age 65, angioplasty is slightly more effective than clot-busting medication.

Nathan R. Every, MD, MPH, associate professor of medicine, University of Washington School of Medicine, Seattle.

ELDERLY DEPRESSION

Depression often goes untreated in the elderly. Some doctors decline to treat depression in elderly patients because they consider the condition "understandable" in light of elderly people's myriad medical problems. Other doctors simply fail to recognize depression. In people over age 65, depression often manifests itself as irritability and/or apathy rather than deep sadness.

Trey Sunderland, MD, chief, geriatric psychiatry branch, National Institute of Mental Health, Bethesda, MD.

Secrets of Much Longer, Happier, Healthier Lives From Happy, Long-Living Doctors

T. Franklin Williams, MD, former director of National Institute on Aging and now professor emeritus of medicine and attending physician at Monroe Community Hospital at University of Rochester, NY.

William C. Dement, MD, PhD, professor of medicine at Stanford University and director of Sleep Disorders Center at Stanford University School of Medicine, Palo Alto, CA. He is author of *The Promise of Sleep.* Delacorte.

Evan Calkins, MD, professor emeritus of medicine at University of Buffalo and senior editor of *New Ways to Care for Older People.* Springer Publishers.

Everyone wants to live a long, healthy life. To find out what steps you should take now to boost your odds of staying energetic, we asked three doctors in their 70s for their secrets…

T. Franklin Williams, MD

When you hold the conviction that you are capable of living a long, active life, you are more likely to take the steps to attain it—according to study after study. Think positively…stay physically and mentally active…and you will probably be able to live without dementia and other serious health problems for a long time. *Specifics…*

TESTS THAT CAN SAVE YOUR LIFE

Reminder: Lifesaving tests—Colon-cancer screenings. People over age 50 should be screened regularly. *Tests:* Stool-blood can be done at home/$5 to $20…flexible sigmoidoscopy, which takes about five minutes in a doctor's office/$100 to $200…colonoscopy, which views the colon and is often done in a doctor's office/$500 to $1,000.

Bruce Yaffe, MD, internist and gastroenterologist in private practice, New York.

■ Don't retire.

Stay employed into your late years, and find ways to do productive work, whether it is volunteering or caring for your grandchildren.

■ Maintain social ties, especially with your own family.

Work to strengthen such ties over the years and to play an active role in your family.

These very personal relationships, such as a close relationship between a grandmother and a granddaughter or between spouses, keep people alert, optimistic and functioning better.

■ Stay mentally stimulated by engaging in work and activities that you enjoy and that challenge you.

It will actually prevent dementia. The brain nerve circuits are stimulated by mental activity. Use your brain, and you won't "lose" it.

■ Plan ahead for stress.

It is impossible to prevent stress, but at least you can minimize its impact if you expect it.

By being aware of potentially stressful situations and preparing for them mentally, you can deal with them when they come.

■ If you become depressed, get a checkup.

There may be a physical cause for your feelings.

Depression should always be treated. Your mental attitude should be positive and forward-looking.

William C. Dement, MD, PhD

There is evidence that healthful sleep patterns and longevity are related. I suspect that there is an enormous shortening of life span caused by undiagnosed and untreated sleep disorders.

I wake at 4 am—too early for most—so I am in bed every night by 9 pm. I will walk out of movies, concerts and dinner parties to keep my schedule. That will frequently cause raised eyebrows...but if I don't put my sleep first, who will? *My advice for sleeping well at night...*

■ Readjust your sleep patterns in order to go to sleep earlier.

Set your alarm one hour earlier in the morning, but go to bed at your usual time. You'll just lie there in the dark if you try to fall asleep earlier.

When you wake up, it's a good idea to expose yourself to bright light for at least two hours. Artificial light is okay in the winter, but it should be bright.

Do not nap! That night, you'll feel sleepy a bit earlier than the night before. Go to bed when you're tired. Set your morning alarm back another hour each night until you've achieved the sleep schedule you want.

Biggest myth: Anxiety keeps people awake. If you're having trouble falling asleep, it's probably because your biological clock is off—not because you're worried. If you're so worried, why do you suddenly fall asleep at 3 am?

■ Develop a comforting routine before bedtime.

A light snack an hour before bed is fine.

Making love helps many people sleep well. Or fall asleep by reading a good book.

■ Avoid excessive alcohol.

While it will induce sleep, it will also wake you up much too soon.

■ Avoid caffeine for the last half of your day.

■ Use sleep medications with caution.

If you are sleep deprived because of insomnia, you may require less than the standard dose.

Speak with your doctor about the appropriate medication. If you require these sleep aids for longer than a few days, ask your doctor about strategies to sleep without medication.

Evan Calkins, MD

Longevity comes in some part, I've observed, from a Teddy Roosevelt–style commitment to the active life. Although physiological functions peak at age 25, we can accelerate aging by our bad habits…or we can slow aging with good habits. *Some good habits…*

▨ Make physical activity routine.
Park your car a few blocks from your place of work.

Take the stairs instead of the elevator. A lot of people play golf on the weekends at the same time they're paying someone to rake the leaves at their home. Rake your own leaves.

▨ Work out with a trainer once or twice a week for one hour.

The trainer will develop a regimen based on your level of fitness. But he or she will also challenge you so that your goal is always being moved ahead.

▨ Exercise should be weight-bearing.
This means that if you swim, which helps people feel limber, you need to supplement it with other forms of exercise.

One-half hour of brisk walking five times a week will do it.

Weight-bearing exercise is especially important because of its bone-strengthening effects. Having a bone fracture puts all other body systems at risk.

▨ Calcium and vitamin D are crucial at every age—but if older people would have one big glass of milk every day, a supplemental pill of 600 mg of calcium and 800 international units (IU) of vitamin D, which allows for the absorption of calcium, their risk of fractures would diminish greatly.

Great nondairy sources of calcium include soy foods, broccoli and calcium-fortified orange juice.

▨ Control cholesterol.
This is one of the best ways to protect the heart.

Studies have proven that low-cholesterol diets and cholesterol-lowering drugs not only delay the onset of clogged arteries but also help to reverse the process.

▨ Avoid nutrition fads.
All these potions and pills cost vats of money—and can create new problems.

But I do recommend vitamin C (I take 500 mg or 1,000 mg daily) and vitamin E (I take 400 IU three times weekly) to help remove harmful free radicals from the body.

Osteoporosis—Prevention And Treatment

Miriam Nelson, PhD, associate professor of nutrition and director of the Center for Physical Fitness at the School of Nutrition Science and Policy at Tufts University, Boston. She is coauthor of *Strong Women, Strong Bones—Everything You Need to Know to Prevent, Treat and Beat Osteoporosis.* Putnam.

Osteoporosis, or thinning of the bones, develops invisibly as we age. Starting at around age 35, the average woman loses up to 1% of her bone mass each year, increasing the risk of fractures in the hips, wrists, spine and elsewhere as she gets older.

Approximately one out of three women will have some degree of osteoporosis in her lifetime.

Osteoporosis tends to occur later among males because their bones are heavier to start with. But it will still affect one out of five men.

Fortunately, osteoporosis is both preventable and treatable.

PREVENTION

◾ Avoid cigarette smoking, excessive intake of alcohol and caffeine and radical dieting.

▶ **Smoking decreases estrogen levels,** and women with a smoking history have significantly lower bone density and are at much higher risk of osteoporosis-related bone fractures than those who have never smoked. If you quit, your risk will be considerably lower than before, though still higher than that of lifetime nonsmokers.

▶ **Drinking more than seven alcoholic drinks a week** is also associated with increased risk of low bone density and fractures.

▶ **Caffeine intake of more than 400 mg per day**—the equivalent of four cups of coffee—doubles the risk of hip fractures. Caffeine has a diuretic effect, which increases excretion of calcium in the urine.

▶ **Yo-yo dieting and/or excessive weight loss** also harms your bones.

◾ Consume a diet high in calcium and vitamin D including supplements when necessary.

▶ **The average American diet doesn't contain enough calcium** to meet the requirements of older individuals. For this reason, women age 50 and over should take daily calcium supplements—preferably in the form of calcium citrate. It is absorbed better than other calcium compounds. In particular, calcium phosphate supplements should be avoided, since phosphorus can interfere with calcium absorption.

How much you should take depends on how much calcium you're getting in your diet. Women and men over age 50 require 1,200 mg of calcium *per day. That's the equivalent of...*

▷ Four eight-ounce servings of milk or yogurt.

▷ Six servings of hard cheese—or calcium-fortified soy milk or orange juice.

▷ 10 servings of spinach.

If you're getting 1,000 mg from these sources, you only need a single 200 mg supplement taken at night. If your diet indicates you need more calcium than this, take an additional 200 mg supplement in the morning, and another at midday, if necessary.

▶ **While calcium is important for building and maintaining strong bones,** it's not the whole story—vitamin D is needed too, in order to absorb the calcium you take in.

It's hard to get enough vitamin D from foods alone, so I recommend that women and men over age 50 take 400 IU of vitamin D each day (or 600 IU, if you're over 70) in supplement form—especially in the months from October through March, when sunshine (another source of vitamin D) is limited.

Best choice: A calcium supplement that also contains vitamin D.

▶ **For bone health, it's also important to eat plenty of fruits, vegetables and whole grains.** Avoid a high-protein diet—it can cause increased excretion of calcium.

◾ Follow an exercise program designed to stimulate bone growth.

Light cardiovascular exercise—such as walking—is important for your overall health, but in later years, the impact of walking is simply not enough to stimulate the development of bone mass.

Our research indicates that strength training is essential for women and men over age 50. Not only does strength training promote bone development, but it also builds muscle, reduces body fat, improves balance and tends to encourage better eating habits.

Our program at Tufts introduces 10 strength-building exercises over a period of 12 weeks using dumbbells. All movements should be done to a slow three-count, with a minute or two rest between sets. As the exercise becomes easier, substitute slightly heavier dumbbells.

WEEKS ONE TO THREE

◾ The wide-leg squat.
Lower yourself onto a chair, then stand up again (two sets of eight repetitions).

◾ The step-up.
Step onto the first step of a staircase, then slowly return to starting position (two sets, each leg).

Seated overhead press.
Push dumbbells up—with two three-pound dumbbells (two sets).

Seated forward fly.
Holding two three-pound dumbbells in front of you, pull your shoulder blades back, then return to starting position (two sets).

WEEKS FOUR TO SEVEN
Back extension.
Lying on your stomach, lift your left arm and right leg off the ground eight times, then switch to right arm, left leg (two sets each side).

Abdominal tummy tuck.
Lying on your back with knees bent, press your lower back against the floor and contract your abdomen (two sets).

WEEKS EIGHT TO 11
Side-leg raise.
With 10-pound ankle weights on each leg, lie on your side and lift your top leg off the ground (two sets for each leg).

Standing calf-and-toe raise.
Stand, holding a countertop for balance, and raise yourself up on the balls of your feet (two sets).

WEEK 12 ONWARD
Chest press.
Lying on your back with knees bent, hold a three-pound dumbbell in each hand and press the weights straight upward (two sets).

Biceps curl.
Sit holding a three-pound dumbbell in each hand, and lift one hand up toward your shoulder, then lower it again and do the same with the opposite hand, until you've done eight repetitions with each arm (two sets).

TREATMENT
If testing indicates a loss of bone density, medication is also recommended.
The best bone-density test is the widely available dual X-ray absorptiometry, or DXA ($150 to $200), used to measure bone density in the hip and spine. Women should get their first bone-density test at age 50, to spot early bone loss and provide a baseline for future tests.

Men can usually wait until their 60s. However, if there is a family history of osteoporosis, or a personal history of bone fractures or eating disorders, testing should be started even earlier.

If your test indicates that your bone density is relatively low, you should talk with your doctor about medication options. While hormone replacement therapy (HRT) with estrogen and progesterone used to be the only option, we now have several drugs approved for the prevention and treatment of osteoporosis, all of them quite safe. *The options...*

▶ *HRT* can reduce risk of spinal fractures by 75% over 10 years, but is being prescribed less due to the risk of side effects.

▶ *Alendronate* (brand name Fosamax), shown to actually stimulate bone growth in the spine.

▶ *Raloxifene* (Evista), which has mild estrogenic effects, but which does not appear to increase breast cancer risk.

▶ *Calcitonin* (now available as a nasal spray, under the brand name Miacalcin). Other, similar drugs are also now in development.

Note: Both alendronate and calcitonin are effective in treating men as well as women. It's up to you and your doctor to decide which medication is right for you—taking into account factors such as your medical history, severity of your bone loss and whether you experience any side effects.

Index